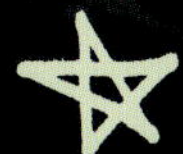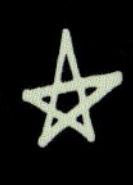

60 Macabre Projects for Peculiar Adults

Creepy Crafts

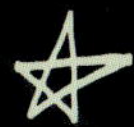

Ashley Voortman, Creator behind @peculiarlyashley

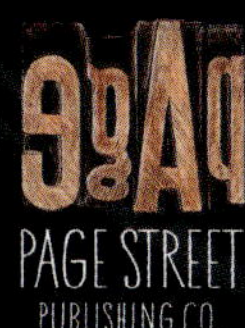

PAGE STREET
PUBLISHING CO.

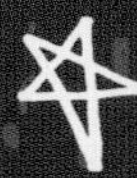
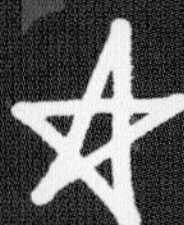

To my husband, Jake—

Who won't let me get a circle window.

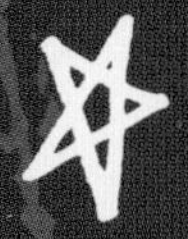

To my daughter, Iris—

Who fully supports my circle window dreams.

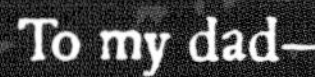

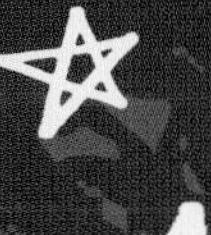

To my dad—

Who's totally onboard with building a circle window.

To my mom—

Who thinks I might be too obsessed with circle windows.

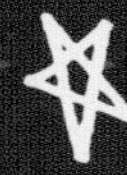

Contents

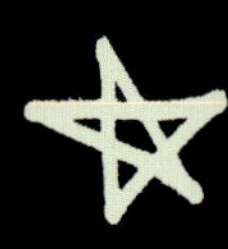

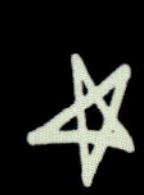
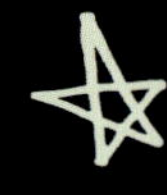
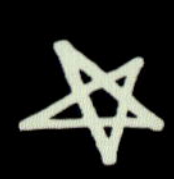

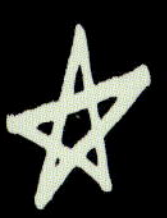

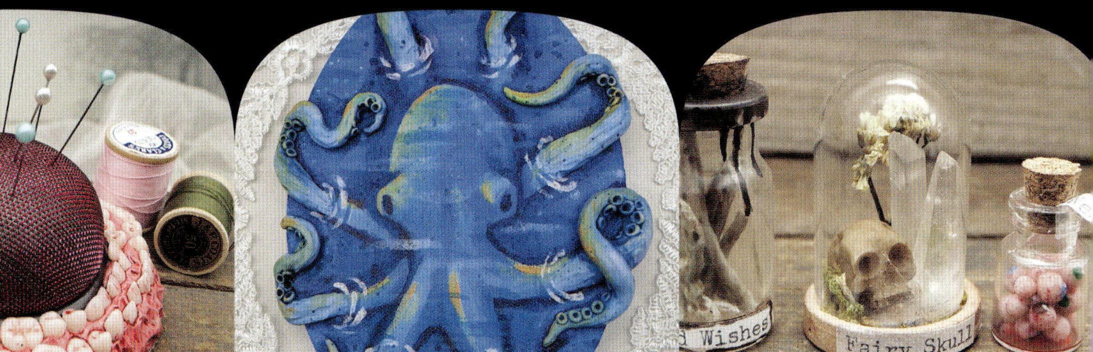

d Wishes
Fairy Skull

Introduction

Hello, fellow creepy crafters, I'm Ashley, your guide to the spooky side of DIY. In this creepy craft book, you'll discover projects to haunt every dark corner of your imagination! Whether you're a crafting pro or just starting out, there's something chilling here for all your dark hearts.

My main goal in life is to upcycle. I love reducing waste and saving things from the trash. That's why most of the projects in this book are made from secondhand stuff, so when I mention something in the materials list, think of it as a hint, not a rule. I also try to stick to similar materials throughout, so you won't end up buying a bunch of things you'll never use, because wasting time, money and materials is the creepiest thing of all!

Here's a basic list to start your creepy crafting:

- 2 lb (908 g) of epoxy clay, white or bronze (e.g., Apoxie® Sculpt)
- Disposable gloves and a silicone mat
- 1 lb (454 g) of white polymer clay
- Basic sculpting tools
- 2 oz (56 g) of Swellegant metal coating (copper)
- 2 oz (56 g) of Swellegant (patina)
- Acrylic paint in various colors
- 8 oz (226 g) of black chalk paint
- 8 oz (226 g) of matte Mod Podge
- 22 yd (20 m) of cheap floral wire
- Glass eyes in various sizes
- 5 to 20 sets of resin teeth
- Everyday recycling finds

Notes on Epoxy Clay: Always wear disposable gloves when working with epoxy clay. If you are in a small, enclosed area, open a window or use a fan for ventilation. Wear eye protection and a dust mask when sanding hardened clay.

Notes on Sculpting: In some projects, you'll need to carve or sculpt some creepy features. Below is a list of the types of tools I use. These aren't all the tools out there, but these are the most common and the ones I use the most. If you buy a sculpting tool kit, most of them will come with these tools.

Ball-tipped or **round-tipped tool.** This is my most used sculpting tool. They come in many sizes and are made of metal. They are perfect for blending seams, adding texture and putting holes in clay. If you only use one tool for sculpting, get a few sizes of this tool.

Silicone-tipped tools. These come in many shapes. I use the tapered point and angled chisel the most. They are great for most clays. You do have to be careful with epoxy clay, though, because if you don't clean it off it can ruin the tips.

Flat-edged tools. These are great for adding sharp, straight lines or cutting clay.

Toothbrush or wire brush. I know this seems like a strange sculpting tool, but it is great for adding skin texture or rock texture. I also use it to make epoxy clay more paintable. When epoxy clay hardens super smooth, the paint tends to bubble up on the surface. You can of course sand the piece or paint the piece before it hardens, but you can also add microscopic holes before it hardens to hold the paint on the surface.

Acrylic rolling pin. I love mine! It's easy to remove clay from (unlike wood) and you can use it to flatten any clay.

Toothpicks. These are great for poking holes in clay or adding support. They are cheap and abundant.

Silicone mat. This is another must-have in your sculpting tool kit. You may not use it to add texture or detail to a sculpture, but you will 100 percent love it for the cleanup! Hardened epoxy clay peels right off of it and paint or glue easily washes away. Do yourself a favor and get a silicone mat; your countertop will thank you!

Last but not least, remember, you can make your own sculpting tools using clay! Some of my favorite tools are ones I made.

Gather your creepy materials and tools and get ready to craft something that will scare all your guests away! Because who needs them anyway?

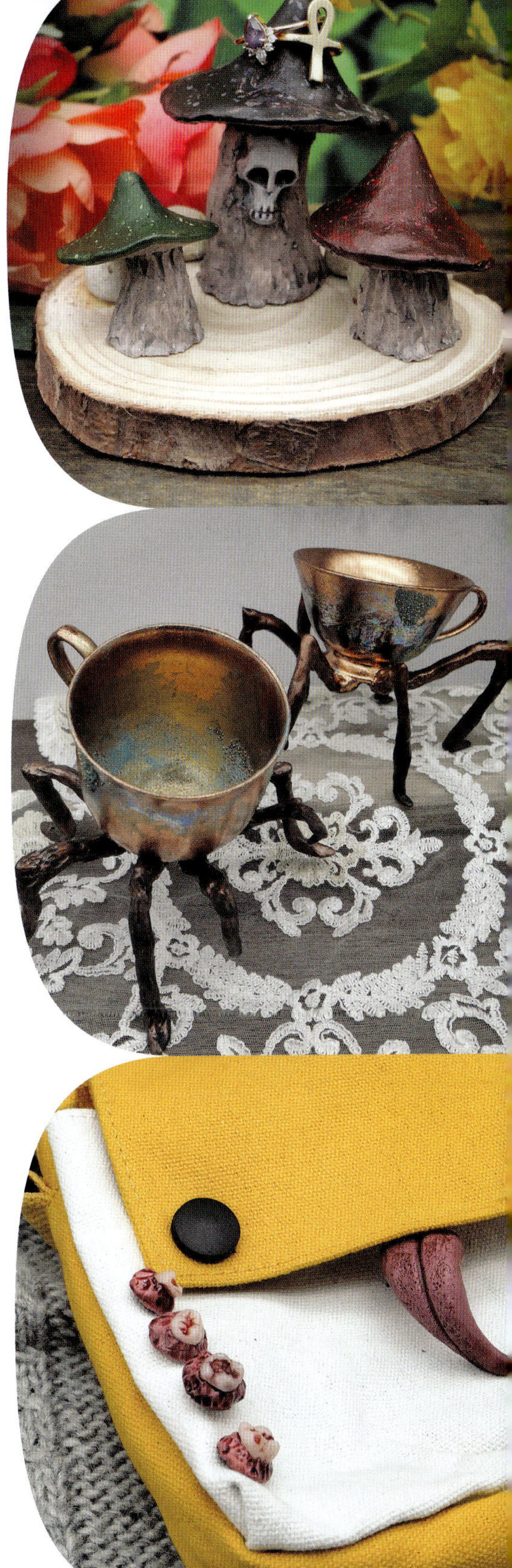

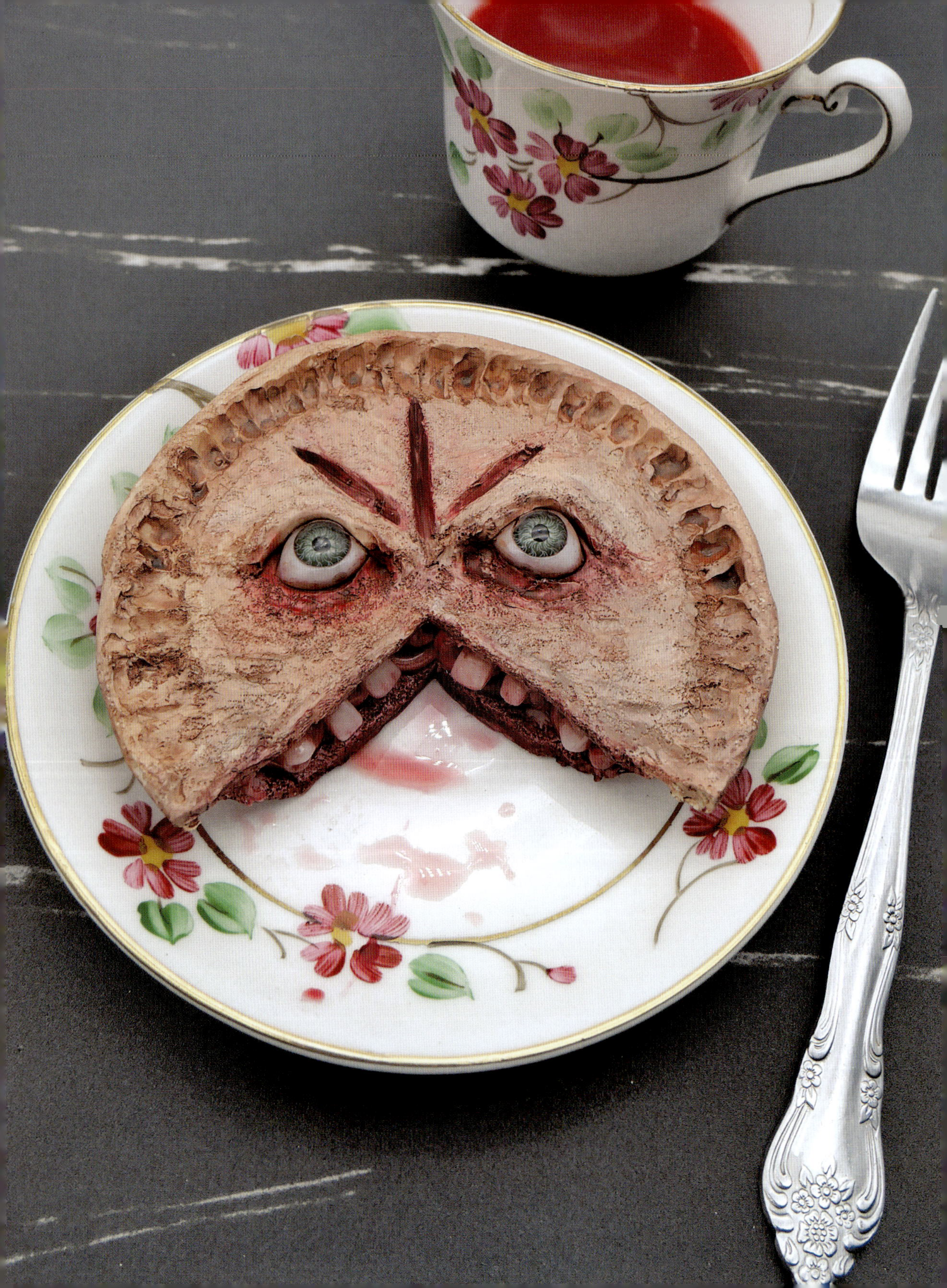

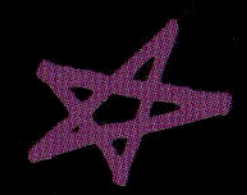

The Eyes Have It

What is it about eyes that draws our attention? I have heard it said that eyes are the circle windows to our soul. So that must be why I love eyes! Okay, say EYE if you think I should get a circle window! I see the EYEs have it . . . (Now tell my husband.)

Ahem, so, in this section I will show you all the creepy, spooky crafts you can make with eyes! We will make eyes out of wooden beads, and I'll show you how to use plastic eyes in your art. There are lots of different ways to use your eyes . . . I mean, I use my eyes every day to look at my blank, circle window–less wall.

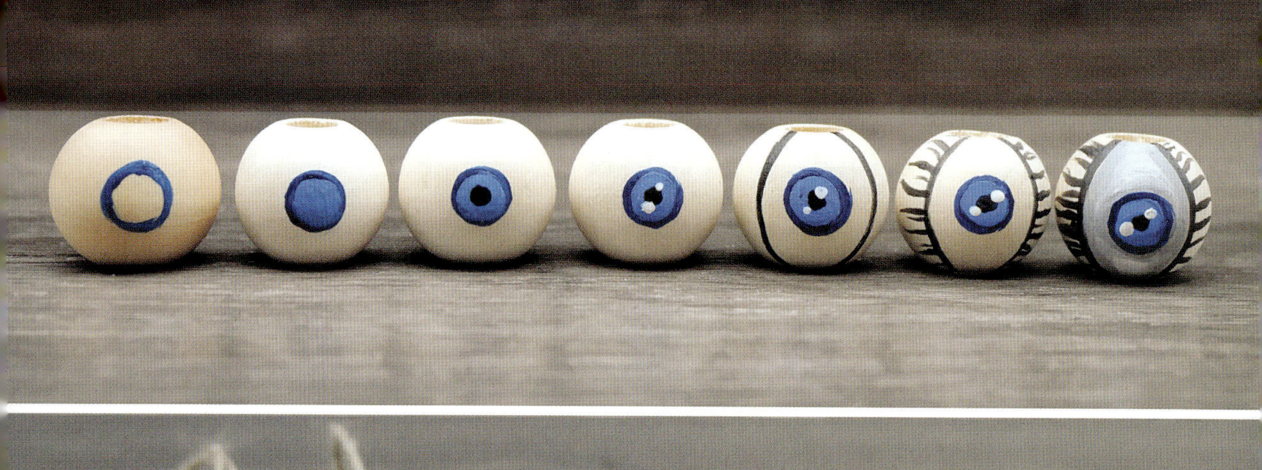

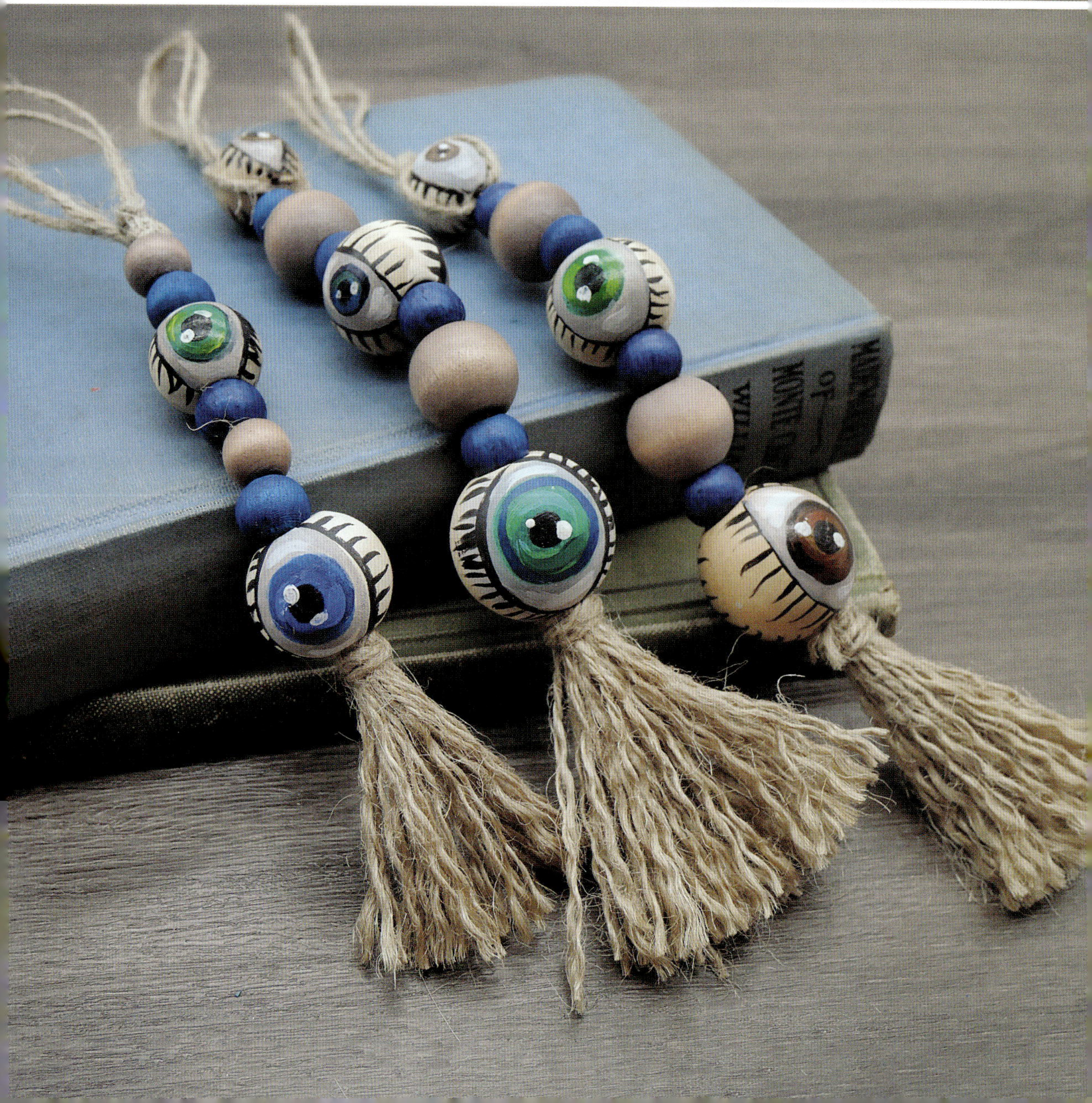

Gazing Garland

Have you ever wondered what people use a beaded garland for? Me too. From what I gather, a lot of people use it for decorating their houses, so I figure why not also use it in my house? Only I don't want to be a basic garland gal . . . Oh no, it should be creepy! So, let's make an eye garland.

This project is so easy! You can do it in just an hour or two depending on how long you'd like your garland and how many eyes you want to make.

Skewer your largest wooden bead with a chopstick. On the front center, paint a dark blue circle about half the size of your bead. Fill in the circle with lighter blue. Add a small black circle in the middle. Paint two smaller white dots on either side of the small black circle overlapping it slightly. You just painted an iris.

Now let's add the lids. Paint two black arches stretching from each hole on each side of your iris. Add radiating lines coming off the arch for lashes. Fill in between the lid and the iris with light gray. Paint white in the middle of that. Repeat on the back of your bead. IT DOESN'T HAVE TO BE PERFECT! Seriously, it's okay if it looks wonky. I promise no one will notice.

Repeat this process on all of your large beads. If desired, swap out the blues for greens and browns. Then paint your four small beads a solid blue.

Now that you have a small pile of eyeballs and beads (yes, that is a weird phrase), let's string them all together. Take 3 to 4 feet (0.9 to 1.2 m) of twine and fold it in half. Tie a knot in the looped end and string the beads on in this order. L, S, M, S, L, S, M, S, L. Or have fun with it and make your own pattern.

(continued)

Materials

- Wooden beads: 3 large, 2 medium and 4 small
- Chopstick (or skewer of some sort)
- Acrylic paint and brush
- Twine or hemp
- 3–4" (7.5–10 cm) piece of cardboard
- Scissors

Tip: Painting eyes on a large wooden bead can be tricky, but if you skewer it with a chopstick like a demented marshmallow on a stick, it helps hold your bead still.

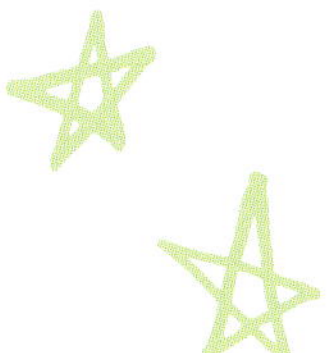

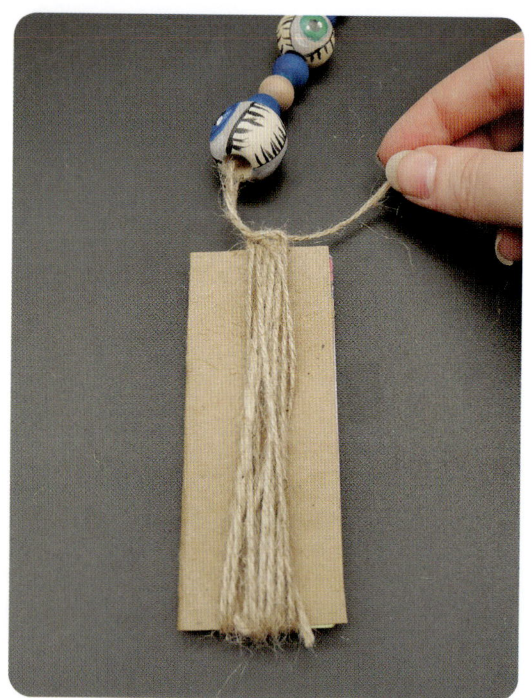

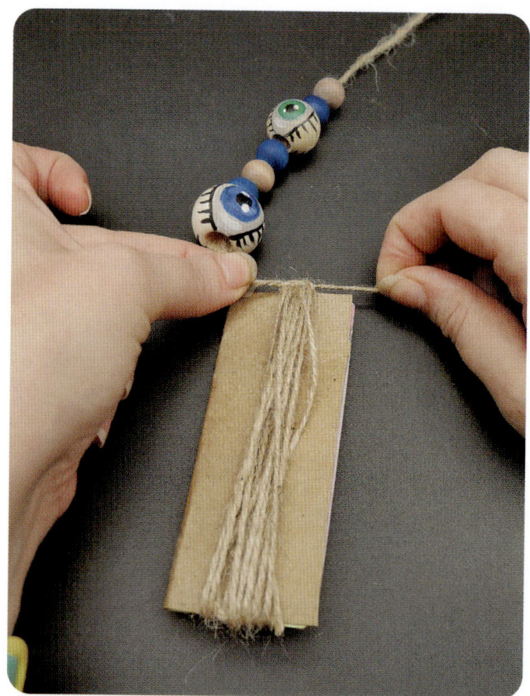

Let's finish it off with a tassel! Wrap twine 10 times around the piece of cardboard. Tie the end string from your eyeball garland around the top loops and slide it off the cardboard. Slip the knotted end into the hole of the last eye bead. Tie a second string around the top of your tassel a few times and tie it off. Cut all the loops on the opposite side and unravel the ends a little bit. You just created a tassel! For more in-depth photos, see the Webby Bookmark (page 207).

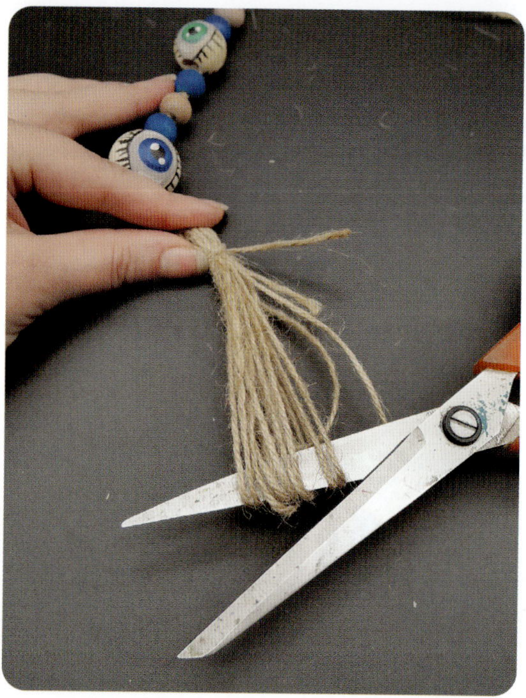

The Blooming Iris

I've had this terrarium for years and I could never think of a project good enough to place inside. So finally, I sat down determined to use this stupid thing and came up with an eye plant. If you don't have a terrarium, you can glue your eye plant onto a circular canvas or a small glass jar. Really, what doesn't need a flower eyeball glued to it? The possibilities are endless!

I used polymer clay, but you can just as easily use epoxy clay. If you use epoxy, be sure to wear gloves and work on a silicone mat.

Fill the hole in your bead with polymer clay and use a round-tipped sculpting tool to make a dimple in the middle. This will be the eyeball, and the hole will be the iris.

Now let's add the petals. Flatten a small marble-sized ball of clay with your thumb into a disk about the size or smaller than your eyeball and pinch the bottom to create a petal shape. Surround your eyeball with four of these petals, pressing the pinched end onto the back of your eyeball. Press on eight or more petals overlapping the initial four to create your flower. If your flower feels too closed, you can gently open it up with your finger. Bake according to the package directions.

(continued)

Materials

- Large wooden bead
- ½–1 oz (14–28 g) white polymer clay
- Sculpting tools with round tip
- Toothpick
- Acrylic paint and brush
- Paper towels
- Hot glue and gun
- Pencil
- Mini glass terrarium
- Floral foam or Styrofoam (big enough to fill the bottom of your terrarium)
- X-ACTO® knife
- Heat gun
- Moss
- Small fake plants
- Pebbles

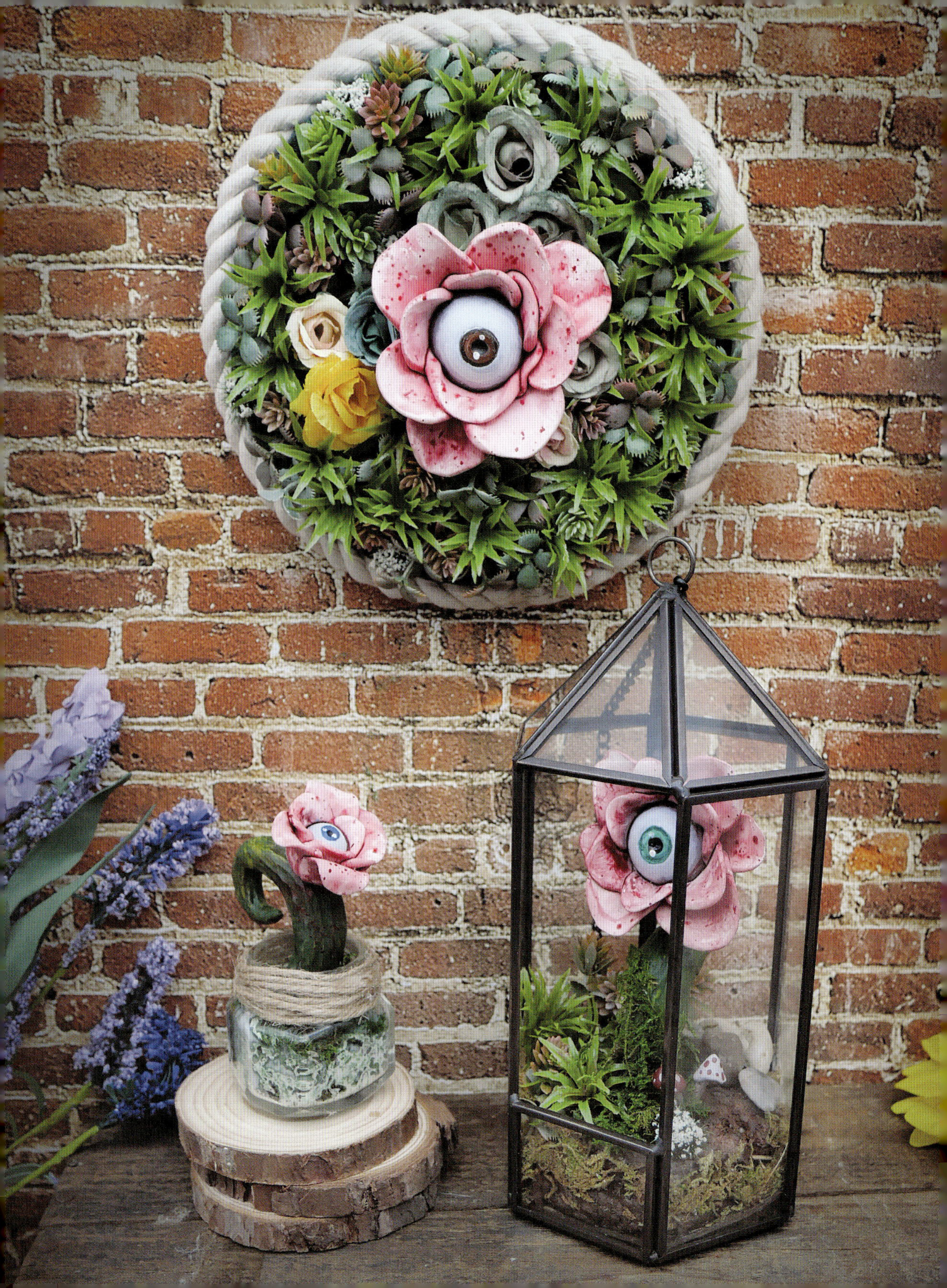

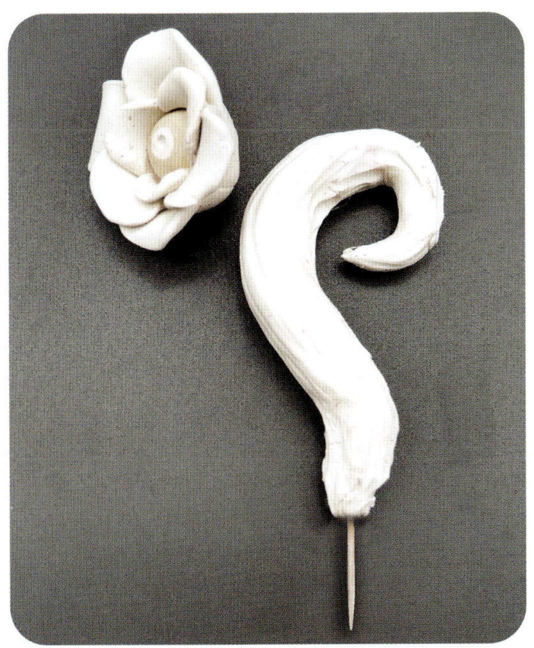

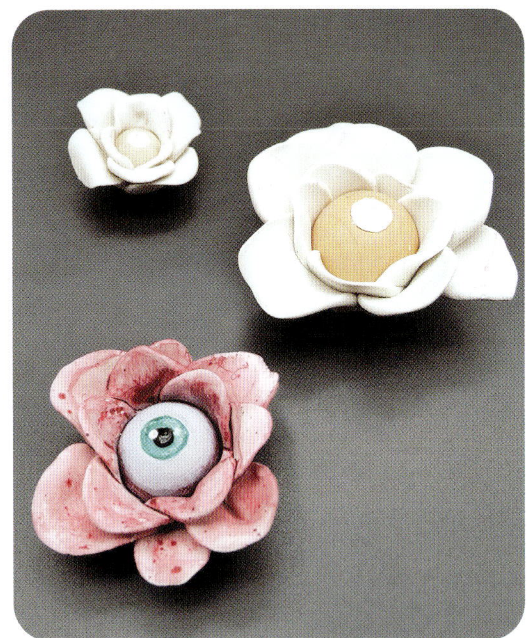

Next, we need to sculpt a stem. Roll a piece of clay and taper it at the end. Shape this into a swirl (make sure this isn't taller than your terrarium). Using your round-tipped sculpting tool, carve lines into the swirl to give it texture. Push a toothpick into the bottom so you can easily add it to your terrarium later. Bake according to the package directions.

Let's add some color. Paint your eye and petals a dark mauve color and wipe away any excess paint with a paper towel. Splatter mauve paint to make the petals look bloodstained. Paint your eyeball (see the Gazing Garland project on page 11, leaving off the eyelashes).

Paint your stem green and hot glue your eye flower onto your stem.

Now that we have an eye plant, it needs a home. I used a bit of leftover packing foam, but you can use floral foam. With a pencil, trace the bottom of your terrarium onto the foam and roughly cut it out with an X-ACTO knife. In a well-ventilated area, use your heat gun on low

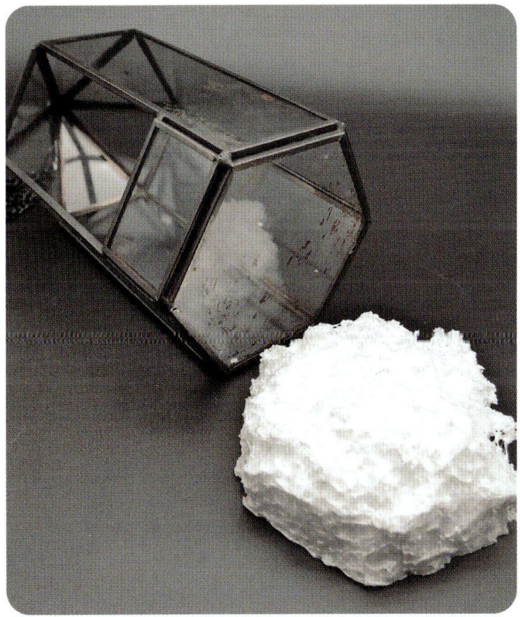

to slowly sculpt the foam into a more natural mound shape. This will also shrink your foam a bit, so if it doesn't fit, just use your heat gun to shape it until it does.

(continued)

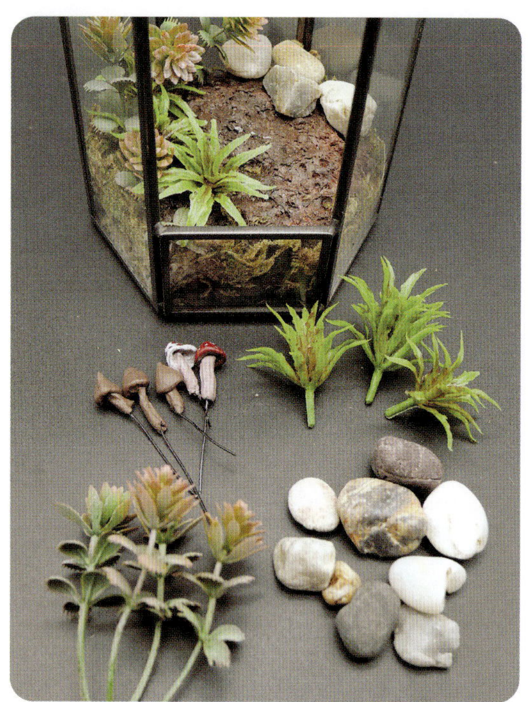

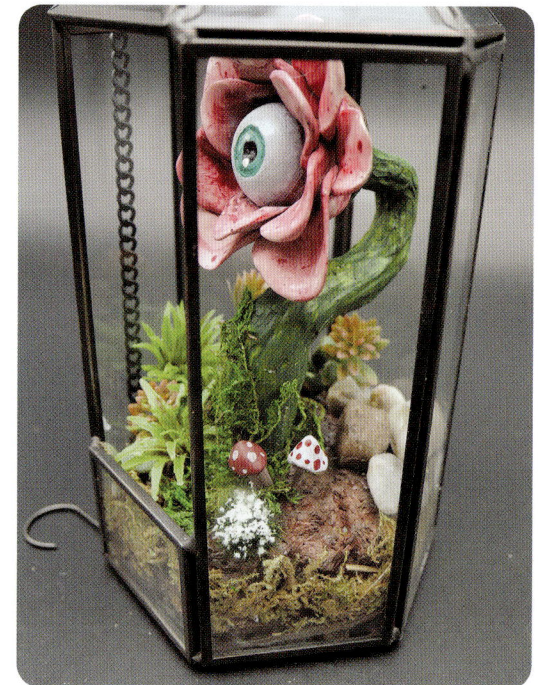

Once you're sure the foam fits in the bottom of your terrarium, paint it brown and hot glue it in. Tuck moss in between the glass and the foam to fill the gaps. Decorate the rest with small fake plants and pebbles. *Because I'm "extra," I sculpted little mushrooms out of clay for the inside. Before baking, I pushed a short piece of wire into the stems so I could easily add them to the foam. But, this step is totally optional, and to be honest, it's barely visible. So you'll have to ask yourself if it's really worth the extra effort.*

In the middle of your foam, poke your flower stem through to the bottom. If it's too long, cut the toothpick a little. You want the stem bottom to be touching the top of the foam. Using the lower temperature setting on your hot-glue gun, glue it in. Glue moss near the base of your flower to hide any hot glue spillover. You're finished!

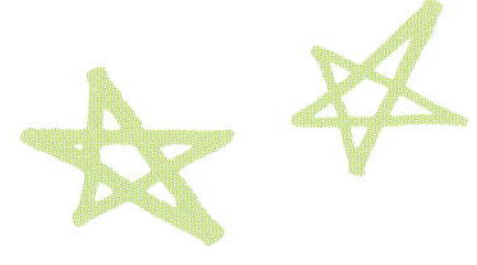

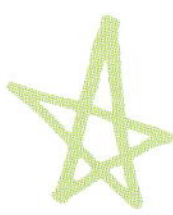

One-Eyed Pumpkin

I thought of this project when I saw a huge bag of foam pumpkins at Dollar Tree, and I had to snag them! Now that I was swimming in boring foam pumpkins because I have no impulse control when it comes to Halloween decorations, I had to make them more interesting.

This project is moderately difficult. If you're comfortable with painting, you should be fine. The sculpting part is pretty easy.

Start by cutting out a mouth hole with your X-ACTO knife on the front of your pumpkin. Scoop out a bit of the innards. *Not too much, just a mouthful.* The mouth should be wide enough to hold your wooden bead.

Lay down a silicone mat and put on your gloves. Mix a small amount of epoxy clay. Smooth a layer of clay in the mouth hole and create wavy lips on the outside with your fingers. Dip your fingers into water to help smooth out the clay. Blend it into the side of your pumpkin.

(continued)

Materials

- X-ACTO knife
- Small foam pumpkin 3" (7.5 cm) wide
- Silicone mat
- Disposable gloves
- Epoxy clay (e.g., Apoxie Sculpt)
- Large wooden bead
- Sculpting tools with round tip or silicone point
- 6 fake resin teeth
- Acrylic paint and brush
- Paper towels
- Glossy Mod Podge (e.g., Magic Modge)

Tip: If your pumpkin keeps falling face-first due to the weight of the clay, you can sculpt a little butt on the back of your pumpkin. Or, you know, just add a butt to it because butts are cute . . .

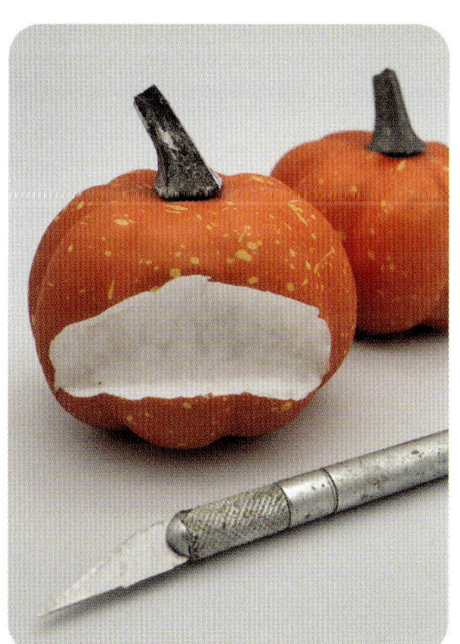

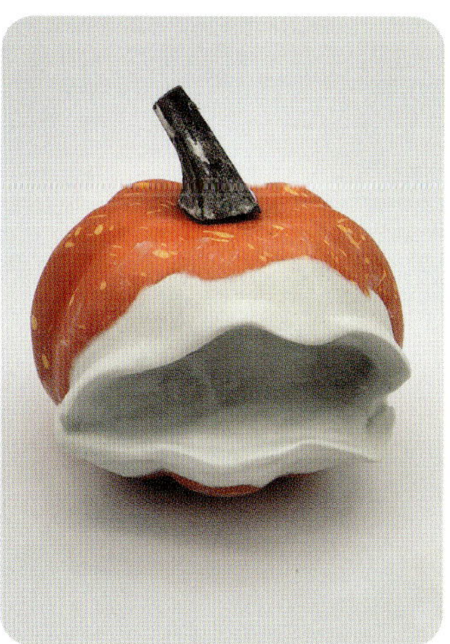

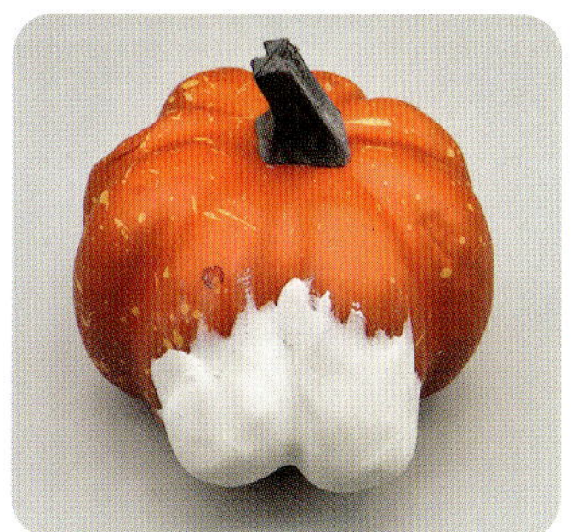

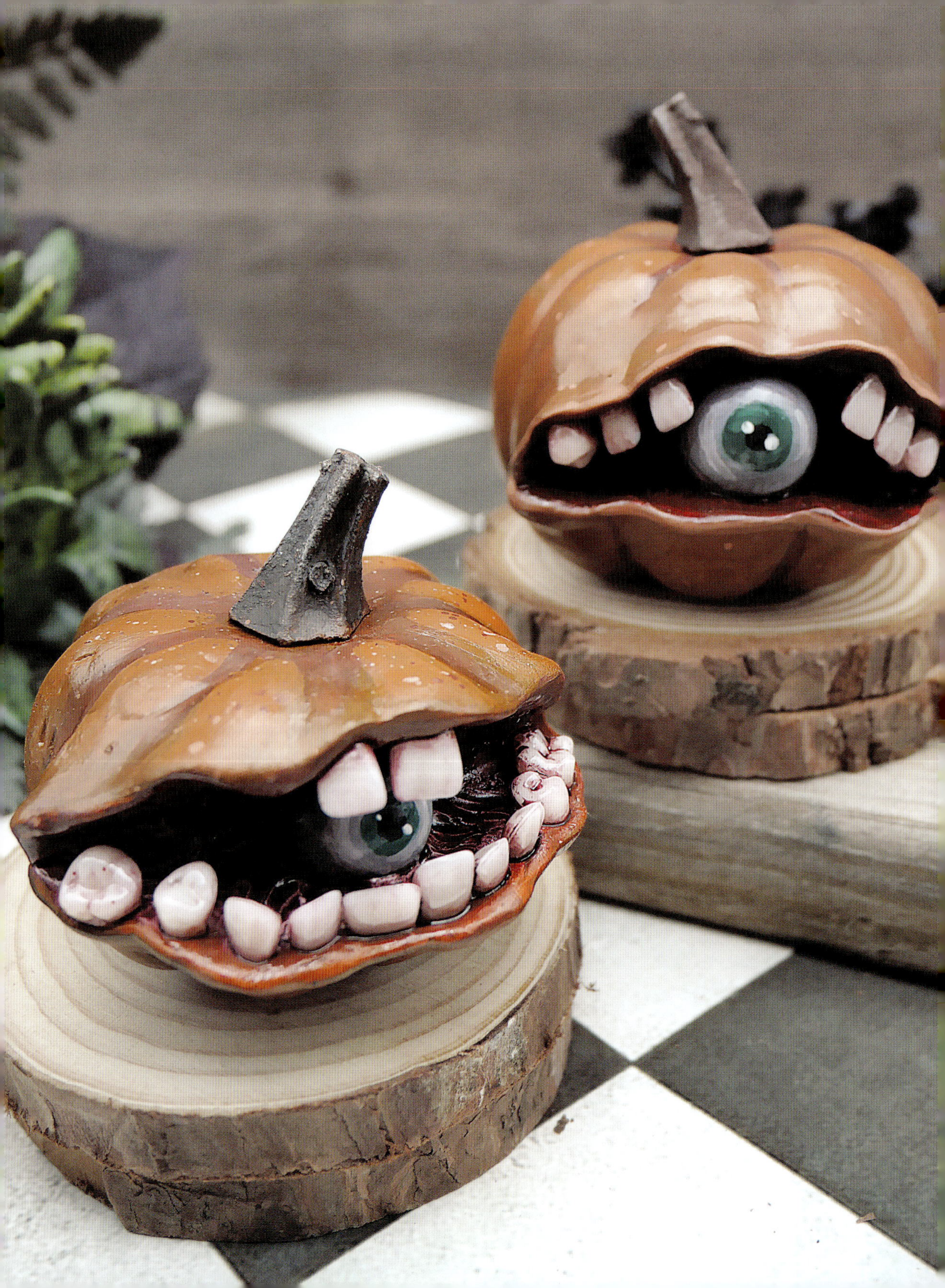

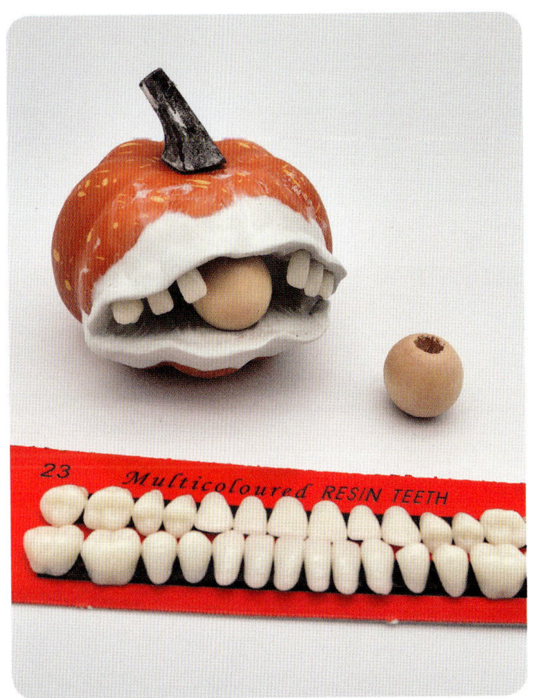

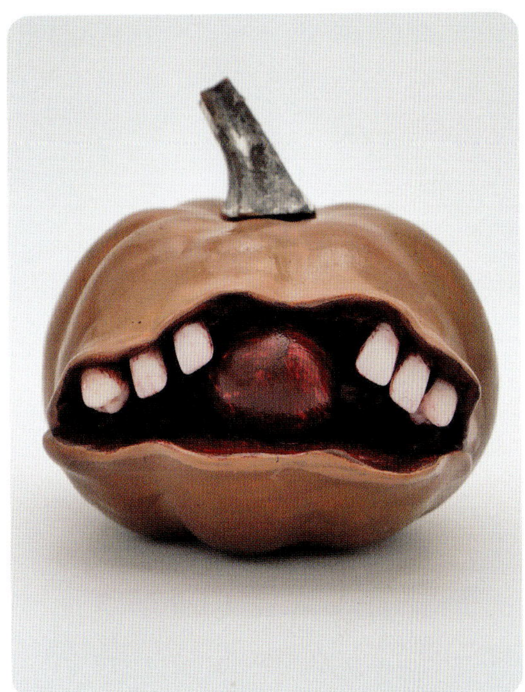

Put your wooden bead inside the mouth hole with the bead hole facing the roof and floor of the mouth. It should look like a solid ball inside your pumpkin's mouth. Add texture on the inside of the mouth by making lines radiating outward with your sculpting tools.

Press three teeth on either side of the bead into the top lip. *You could fill in the whole mouth with teeth, but by leaving a space in the middle it gives you better access to the bead later when we go to paint it. Let your clay set overnight to cure.*

Paint your entire pumpkin a rusty orange rather than that bright orange it came with. Flick brown and light orange paint on the outside to give it a pumpkin texture. Paint the inside of the mouth and eyeball maroon. Wipe the teeth off with a paper towel as you go to keep them whitish. Then paint your eyeball (see the Gazing Garland project on page 11, but leave off the eyelashes). Finally, paint a coat of glossy Mod Podge inside the mouth to make it look wet, and you're finished!

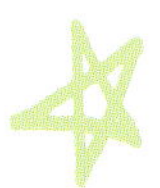

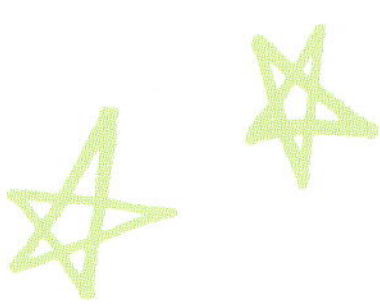

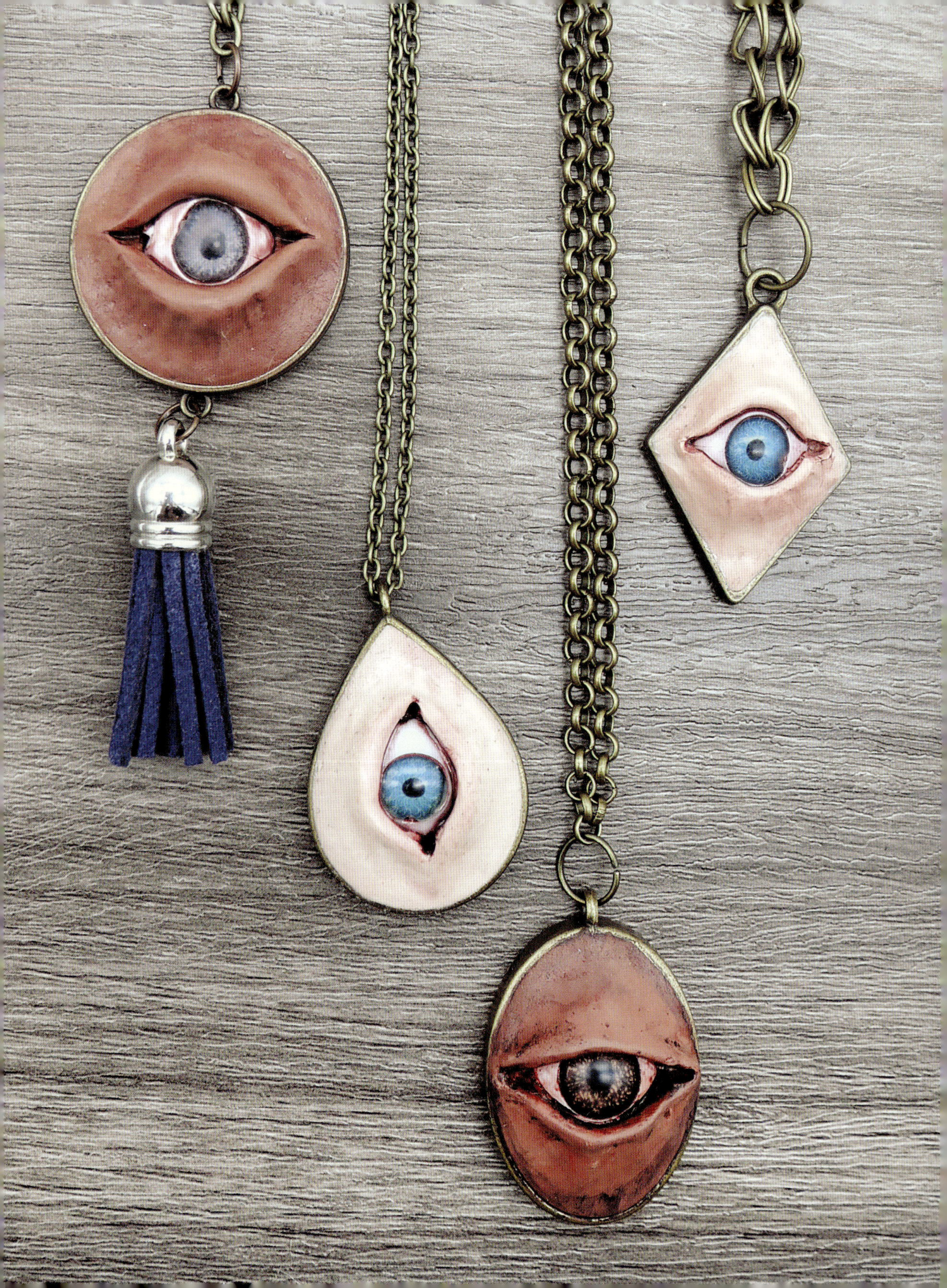

The Necklace of Sight

Do you feel like your neck doesn't get the attention it deserves? Do you want a conversation starter that you can wear? Have you tried adding more eyeballs to your wardrobe? No? Well, maybe you should! I'm here to show you how. Let's make an eye necklace!

An eye necklace is a pretty simple project. You can easily finish it in an afternoon and still have time to learn a foreign language or complete a marathon. Okay, maybe not those, but you get the idea.

Let's fill your frame with clay. Roll a ball of polymer clay into a marble, then push the clay marble flat inside your metal frame with your fingers so it fills the frame evenly without mounding over.

Push your plastic eyeball into the middle of the clay and cover the top and bottom half of the eye with a thin strip of clay. This will act as the eyelids.

Take a round-tipped sculpting tool and smooth the seams of your eyelids into the rest of the clay. Use the same tool to make a dimple in the left corner of the eye.

Bake according to the package directions but keep a close "eye" on it! *The plastic can melt if left too long in the oven, making your eye look like it has cataracts, which might not be a bad thing, but if you're worried, you can lower the baking temperature 10 to 15 degrees.*

After your eye has cooled down, let's add some paint! Use a watered-down maroon and paint the edges of your eye. Make sure it seeps into all the cracks and crevasses. Wipe away any excess paint with a paper towel.

Last thing to do is add a loop ring to the top and thread your necklace chain through. You now have a lovely (slightly disturbing) necklace!

Materials

- ½ oz (14 g) skin tone polymer clay
- Metal frame necklace pendant
- Plastic eye
- Sculpting tools with round tip
- Acrylic paint and brush
- Paper towels
- Loop ring
- Necklace chain
- E6000 or super glue (if needed)

Tip: *Your eye might fall out of the frame while wearing it, depending on your clay. You can glue it back in with E6000 or super glue.*

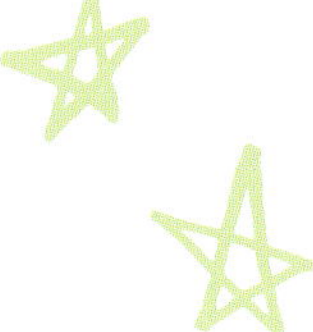

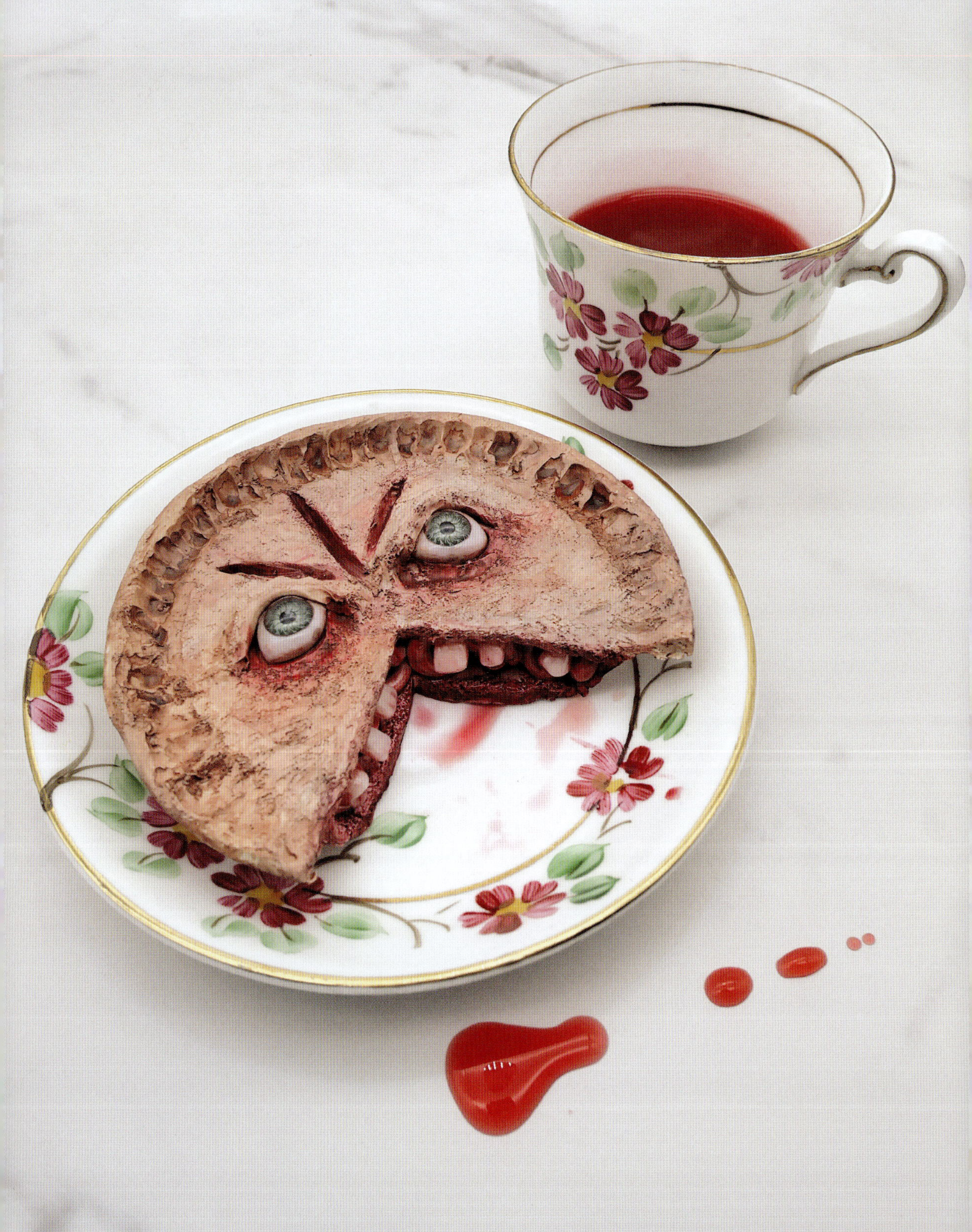

Delicious P-eye

Is pie inherently creepy? No . . . but if you start adding teeth and eyes to it, suddenly guests question whether they should call the authorities or just leave. I suggest sprinkling these types of creepy décor items among "normal" décor. The longer people stay at your house, the more the "weird" décor gets noticed, making your guests stay a little bit shorter and giving you the personal time you desire!

I like this project because it's a lot easier than it looks. It's just a few simple techniques that with a little practice anyone can do.

I got my pie tin with pie already in it. After devouring the delicious pie held within, I washed out the tin and saved it. But if you weren't fortunate enough to eat a delicious pie, you can pick up a pack of small pie tins at your local grocery store.

Materials

- 2 oz (56 g) white polymer clay
- Acrylic rolling pin
- 5" (12.7-cm) disposable pie tin
- X-ACTO knife
- Aluminum foil
- Sculpting tools with round tip
- 2 plastic eyes
- Fake resin teeth (optional)
- Acrylic paint and brush
- Paper towels

Roll out a thin layer of polymer clay with your acrylic rolling pin ⅛ to ¼ inch (3 to 6 mm) thick. Using the bottom of your pie tin as a template, cut out a circle with your X-ACTO knife for the bottom crust. Cut a quarter wedge of the circle so it resembles a Pac-Man of sorts . . . or should I say Pie-Man? Press this into the bottom of your tin. Then cut out a thin strip of clay that's the same height as your tin and place it around the edge, stopping where your Pac-Man mouth is.

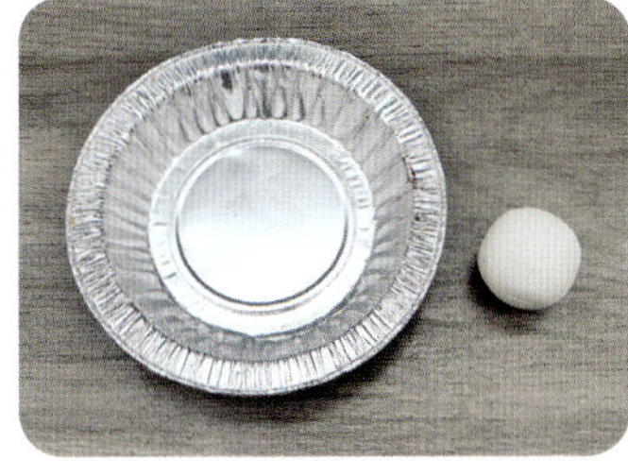

Ball up some aluminum foil and mold it into a smaller Pac-Man shape. This is the filling. If your filling is too tall, use your rolling pin and smash it down before adding it to your pie. We're just trying to save clay, but if you're not worried about waste, then just fill this in with clay.

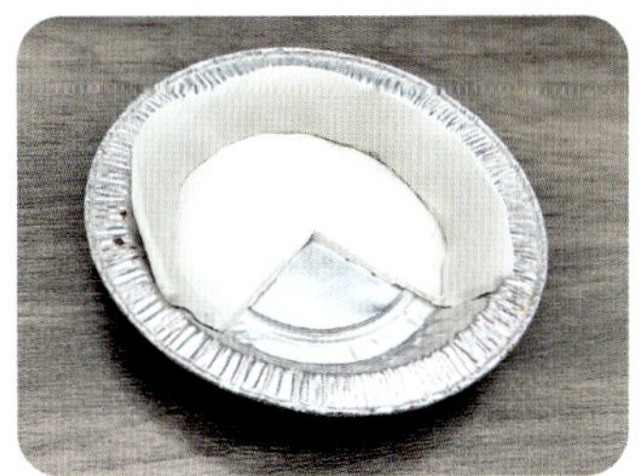

(continued)

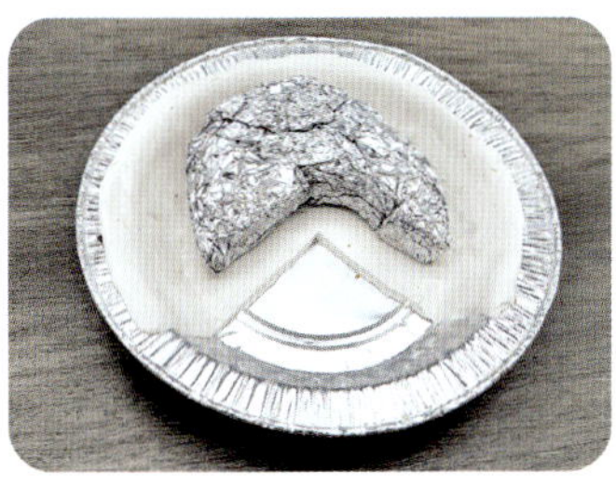

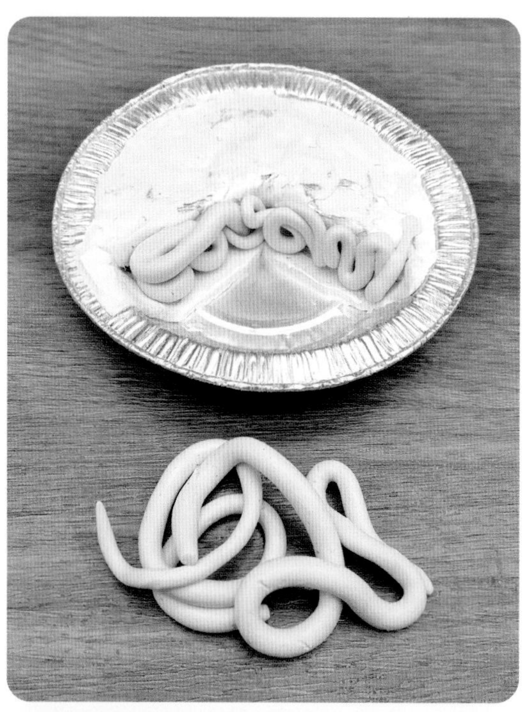

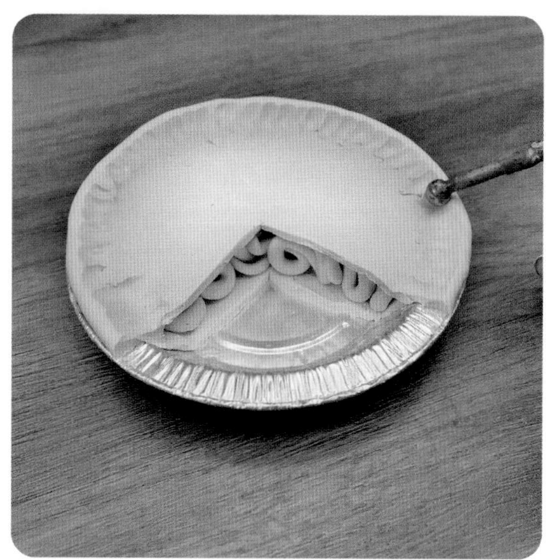

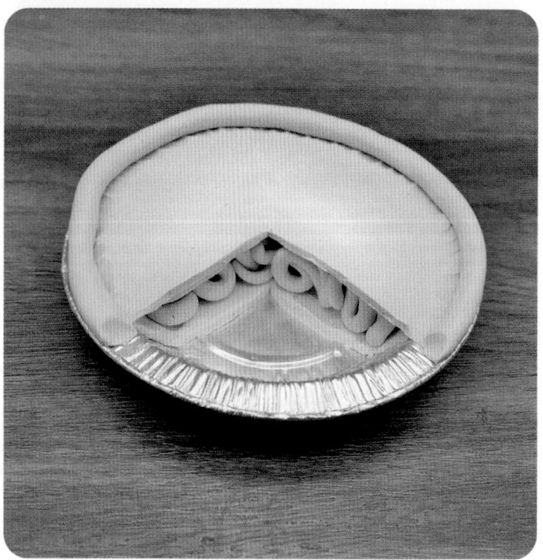

We want to hide the fact that your pie is full of aluminum foil . . . So, let's cover it in guts! Smear or push clay into all the gaps around the foil so we have something to attach our guts to. Using your palms, roll out a long clay snake about ¼ inch (6 mm) thick. Snake and loop it onto the mouth of your Pac-Man.

Using your rolling pin, roll out another ⅛- to ¼-inch (3- to 6-mm)-thick layer of clay and cut out a larger Pac-Man shape. Lay it on top. Trim any excess hanging over the edge with an X-ACTO knife.

Finish off the edge of your pie crust with a rope of clay around the three-quarter circle. Use a larger round-tipped sculpting tool to squish your rope's edge down onto the top crust.

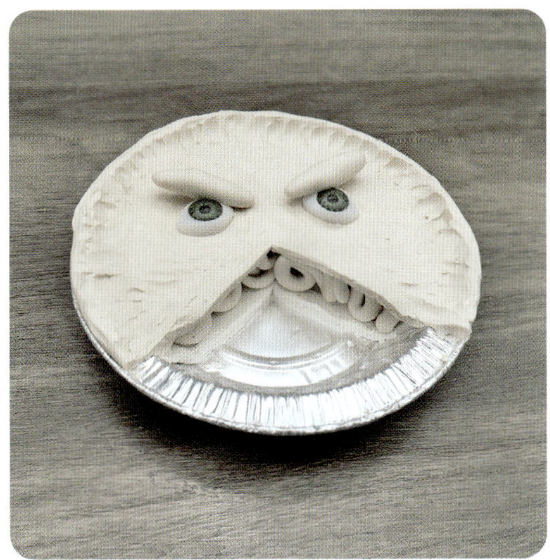

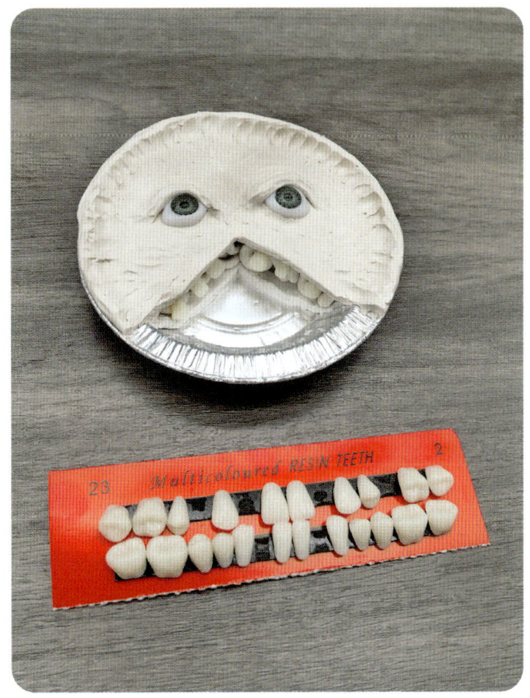

Press the eyeballs onto the top crust and add lids to the top with clay. You can make your pie happy, angry, or like it's contemplating life. If your pie truly has sentience, then I'm sure it has some feelings about being half-eaten.

If you want your pie to be totally terrifying, add teeth. If you're uncomfortable with your pie having the ability to bite you, then leave this part out. To add the teeth, press each tooth in front of the "guts" just under the top crust.

Bake according to the package directions but keep a close "eye" on it! *The plastic can melt if left too long in the oven, making your eye look like it has cataracts, which might not be a bad thing, but if you're worried, you can lower the baking temperature 10 to 15 degrees.*

After baking, pop the pie out of its tin and paint. Coat the whole pie crust in a light tan. Paint the nooks and crannies a maroon and wipe off the excess paint with a paper towel. As for the guts, use a watered-down maroon and drip it in the mouth, smushing it around with a paintbrush. Wipe off any paint that gets on the teeth or eyeballs. Adding pinkish red around the eyes makes your pie look tired and angry. Perhaps hangry?

Now you can impress your friends and hopefully freak them out when they see your delicious creepy pie!

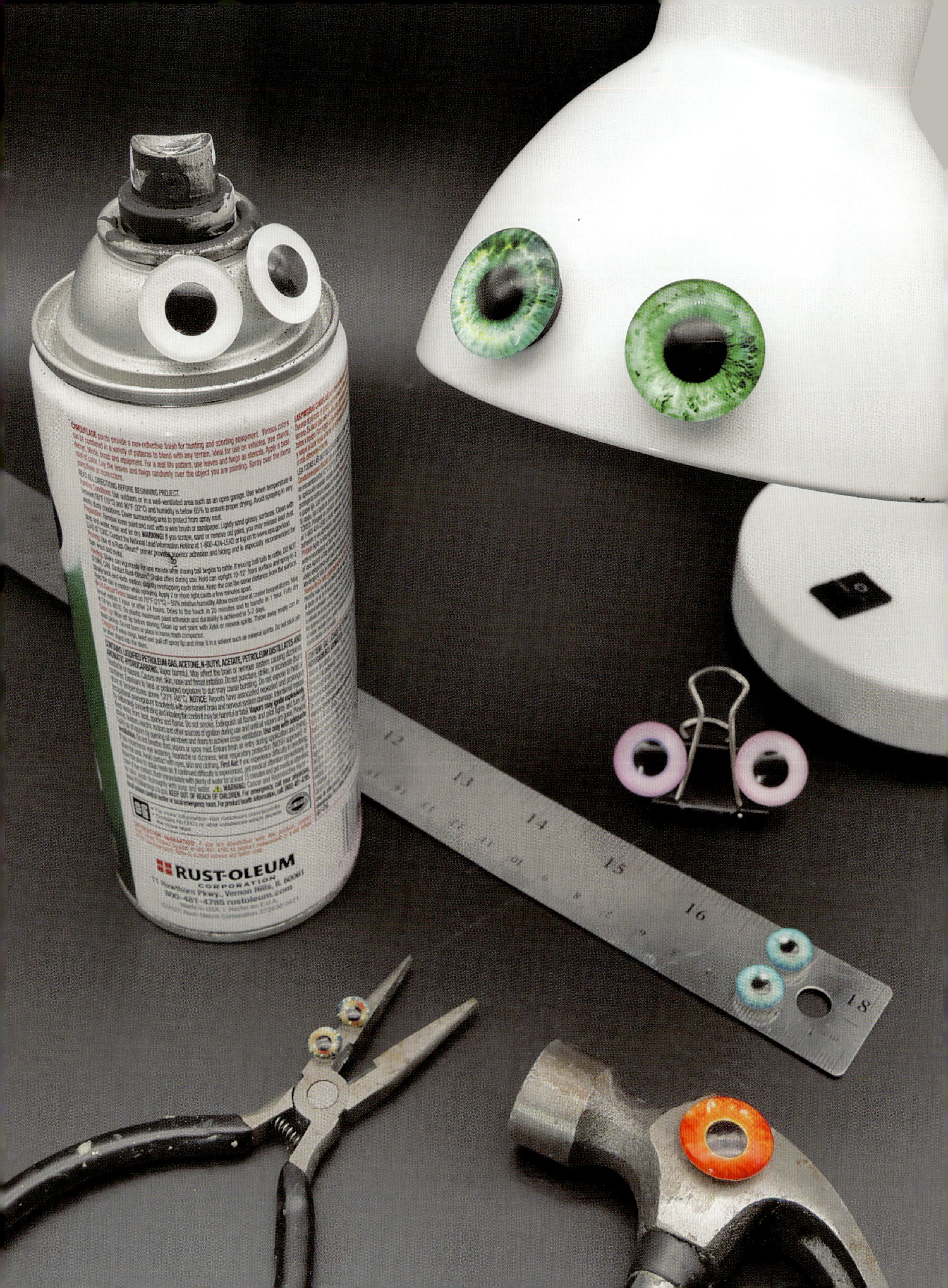

Eye Magnets

Feel like creepy crafting but don't have the time? This is a quick and super simple craft that will only take a few minutes of your time. I bet you never thought to glue eyeballs onto magnets! Think of all the possibilities! Filing cabinet eyes! Lawn mower eyes! Eyes on your pickle jar! Eyes on your lamps! Why would we do this? Because everything is just a little bit creepier if it's staring back at you.

- Super glue
- Small powerful magnets
- Plastic eyes

Squeeze a single drop of super glue onto a magnet. Place your eye on top. Repeat for even more eyeball fun!

Bam! You're done! Now go creep out your coworkers, or family, or strangers or whomever.

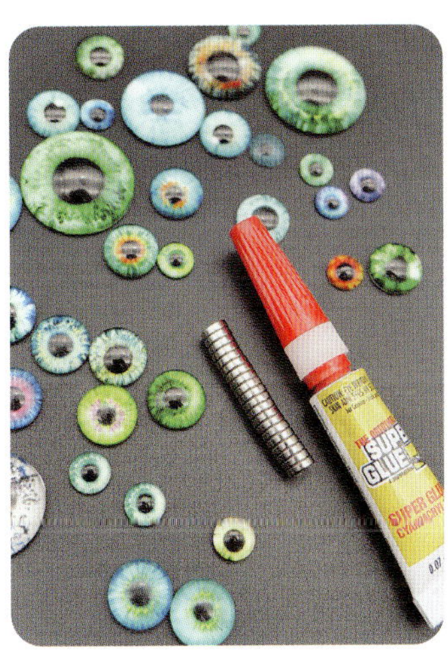
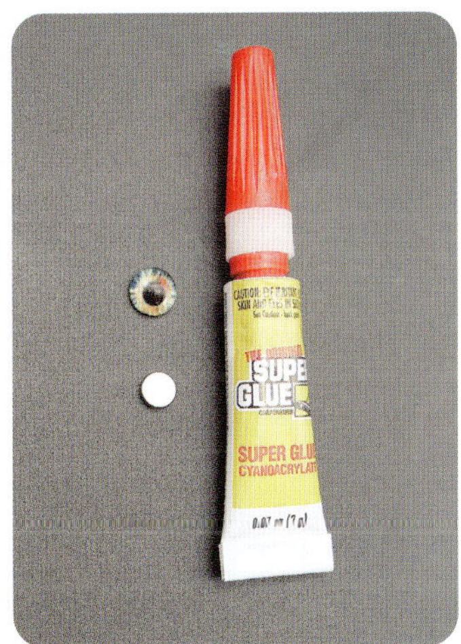
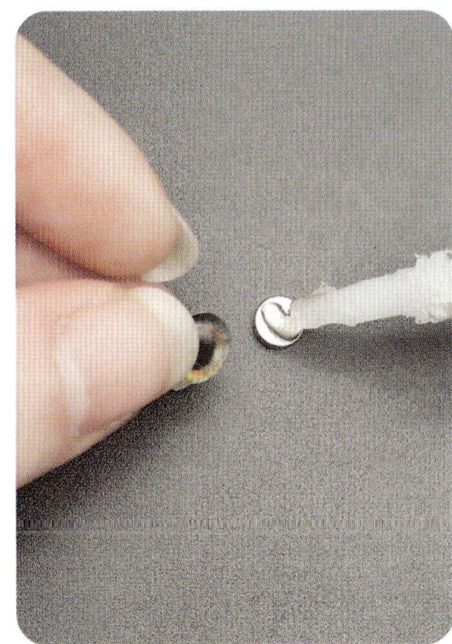

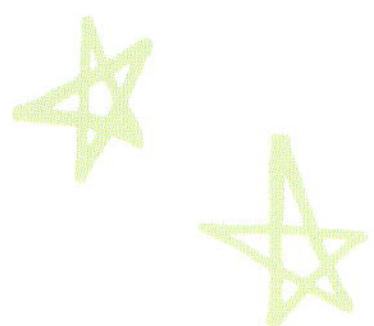

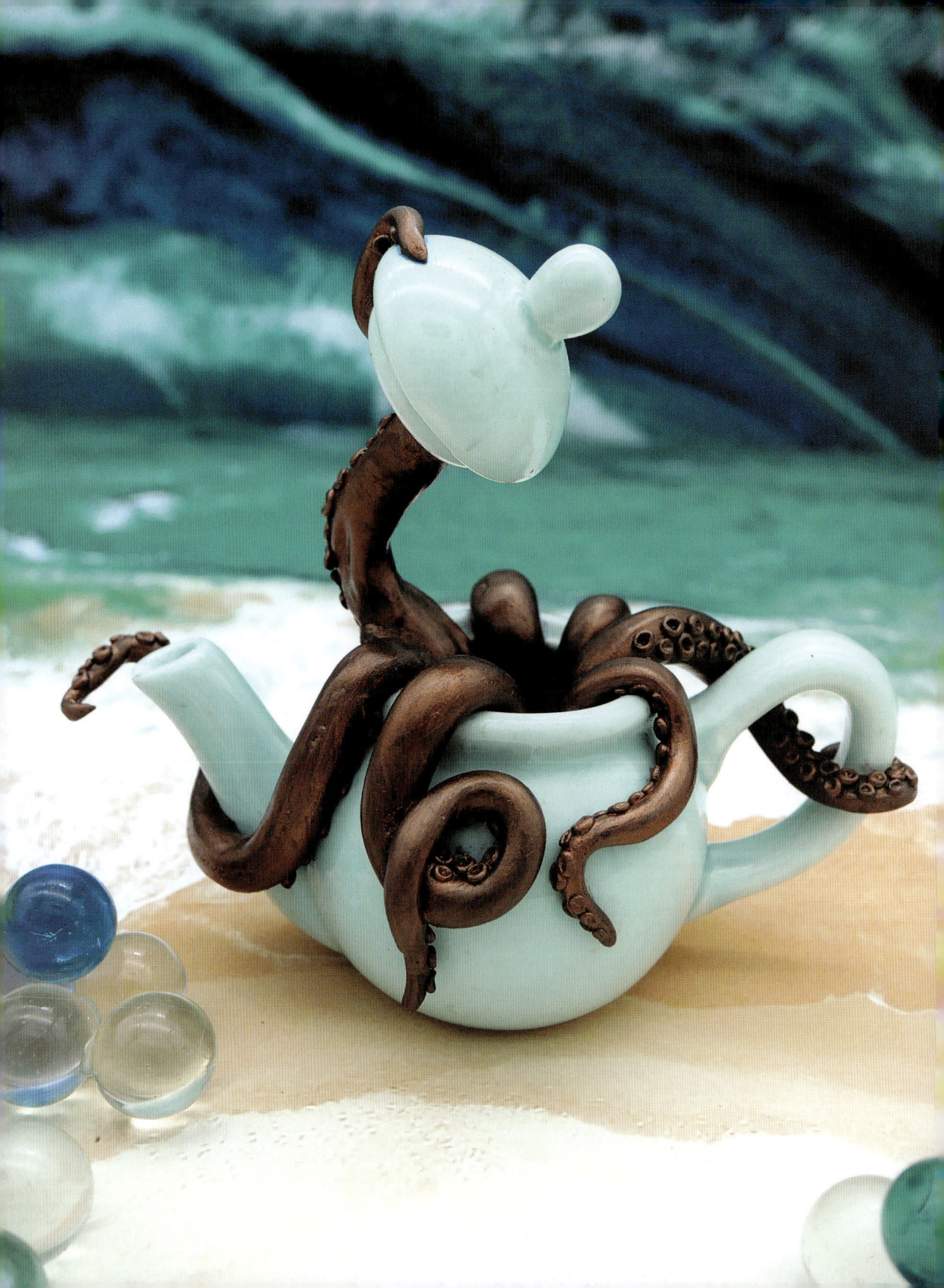

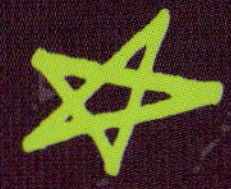

Not Your Grandma's China

Did Grandma leave you with a bunch of old china that you'll never use? Did you find a really cool teapot or sugar spoon at the thrift store that was calling your name? Rather than put it in a china hutch and stare at it collecting dust, you can make it into a real conversational piece, because who stands around talking about boring china when they could be talking about your new teeth pot or spoon with eyes!

Whether you inherited your china or bought it secondhand, with just a little paint, glue and clay you'll be making a whole curio cabinet full of creepy crockery!

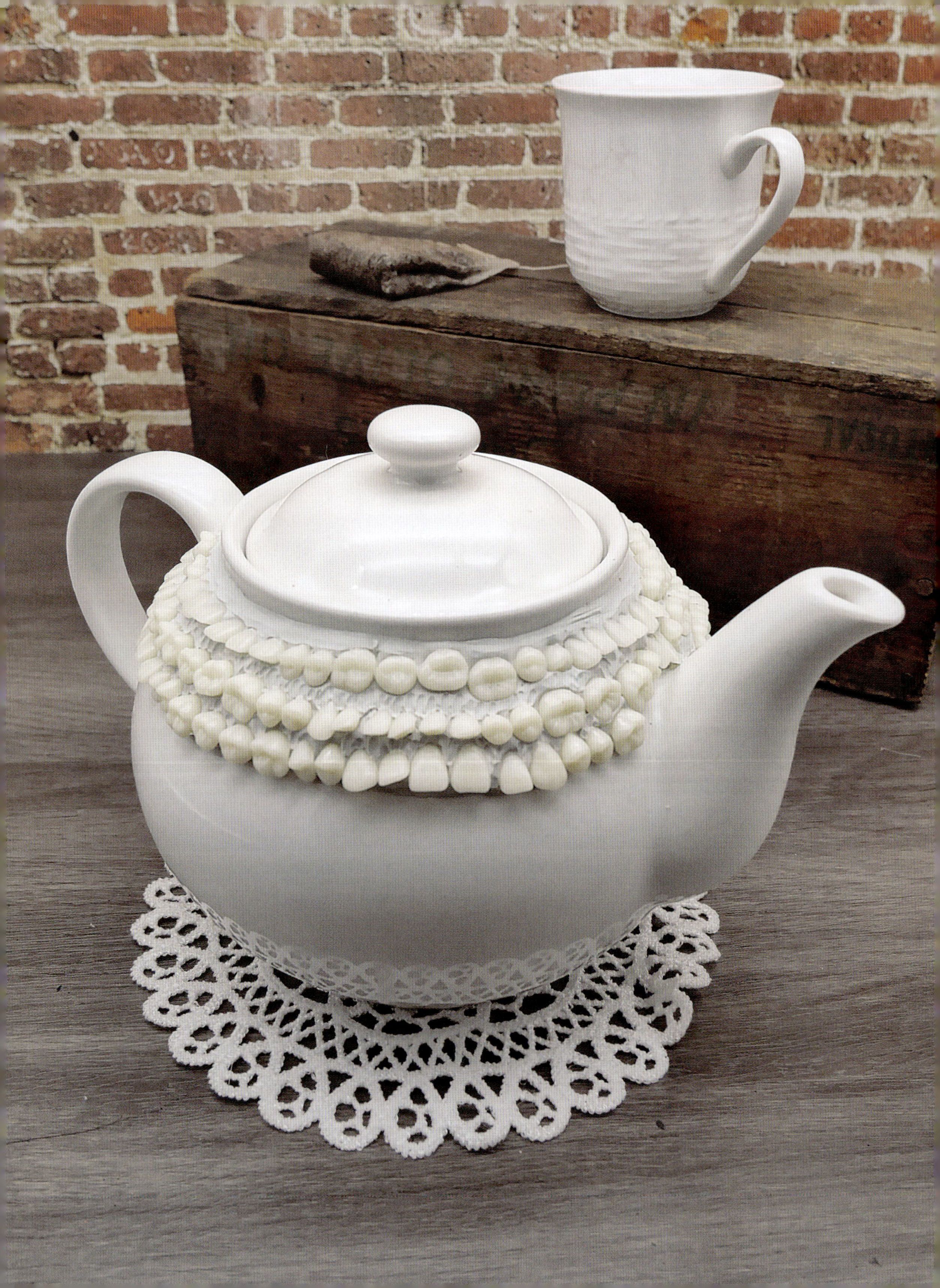

Teeth Pot

Should you drink out of this teapot? You could, but unlike real teeth, cleaning and brushing them might make them fall out. But it's going to look pretty stellar in your china cabinet!

Alternatively, you could make a Teeth Cup instead of a Teeth Pot. You'll just use less clay and fewer teeth.

Materials

- Silicone mat
- Disposable gloves
- White epoxy clay (e.g., Apoxie Sculpt)
- Teapot (or teacup)
- 5 full sets or more fake resin teeth
- Sculpting tools with round tip or silicone point

Lay down your silicone mat and put on your gloves. Mix together your epoxy clay. How big your teapot is will determine how much clay you mix. You can always mix more if you run out, but it's a waste if you mix too much. Start with a few gumball-sized amounts until you get a feel for how much you might need.

(continued)

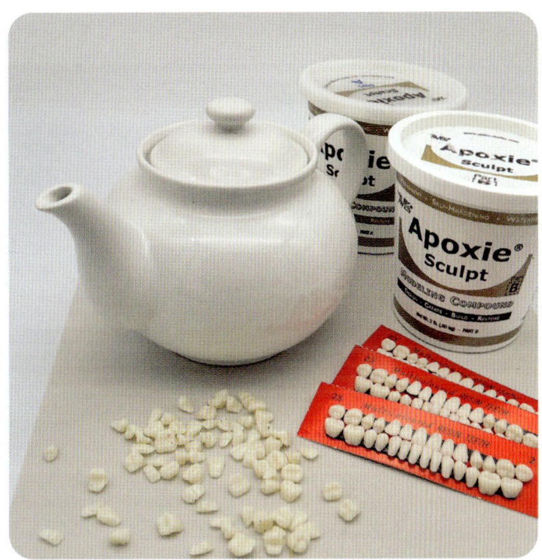

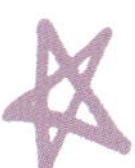

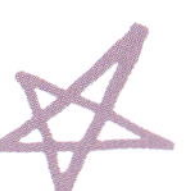

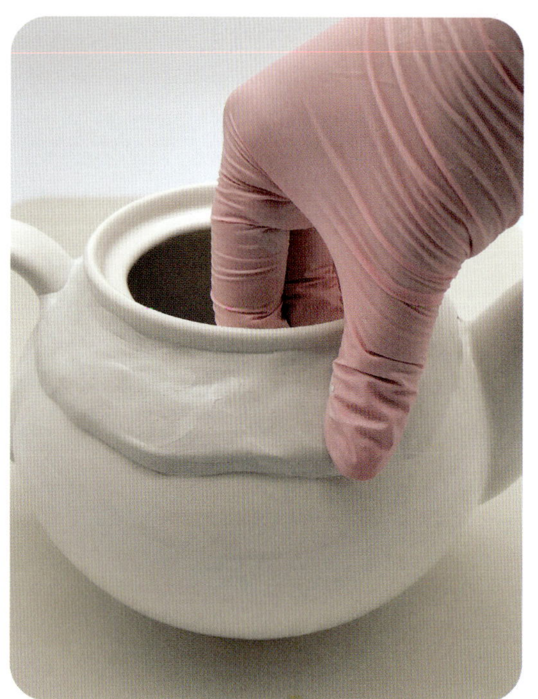

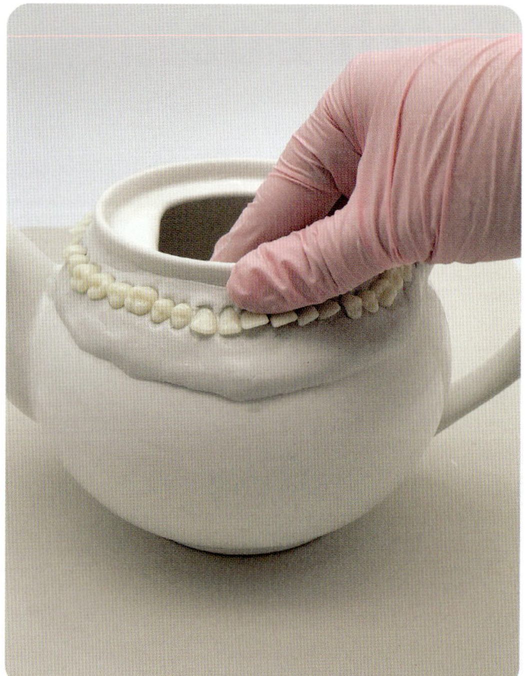

Smooth on a ¼-inch (6-mm)-thick coat of clay around the upper half of your teapot. Dip your gloved fingers into water to help smooth out the clay. Only smooth the clay 1 to 2 inches (2.5 to 5 cm) down from the top of your teapot.

Starting at the top of your teapot, push each tooth in side by side up and into the clay, burying the top part of each tooth in the clay. Work all the way around to make a complete circle, then start a second row under the first. I made three rows in total, but do what feels right to you. *If you're using a teacup instead, make rows all the way down until you reach the bottom.*

Using your round or silicone-point sculpting tools, form gums around each row of teeth. Let your monstrosity sit and harden for 24 hours.

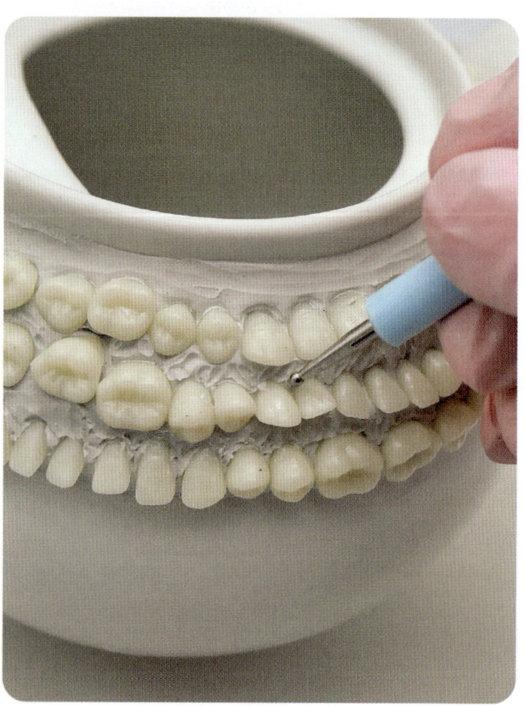

Spider Teacup

Over the years I've made a bunch of these spider teacups! For one, they are a lot easier to make than they look, and two, there's nothing better than seeing a whole shelf of spider cups coming at you. You can even make a whole spider family with a kid's tea set. This project will take a few days to complete, but I promise it's well worth it!

Unroll three 5-inch (12.7-cm) lengths of wire and pinch them together at the ends. Without cutting your wire, tightly wrap the wire around the strands starting at the top going down to hold them together. This should look like a stick wrapped in wire around 5 inches (12.7 cm) long. Do this five more times for a total of six wire sticks. These will be the frame for our spider legs. *You can do eight legs if you want; I just find six more manageable.*

Flip your teacup upside down and use a small amount of hot glue to evenly space your legs around the bottom of your teacup. DON'T USE TOO MUCH HOT GLUE! The hot glue is just meant to temporarily hold your legs.

(continued)

Materials

- Floral wire (any color)
- Teacup
- Hot glue and gun
- Disposable gloves
- Silicone mat
- Bronze epoxy clay (e.g., Apoxie Sculpt)
- Sculpting tools with round tip and silicone point
- 2" (5-cm) block or container (to set spider on)
- Cling wrap
- Matte black spray paint
- Swellegant copper metal coating
- Paintbrush
- Metal leaf gilding glue
- Imitation copper metal leaf
- Metal leaf varnish
- Tacky glue
- Gold embossing powder
- Heat gun
- Turquoise chalk paint (optional)
- Paper towels (optional)

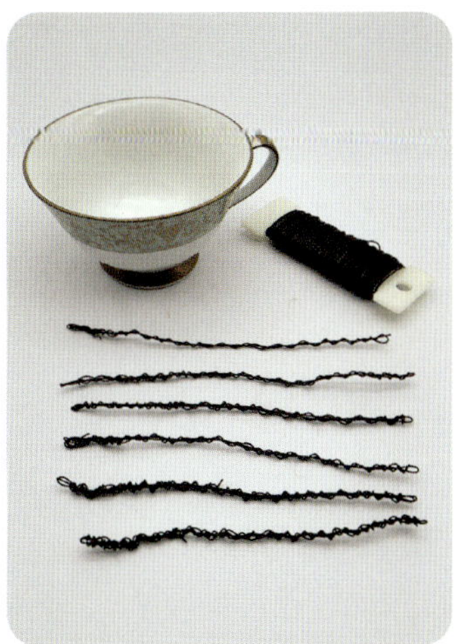

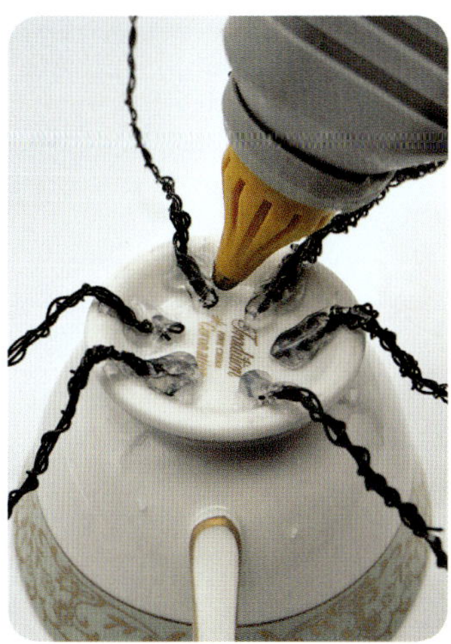

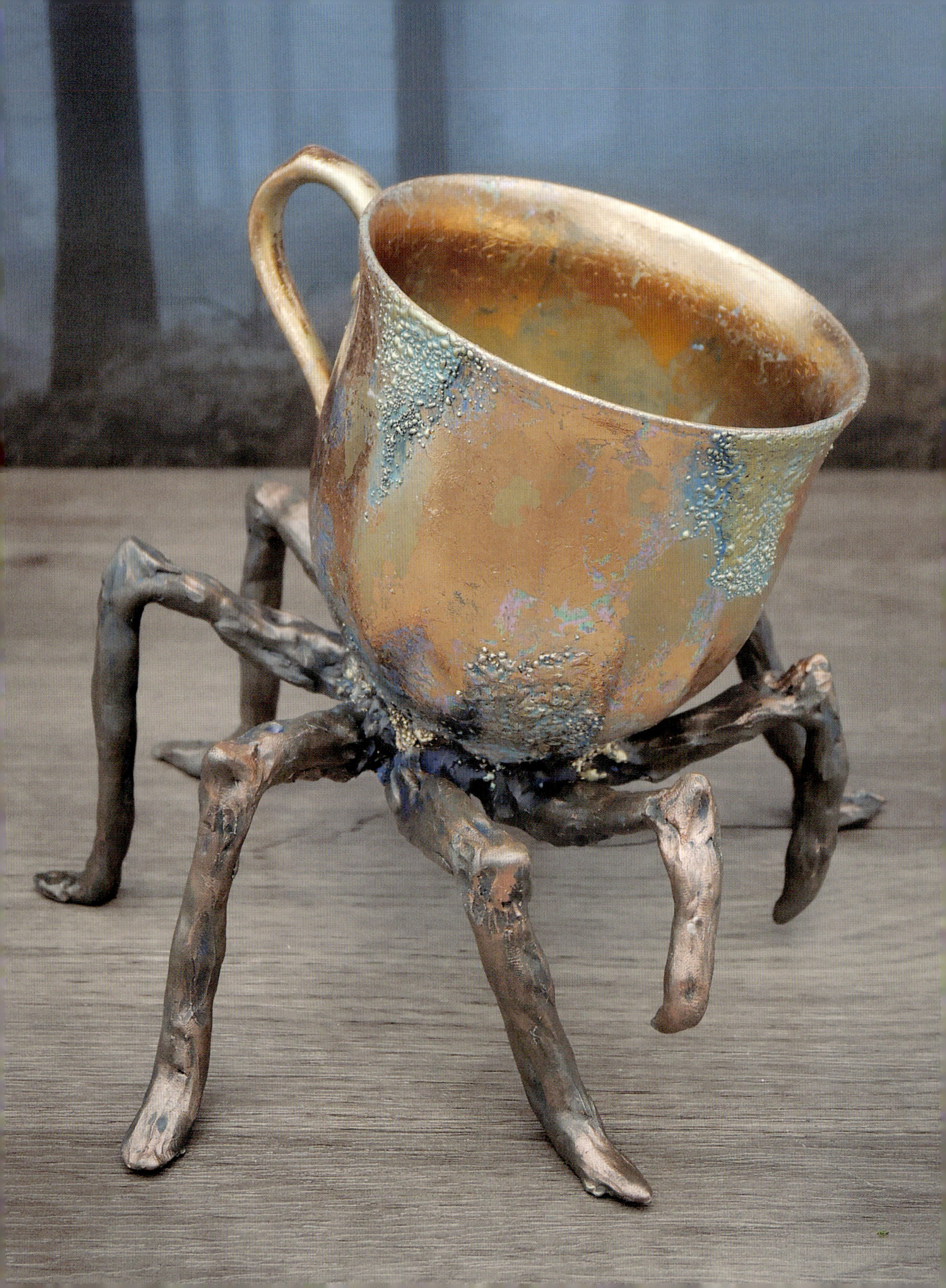

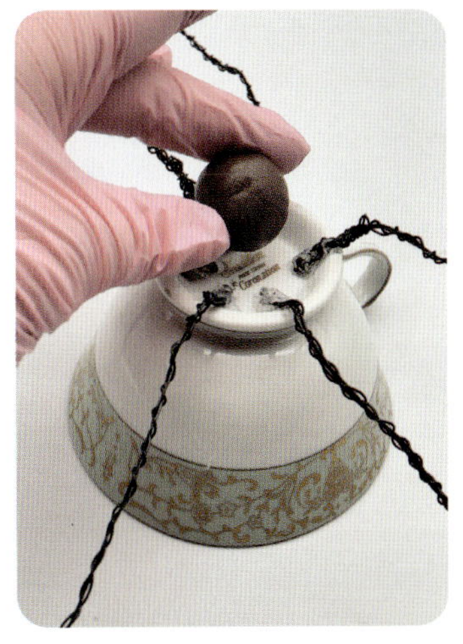 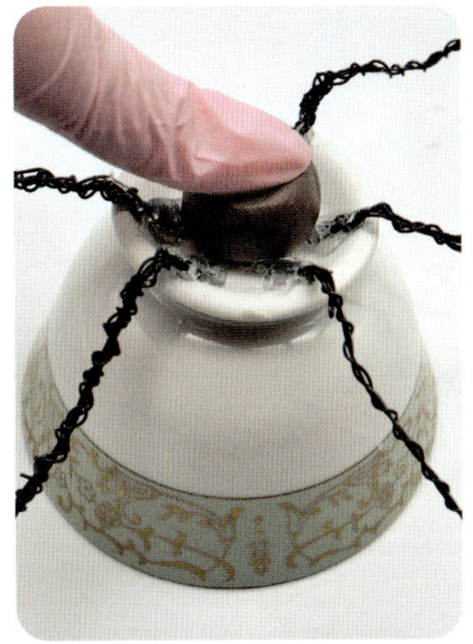 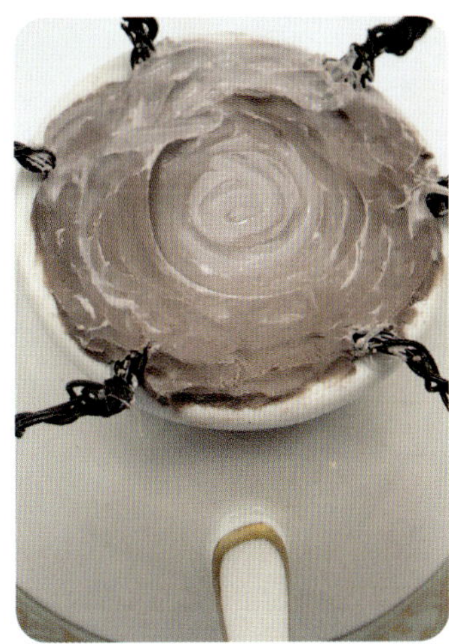

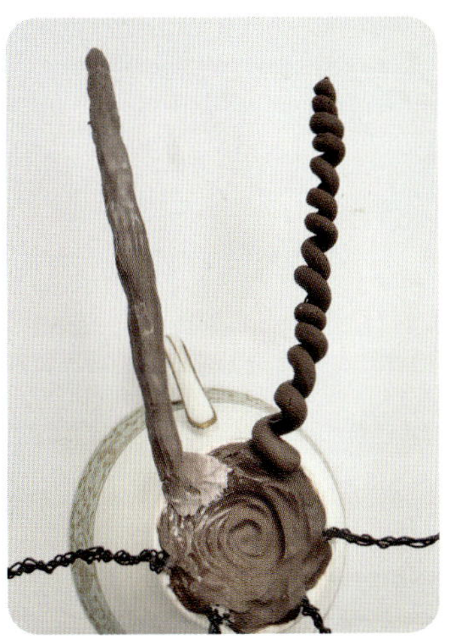 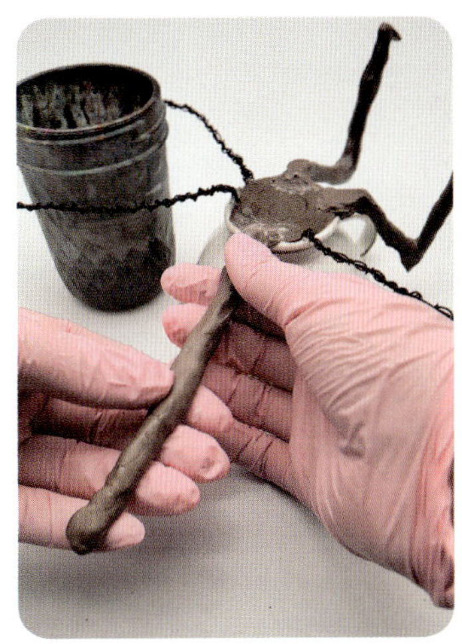 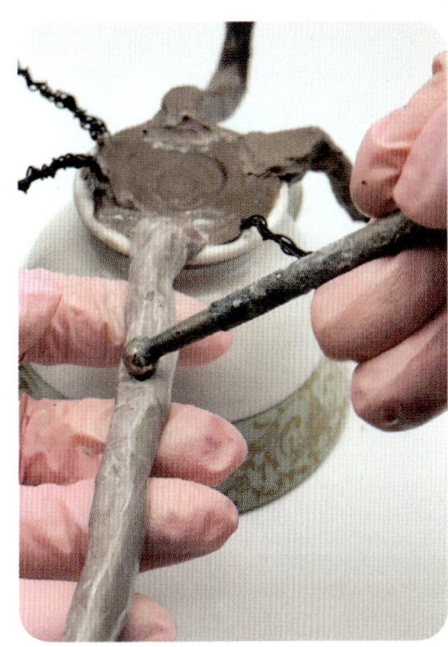

Put on your gloves, roll out your silicone mat and mix a small ball of epoxy clay that is just big enough to cover the bottom of your cup. Press the clay into the "crotch" of your spider. Dip your gloved finger into water and smooth it out over where you hot glued the legs onto your cup. Add a spiral on the bottom of your cup with a round-tipped sculpting tool. Wait 24 hours to cure.

Let's flesh out these legs! Mix a gumball-sized amount of epoxy clay and use your palms to roll a long rope about the thickness of a pea. Spiral it around one of the legs so that it covers it from top to bottom. Smooth it out by dipping your gloved fingertips in water and massaging the clay smooth. Repeat for the remaining legs. Once all your legs are covered, add tree branch texture by dragging a silicone-point sculpting tool up and down each leg.

Tip: Only mix enough clay to cover one leg at a time. This will help keep the clay from hardening too quickly as you work.

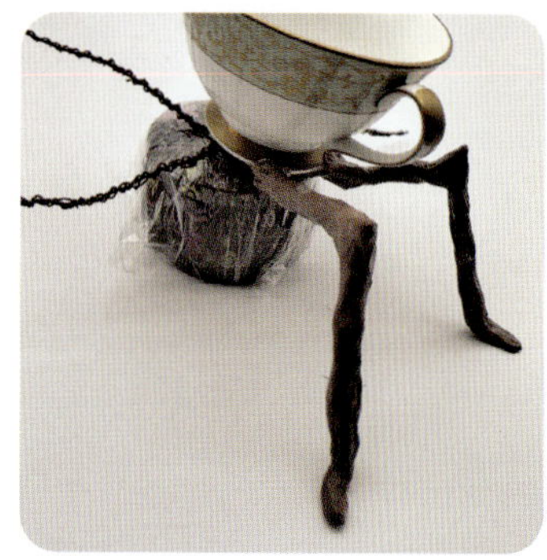 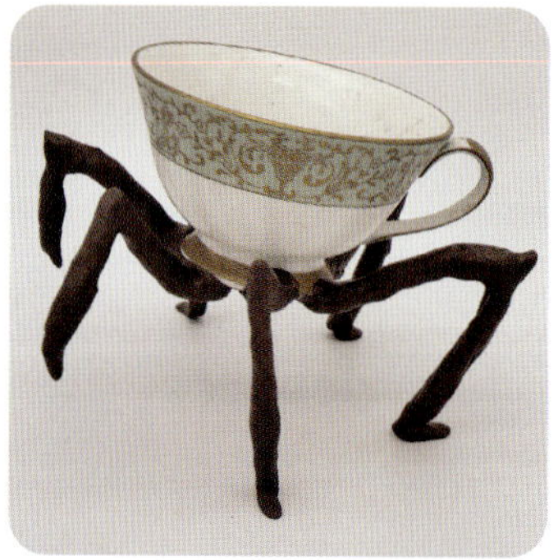 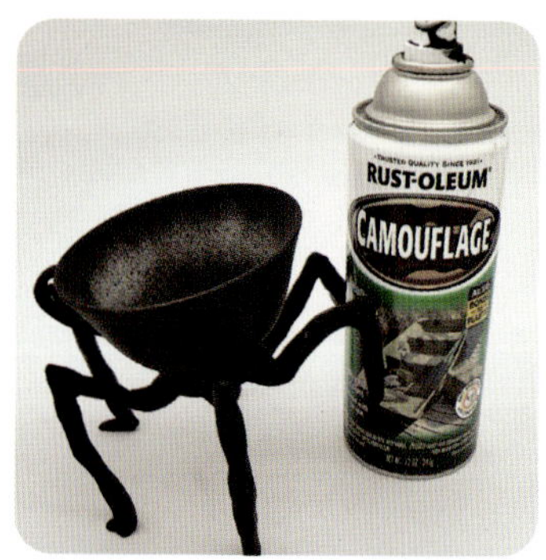

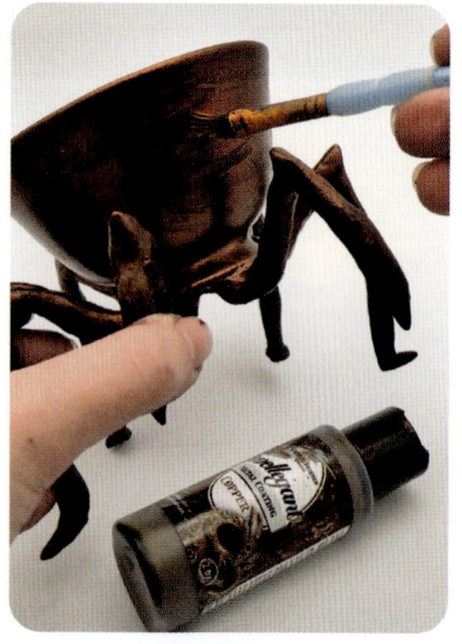 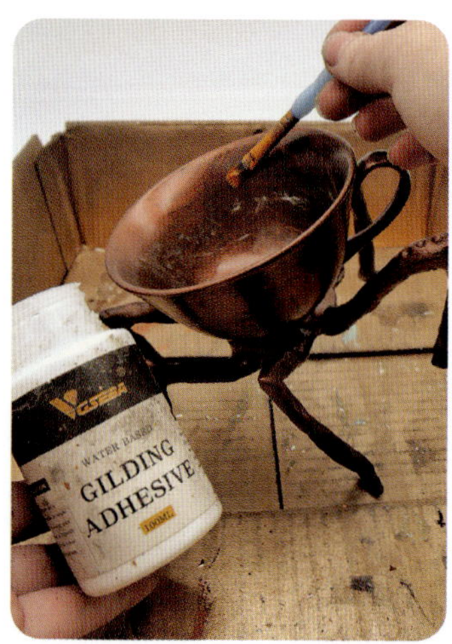 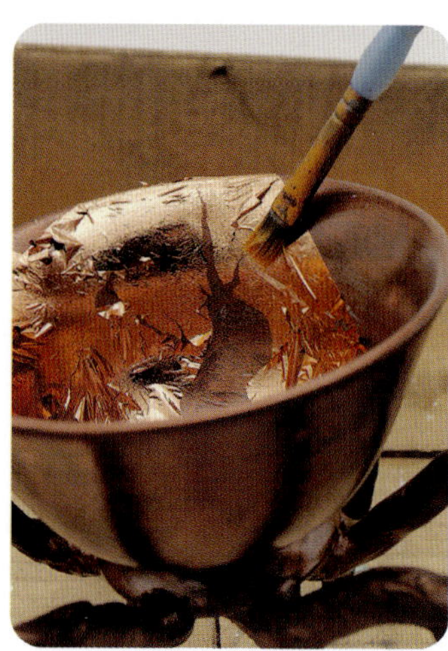

Now that our spider feels less vulnerable and naked, let's mold these legs into a more spidery shape. Cover your block or container in cling wrap and set your spider crotch on top. This will act as a stand while your legs harden. Fold each leg from the base up into the air and then in the middle, making an upside-down V shape. Make sure each foot is touching the mat. Using leftover clay, form a spider foot at the bottom of each leg.

Set your spider in a safe space for 24 hours to contemplate its new spider life. Once it's hardened, peel it off the cling wrap. It should now stand on its own.

Spray-paint your entire spider cup matte black. Let this dry for 1 to 4 hours, but check your package for more accurate dry times.

Next, let's add some color by painting the entire spider cup with copper paint. Let this dry for 20 minutes.

Apply a thin layer of gilding adhesive to the inside of your cup, around the rim and randomly around the leg joints. Wait for it to get tacky (usually 10 to 20 minutes). Make sure you don't leave any wet puddles of glue, as the foil won't adhere to wet puddles. Then slap that foil on! Brush any excess foil off.

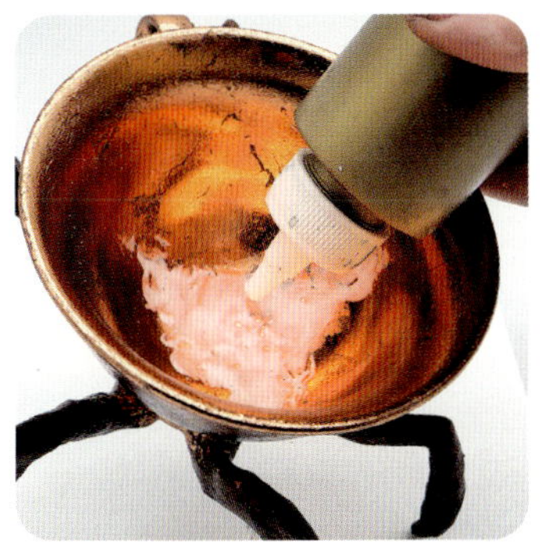 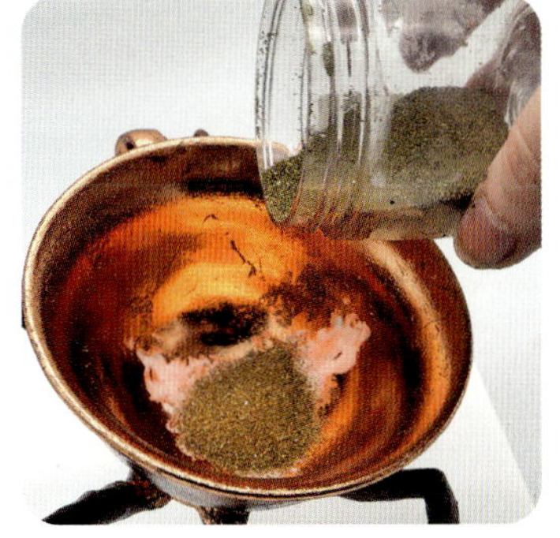 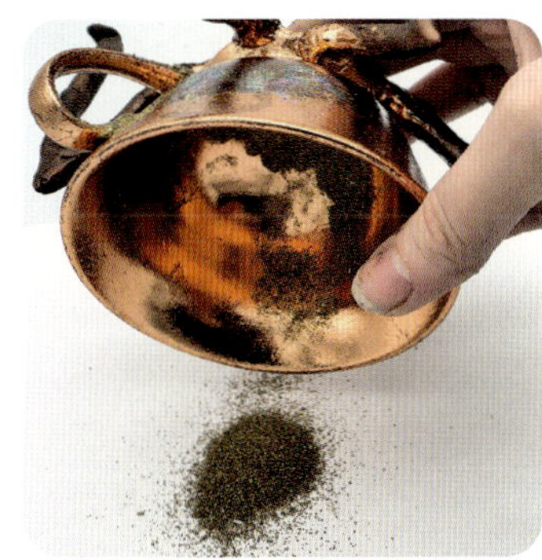

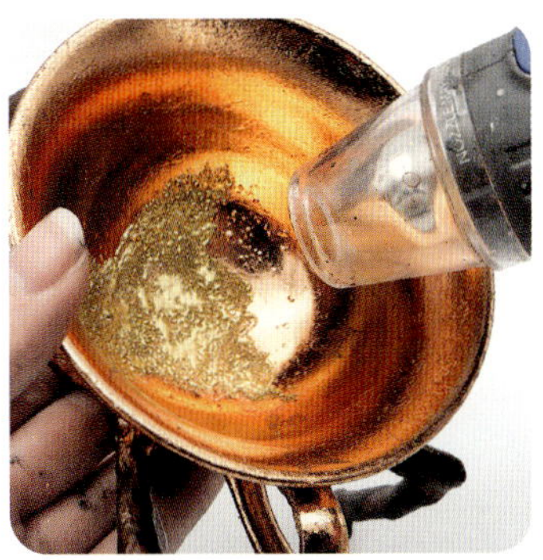 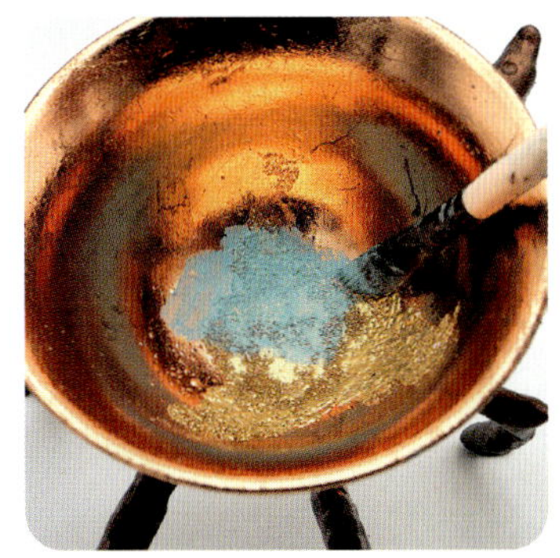 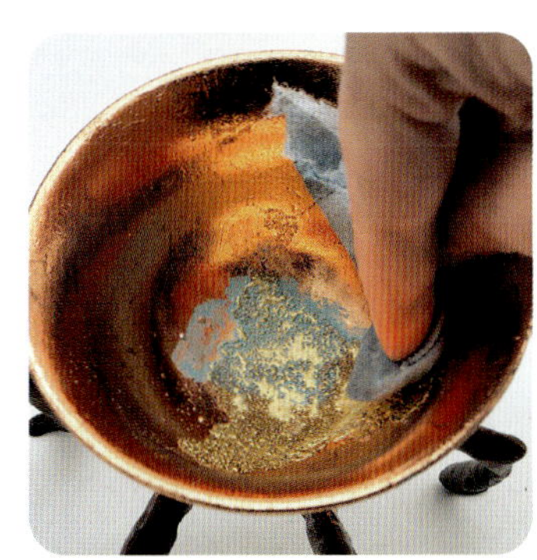

Clear coat over all the foil with metal leaf varnish to keep it locked in place.

Squeeze a small amount of tacky glue inside your cup and smooth it out with your finger. Before the glue dries, sprinkle on your gold embossing powder. Tap any excess off and heat what's stuck onto your cup with your heat gun until bubbles form. Repeat this process on the outside, around the leg joints and/or handle if desired.

Optional Details: Adding turquoise paint is an optional step that I feel pulls it all together. Coat each bubble cluster in paint and wipe it away with a paper towel. This leaves paint inside the crevasses and makes it look tarnished.

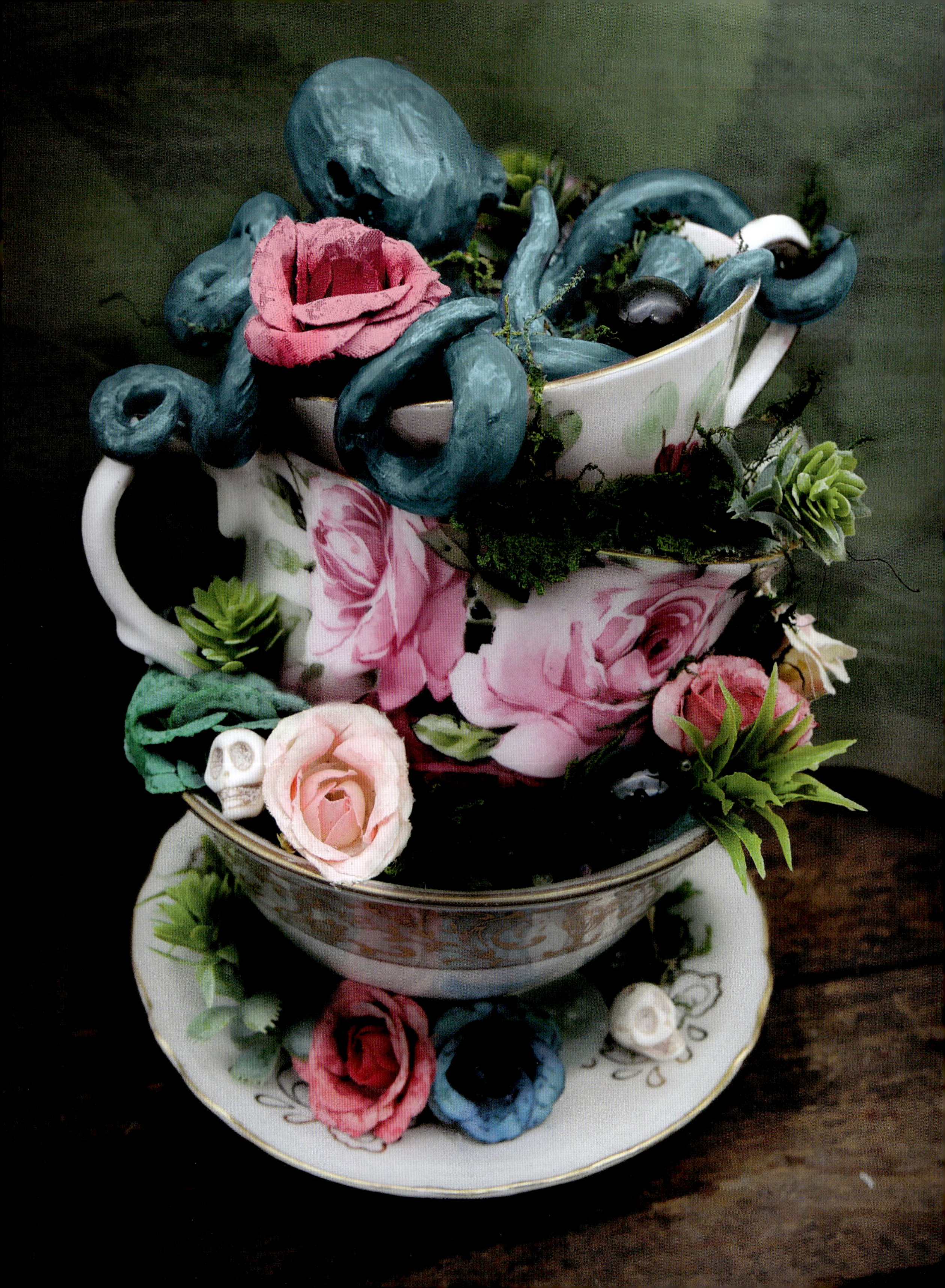

Tipsy Teacup Tentacles

Why is an octopus lurking inside teacups? Maybe you should ask her, since she's the one being mysterious here . . .

My cupboard became a haven for the mismatched cups in the world! So much so that at some point I decided it was time to grow up and get matching cuplery. (*You know, cutlery but with cups. IDK, what would you call it?*) However, I have a weakness for shiny objects and that led me right back to collecting more mismatched cups. Anyway, that's how this project grew out of a need to use them all up.

Materials

- 3 teacups and 1 saucer (mismatched)
- Aluminum foil
- Hot glue and gun
- Silicone mat
- Disposable gloves
- Epoxy clay (e.g., Apoxie Sculpt)
- Sculpting tools with round tip and silicone point
- Acrylic paint and brush
- Moss, fake flowers and/or plants
- Precision craft glue (e.g., Bearly Art®)
- Marbles

First, we have to plan our cup tower. Start off with your three teacups and one saucer and place them inside of each other, alternating handle placements with the saucer at the bottom. Assuming your teacups are all different, we need to get a sense of which teacups should go first, second and third. Once you've arranged them the way you like, fill the top cup with tightly packed aluminum foil ½ to 1 inch (1.3 to 2.5 cm) below the rim. Pull out your wad of aluminum and hot glue it back in place.

(continued)

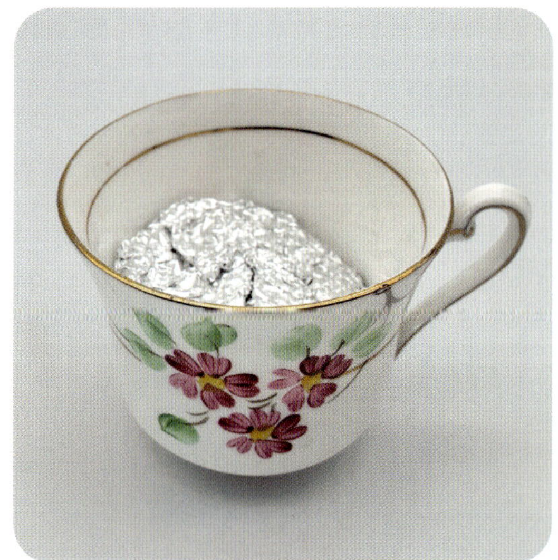

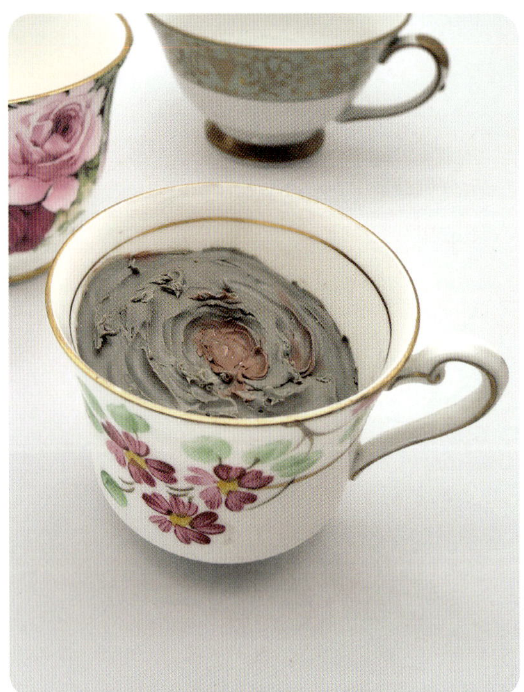

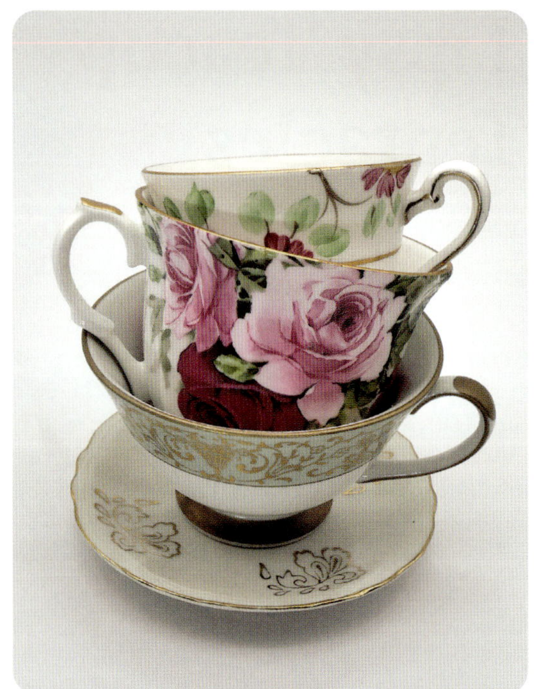

Lay down your silicone mat and put on your gloves. Mix four gumball-sized epoxy clay balls. Use one ball to cover the foil in your top cup (around ¼ inch [6 mm] thick). Place one ball in the bottom of each of the other two cups and in the middle of the saucer. Then assemble your tower. These clay gumballs will be the glue that holds it all together and also act as spacers between your cups. Adjust the cups so that the handles are alternating sides and everything looks a little askew.

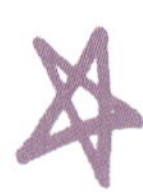

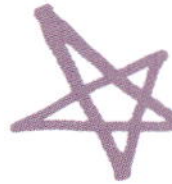

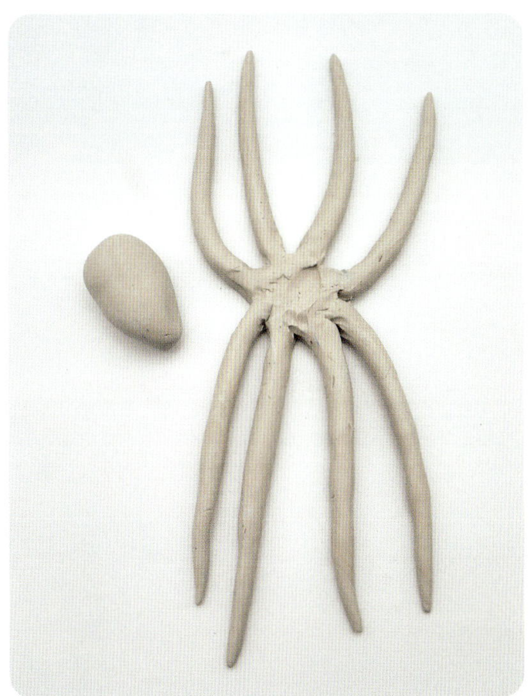 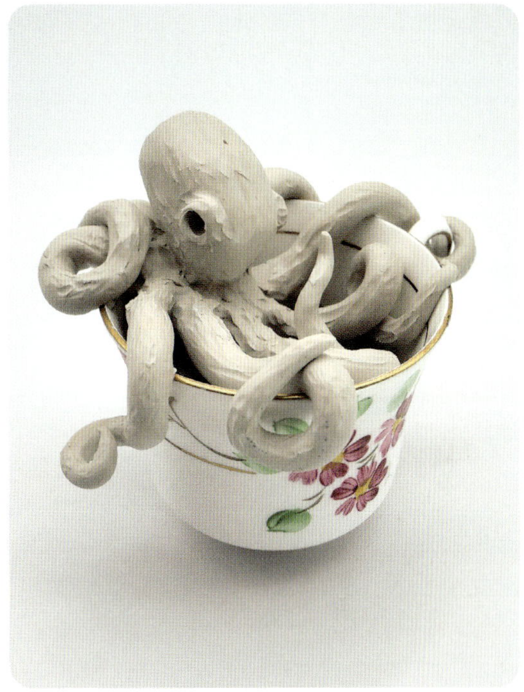

Let's make a puss! Working on your silicone mat, mix two golf ball–sized amounts of epoxy clay. Divide your clay into nine equal parts, eight for the legs and one for the head. Roll the legs out into a tapered cylinder and mash the thicker ends together using your fingers, making a pinwheel shape. Smooth the seams together with water and your gloved finger. Roll an oval ball and attach it to the middle of your pinwheel. Secure it by smoothing the edges with a round-tipped sculpting tool. Using your sculpting tools, add eyeholes on either side of the head. Add texture with your round-tipped sculpting tool to give your octopus more character.

Shape your clay octopus into the top cup of your teacup tower. Wrap a leg around the handle and droop other legs down the sides. Really let your octopus appear at home in your cups. Set aside for 8 or more hours to set.

Let's add the finishing details! An octopus can change its colors, so paint your octopus any color you like. Tuck moss in between the cups and secure with precision craft glue. *Don't use hot glue on moss, or it will dry it out and make the moss brittle.* Use hot glue on any artificial plants, marbles or other embellishment. *I think the marbles look like bubbles!*

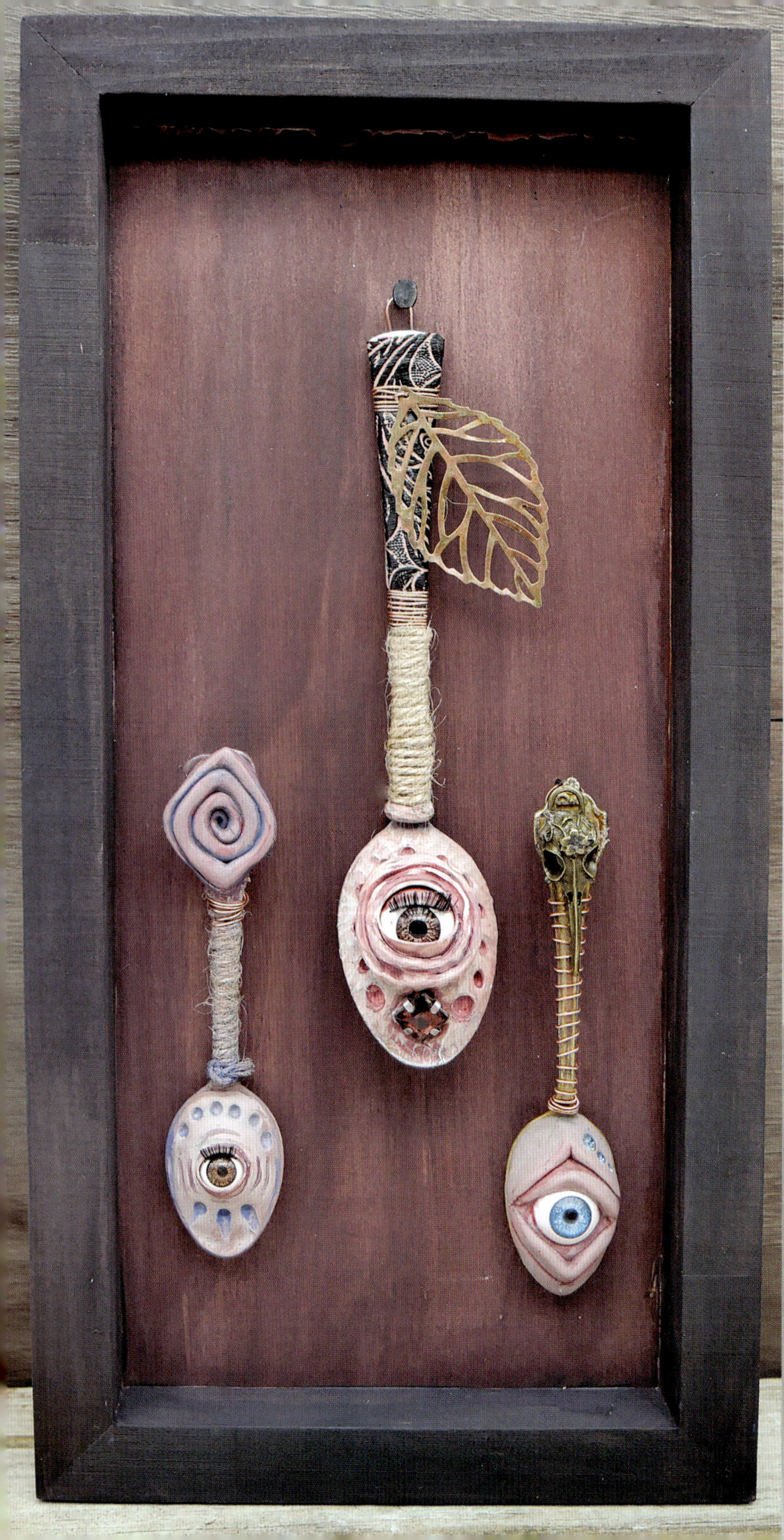

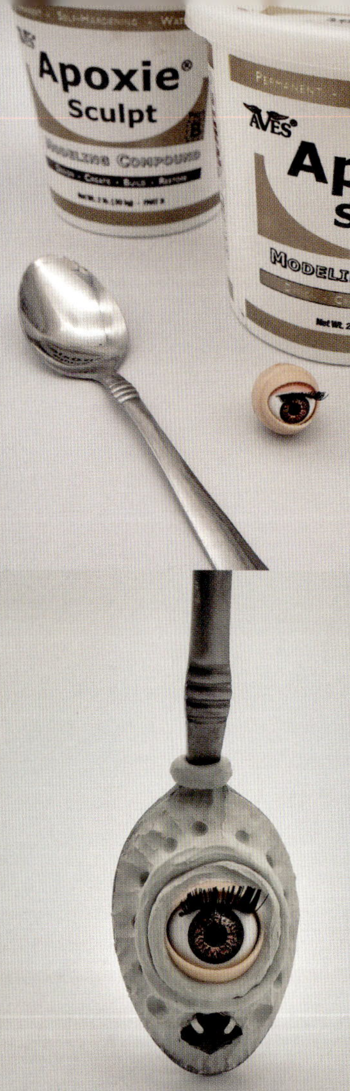
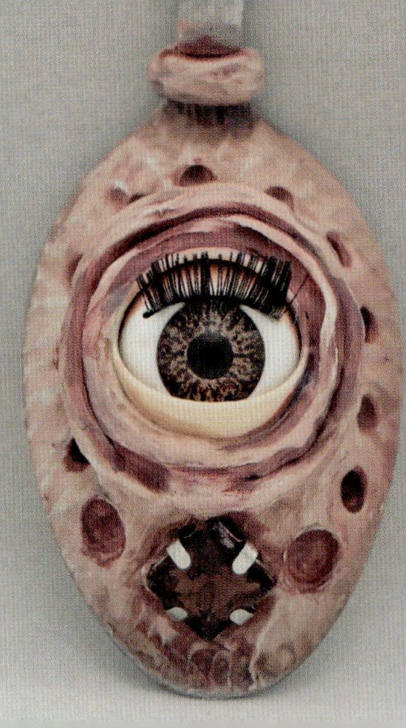

All-Seeing Sugar Spoon

I have a few spoons that are unusable because they took a journey into the garbage disposal. Should I have checked the garbage disposal before turning it on? Yes, but don't you watch horror movies?! I'm positive that's how my hand gets cut off! So, I ended up with a handful of spoons that make me feel like the Joker when I sip soup from them. This is a great craft to save your dinged-up spoons from the trash!

This is a pretty easy project to do and doesn't require a lot of skill. The hardest part is waiting for your clay to harden.

Materials

- Silicone mat
- Disposable gloves
- Epoxy clay
- Metal spoon
- Plastic eye
- Sculpting tools with round tip and silicone point
- Gem
- Acrylic paint and brush
- Paper towels
- Twine or fabric (optional)
- Craft glue (if needed)
- Floral wire
- Rectangular wooden canvas or frame (optional)
- Small finishing nails and hammer

Lay out your silicone mat and put on your gloves. Mix enough epoxy clay to fill the bowl part of the spoon. Push the eye right in the middle of your spoon. If you have an eye that blinks, make sure you don't get any clay on the lid so that it still freely blinks.

Add details around the eye using your sculpting tools. Use a round-tipped sculpting tool to make holes and/or a silicone-point sculpting tool to add a few wrinkles. Let the clay set for at least 2 hours.

Let's make your spoon fancy by adding a gem to the bottom with epoxy clay.

Paint the clay a skin color of your choice. Let the paint dry for 5 to 10 minutes. Then fill in all the "wrinkles" of your eye and surrounding clay with a darker maroon paint, wiping off any excess with a paper towel. We only want the darker color to fill in the "skin" folds.

Now for the handle. You could leave it as is, or if you want to be "extra," wrap it in twine or fabric. Secure the twine or fabric with craft glue if needed. Wrap a small amount of wire at the top and close it off with a loop at the back. This is so you can hang your spoon.

Lastly, it needs a home. You can use a picture frame, shadow box or wooden canvas, or anything you have on hand that you can put a nail through. Or just skip this part and hang it directly on the wall. I'm using a 6 x 12–inch (15 x 30–cm) wooden canvas flipped around. Hammer a small finishing nail in the top center of your wood. *Be careful what's behind it while you hammer.* Then hang your spoon on the nail. Everyone will be quite jealous when they see your All-Seeing Sugar Spoon.

Add more spoons for more spoony goodness!

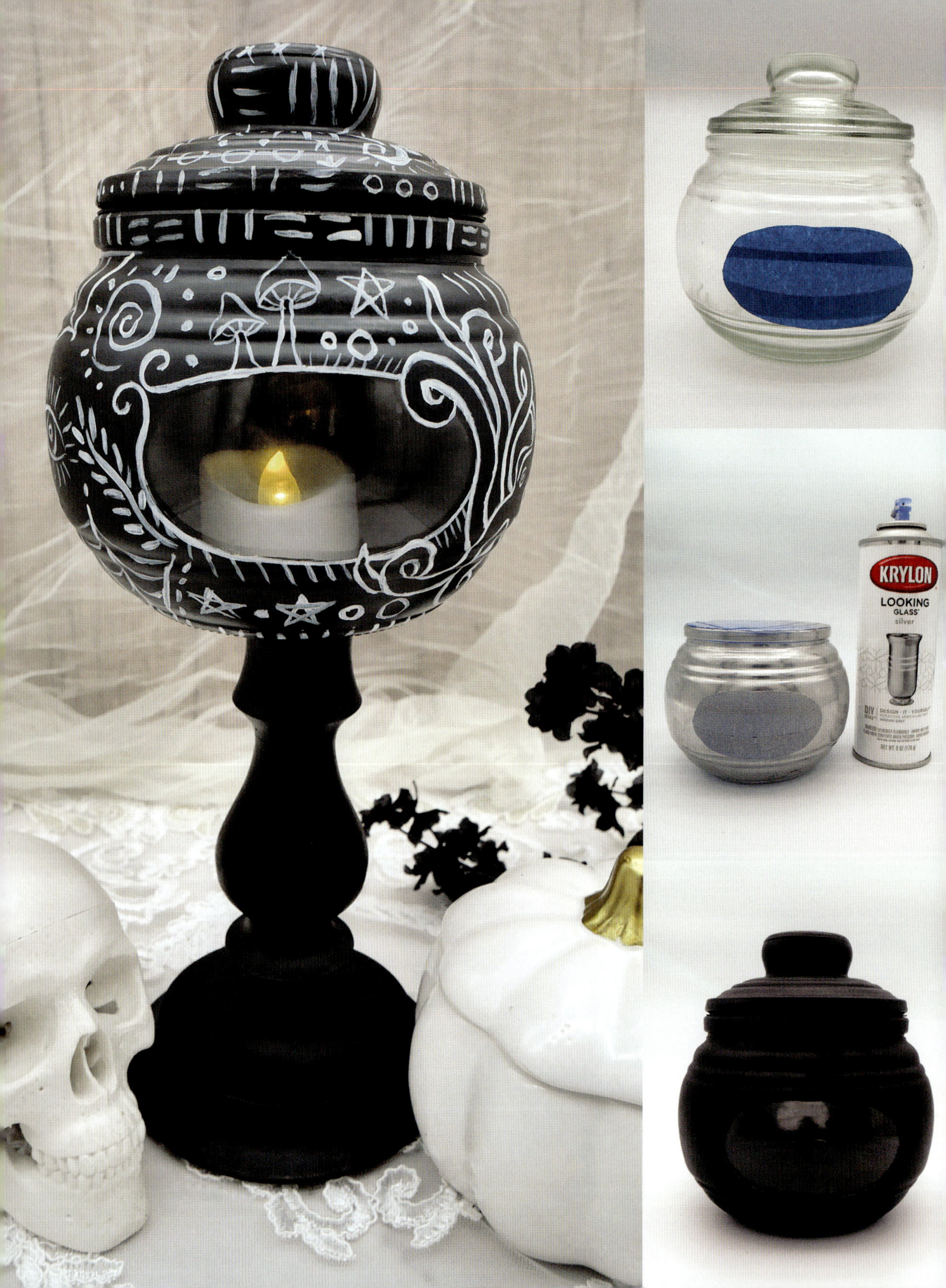

KRYLON
LOOKING
GLASS
silver

Candy Dish Candle

I found this super cute candy dish at the dollar store and I initially thought, "What a cute way to display candy for my family and guests!" Oh boy, was I wrong! I didn't take into account that my family is a bunch of scavengers. The second I'd fill it *(and I am the only one who fills it, by the way)* it would be empty. Or worse, they'd complain about what candy was in it! I was done. You barbarians lost all candy dish privileges! So instead, I made it into a candleholder!

This project is super easy. You can upscale your current candy dish or turn it into a candleholder, it's up to you! If you can draw a few squiggles and lines, you can do this project!

Using rubbing alcohol and a paper towel, wipe down your candy dish and let it air-dry. This gets the oils from grubby little fingers off the surface and helps the paint stick. Place masking tape in overlapping strips on the front of your bowl and use an X-ACTO knife to cut an oval. Peel off the excess tape around the oval. Cover the opening of the bowl with tape. *We don't want any paint to end up on the inside because that's not yummy!*

Spray-paint the whole bowl with silver mirror paint. *I like the mirror paint for candles because it will reflect the light.* Let it dry for 30 to 60 minutes.

Once it is fully dry, spray-paint the whole thing black. Let this paint dry for 30 to 60 minutes. Carefully peel off the tape.

Using a small paintbrush, paint on some white details. You could do abstract squiggles, or you could paint mushrooms, octopuses, mushroom octopuses . . . whatever you like. Just keep it simple. Once your white paint is dry, clear coat your work with Mod Podge.

Lastly, hot glue a candleholder to the bottom of the dish. This is totally optional, but I think it gives it a classier look. Put in your candle or candy and TA-DA! You now have a fancy holder!

Materials

- Rubbing alcohol and paper towel
- Clear glass candy dish or bowl
- Masking tape
- X-ACTO knife
- Silver mirror spray paint
- Black spray paint
- Acrylic paint and brush
- Mod Podge
- Hot glue and gun (optional)
- Candleholder (optional)
- Candle or candy (optional)

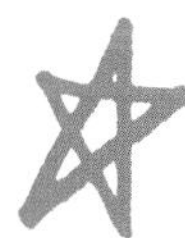

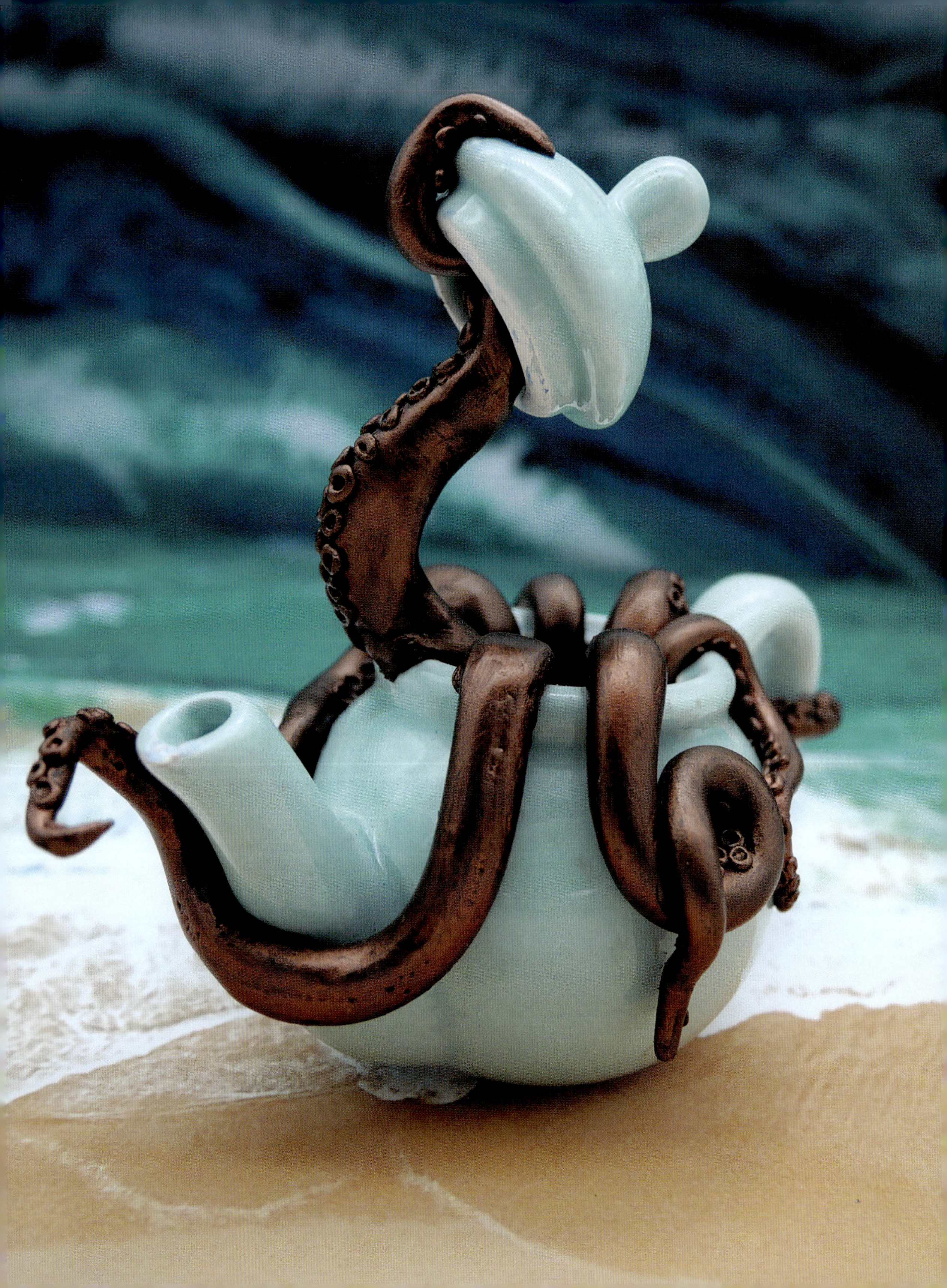

Tentacled Teapot

I like this project because it combines my two favorite things: teapots and octopuses! You could use a regular-sized teapot for this project if you like, just use a lot more clay. Epoxy clay comes in different colors. I used bronze, but use whatever color you have. Additionally, you can swap out the epoxy clay for polymer clay on this project, but keep in mind that polymer clay isn't as strong and you'll have to forgo the tentacle sticking up.

Lay out your silicone mat and put on your gloves. Mix a small amount of epoxy clay. The amount will vary depending on how big your teapot is. Keep in mind that you can always mix more, but you can never mix less. For my tiny teapot I started with a gumball-sized amount.

Using the palm of your gloved hand, roll your clay into a tapered tentacle shape. Roll 10 to 15 tiny peppercorn-sized balls. These will be your suction cups. Stick them in a row going down your tentacle. Using a small round-tipped sculpting tool, push a dimple in the middle of each ball. Repeat until you have five tentacles.

(continued)

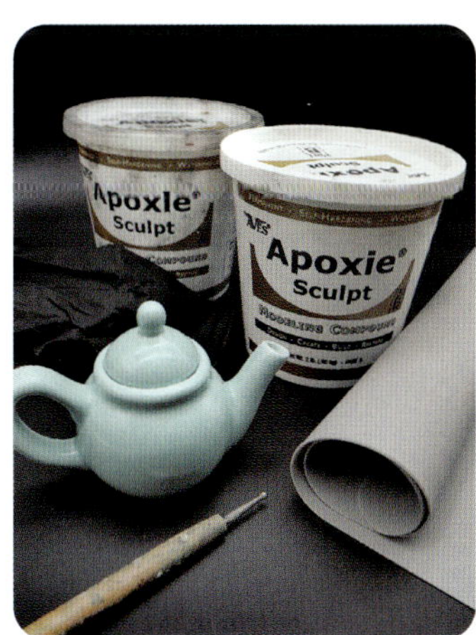

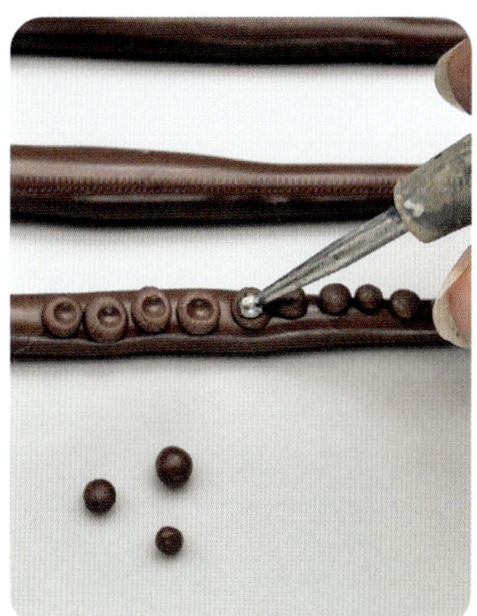

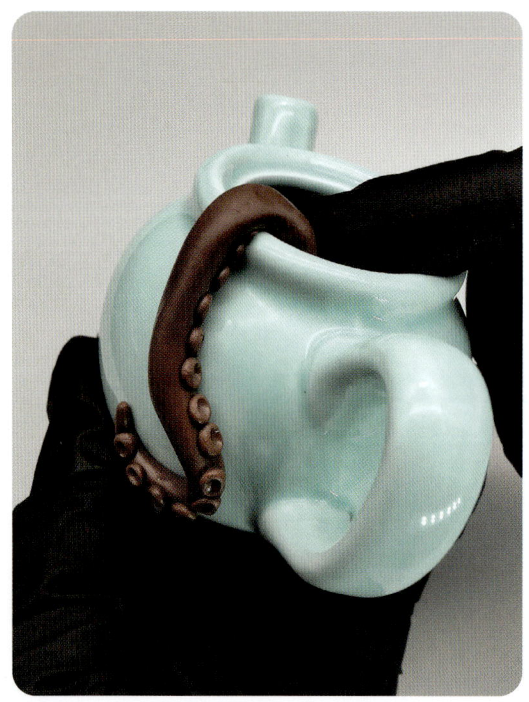

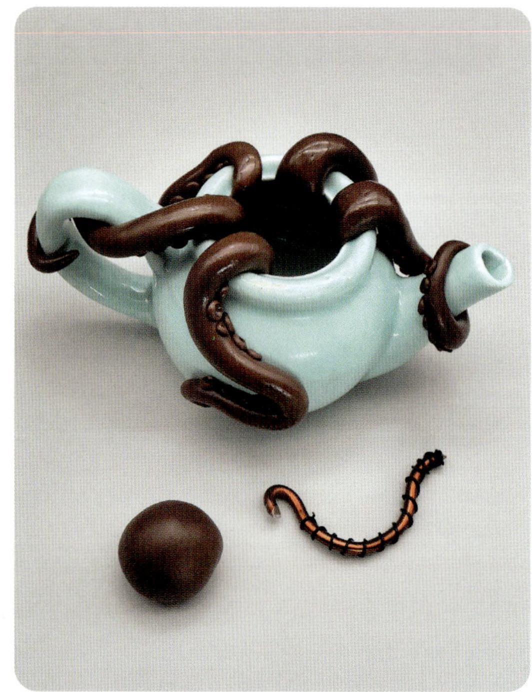

Start on the inside of the teapot and press the thicker side of your tentacle along the inside edge of the teapot hole. Continue to add two more tentacles around the hole, then wrap one tentacle around the handle and one around the spout. You should have five tentacles attached to your teapot. Leave room for a sixth tentacle on the side. *You can do seven tentacles if you're using a bigger teapot. Unfortunately, the real estate on this tiny teapot is small, so I did five.*

Take your 3 mm wire and cut it about the length of a tentacle. Wrap this wire with thinner floral wire, spiraling up. *The floral wire makes it so the clay will stick.* Shape your wire into a crude S shape with a small hook on the end. Make sure the hook is large enough to wrap around the edge of your teapot hole. Cover your S wire with clay, leaving the hook part open. Wrap the hook around the edge of the teapot hole. Using a small amount of hot glue, glue it to the inside of your teapot.

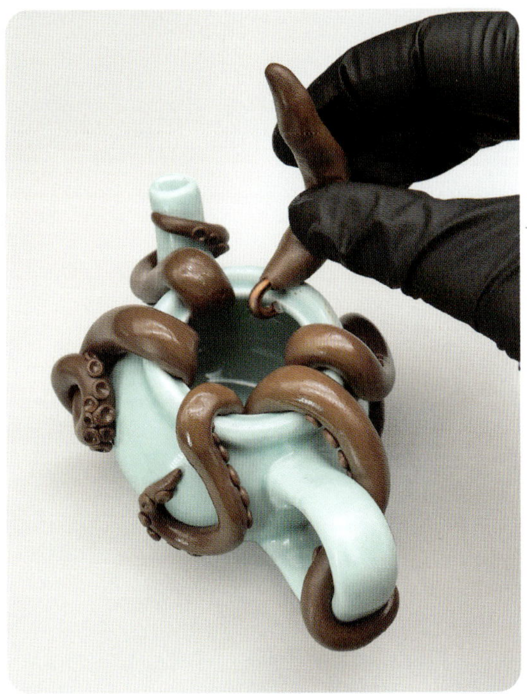

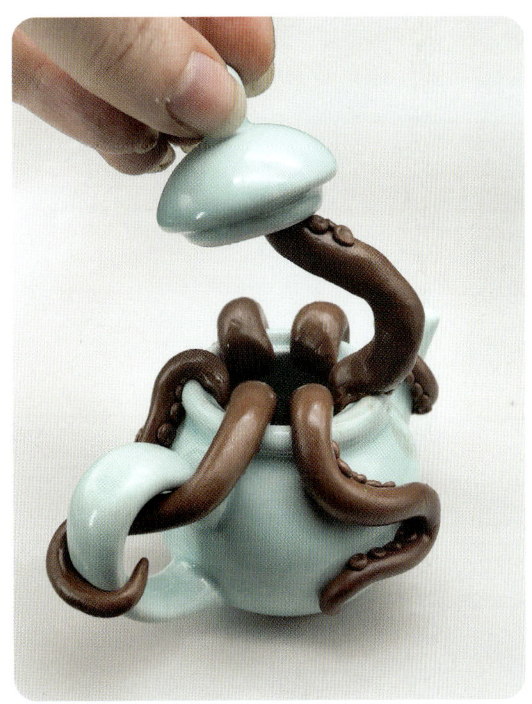

Cover the hot glue and wire hook with epoxy clay. Make sure you have clay touching the inside of your teapot. *Because hot glue SUCKS and epoxy clay will be what adds the strength once it hardens.* Make this tentacle look like the rest of the tentacles only going straight up in the air. Let this set for 24 hours.

Put on your gloves and mix up an olive-sized amount of clay. Sculpt a tentacle tip coming out of the underside of your teapot lid. Use any excess clay to attach the lid to the tentacle sticking up. Let it sit for 24 hours. Paint your tentacles if desired.

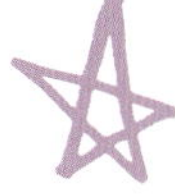

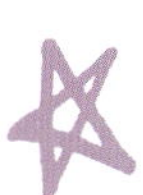

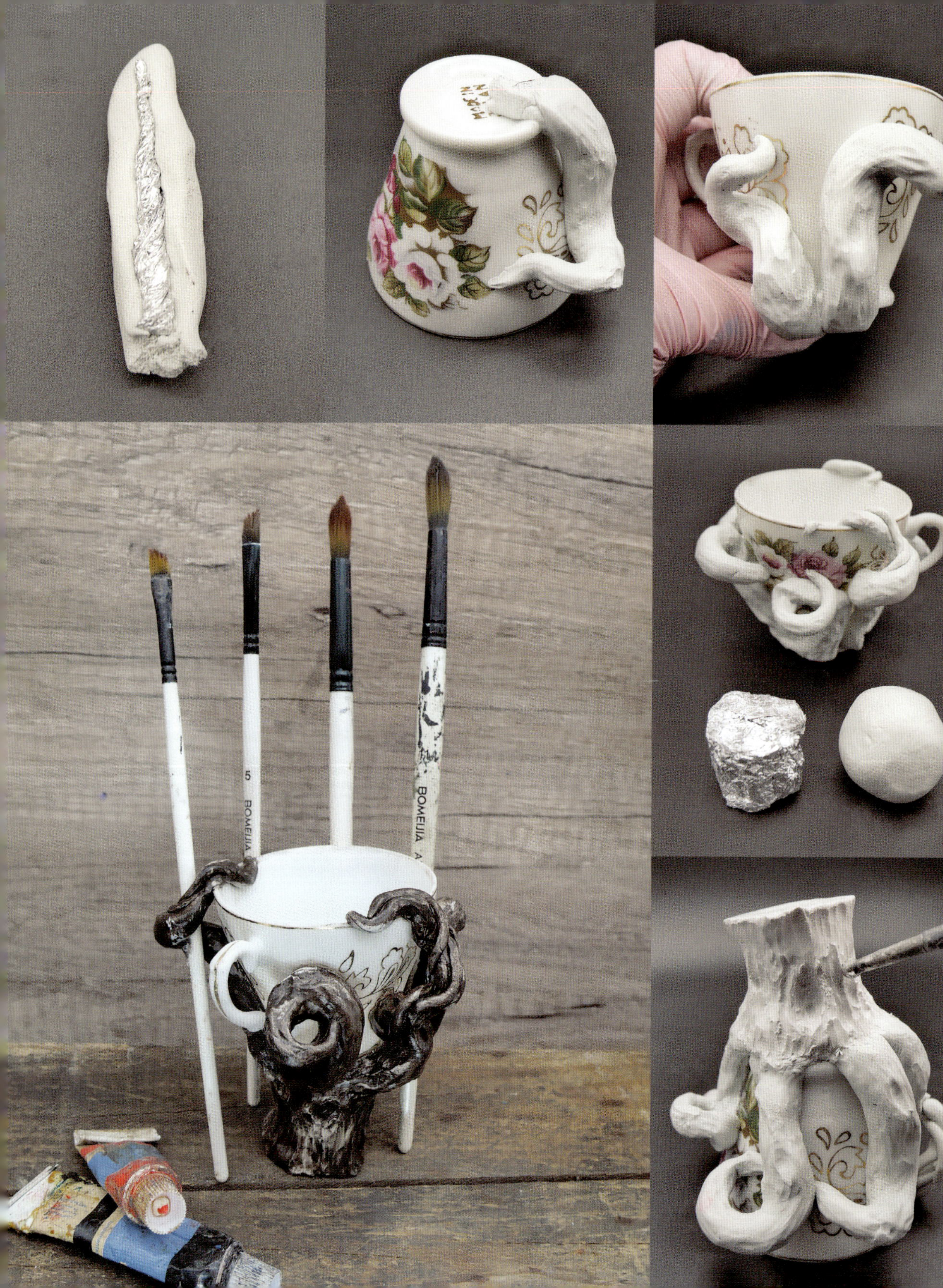

Twisted Tea Tree

Materials

- Aluminum foil
- Disposable gloves
- Silicone mat
- Epoxy clay (e.g., Apoxie Sculpt)
- Teacup
- Sculpting tools with round tip
- Acrylic paint and brush

I began this project with the intention of making it hold my toothbrush. But then I wondered, what purpose would the cup part serve? Perhaps floss? Who actually flosses anyway? We all tell our dentist that we do, but let's be honest, you don't. Instead, I decided to make this a paintbrush holder. In the middle you can put water or paint, making it a far better use of space.

To start off we'll make four to six branches out of aluminum foil. Crumple the foil into a skinny leg roughly 3 to 5 inches (7.5 to 12.7 cm) long and no thicker than a pencil on the thickest end. Put on your gloves and lay down your silicone mat. Mix together a golf ball–sized amount of clay for each branch and wrap each branch with clay.

Press one of your branches onto the bottom of your cup and make a loop. Keep working until all your branches are attached to your cup. Make sure each loop is large enough to hold a paintbrush or pencil, whatever you decide your cup should hold.

Drag a round-tipped sculpting tool the length of each branch to add texture. Add knots to your branches by pushing that same tool into the clay and making circles radiating out. Set this on a silicone mat to harden overnight.

Crumple up a ball of aluminum foil and flatten the ends to make a short cylinder about the same diameter as your cup bottom.

With gloves on, cover your foil cylinder with a thin layer of epoxy clay. Flip your cup upside down and attach your cylinder to the bottom. Smooth out the seams with a round-tipped tool. This will be the trunk of your tree. Add texture to your tree trunk to match your branches.

Flip your cup back over and make sure your branches will hold your paintbrushes or pencils without falling out. If they do fall out or don't want to stand up correctly, add clay vines or bumps to make them more secure. Don't let your clay harden with these brushes in the loops unless you want them to be permanent structures. Set your tree aside for 4 or more hours to cure.

Finish off your tree by painting it the color of your choice.

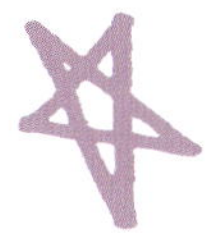

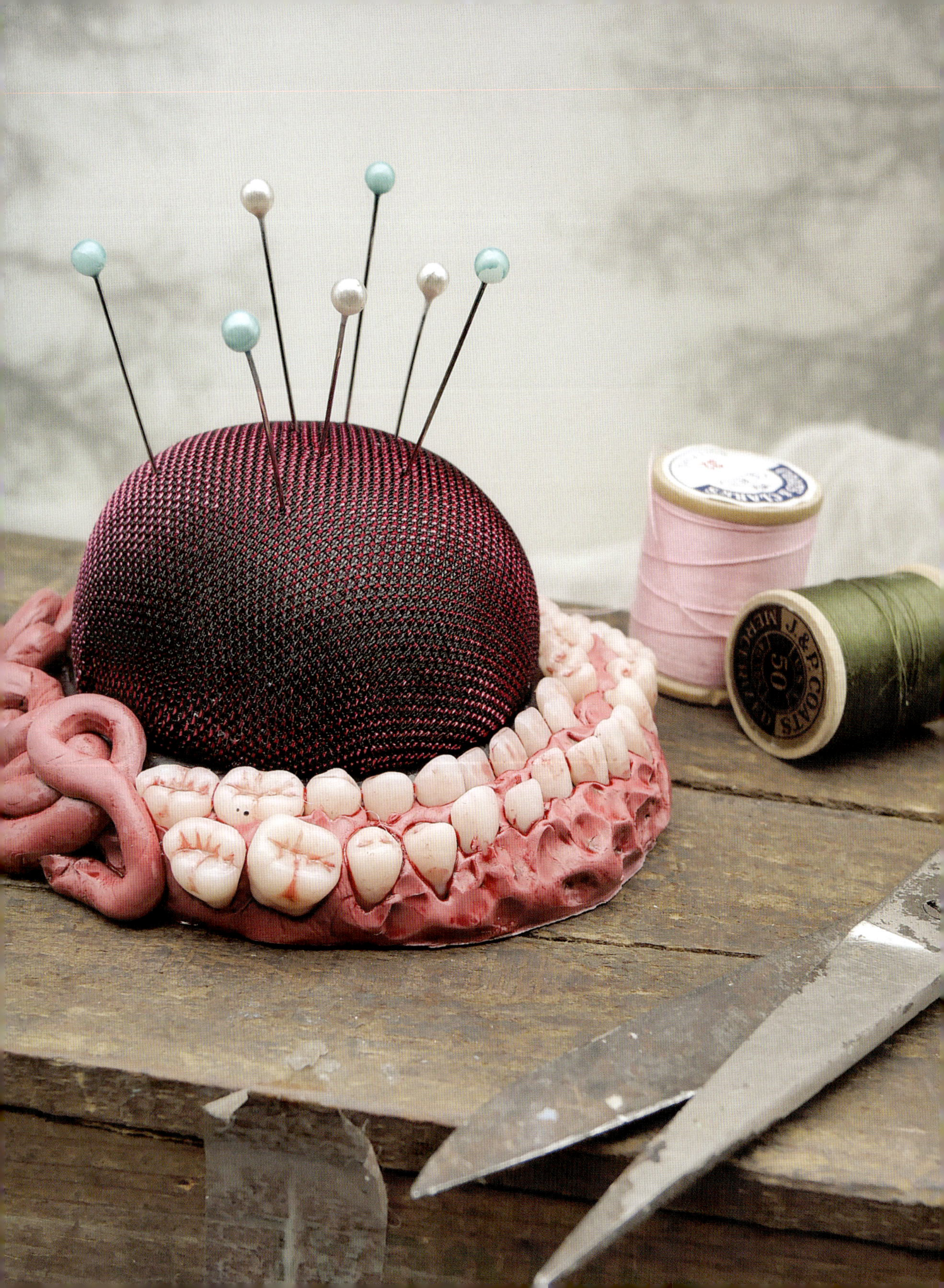

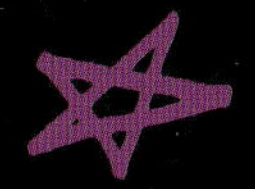

Reborn Relics

From antique hand mirrors (definitely not haunted) to old photo frames (also, I swear, not haunted), we're rebirthing old forgotten relics into something new! And yes, it is as messy as it sounds. What did you expect? This is a craft book, not an owner's manual! Just keep the mess off the carpet and you'll do fine.

There's only one rule (well, besides the "no mess on the carpet" rule): Avoid upcycling something that *Antiques Roadshow* might appraise for ten times the price you paid. However, if you do, remember, ignorance is bliss, so maybe don't google its value.

Upcycling can be a great way to save things from the trash. So not only can you fulfill your creepy crafting craving, but you can feel good about it too!

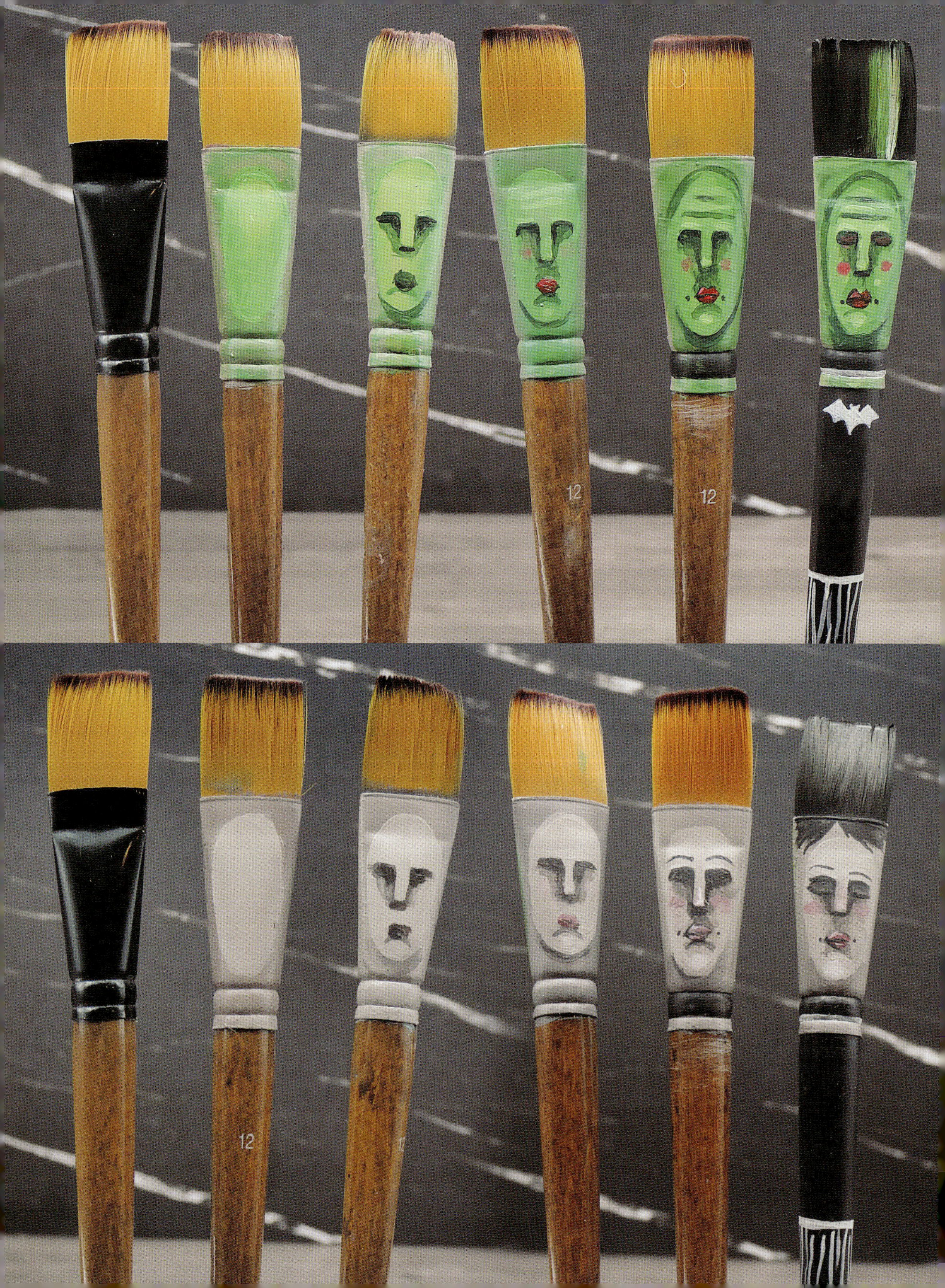

Monster Brushes

The one time I threw away my old, beat-up, falling-apart paint-brushes they looked up at me from their new trashy home and I questioned whether inanimate objects had feelings. So, I dug them back out and put them in a jar. You know, just in case . . . If this sounds familiar, then oh boy, do I have the project for you! Get your jazz hands ready for MONSTER BRUSHES! Did you use your jazz hands? Just in case, let's do it again . . . Ready? MONSTER BRUSHES!

Is using a new paintbrush to paint an old paintbrush weird? Only if we make it weird.

Materials

- Old paintbrush
- Sandpaper
- Acrylic paint and brush
- Fine-tip black marker
- Mod Podge

Look at your old brush and decide what kind of brush/monster it is going to be. *Example: werewolf, vampire, monster, ghost.* Once you've looked into its soul and decided, sand down the metal flat part of your old paintbrush. Then paint one side a "normal" skin tone and the other side a "monster" skin tone. Add a lighter-toned oval in the center of both sides. Be sure to leave room for the neck.

Tip: A heat gun is handy for this project so you can quickly dry your paint in between details, but it's not necessary.

Take a darker skin tone and draw the bottom outline of a T in the middle of your oval. The shaft of the T is the nose, and the two lines are the eyes. Darken the underside of the T to define the eyes and nose more. Paint a small oval for the lips. Paint the bottom half of the oval darker than the top half.

Let's add some makeup. Dab a little pink under each eye. *Are they blushing? Probably, we haven't painted on the clothing yet!* Fill in the lips with a pink or red. Remember, keep the top lip lighter than the bottom.

Use a fine-tip black marker to draw on the eyebrows, eyelashes, lip liner and dimples.

Let's give your brush some clothes! Paint the entire handle one color (I went with black). Paint buttons, pants, a collar, whatever you think your brush would wear. Add a necklace if your brush has a dent there like mine does.

A little hair dye can boost the confidence of your brush. You can paint all the bristles or add a little pop of color with a stripe. Paint bangs on the human side.

Lightly coat your finished brush monster with a clear layer of Mod Podge. *Be careful for a few days around your monster! No, they won't bite you, but the paint can easily scratch off. Once the paint has time to harden, the brush is much less delicate. Sort of like real people . . .*

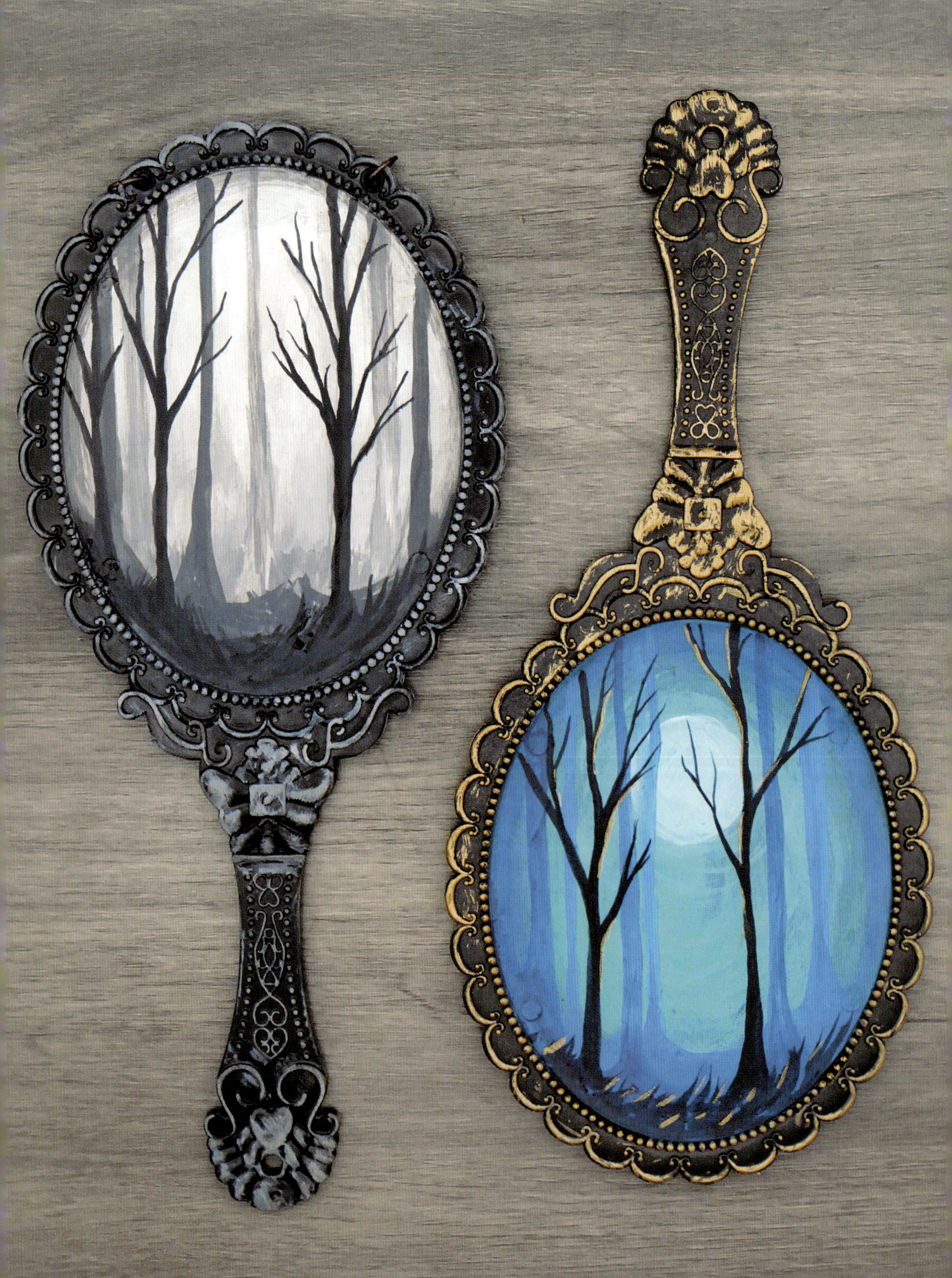

Mirror, Mirror

Vintage hand mirrors and antique brushes always catch my eye while rummaging through my local secondhand shop. I can't help but wonder about their story. Who owned them? How did they end up here? Did someone pass away and they ended up in a donation box? They are such personal items that you typically use them until they wear out or you do.

I think these items deserve all the love we can give them. That's why I came up with this project. It's so simple you can either finish it in an hour or take your sweet time with it.

Materials

- Hand mirror
- Heat gun
- Flat object (e.g., butter knife)
- Sandpaper
- Acrylic paint and brush
- Mod Podge
- Wood burner (optional)
- 2 loop rings (optional)
- 6" (15-cm) chain (optional)

You'll need to pry the mirror portion off your hand mirror. To do that, use your heat gun and heat up the mirror. Move the heat gun continuously so you don't melt the plastic. After 10 to 20 seconds, very carefully wedge a flat object in between the mirror and the back. Slowly pry and move around the outer edge. The mirror will begin to loosen and pop off.

Peel off any leftover residue. Use sandpaper to roughen up the surface where the mirror was.

Paint the now mirrorless frame white. You may need a few coats depending on your paint and the material your hand mirror is made of.

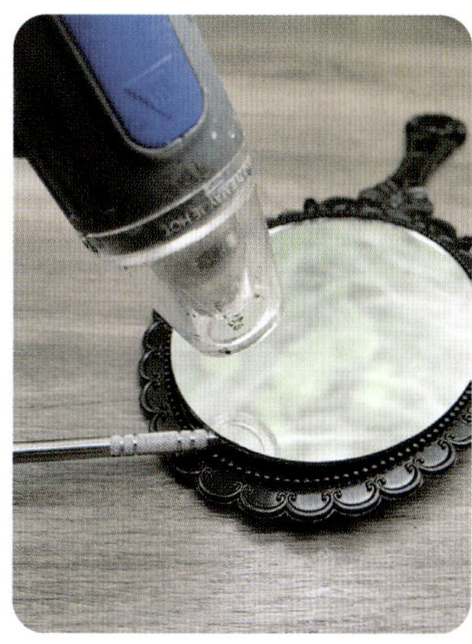

(continued)

> **Tip:** You can alternate coats of paint and heat gun drying to get a nice even coat. Just be careful not to melt any of the plastic.

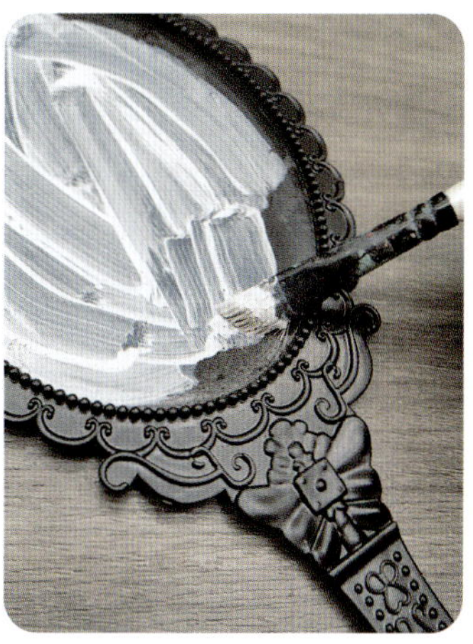

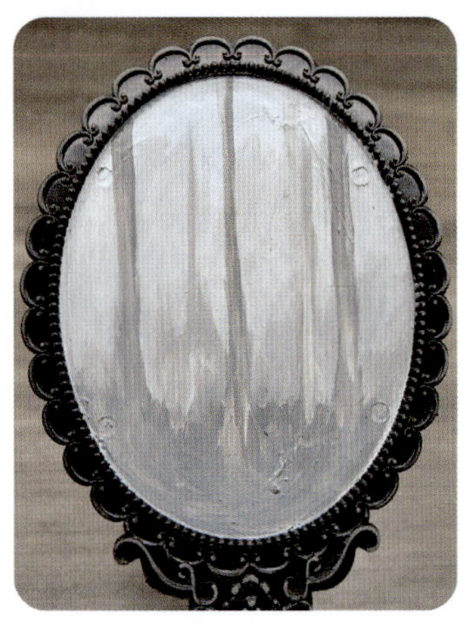
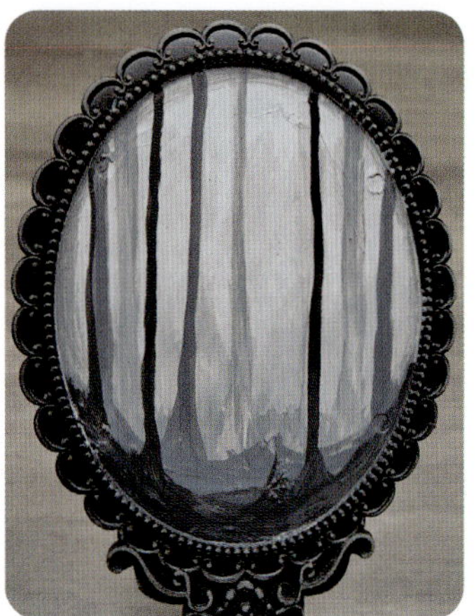
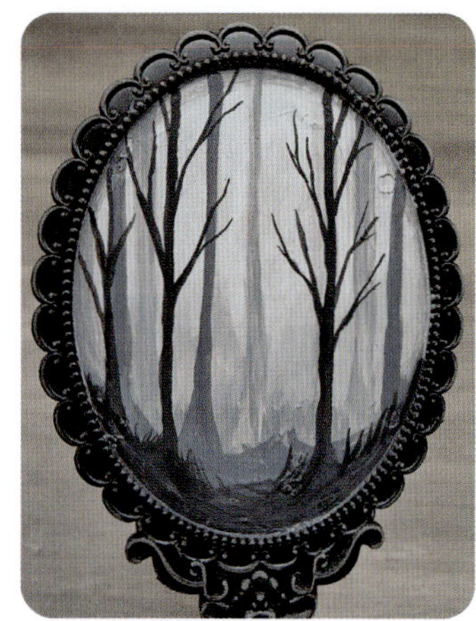

With a light gray color, paint a few skinny lines coming up from the bottom of your white frame along with some grass lines at the bottom. *They don't have to be perfect; we're just doing basic shapes.*

Mix a small amount of black into your light gray and paint more tree lines overlapping the ones you just painted. Add more overlapping grass a little below the lighter gray grass.

Using black paint, add one last layer of overlapping trees. On these black trees, paint more detailed tree branches reaching out across your frame. Dry all your trees with a heat gun for a few seconds. Clear coat your entire forest with Mod Podge.

Options for Displaying: You could leave it as is and place it on a shelf, you could frame it or you could use a wood burner to melt holes through the top. Attach a chain to the holes with the loop rings and hang it that way. *I like to think of this like a small handheld circle window, looking out at a haunted forest! Oh, how I wish I had a circle window . . .*

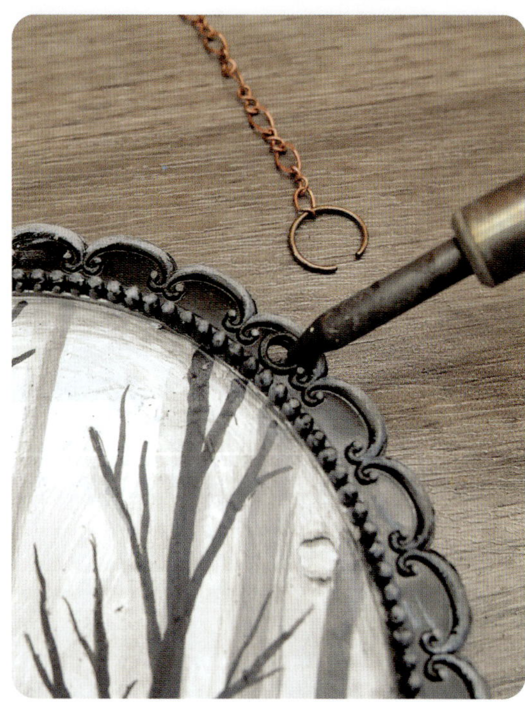

Pincushion of DOOM

I needed a creepy place to put my sewing needles and pins. All the cushions you can buy are much too "normal" for me. So, I came up with this project! I bet you never thought of a pincushion with teeth. Or maybe you have but didn't know where to start. Well, this is a pretty easy one and you can start right here!

Lay out your silicone mat and put on your gloves. Mix together about an egg-sized amount of epoxy clay. *I didn't have pink epoxy, so I mixed red and white to make pink. Alternatively, you could also paint the clay at the end.*

Cut the clay in half and roll out a rope long enough to wrap around the base of your pincushion.

(continued)

(continued)

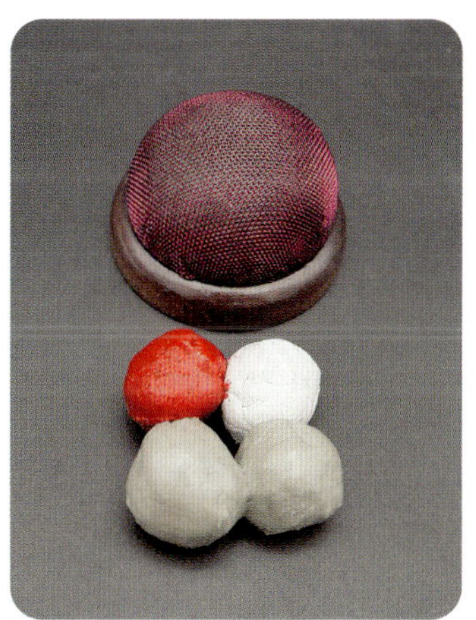

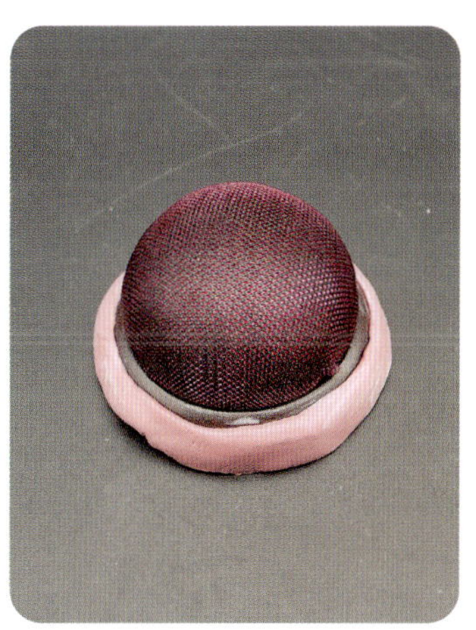

Materials

- Silicone mat
- Disposable gloves
- Red and white epoxy clay (e.g., Apoxie Sculpt)
- Pincushion (with a base)
- Set of fake resin teeth
- Gloss Mod Podge (e.g., Magic Modge)
- Acrylic paint and brush
- Paper towels

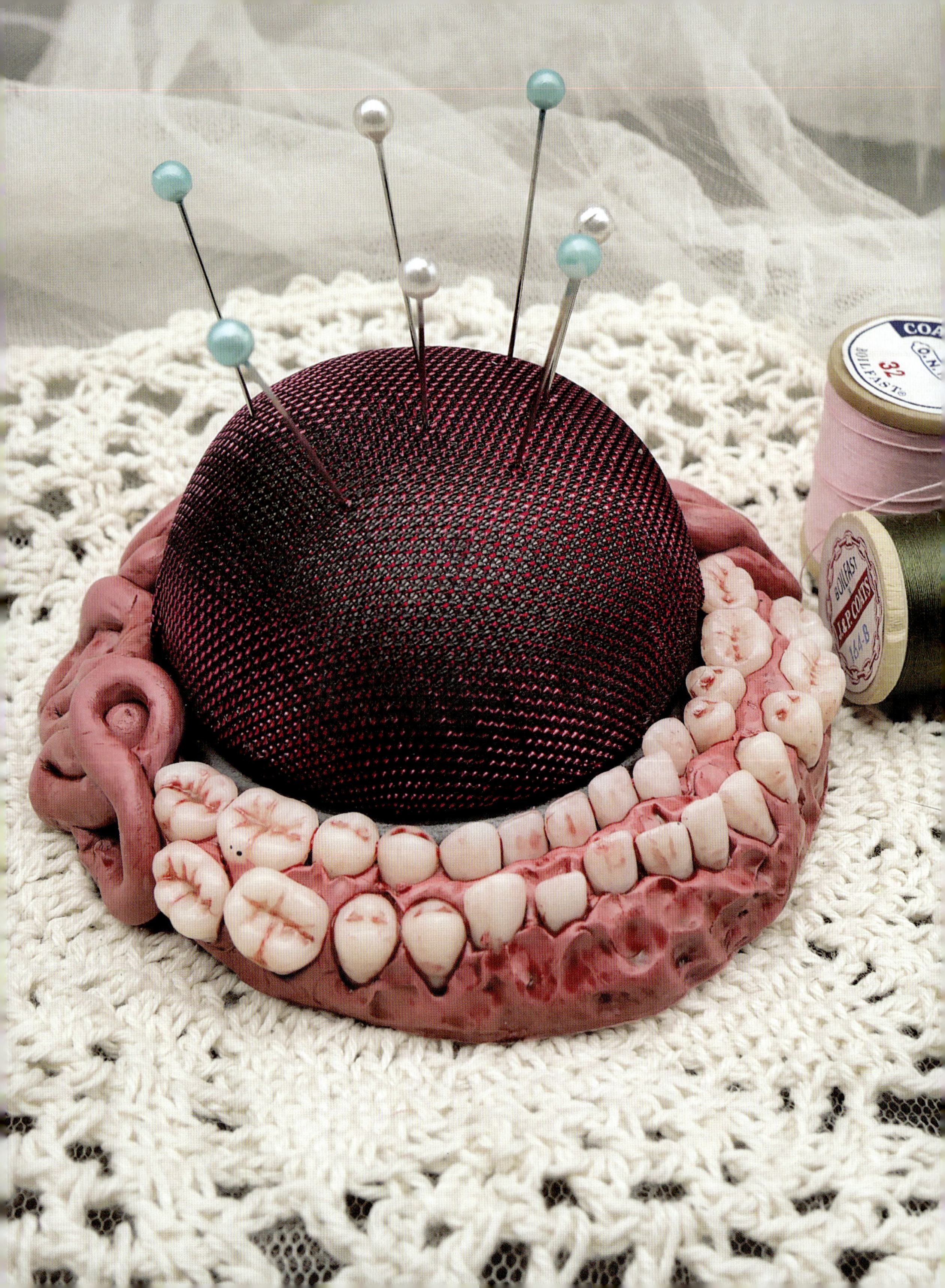

COA
O.N.T.
BELFAST
32
BELFAST
J.&P.COATS
164-B

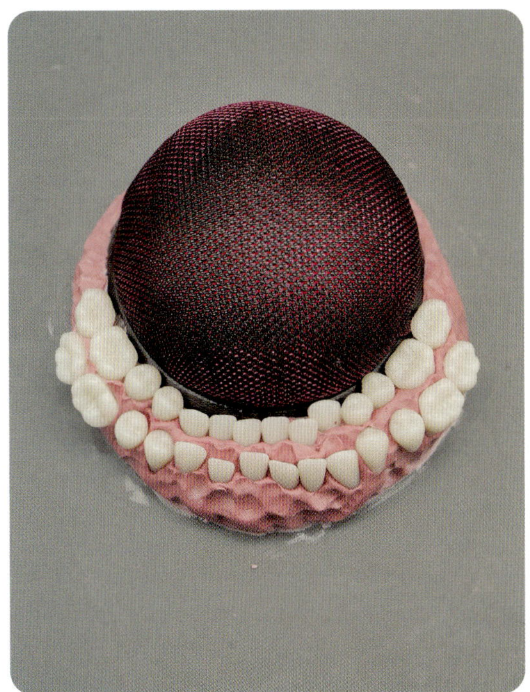

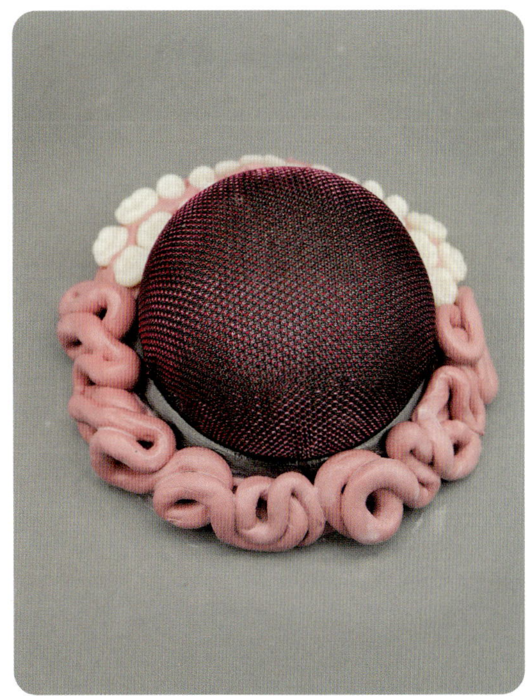

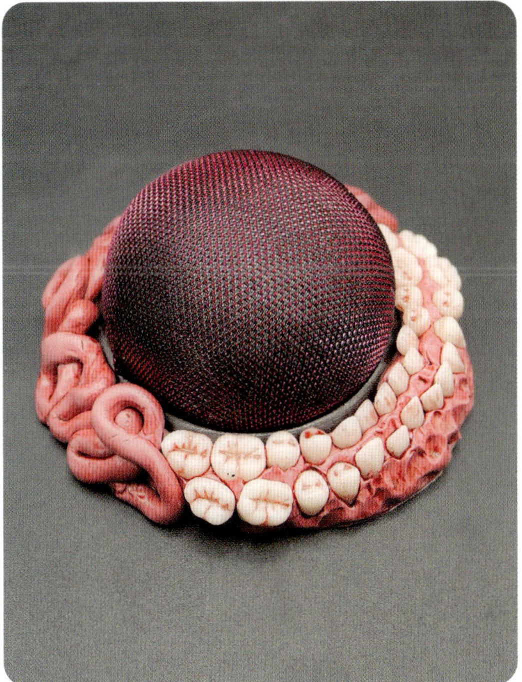

Using the remaining clay, wrap another rope halfway around on top of the first layer of clay. Smooth and flatten it out a little with your fingers.

One by one, press two rows of teeth into the thicker side of the clay.

Roll out a long rope of clay about as thick as a pencil and loosely loop or squiggle it around the opposite side of the teeth. You can do this with one long rope or if it's easier split your rope up into two or three pieces. This should resemble intestines or brains. Set it on your silicone mat overnight to harden.

Once your clay has set, tint a small amount of gloss Mod Podge with red acrylic paint and paint all the clay. Make sure to get it in all the nooks and crannies. Wipe off any excess, especially on the teeth, with a paper towel.

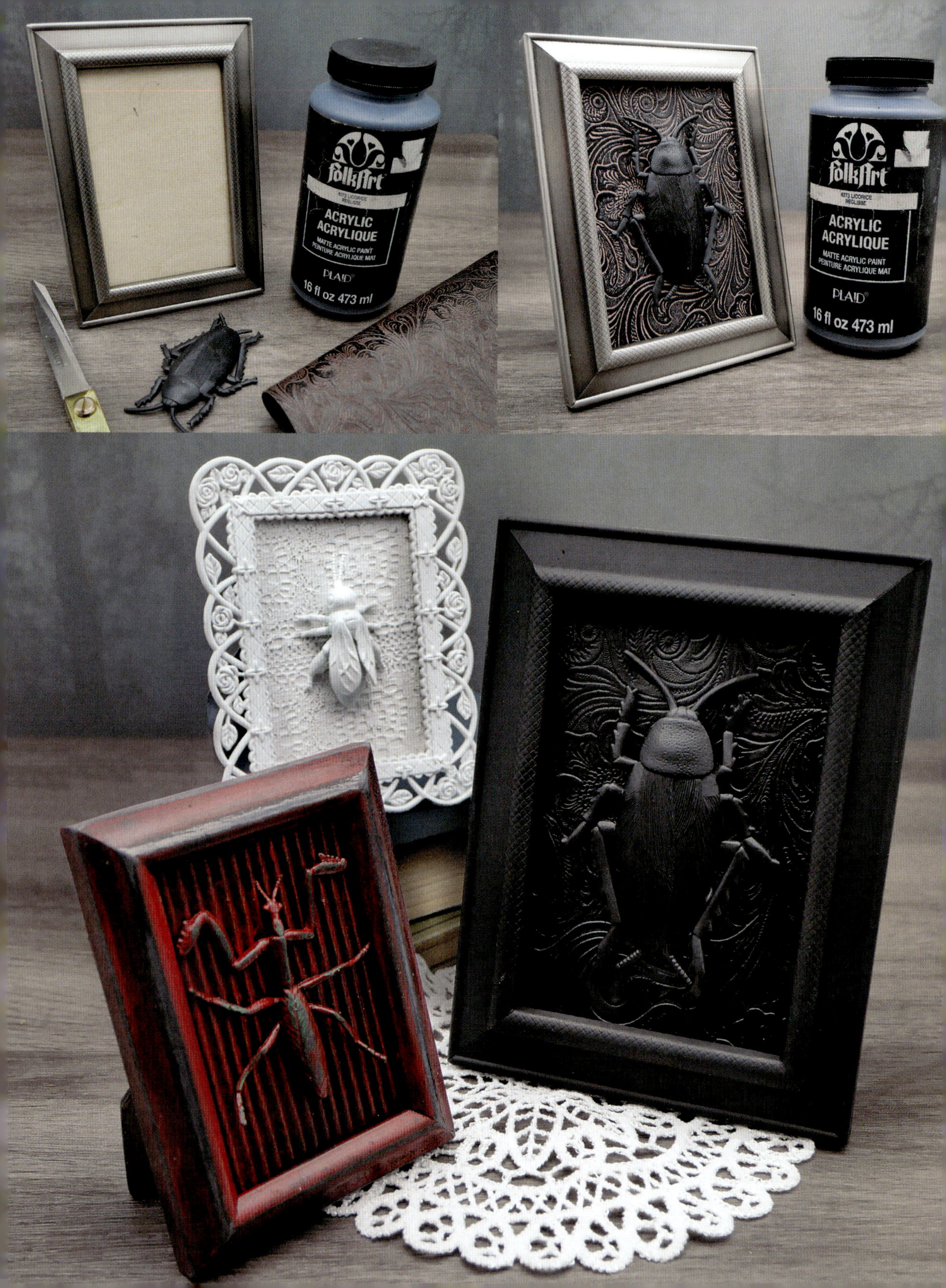

Bugging Out Frames

I was just cleaning out my junk drawer one day and found a whole handful of plastic bugs! My first thought was perhaps this is a new species of bug, the *Junkus bugus,* and if left in a junk drawer too long they multiply. But then I remembered they're leftover Halloween decorations that I threw in the junk drawer. Hey! I'm not unburying the Halloween storage box for three plastic bugs! So, with the promise that I would make them into something someday, into the junk drawer they went.

This is one of the easiest projects in this book! Plastic bug, frame, paint! Super easy! SO easy, in fact, that instructions are not needed and you can make it from just looking at the photos. However, this is a book, and the publisher wants me to write something. I know . . . I know . . . But feel free to not read and just look at the pretty pictures instead.

Materials

- Small picture frame (big enough to hold your plastic bug)
- Textured paper (for background)
- Scissors
- Craft glue
- Plastic bug
- Hot glue and gun
- Acrylic paint and brush or spray paint
- Sandpaper (optional)

Take the glass out of your picture frame and use the glass as a stencil for your interesting textured paper, and then cut it out. Using craft glue, adhere it to the cardboard backing of your frame.

Some Ideas for Finding a Textured Background: Peel a layer off corrugated cardboard and use the bumpy side, crumple up some paper and lay it flat, use old lace off clothes destined for the trash or cut up an old purse. The possibilities are endless!

Take your best-looking bug (that's a phrase I never thought I'd say) and hot glue it onto the textured background in the center of your frame.

Lastly, either hand-paint or spray-paint the entire thing, frame and all, one color. For a distressed look, lightly sand the top of your frame and bug to reveal the color beneath. Now you have a framed bug, how lovely! *Did you actually read this? Just checking . . . No, no, I get it, you wanted to make sure you were doing it right.*

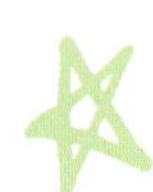
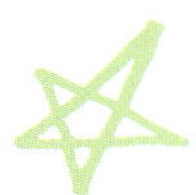

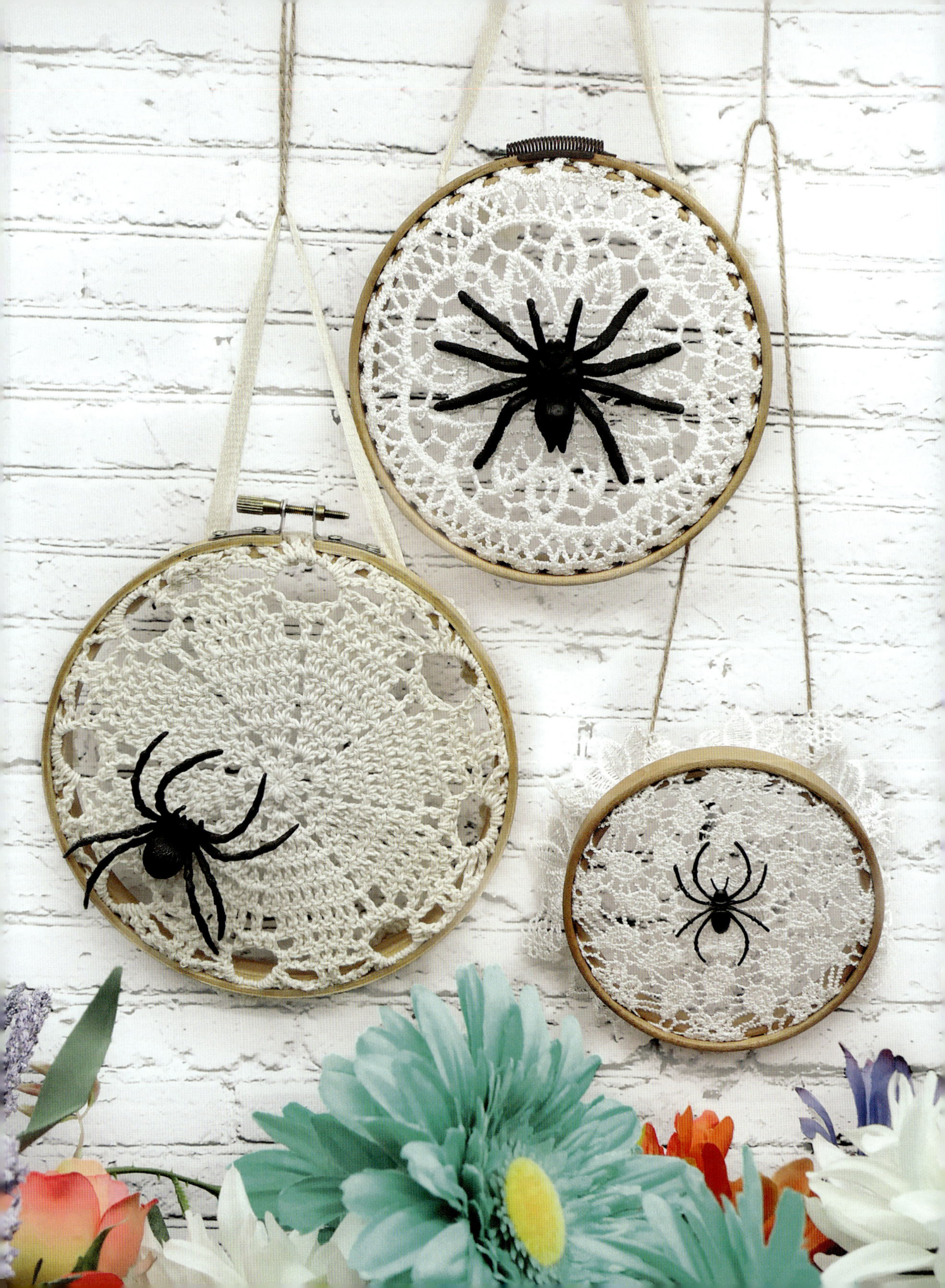

Embroidery Webs

Materials

- Embroidery hoop (slightly smaller than your doily)
- Old doily
- Needle and black thread
- Black plastic spider
- Antique white craft ribbon

Grandma left behind a lot of stuff, or if your grandma is still alive, perhaps she tried to give you a lot of stuff hoping you'd get into embroidery. *A nice, sensible hobby instead of that weird hobby you're currently into.* Well, joke's on her! We're merging our weird, creepy hobby with her "nice, sensible" hobby! We're making creepy embroidery hoops!

This is a quick and easy one. The time for this is around 15 to 30 minutes depending on how long it takes you to thread a needle because, let's face it, it can take me 15 minutes to get that stupid thread inside that damn hole!

Separate your embroidery hoop and smash Grandma's old doily in between the two rings.

Thread your needle with black thread and sew the spider onto the doily. Be creative with the placement; you can place it in the center or off to the side.

Once you've finished attaching the spider, tie a piece of antique white craft ribbon onto the back of the hoop for hanging. You're finished! Told you this one was easy! *Now, how long did it take you to thread your needle?*

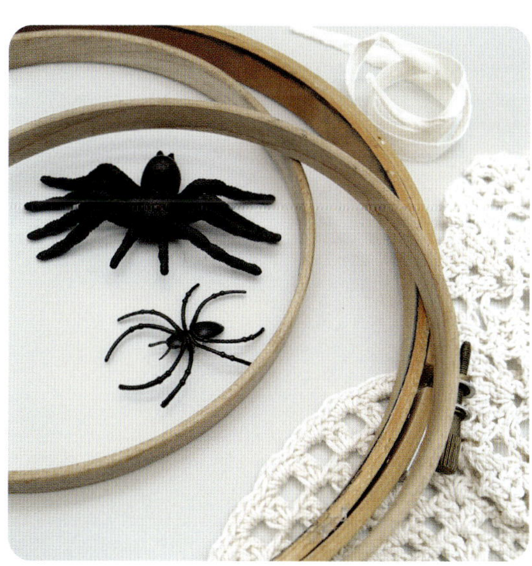

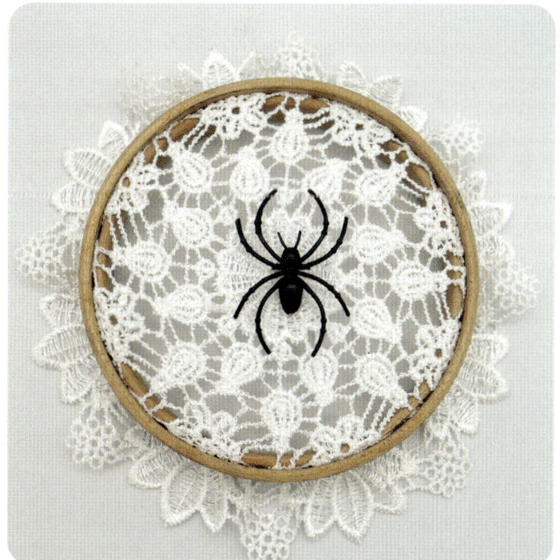

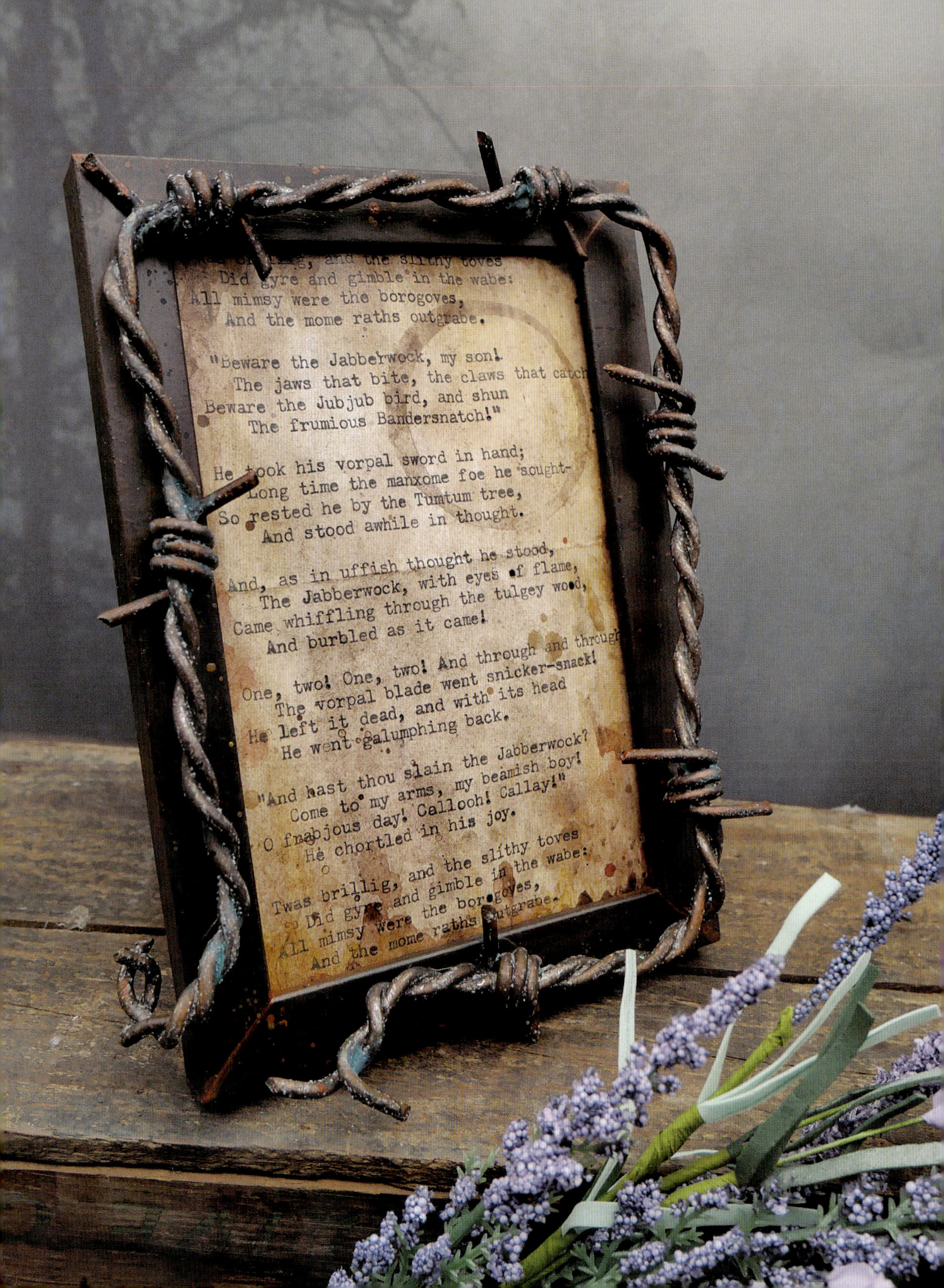
'Twas brillig, and the slithy toves
Did gyre and gimble in the wabe:
All mimsy were the borogoves,
And the mome raths outgrabe.

"Beware the Jabberwock, my son!
The jaws that bite, the claws that catch!
Beware the Jubjub bird, and shun
The frumious Bandersnatch!"

He took his vorpal sword in hand;
Long time the manxome foe he sought-
So rested he by the Tumtum tree,
And stood awhile in thought.

And, as in uffish thought he stood,
The Jabberwock, with eyes of flame,
Came whiffling through the tulgey wood,
And burbled as it came!

One, two! One, two! And through and through
The vorpal blade went snicker-snack!
He left it dead, and with its head
He went galumphing back.

"And hast thou slain the Jabberwock?
Come to my arms, my beamish boy!
O frabjous day! Callooh! Callay!"
He chortled in his joy.

'Twas brillig, and the slithy toves
Did gyre and gimble in the wabe:
All mimsy were the borogoves,
And the mome raths outgrabe.

Barbed Wire Frame

You can use barbed wire on several things. I'll show you how to add it to a frame, but keep in mind, you could add it to a canvas, around a sculpture—really, what can't you barbed wire-ify?

*Tip: The wire sizes are just what I used, but honestly it depends on the project. You want to make delicate barbed wire? Use thinner wire. "Manly" barbed wire? Use thicker wire. I do use the word "manly" loosely because as a woman . . . PSSHHT *insert eyeroll* but you get the idea . . .*

Materials

- Wire cutters
- 80" (203 cm) of wire (3 mm or smaller)
- Vise-grip locking pliers
- Needle-nose pliers
- Super glue
- Sandpaper
- 5" x 7" (12.7 x 18–cm) picture frame
- Swellegant copper metal coating
- Swellegant patina
- E6000 glue
- "Heavy stuff" (e.g., stack of books)

Use wire cutters to cut your wire into two 24-inch (61-cm) lengths and six 5-inch (12.7-cm) lengths. *The color of your wire doesn't matter, as we're going to be painting it anyway.*

Hold the two ends of your 24-inch (61-cm) wire together with your vise-grip locking pliers and start to twist them. Keep your hands close to the twist point. This helps your twists stay even. *But don't worry about them being perfect. Perfection is overrated.*

(continued)

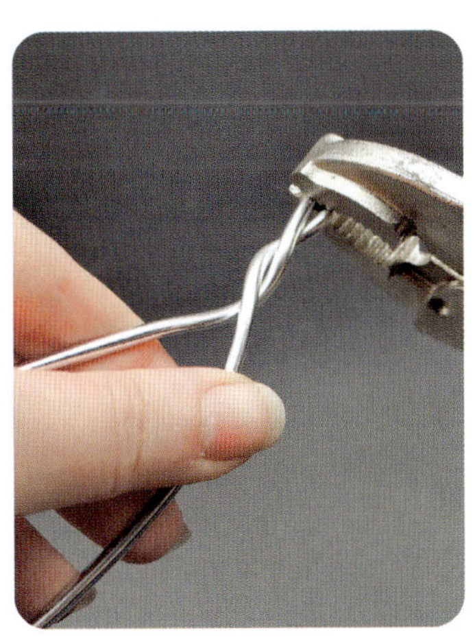

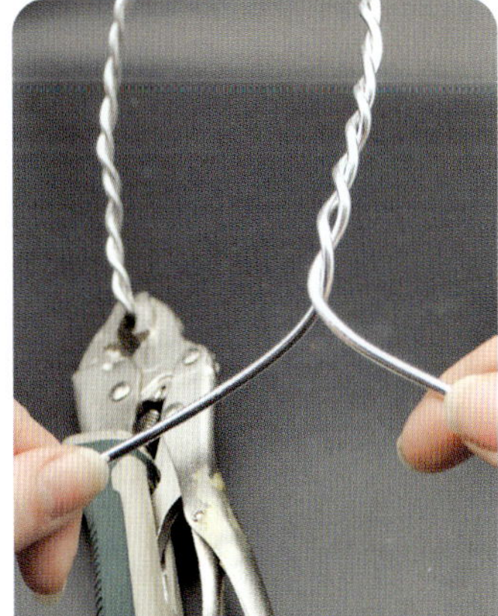

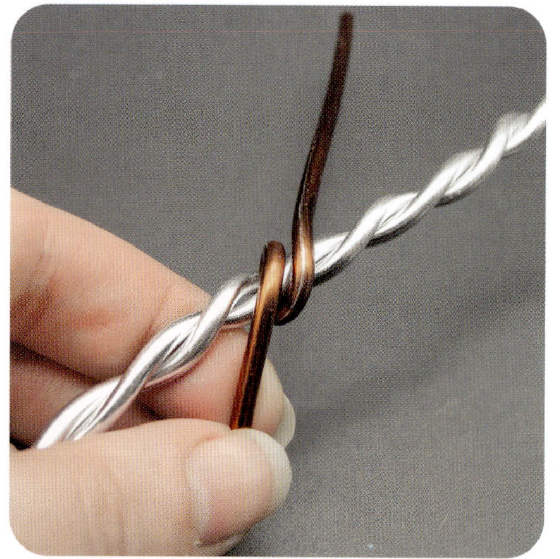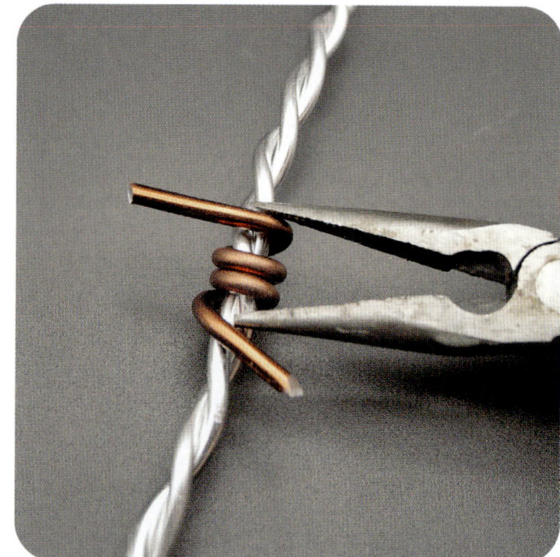

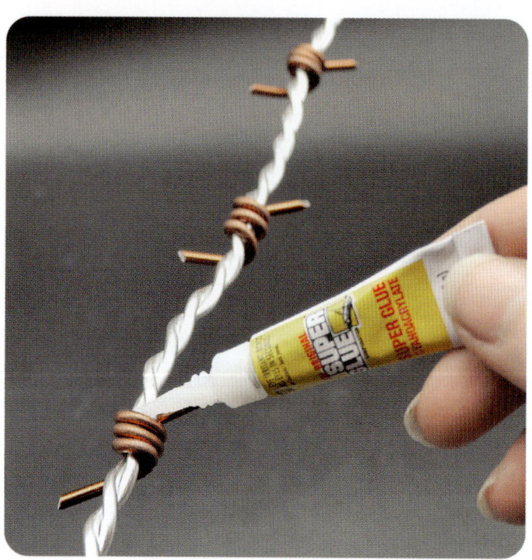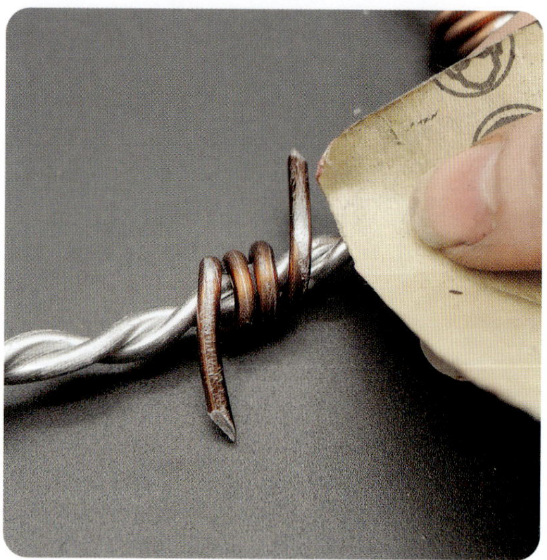

Take one of your 5-inch (12.7-cm) wires and, starting 1 to 2 inches (2.5 to 5 cm) from one end of the long twisted wire, wrap it around three times. Your ends should be going in opposite directions, allowing the barb to lie flat. Move down another 1 to 2 inches (2.5 to 5 cm) and repeat with another short piece of wire. Make sure you are wrapping in the same direction on all six barbs. Squeeze each barb with your needle-nose pliers to secure in place.

Your barbs are going to want to slip. *Can you blame them?* To keep them in order, add a drop of super glue to each. Elevate your barbs off the ground to dry. Once your super glue is dry (5 to 15 minutes), sand everything with sandpaper. It doesn't have to be perfect; just rough up the surface a bit. Then shape your wire into the same shape as your frame.

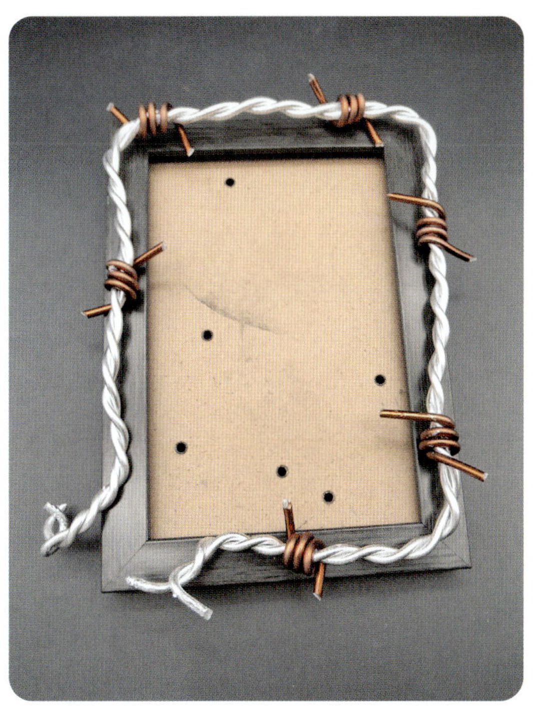

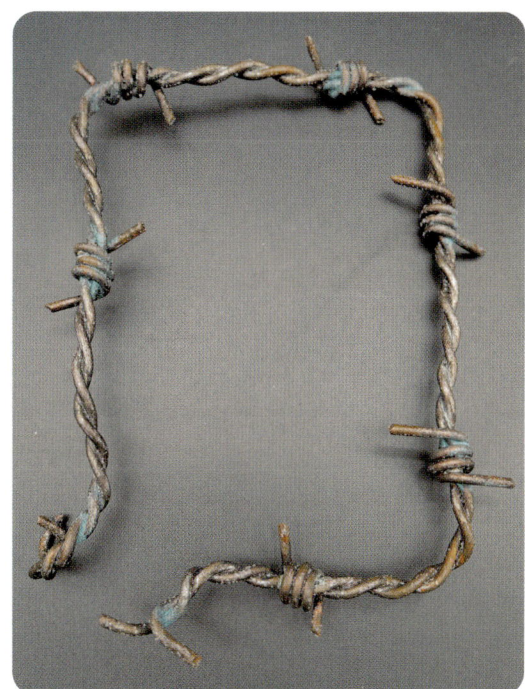

Paint the entire barbed wire and frame with Swellegant metal coating. Let it dry completely.

You could use regular copper paint instead of Swellegant, but I prefer the Swellegant because it has actual metal in it and the patina that we'll be adding next will react to the metals and oxidize them, creating beautiful colors.

Paint your barbed wire and frame with Swellegant patina. *Don't use a heat gun on patina!* The oxidization takes a few hours to show up.

Once you're satisfied with the amount of oxidization your barbed wire has achieved, glue each of the barbs to your frame using E6000. Place something heavy on top, like a dictionary, *though who has a dictionary anymore?* This will ensure all barbs are touching the frame when the glue dries. Wait 24 hours and remove your "heavy stuff." You're finished!

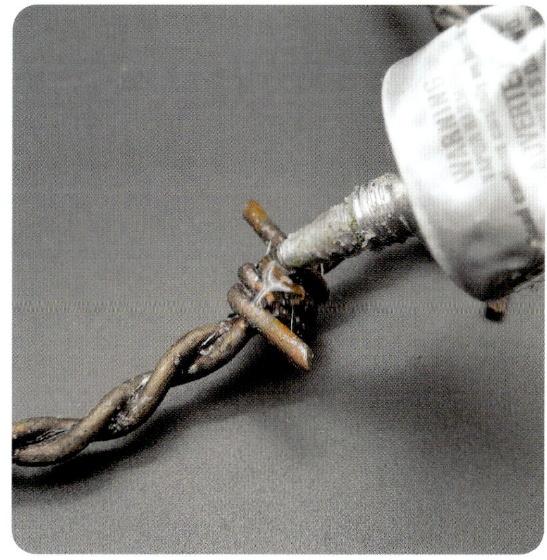

Some ideas of what to put in your barbed wire frame: Perhaps an old-timey photo of Barb, a poem written by Barb or you and Barb playing with Barbie. Have I taken the Barb thing too far? Yes, yes, I have . . .

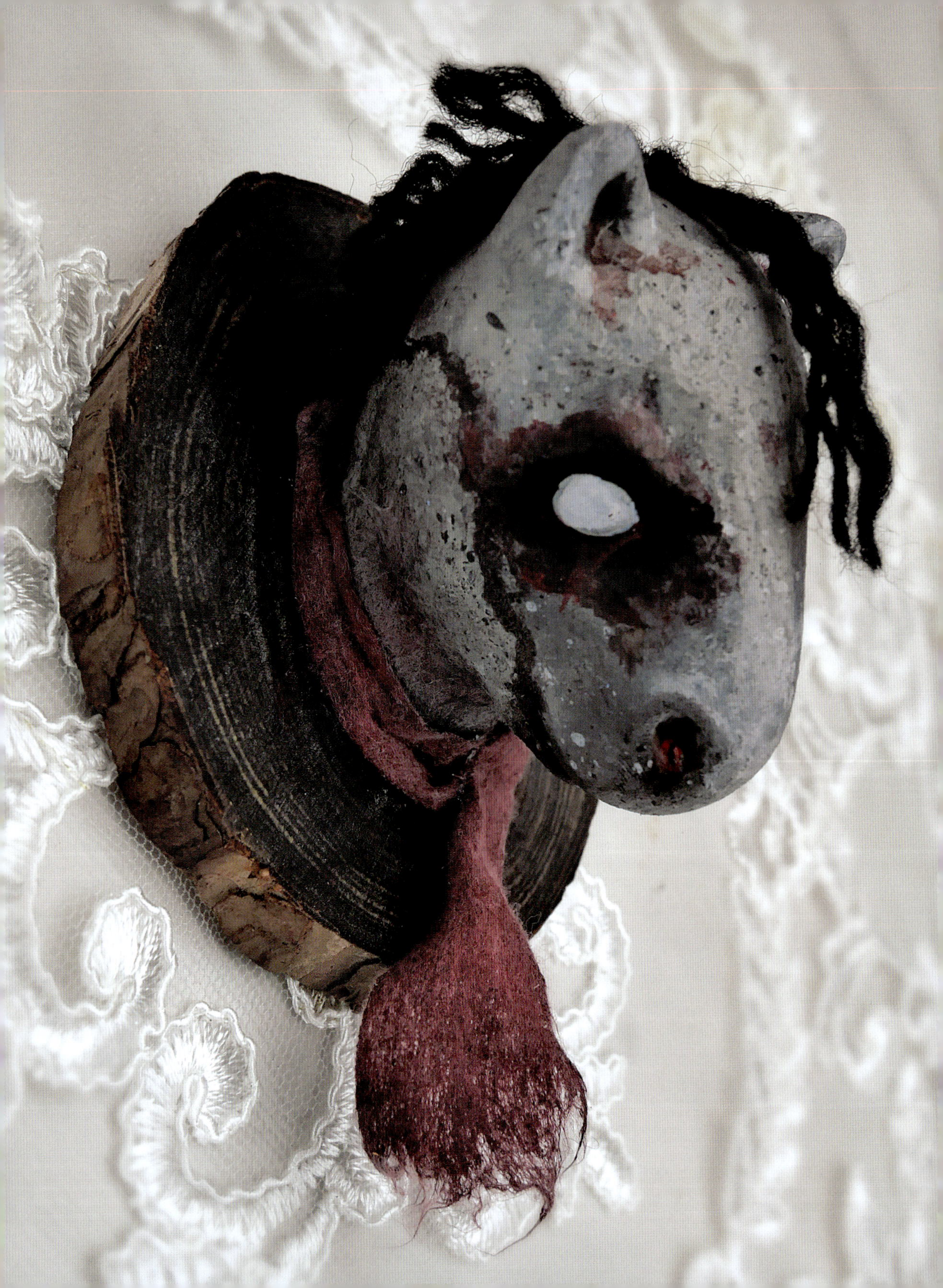

Apocalyptic Pony

Did you want a project the makes you feel nostalgic and creeped out at the same time? Well, look no further! In this project we'll be turning an innocent My Little Pony into an apocalypse pony. Feel like a kid again, ripping the heads off your toys! Oh wait, you didn't do that as a kid? . . . Just me? . . . Well, this is awkward. By the way, don't throw your leftover pony pieces away because we can use them in the next creepy craft, Baby Zebra.

Using scissors, cut or rip the head off your pony and take all the hair out. Set your pony body aside for other projects. *Trust me, she's dead inside and won't feel a thing.*

Paint your pony with black chalk paint and let it dry, 10 to 20 minutes. (The chalk paint makes the other paints stick better.)

(continued)

Materials

- Toy pony head
- Scissors
- Black chalk paint and brush
- Gauze
- Matte Mod Podge
- Pointy object (e.g., thick needle)
- Large jump ring
- Acrylic paint
- Aluminum foil
- Hot glue and gun
- Wooden plaque or wood slice
- Black yarn

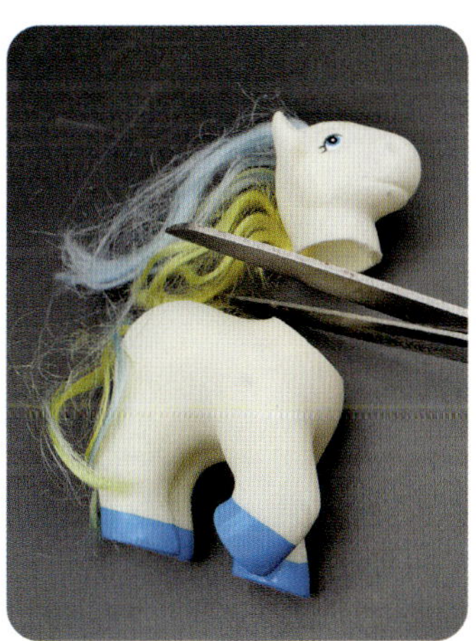

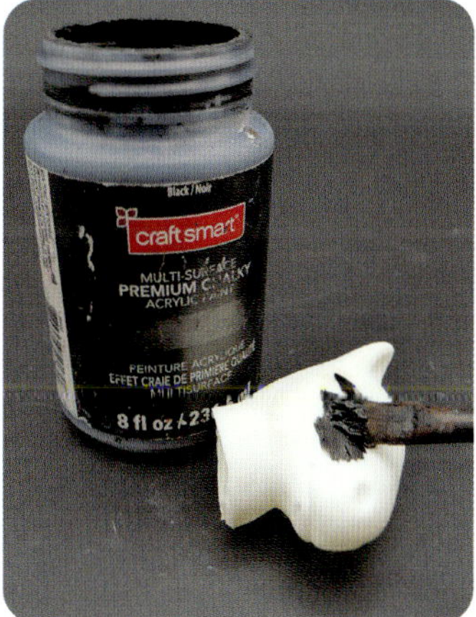

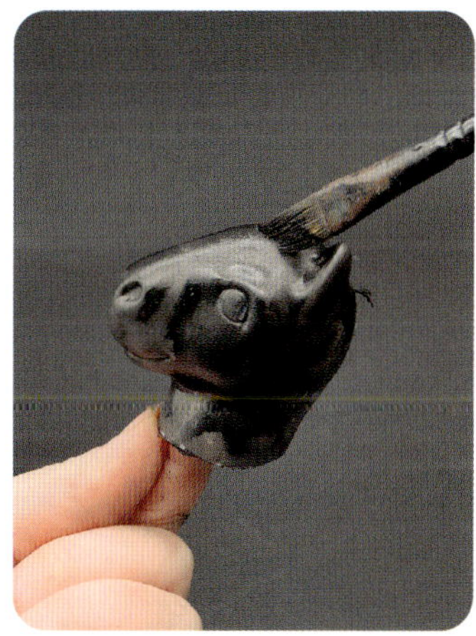

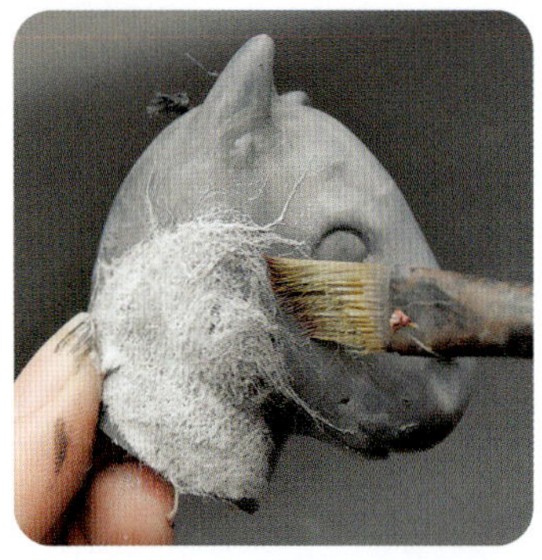
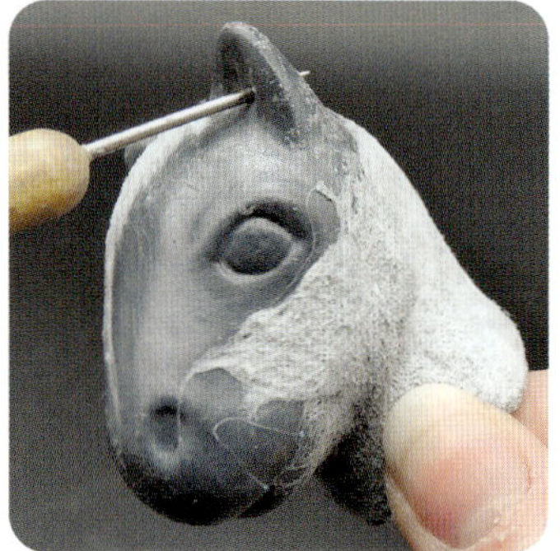
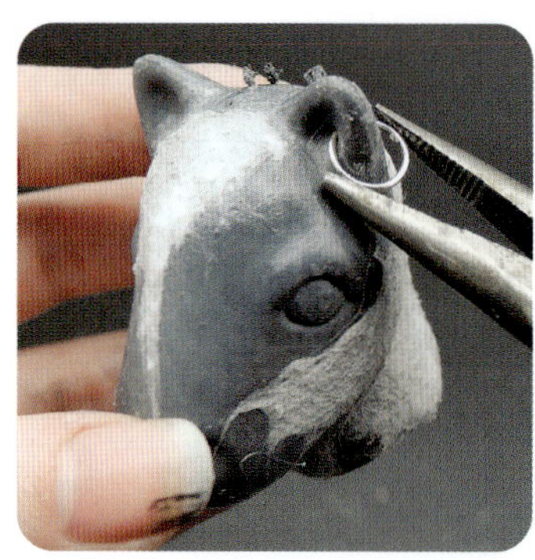

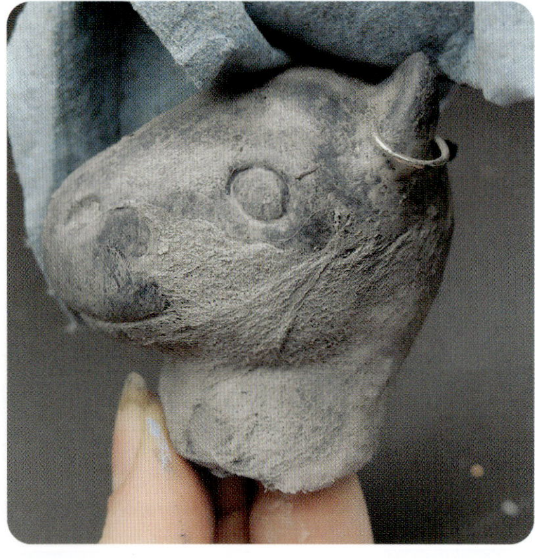
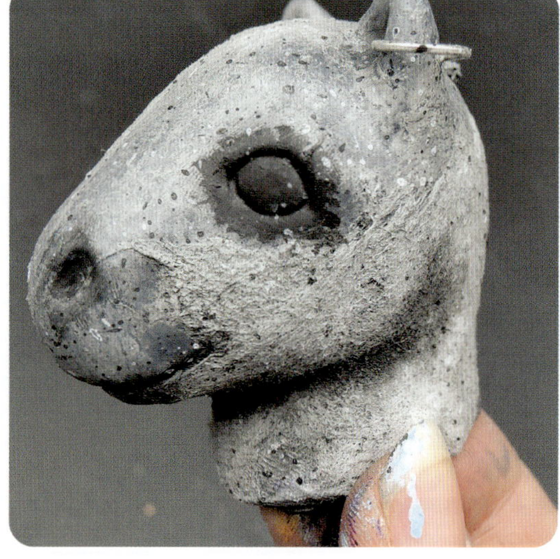

Rip off small pieces of gauze and use matte Mod Podge to adhere it around the face and neck of your pony. Avoid overlapping and covering the eyes and mouth. Coat your entire pony head with matte Mod Podge.

Poke your pointy object all the way through one of your pony's ears. Loop in one large jump ring to make an earring.

Paint your pony head gray and *angrily* flick black and white paint at it to create a speckle effect. *You don't have to be angry; it just helps.*

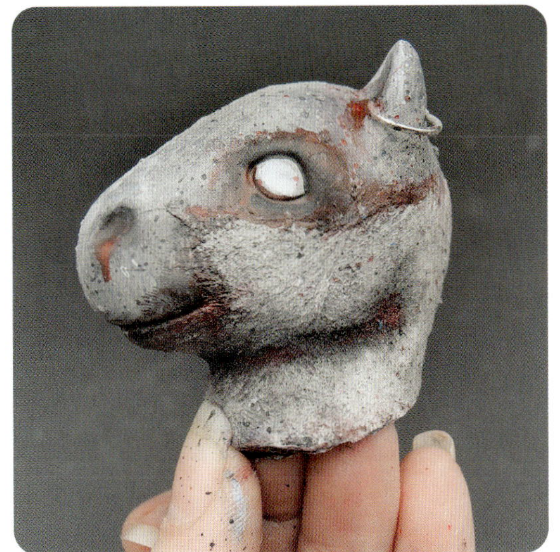

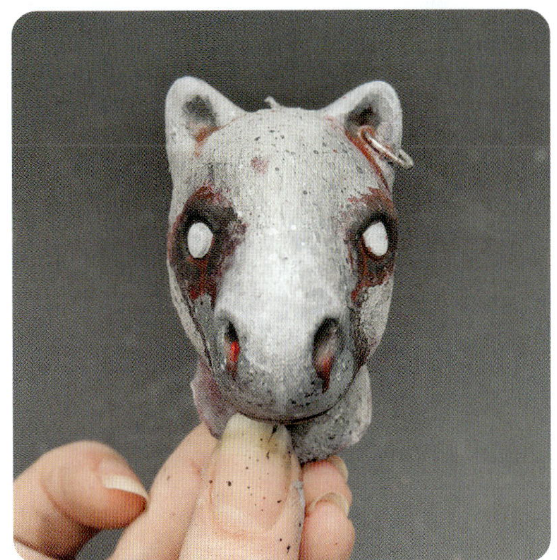

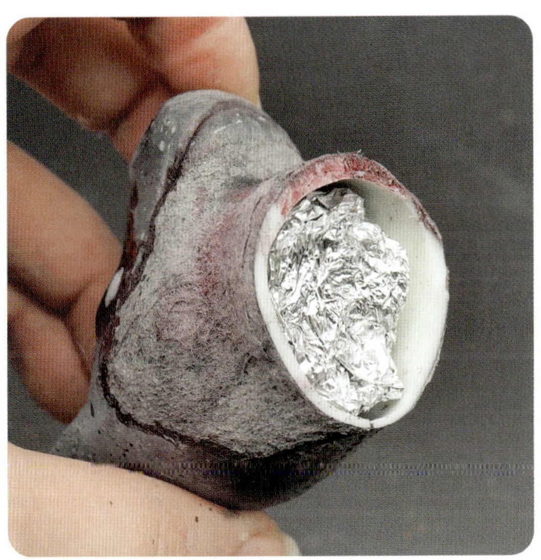

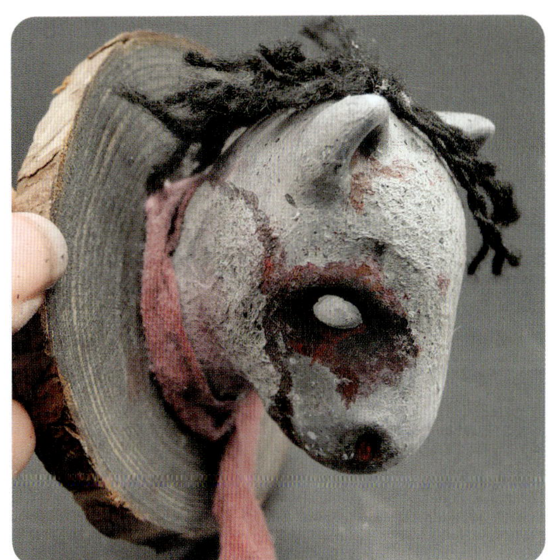

Next, paint around the eyes, in the nose and the mouth with black paint. Add bloody red details along the edge of the gauze and fill the eye with white.

Stuff the inside of your pony head with aluminum foil and hot glue it in place. Then hot glue your pony onto your wooden plaque.

Pull apart a few short strands of black yarn and hot glue it on top of your pony's head to create a mane. For a scarf, I used some of my leftover gauze and painted it red. A scarf helps hide where your pony's neck was cut off.

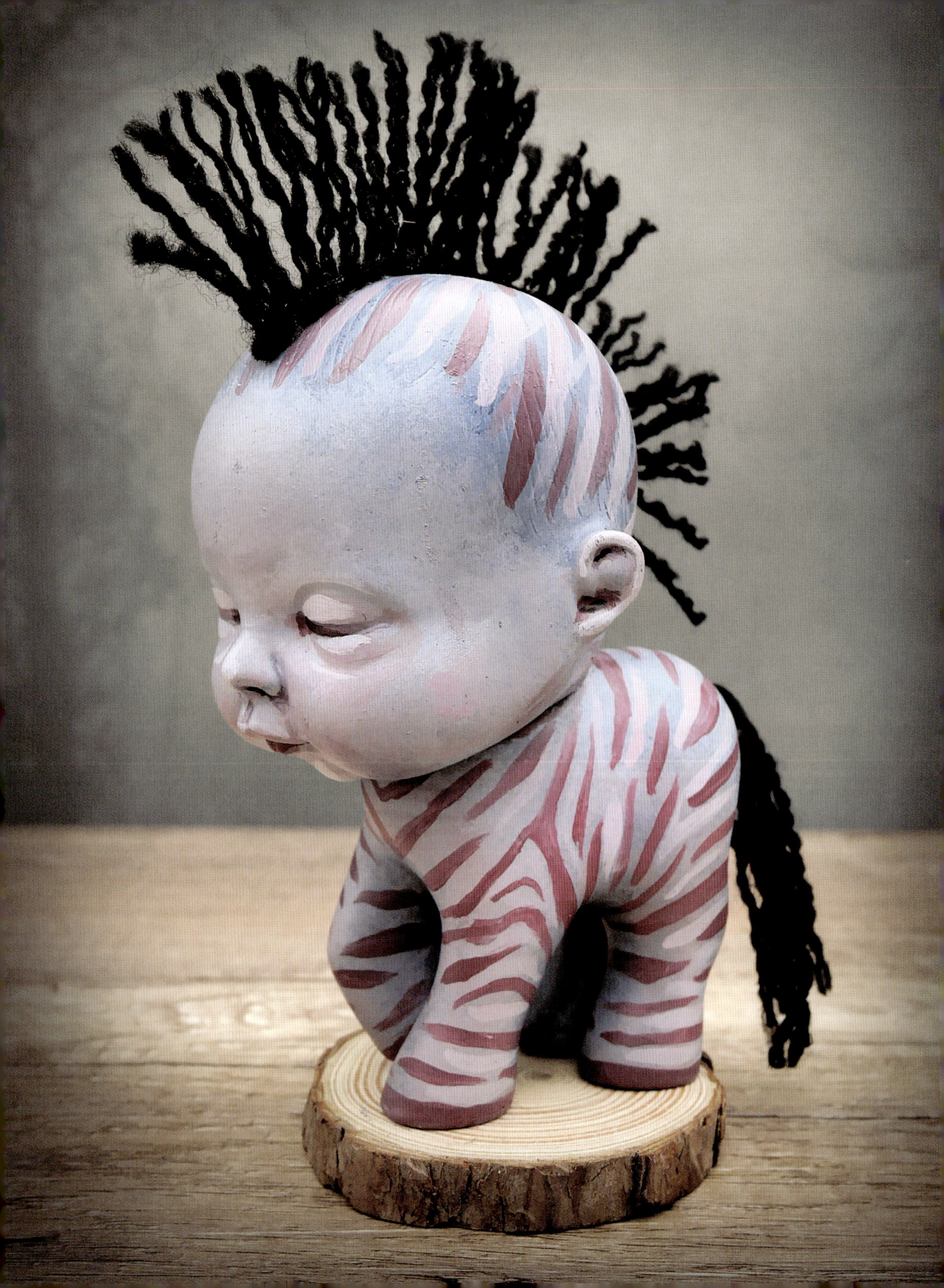

Baby Zebra

Did you save that pony butt from the previous creepy craft? Good. Because we're making a baby zebra! But hold on, because I'm not talking about a little zebra. Nope! I'm combining a pony butt with a baby doll head. Yup, you got that right! A project that's sure to be adorable and terrifying at the same time!

Materials

- Scissors
- Toy pony butt
- Baby doll head
- Aluminum foil
- Hot glue and gun
- Toothpick
- Black chalk paint and brush
- Matte Mod Podge
- Acrylic paint
- Black yarn
- Wood slice (if needed)

With scissors, cut your toy pony in half, *or use the butt from the previous project,* and make sure the neck will fit inside your doll head. If it doesn't, you may need to add foil and glue. Take out any hair from both the doll head and the pony butt.

Fill both the pony butt and the doll head with aluminum foil and hot glue the foil in place. Poke a toothpick inside the pony's butt and jam the doll head on top. Use plenty of hot glue to make sure the two are securely attached.

> **Tip:** *Turn your doll head so it's facing slightly to the side instead of straight forward for a more interesting look.*

(continued)

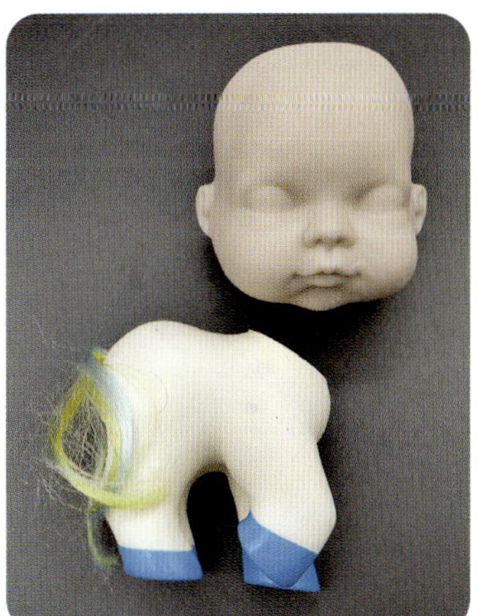

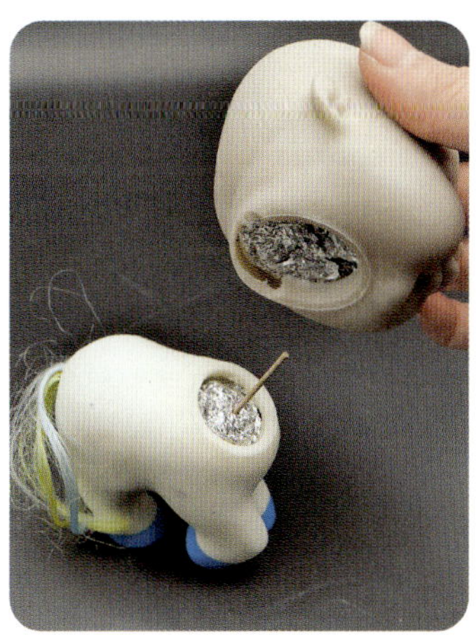

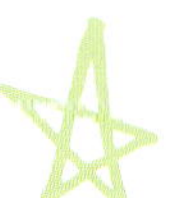

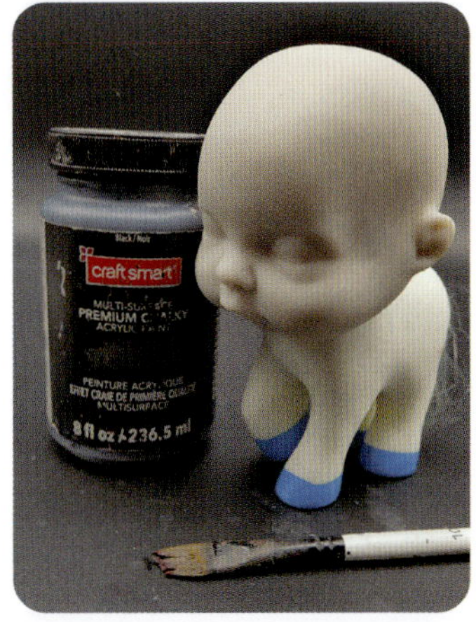 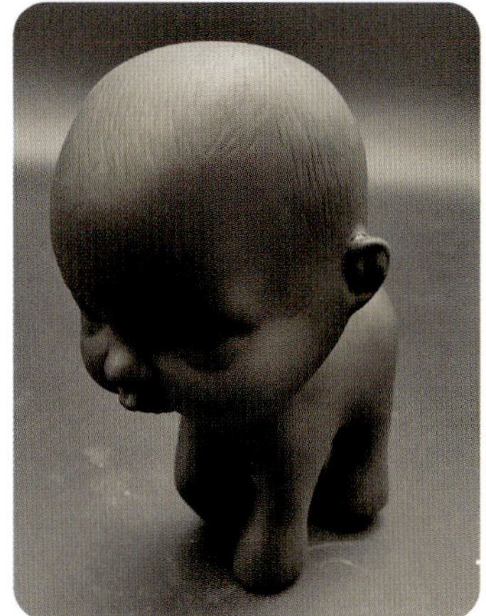 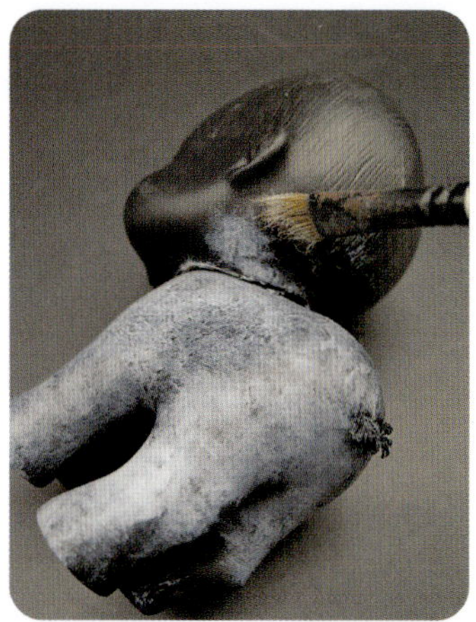

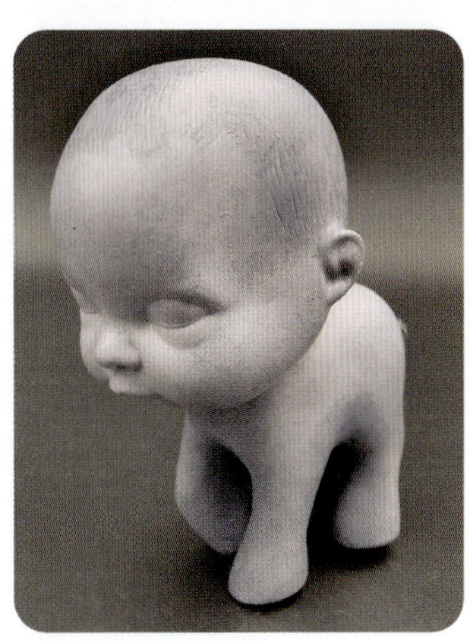 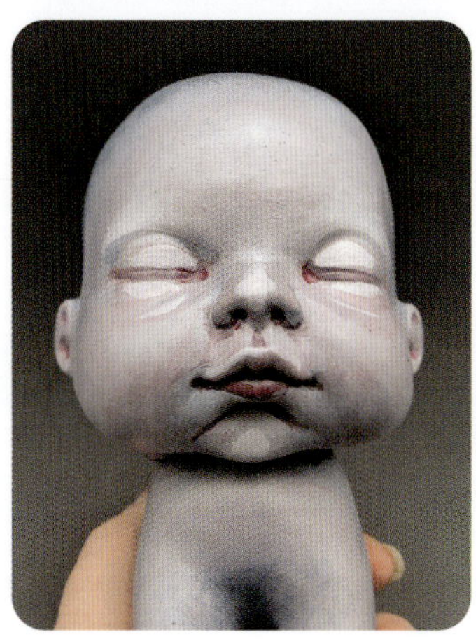 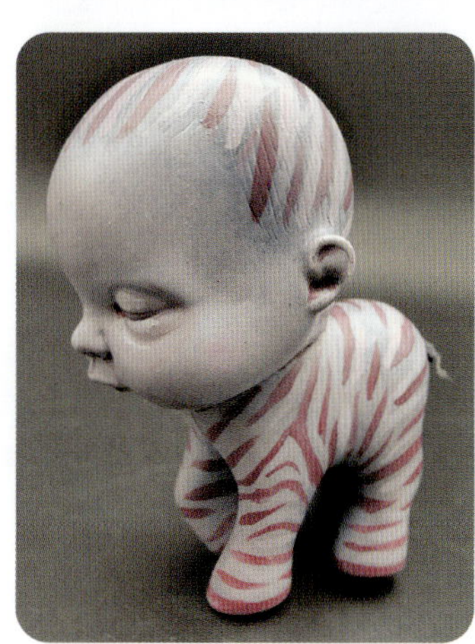

Paint your diabolical creation using black chalk paint. Once your black paint is dry, coat the entire thing in matte Mod Podge. *The black chalk paint will stick to most surfaces, so it's good to have this as a base and paint our skin tones on top.*

Using a grayish skin tone, paint your baby zebra. *I found that patting the paint on with a dry paintbrush makes a more realistic skin texture.*

Paint details onto your baby's face, such as mauve lips. Enhance the shadows and highlights with lighter or darker skin tone paint. Pay close attention to the eyelids, nose and chin. Don't use bright colors; keep everything pretty desaturated.

Using the same color you used for your baby's lips, paint on zebra stripes and caps on each foot. Once the paint is dry, coat it in matte Mod Podge.

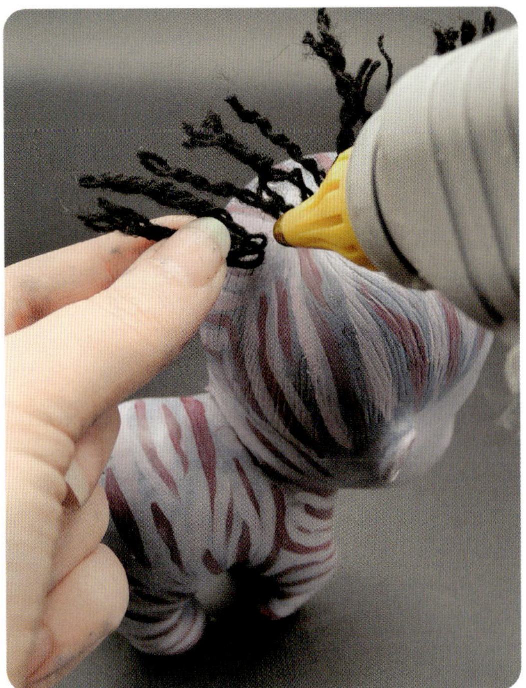

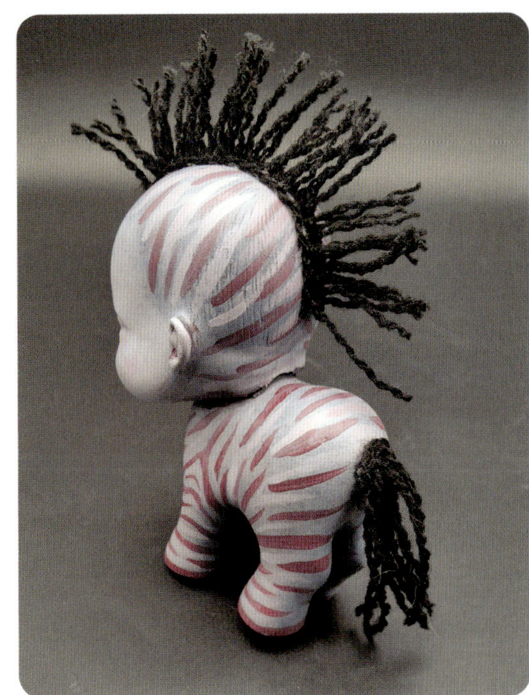

Now for the mane and tail. Cut off short strands of black yarn and unravel them. Hot glue the yarn to the top of your baby's head to make a mohawk. You can trim it all to one length after it's glued on. Do the same for the zebra tail.

My baby zebra didn't want to stand up on its own. *(I can't imagine why, because they're looking pretty fabulous now.)* If you also run into this problem, hot glue it to a flat surface. I used a slice of wood, but you could use a small saucer, a block of wood or really anything you have on hand that will look nice under your baby zebra.

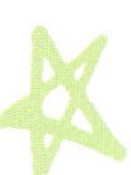

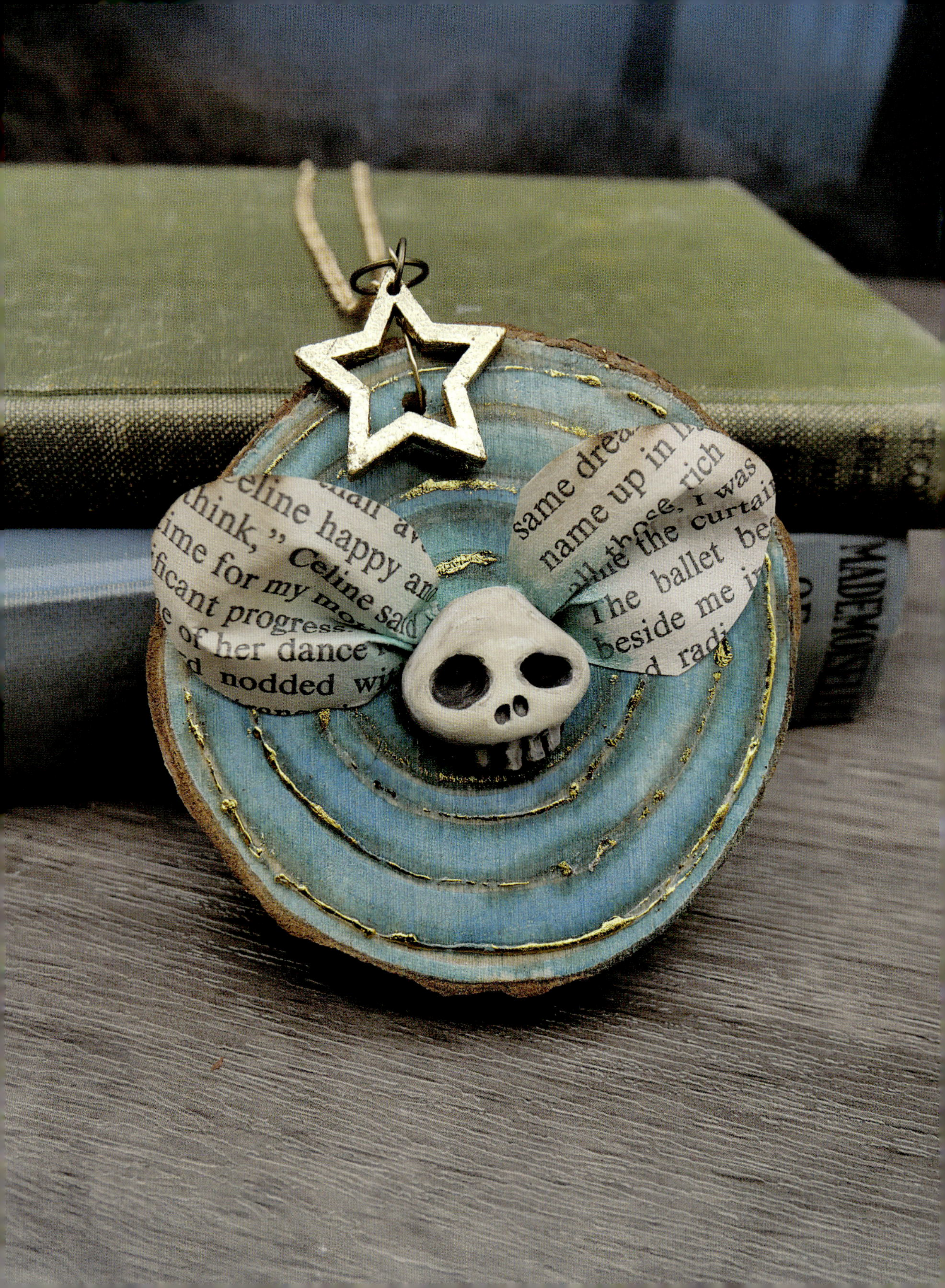

eline happy an
think," Celine said
ime for my mo
ficant progress
e of her dance
d nodded wi
same drea
name up in
the curtai
The ballet be
beside me in
d radi

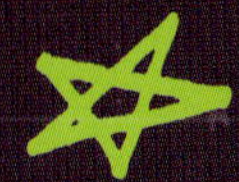

Paper Shredder

Books are in abundance everywhere! I don't want to alarm you, but you're holding one right now! I know, spooky . . . I'm talking to you as if I'm watching you while you read this! Don't worry, I totally didn't see you pick your nose earlier . . .

Good places to acquire books are either from a thrift store or the dollar store. Did you buy my book secondhand? If so, do you plan on making the art in the book? Or making the book into art? Either way, I'm totally stoked to be a part of the art process!

Thrift stores are great because they often sell used books. You can feel confident that the book has served its purpose and can now serve a completely new purpose as art. Secondhand books are also cheap and thrift stores seem to be overflowing with them.

Dollar stores (like Dollar Tree) are another great place to get books. I think Dollar Tree is a book's last stop before the big black nothingness. If someone doesn't buy it there, then it will surely be thrown out or recycled. These books are great if you want one that's in good shape. They have clean pages and sturdy covers.

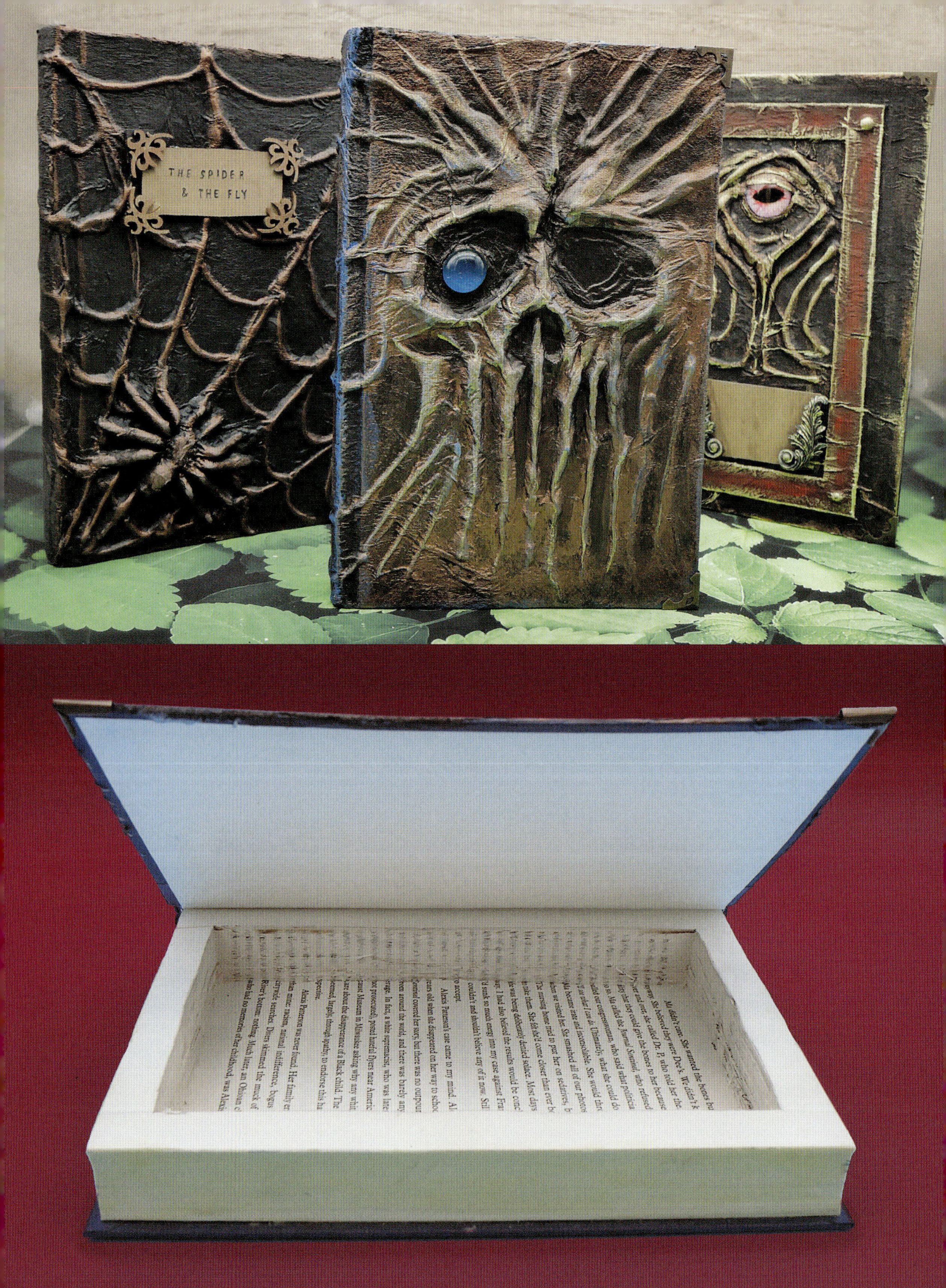

THE SPIDER
& THE FLY

Secret Book Box

A secret book box is exactly what it sounds like: a box that looks like a book for hiding secrets in *(or incriminating evidence. I don't judge!)*. It's relatively easy to make, but it does take a bit of time, patience and hand strength.

Finding a good book is key! Pick a thick one. In fact, the thicker, the better! You'll want lots of space for your secret love letters . . . *or whatever! Again, I don't judge . . .*

Begin by opening the front cover of your book. Lay your silicone mat on the first page and then close the cover. This creates a barrier between the cover and the first page. Next, open the back cover and affix it with glue to the last page.

Hold your book tightly shut and squeeze tacky glue onto the outside edges of the pages. Smooth the glue using your index finger, coating the entire edge of the book. *Imagine it as a large notepad, where all three sides are covered in glue, instead of just one.* Allow the glue to dry for 1 to 2 hours before coating a second time. Stack something heavy on top, such as more books, and let it dry overnight.

(continued)

Materials

- Hardcover book 2" (5 cm) or thicker
- Silicone mat
- Tacky glue
- Ruler
- Pencil
- X-ACTO knife
- Hot glue and gun
- Flat glass marble (optional)
- Matte Mod Podge
- Paintbrush
- Blue shop towels or cloth-like paper towels
- Heat gun
- Scissors
- Acrylic paint
- Metal corner protectors (optional)

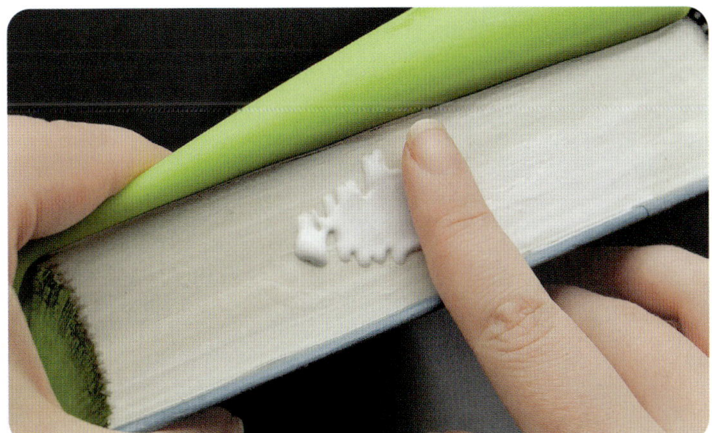

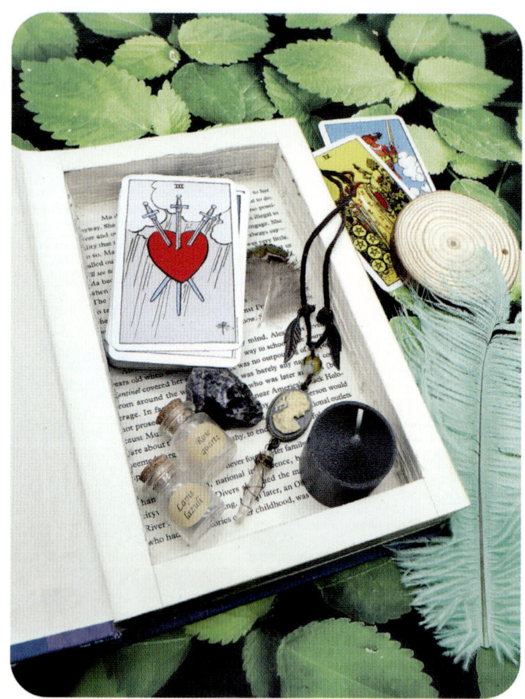

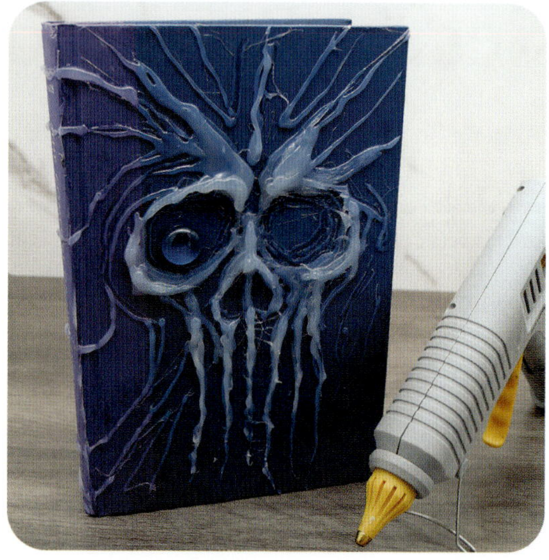

The next day remove the silicone mat and check that everything is securely glued. You should now have a solid block of pages and a cover that opens freely. On the first page, use a ruler and pencil to draw a rectangle, leaving a ½ inch (1.3 cm) around the outside. With an X-ACTO knife and a ruler, carefully begin cutting out the rectangle. Be careful not to rip or cut into the pages outside that rectangle. *This is going to take some time, so put on a good movie and get to work.* Keep cutting until you're a few pages away from the back cover. Save the scrap pages, as we will use them in other crafts.

Using hot glue and a glue gun, "draw" a face with lots of wrinkles on the cover. You can carry your hot glue design to the spine of your book, but stop at the back. Glue on a flat glass marble for an eye. *Alternatively, you can do all sorts of stuff like webs or make a border out of craft sticks. Have fun and don't worry if it looks messy; we're going to cover it anyway.*

Once you have all the texture you want, pour Mod Podge over the cover. Use your paintbrush to get into all the nooks and crannies. Use more than you're comfortable with.

While your Mod Podge is still wet, lay a single towel down onto the cover and start to mold it into all the little spaces. You may need another towel for the spine if it doesn't wrap far enough around. Using your paintbrush or your fingers, go over the top of your book, squishing all the air pockets out. Use a heat gun to really squish everything into place. *It will slightly melt the hot*

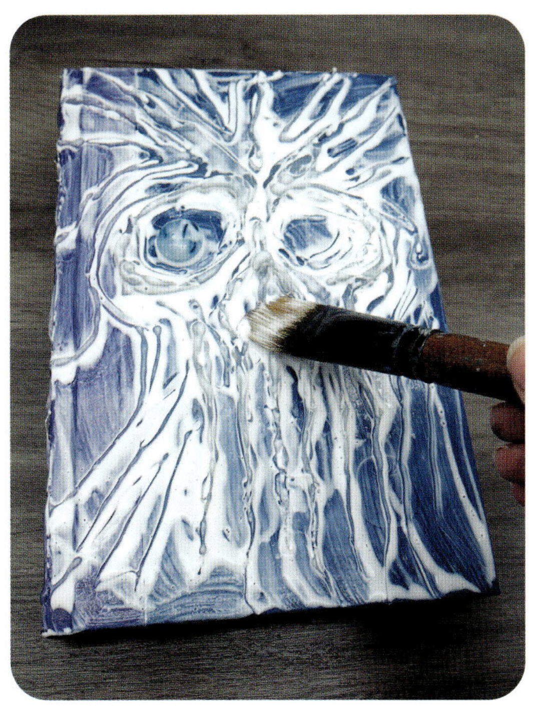

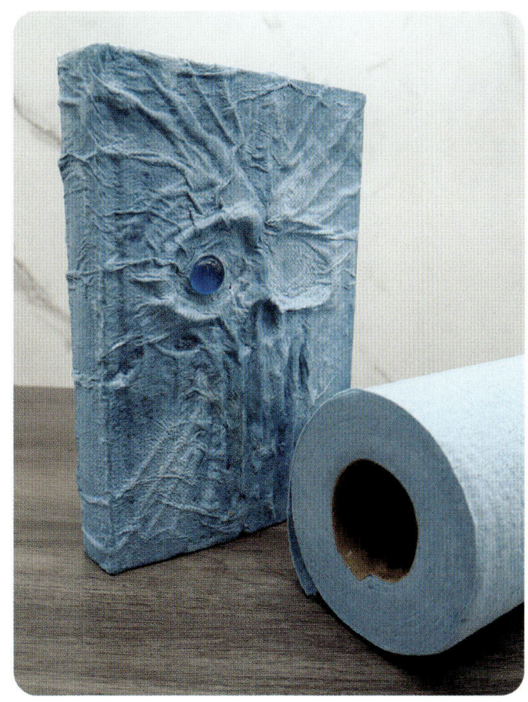

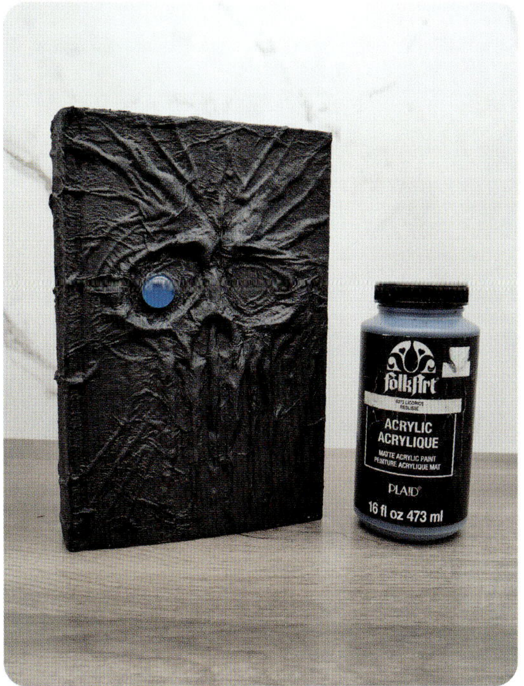

glue under and make it stick better. Just be careful not to go overboard because you'll start losing your hot glue details with high heat.

With scissors, trim any excess towel off the edges of the cover and spine. Lay it on a silicone mat to dry. *If this is getting too messy for you, let it dry for 24 hours before you continue. If you don't mind the mess, you can continue after an hour.*

Paint both covers and the spine in matte black paint. Then dry brush on bronze paint to make those details pop! Dry brushing is when you take a dry paintbrush, dip the tip into paint and lightly sweep it over the surface. You can use other colors too, but keep the base coat dark and the dry brushing lighter. Be careful not to get any paint on the pages!

Finish off the corners of your book with metal corner protectors or other embellishments. *You've just completed a secret book box! What kind of secrets will you stash in it?*

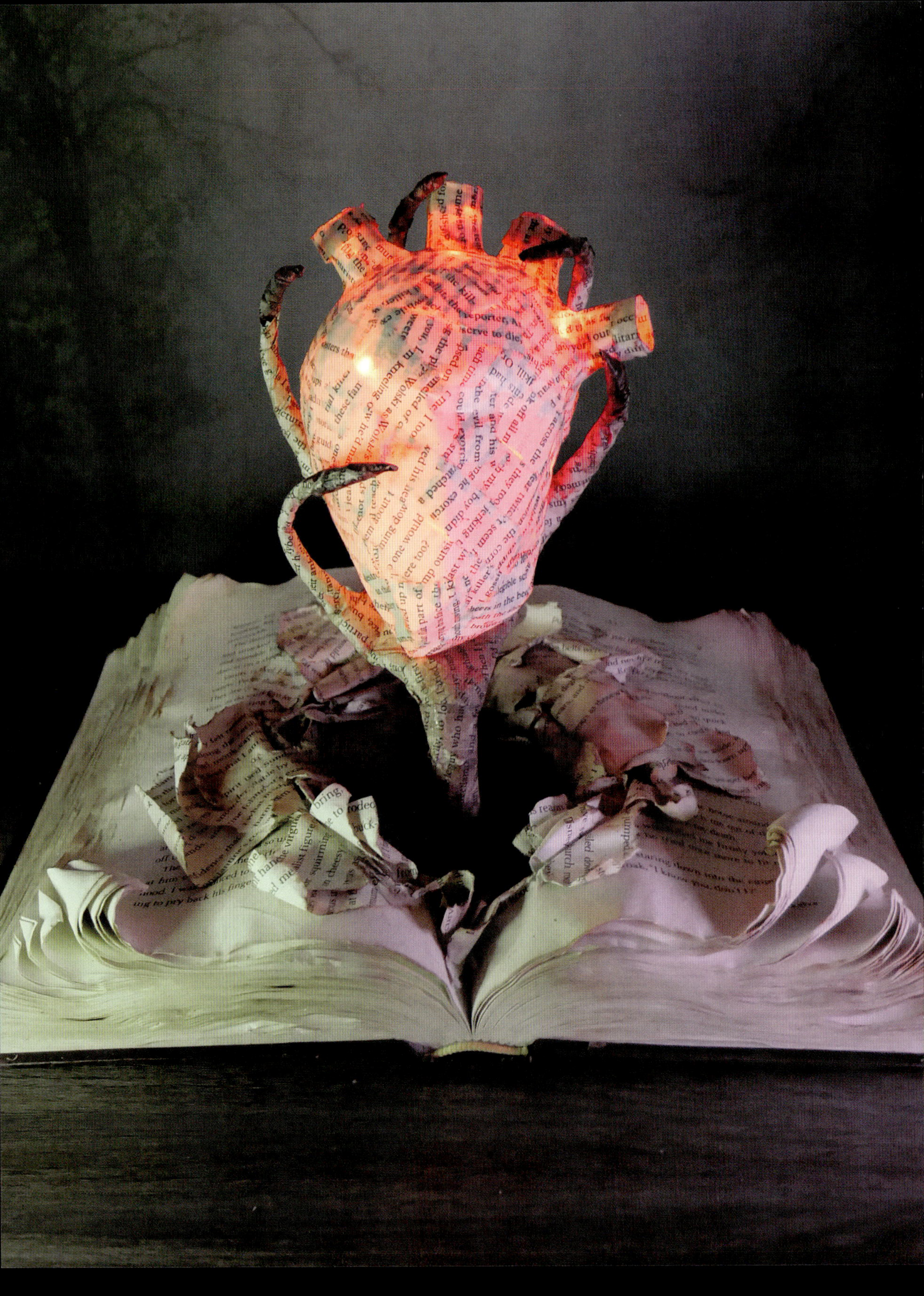

Gripping Story

Have you ever read a book that just gripped you like none other? In this project we'll illustrate that point. This is a medium-difficult project but relatively cheap, so if you screw it up it's no big deal. Just relax and have fun with it.

Where to get pressboard? Nowadays a lot of furniture and easily crushable items are shipped with small pressboards that are extremely durable. I hoard them! They are super useful and make for great cutting surfaces.

Where to get book pages? If you did the Secret Book Box project (page 81) then you should have a ton of leftover pages. If you didn't, then you'll have to rip some out from a second book.

Open your book in the middle and lay it face down. Take your small wood board or pressboard and hot glue it so it's touching both covers and the spine. This is so that your book will stay lying nice and flat.

Cut or rip book pages (NOT FROM THIS BOOK!) into 2-inch (5-cm)-wide strips. Trifold your strips so they are long and skinny. Your strips should be shorter than your book; if they aren't, rip them so they are. Tuck your strips into your book every 5 to 10 pages and secure them using a small amount of craft glue. *These just make the book look fuller.*

(continued)

Materials

- Hardcover book
- Wood board or pressboard (about the size of your book cover)
- Hot glue and gun
- Book pages (from a different book)
- Craft glue
- Squirt bottle
- Strong brewed tea or coffee
- Heat gun
- Pencil (optional)
- Matte Mod Podge
- Wire cutters
- Floral wire
- Masking tape
- X-ACTO knife
- Acrylic paint and brush
- Plate easel or picture hanger (optional)

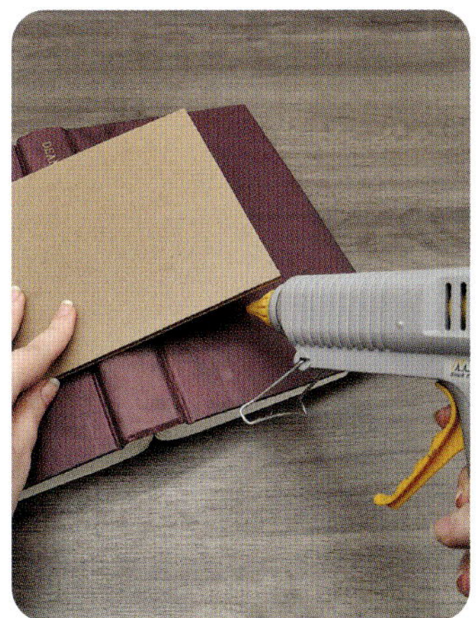

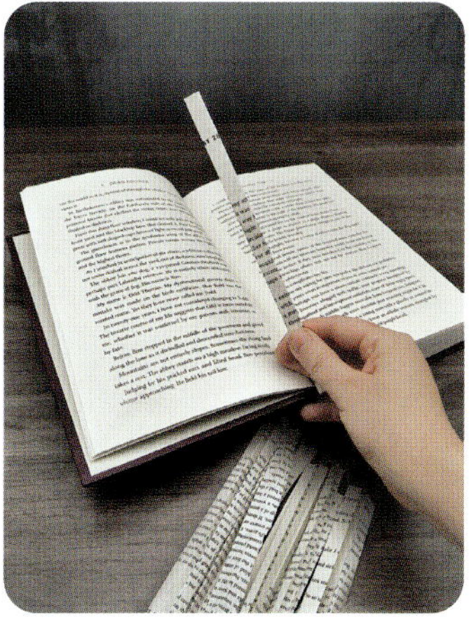

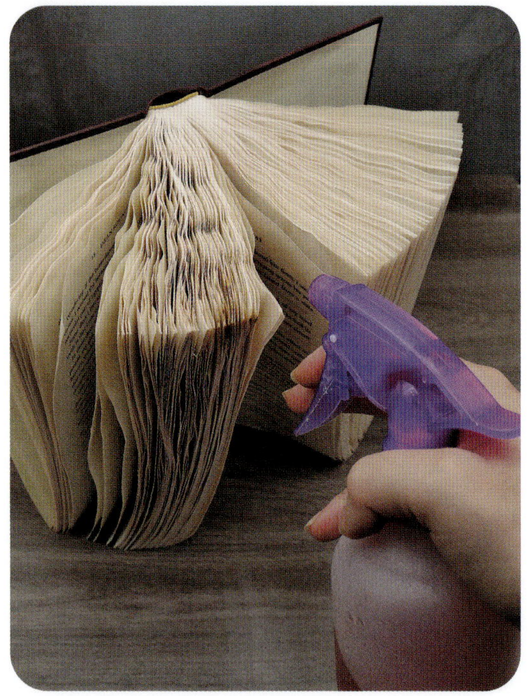
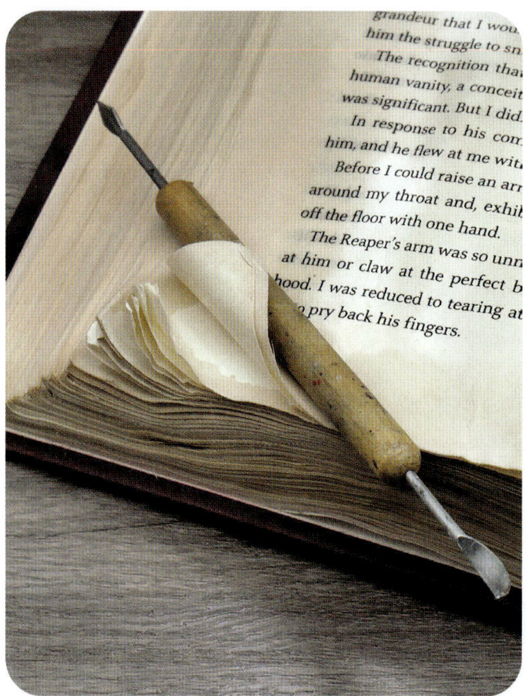

Tip your book on its side and let the pages fan out in front of you. Fill a squirt bottle with strong brewed tea or coffee and spray down the fanned-out pages. Dry it with a heat gun and repeat. *This will take some time. I alternated between spraying and blasting it with a heat gun to get a wavy, weathered look.*

Once your book is old and weathered looking, lay it facing up, open to the middle page. Curl the pages of the open book around anything cylinder shaped, like a pencil or paintbrush handle.

Liberally coat the edges of your pages with Mod Podge. *You don't want your pages to go anywhere. Dry and set the shape with the heat gun. Your book should end up being pretty stiff at this point, almost like a sculpture.*

Now we need to add something to the middle! Cut some floral wire and twist the pieces together in the rough shape of a hand, then cover it with masking tape. Bend your hand's wrist back and position it in your book to get the right shape. *Getting the shape right is key. It should feel like it's holding something or trying to grab someone.* Using Mod Podge and more book pages (again, not from this book!), adhere pages onto the hand. Rip the pages in strips and wind them around the wrist and fingers. Set off to the side to dry for a few minutes.

Using an X-ACTO knife, cut a few small lines radiating into the center of your open book and gently pull the pages back a little. Once you have a small/medium-sized hole in your book, push the wrist of the hand into the spine and hot glue it in. Make sure it's secure. Cover any exposed hot glue with your extra book pages and Mod

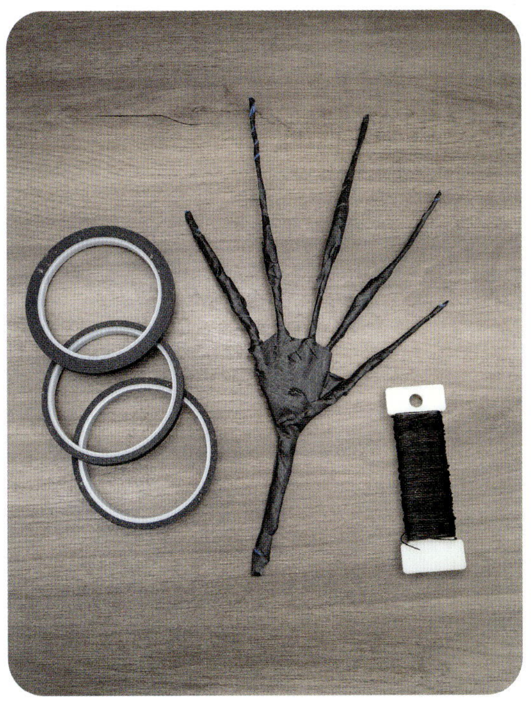

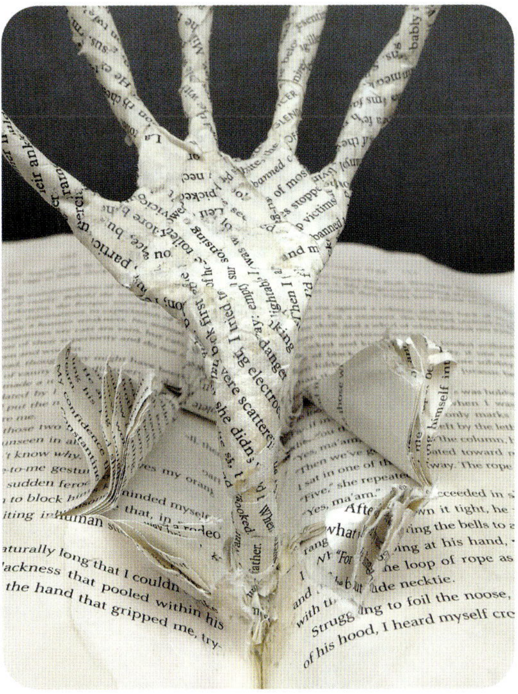

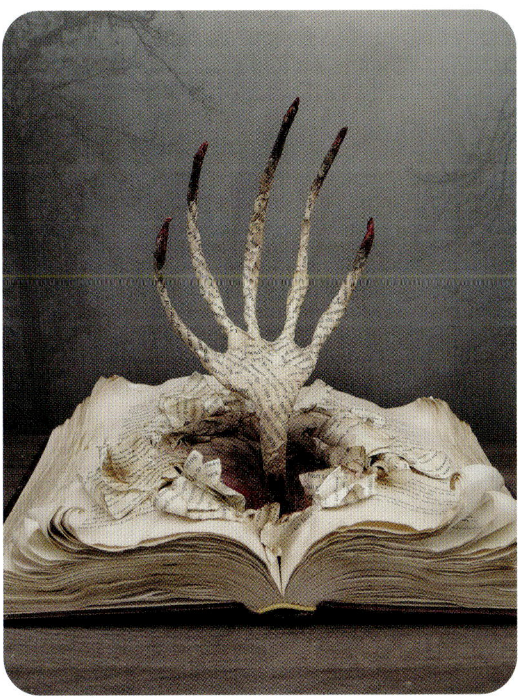

Podge. Slowly distress the hole by ripping pages radiating from the hand. Be very careful not to rip all the way to the edge of the page. Curl the ripped edges with a pencil or brush handle and use Mod Podge where needed to set the shape.

Paint the hole with red and dark brown paint. Make it darker toward the wrist and fade out under the book pages in the hole. Paint the tips of the hand with red and dark brown. You can burn the edges of curled pages with your heat gun. Just be careful not to burn them too much and start a fire! Depending on how you want to display your book you can leave it as is, put it in a plate easel or attach a picture hanger to the back to hang it on the wall.

If you want to add a heart, see page 89 for instructions.

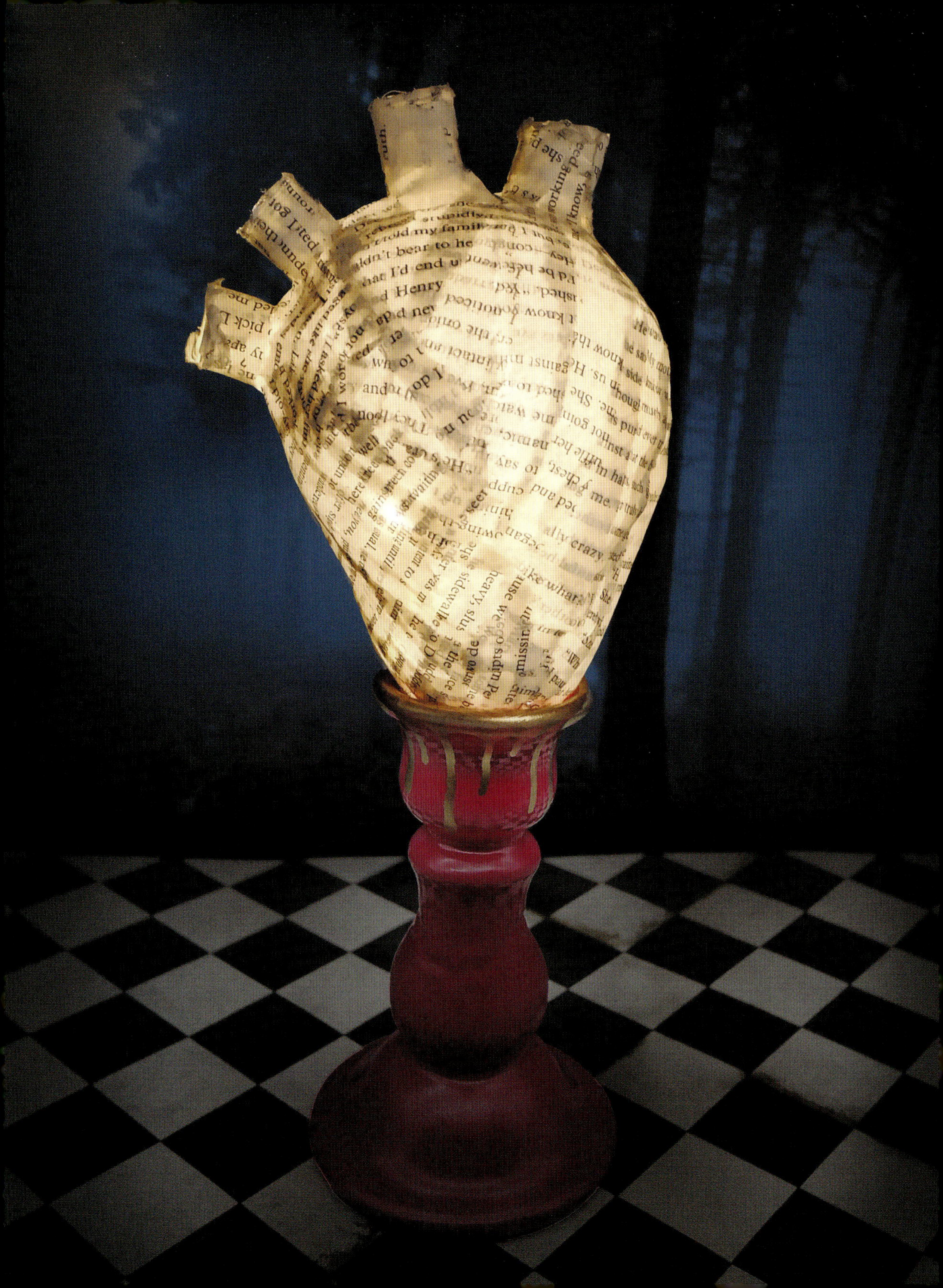

The "Lit" Heart

Whether you want to make this heart for your Gripping Story project on the previous page or as a stand-alone piece, I got you covered. We're making a "lit" heart . . . get it? Lit as in literature and lit as in light? I know, I know, I'm very clever! Anyway, this project will either be amazing for all the literature lovers out there or pure torture because—warning!—you will have to rip up book pages. But if you've done the previous project, then you've already done your fair share of page-ripping.

Materials

- Balloons
- Rubber band or long balloon
- Clear packing tape
- Scissors
- Book pages
- Matte Mod Podge
- Water and small container
- X-ACTO knife
- Battery-operated fairy lights
- Hot glue and gun
- Candleholder (optional)
- Acrylic paint and brush (optional)

Blow up a balloon about the size of a softball and tie a rubber band or long balloon around the middle to make it more of a kidney/heart shape. Use clear packing tape to hold the band down. *Trust me, this is important: I almost lost an eye when a rubber band hurled itself at my face!* Scrunch up balloons at the bottom of your kidney-shaped heart to create more of a point and tape those down with clear packing tape. With scissors, cut the "blow end" off four balloons and fill them with rolled up paper or book pages to keep their shape. Tape these "blow end rolls" onto the top of your heart to make arteries.

> **Tip:** *We don't want any paper to stick to our heart, so everything on the outside should be either tape or balloon material.*

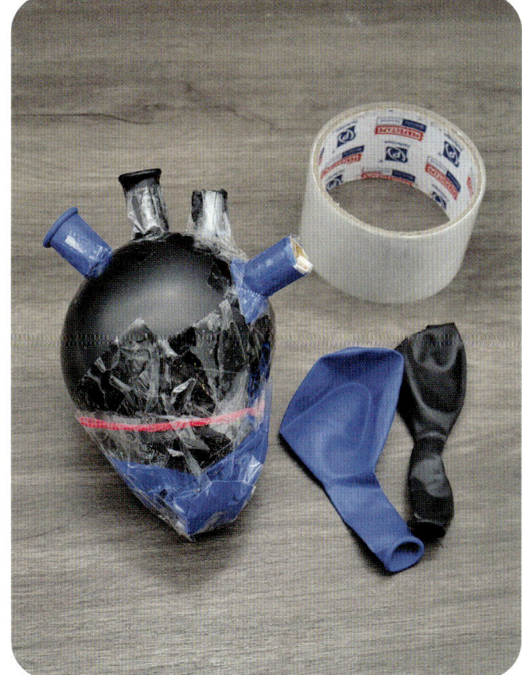

(continued)

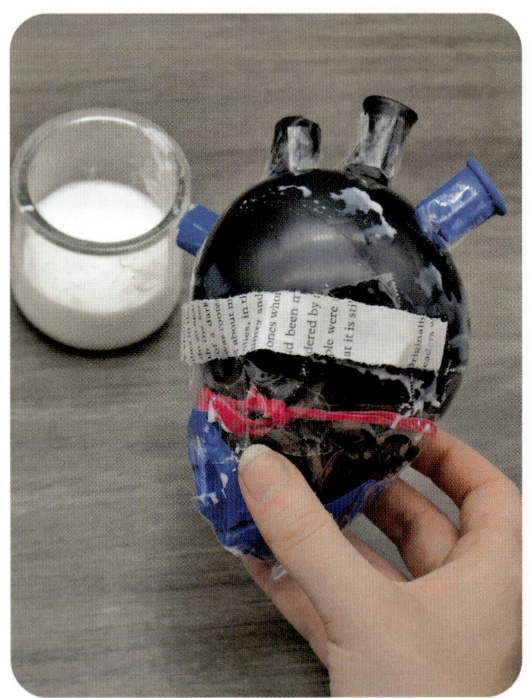 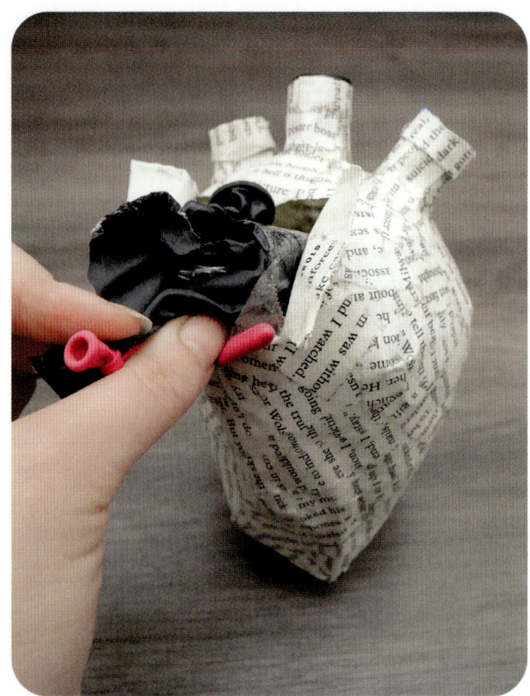

Rip your book pages into thin strips. Mix two parts matte Mod Podge with one part water in a small container and dip your page strips in. Lay them directly onto your balloon heart. Keep working until you have the entire balloon covered. Leave the tops of the arteries open. *Overlap your pages as little as possible. We want our light to shine through.* Coat your entire heart with a final non-watered-down layer of Mod Podge.

Your heart should be hardened by the stresses of life. I mean, the Mod Podge will make it hard in about 24 hours. Cut a little door in the back of your heart with an X-ACTO knife. Pop your balloon and gently pull it out the door. Your heart will want to collapse a bit as you pull out your balloon. Don't panic! Use your fingers to gently pop it back into shape.

 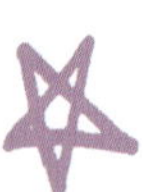

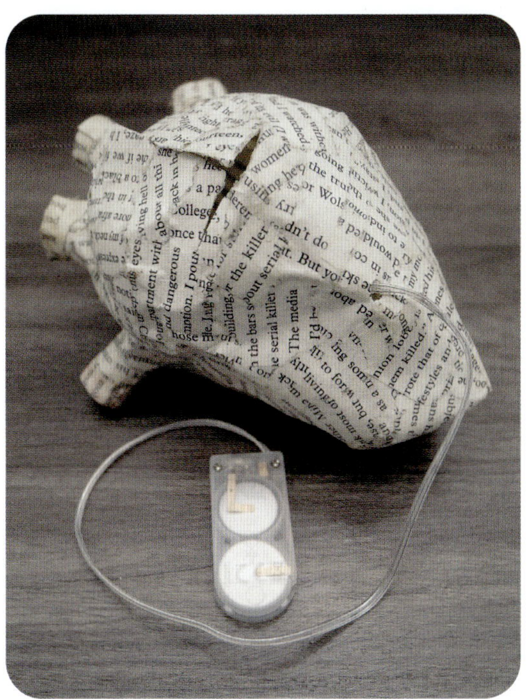

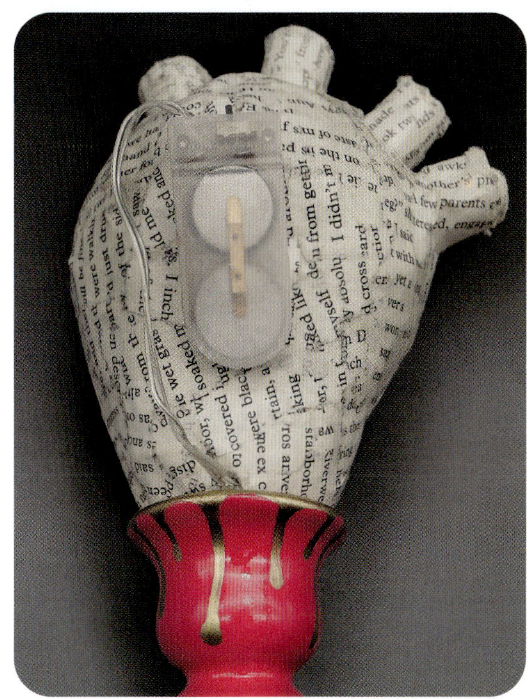

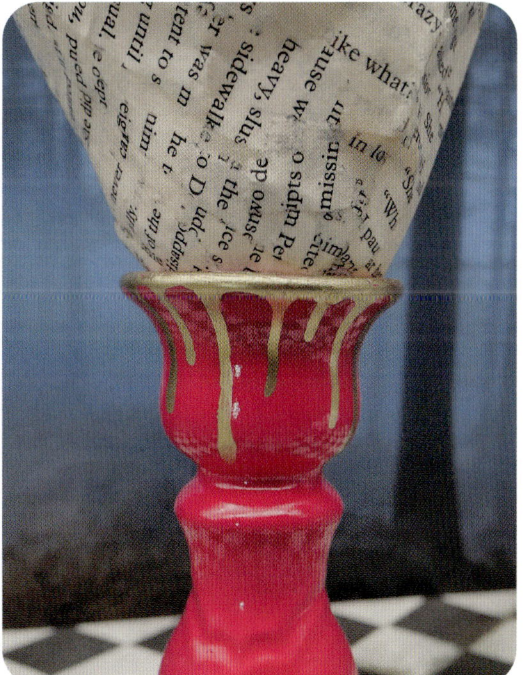

Poke a tiny hole in the bottom with your X-ACTO knife and feed your fairy lights through. Using the door you cut to access the inside of your heart, hot glue your lights evenly inside. Glue some lights into the artery holes. Test out your lighting to make sure it's evenly lit. Seal your door shut with ripped-up book pages and Mod Podge, and hot glue the battery pack on the back.

If you're here from the Gripping Story project, hot glue your heart to your book's hand.

Or if you want a stand-alone heart, hot glue the bottom of your heart to the hole of a candle-holder. Painting your candleholder with a pop of color can add an optional fun touch.

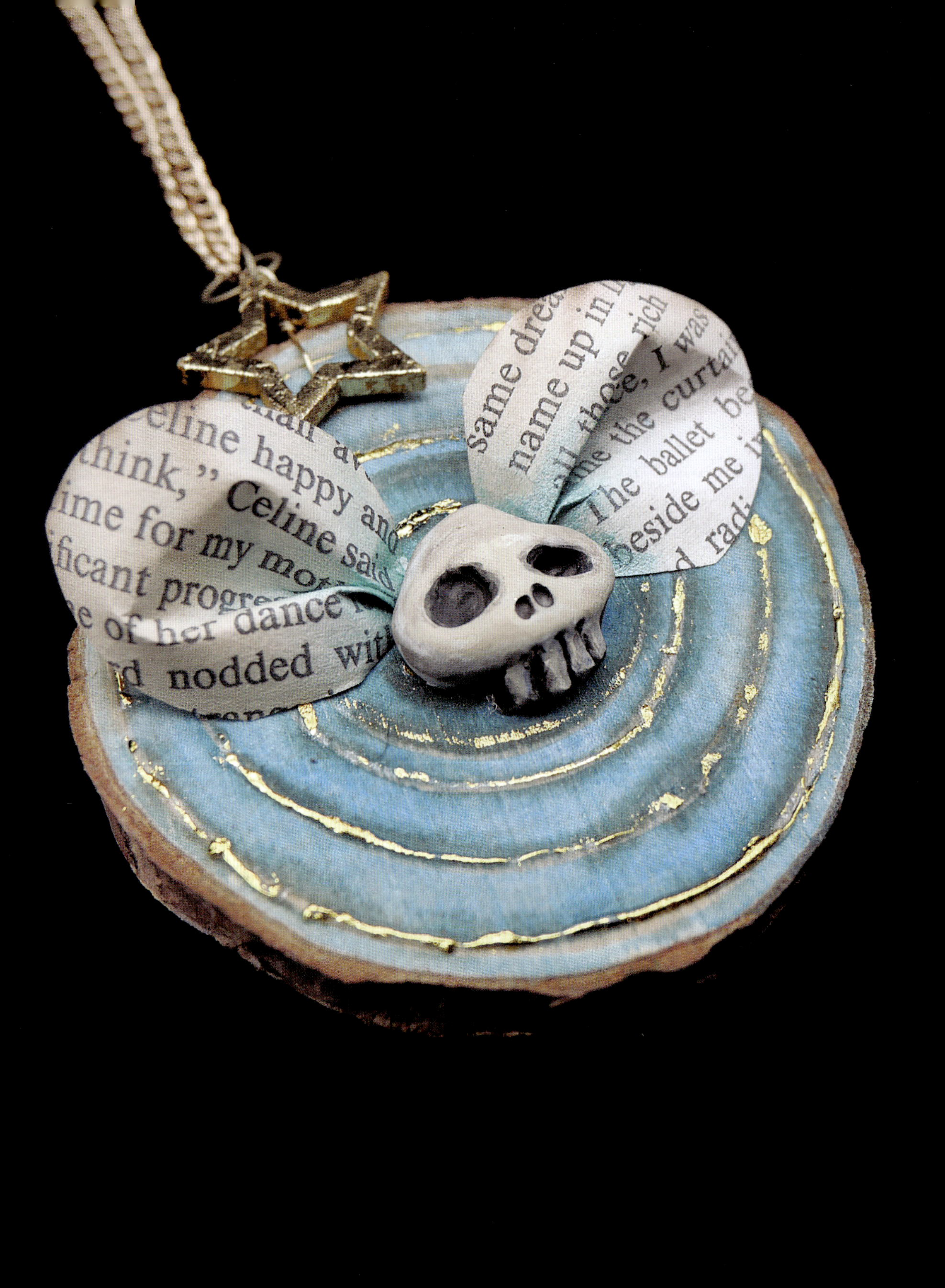

eline happy an
think," Celine said
ime for my mo
ficant progres
e of her dance
d nodded wit
same drea
name up in
these rich
the curtai
the ballet be
beside me i
d radi

Flying Fiction Ornament

Let's be honest, I totally winged this project . . . Get it? Winged it. Anyway, this project makes for a great gift! You can attach it to the outside of your gift wrap as a bow alternative or just give the ornament as the gift itself. It's easy to make and you can create a bunch at once if you like.

I used polymer clay because it's easy, but you can substitute almost any clay.

Roll out a gumball-sized piece of polymer clay. Flatten your ball and sculpt it into a flat mushroom shape. Use a round-tipped sculpting tool to make two eyes and a nose. Use a flat-edged sculpting tool to make indents for teeth. Bake in the oven according to the package instructions. Once it cools, paint the eyes, nose and teeth with black paint. Set aside.

(continued)

Materials

- ½ oz (14 g) white polymer clay
- Sculpting tools with round tip and flat edge
- Acrylic paint and brush
- Scissors
- 1 book page
- Craft glue
- 3" (7.5-cm) circular wood slice with hole
- Foil adhesive (e.g., Deco)
- Imitation gold leaf
- Metal leaf varnish
- Precision craft glue (e.g., Bearly Art)
- 5" (12.7 cm) of floral wire
- 1–2 jump rings
- 8" (20-cm) golden chain
- Star charm (optional)
- Mica powder (optional)

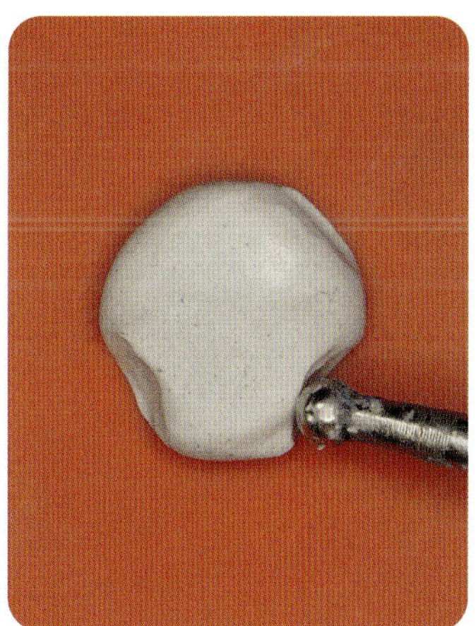
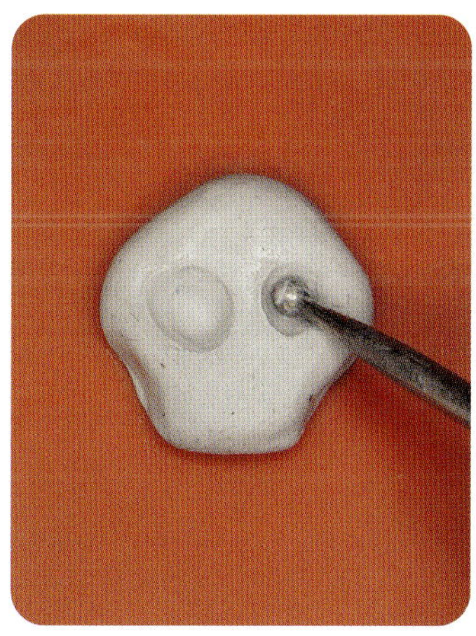
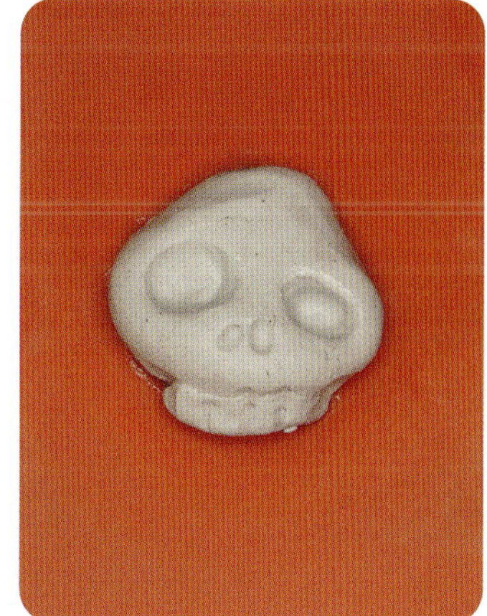

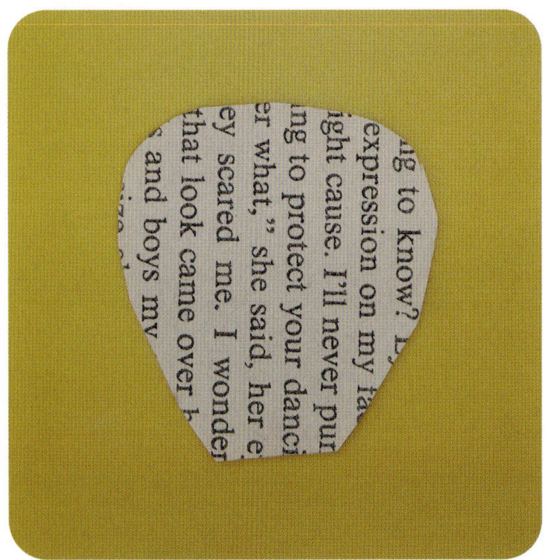

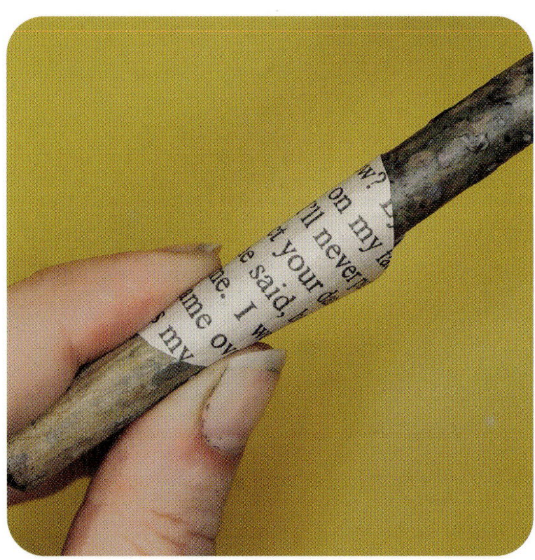

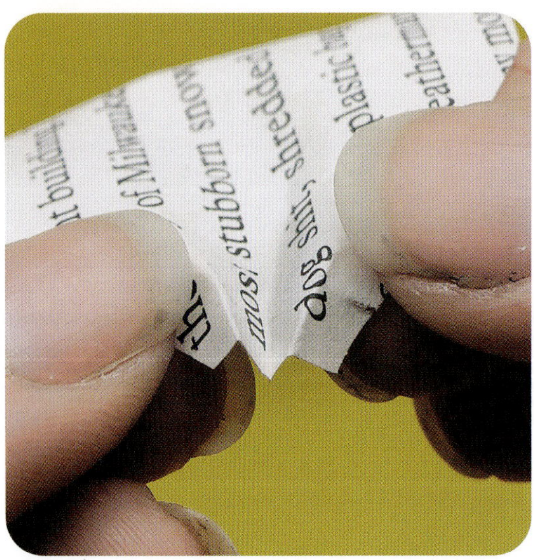

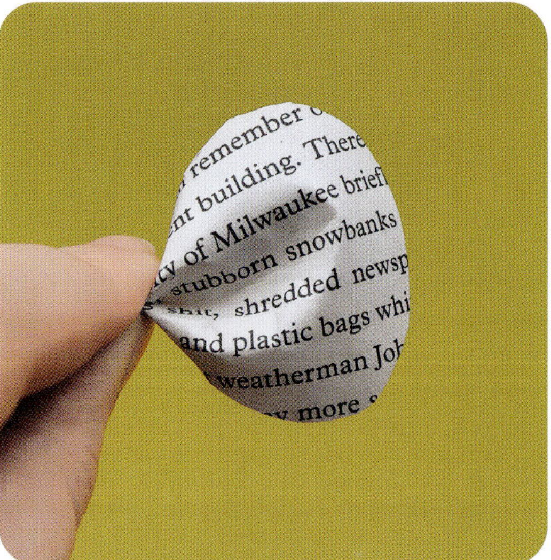

With scissors, cut two wing shapes out of your
book page. Roll your wing around the handle of
a sculpting tool to give it shape. Unroll your
wing and fold the bottom flat part into an M.
Using craft glue, glue the fold together to hold
the wing shape. Set aside.

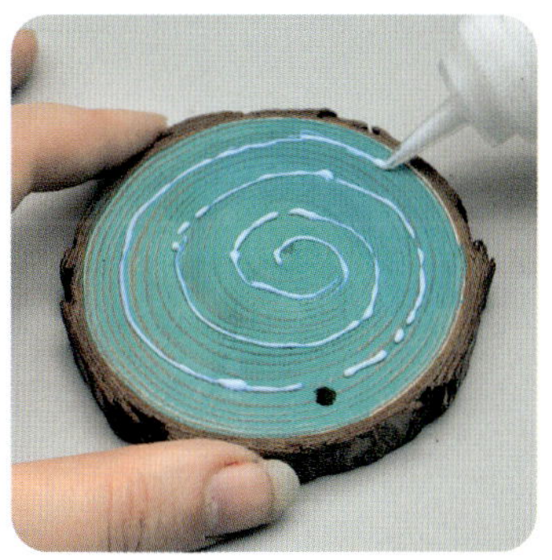
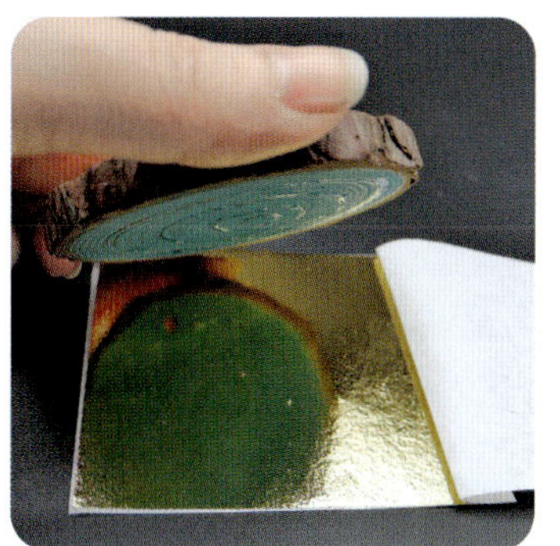
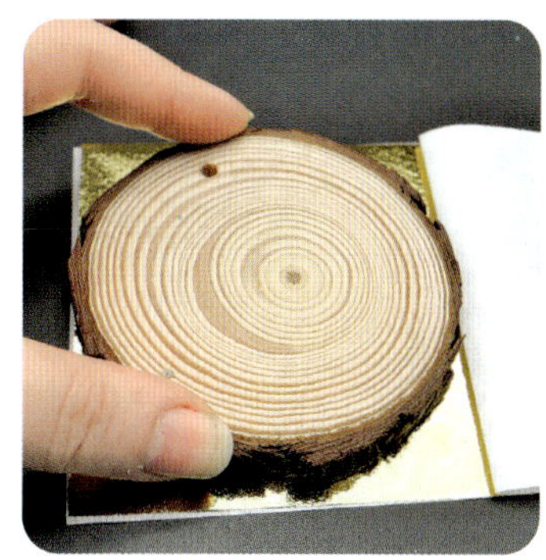

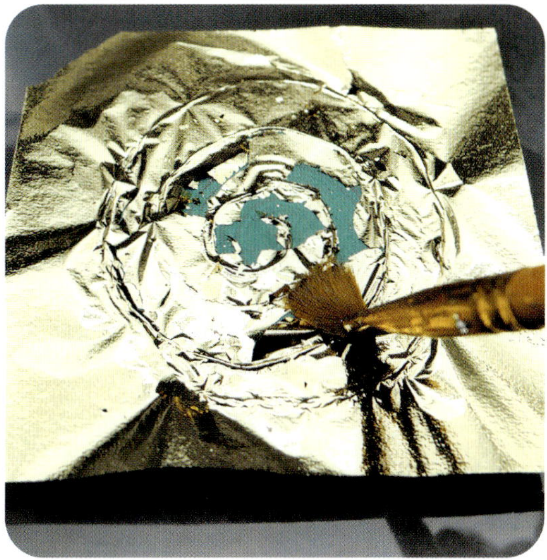

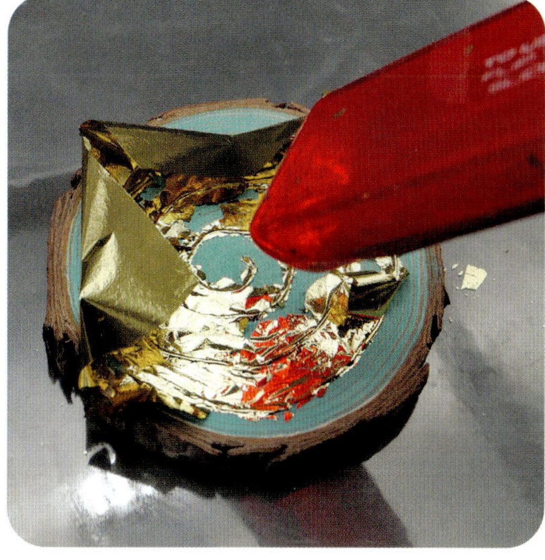

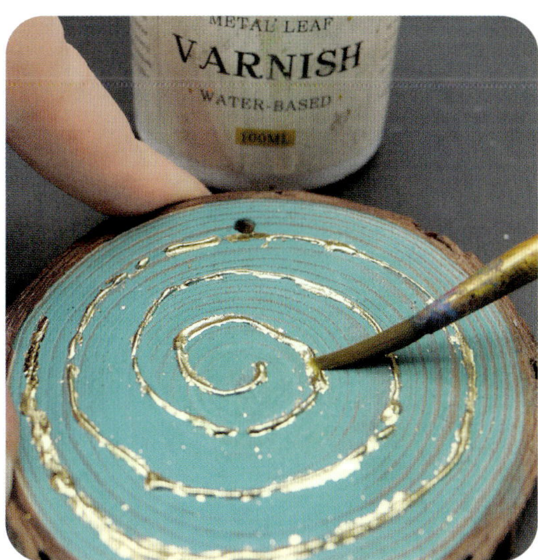

Paint your wood slice with any color of acrylic paint. *I went with teal, but you can do whatever floats your boat.* Draw a spiral on your wood slice with foil adhesive and let it dry. Read the packaging for drying details, but usually it's an hour. Press the wood slice's adhesive side into a sheet of imitation gold leaf and flip it over. Brush away any excess foil. *This can be very messy! I mean extremely messy! Worse than glitter messy! I highly recommend having a small handheld vacuum ready to suck up any stray gold flakes!* Seal the gold leaf with metal leaf varnish.

(continued)

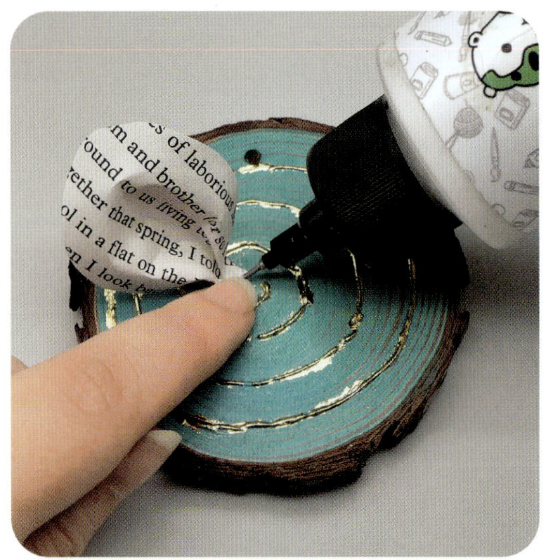

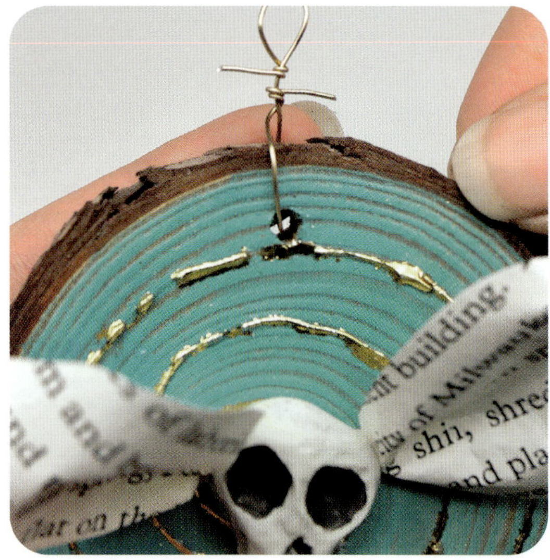

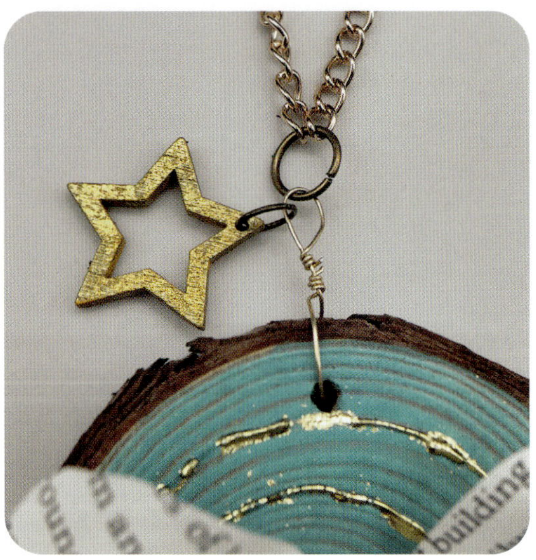

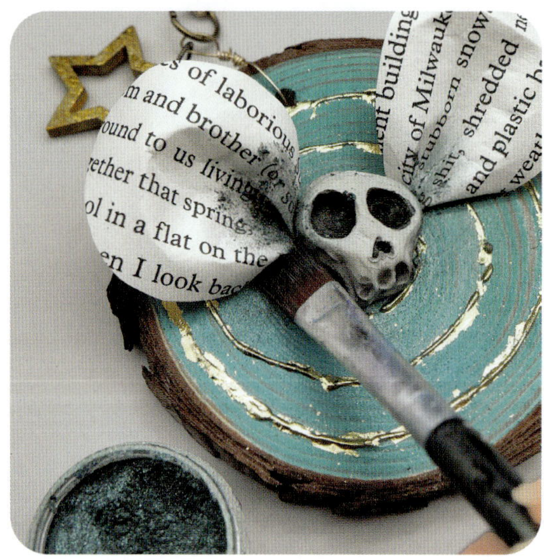

Using precision glue, glue your wings to the center of your wood slice, then your skull in between the wings.

Twist the floral wire into a figure-eight loop in the hole of your wood slice. Add a jump ring to the top loop and feed your chain through the loops. Attach your star charm (if using) with an additional jump ring. *Or if this is too complex, just tie a string in the hole and be done with it. Sometimes simple is better.*

To add depth, brush on dark mica powder around your skull. Wipe or blow off any excess powder that may have found its way onto the skull and wings.

Nevermore Drawer

In a "nevermore" drawer you can keep everything from your past that you'd like to forget. However, if you really wanted to forget them, perhaps keeping them is a bad idea in the first place. Though who doesn't have a few toxic mementos they just can't let go of? In a more "Poe" style, you could store old lovers' notes in there, vowing to "nevermore" revisit the heartaches of the past. Who am I kidding? We don't write notes anymore. Perhaps you could just throw your old phone in there with all their text messages. I don't know, let's not overthink it. I'll probably store beef jerky in mine, because mmmmm . . .

Materials

- Wooden drawer
- Sandpaper
- Book pages
- Matte Mod Podge
- Water and small container
- Heat gun
- Acrylic paint and brush
- Paper and printer (optional)
- Scissors
- Pencil
- Masking tape
- Stamp and ink pad (optional)

Start by sanding your wooden drawer with sandpaper. You don't need to sand down to the wood but just rough it up a bit. *If you're comfortable, try yelling obscenities at it. This helps "rough" it up mentally as well.*

(continued)

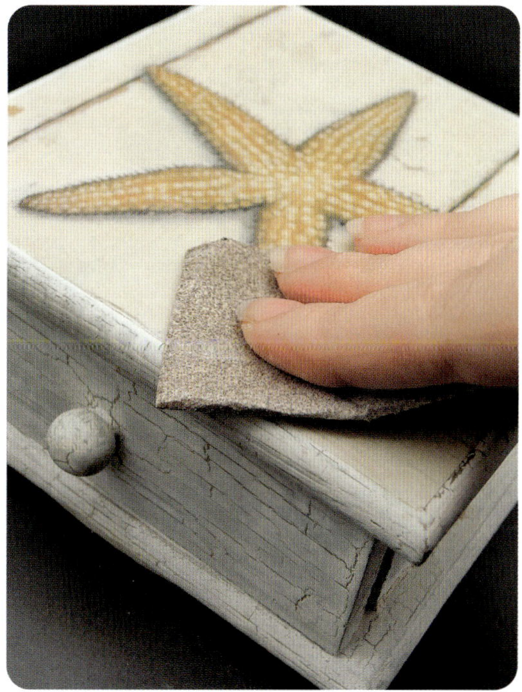

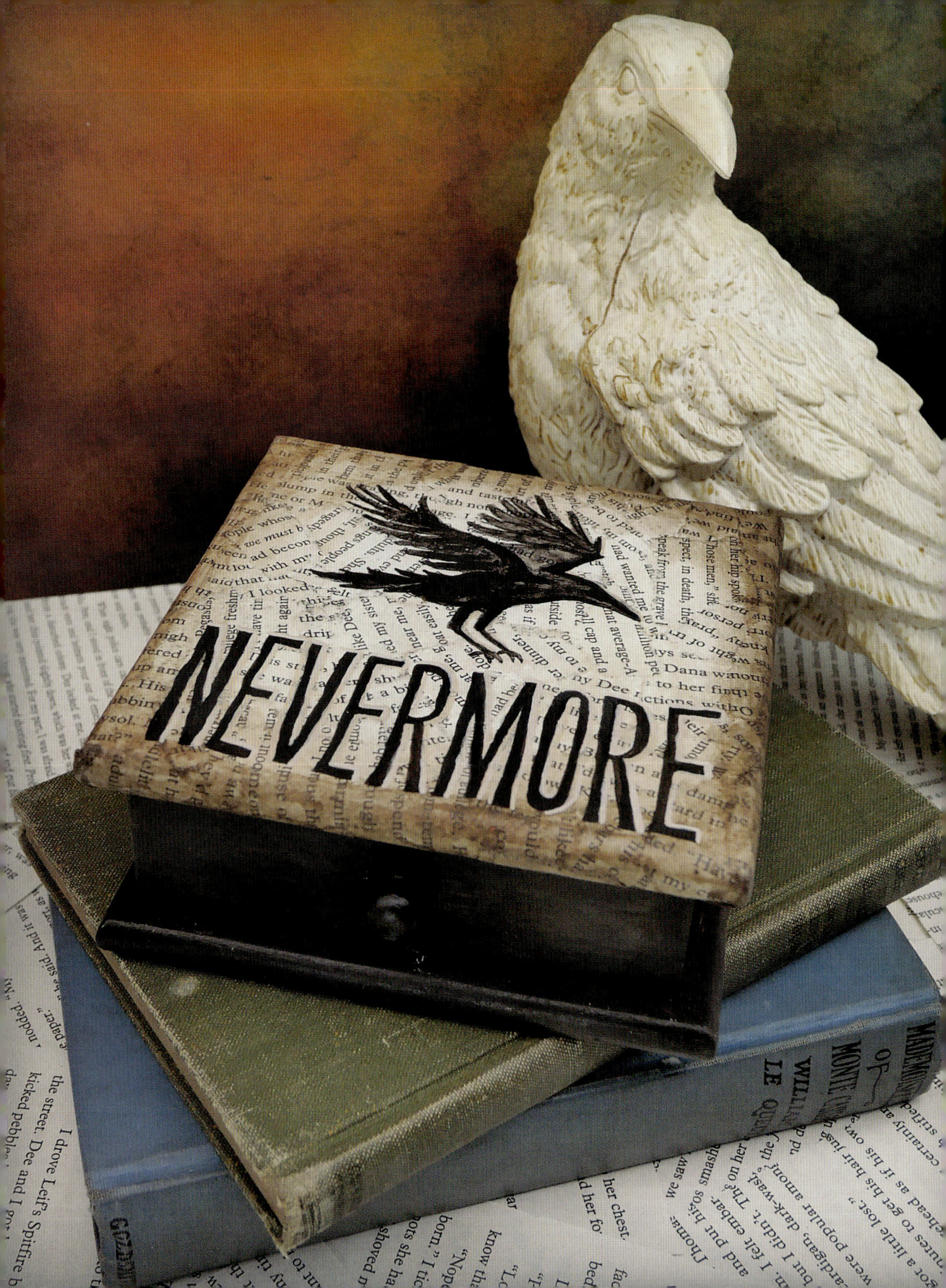

NEVERMORE

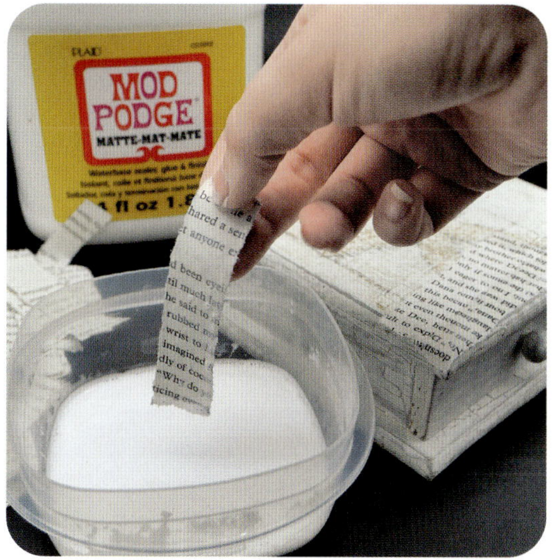 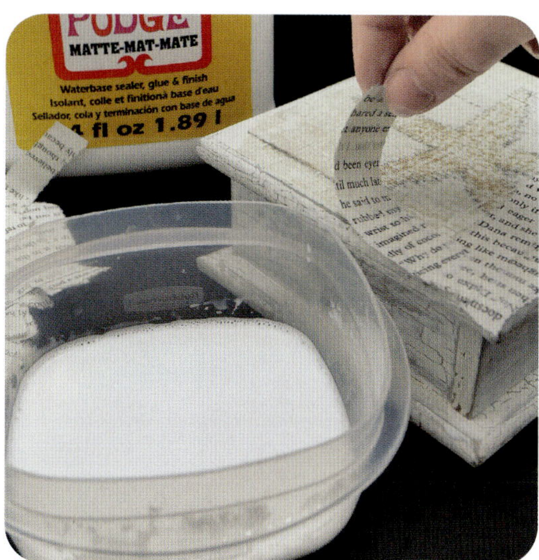

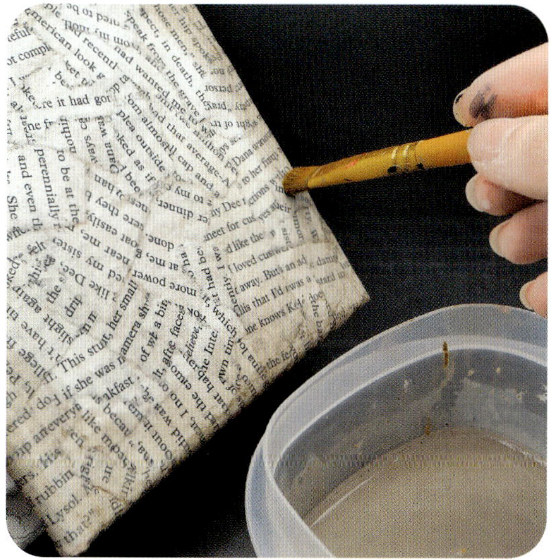 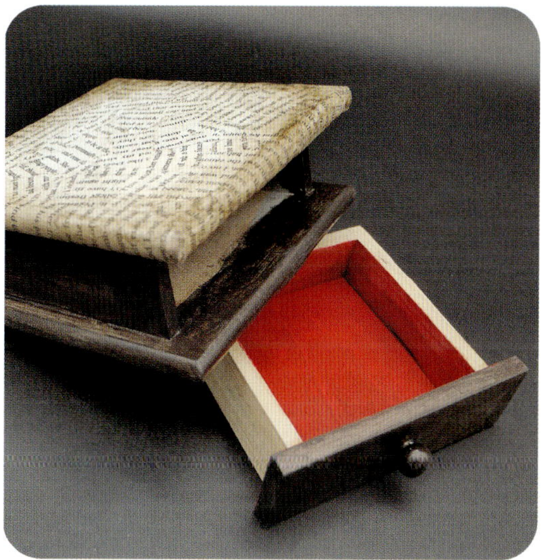

Rip a few book pages into smaller sections. You don't want any clean straight edges, so rip those off. Make a mixture of two parts Mod Podge and one part water in a small container. Dip your ripped-up pages into the mixture and lay them on the top half of your drawer. Don't make it look too organized; your pages should go every which way. Dry it with a heat gun for a few minutes.

Using your leftover watered-down Mod Podge mixture, add a tiny amount of brown and yellow acrylic paint. Paint just the top edges of your drawer and dry with the heat gun. You may want to do this a few times depending on how "aged" you want it to look. Paint the bottom half of your drawer with brown paint (or the color of your choice). I also painted the inside of my drawer a bright red color for extra pizzazz!

(continued)

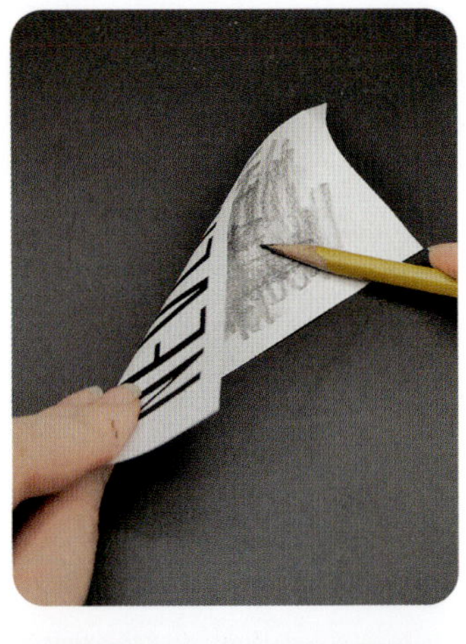
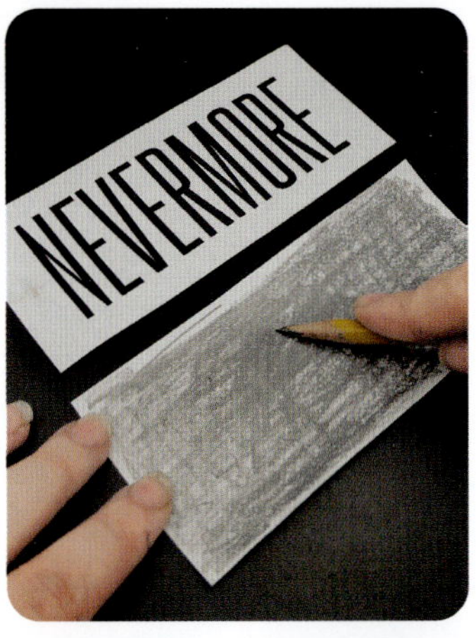
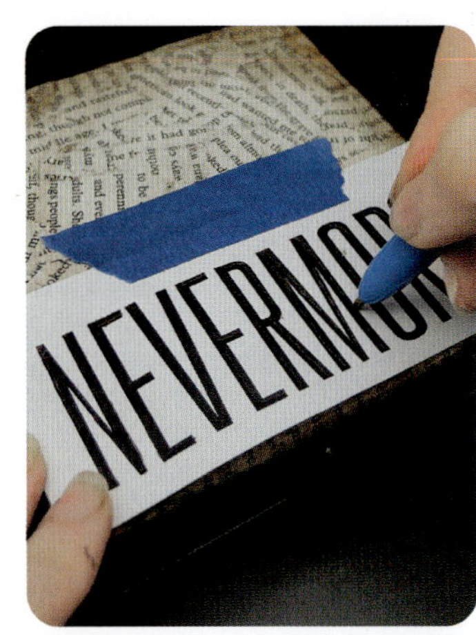

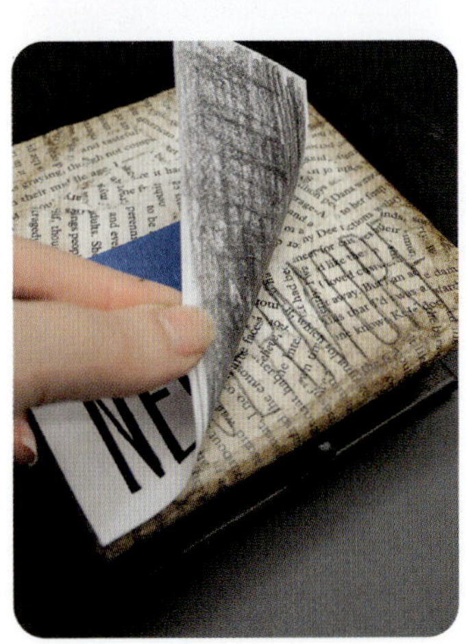
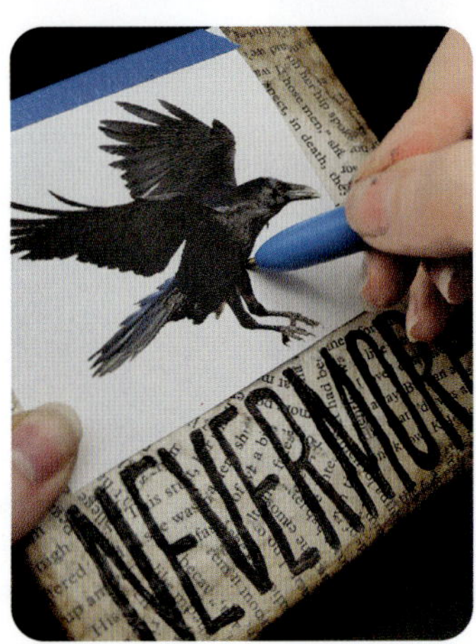
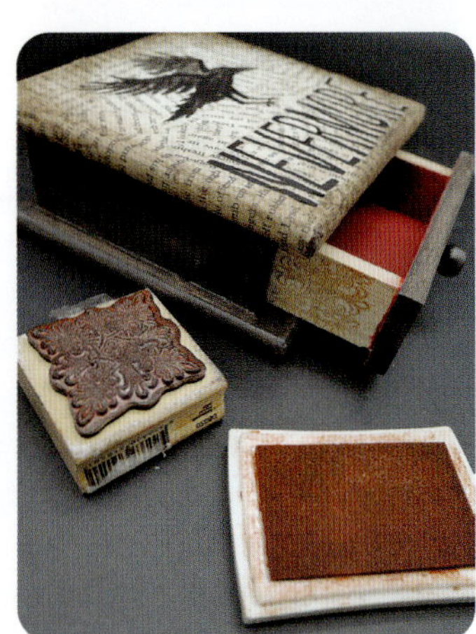

Now for the lettering. If you have terrible handwriting like I do, print out the word "NEVERMORE" in a font you like. Cut it out with scissors. With a pencil, shade or scribble on the entire back of your print. *You can alternatively use carbon paper but not everyone has that, and I wouldn't want you to buy a whole pack for one project. Also, this is great for working out any aggressions!*

Flip your paper over and tape it where you want your word to be placed. Using a pointy object like a pen or pencil, trace the word onto your drawer using a good amount of pressure. *You can lift the flap without taking it off to check that it's transferring. If it's not, you didn't scribble enough on the back, you're not using enough pressure or your drawer isn't fully dry from the Mod Podge paint mixture.*

Once the word "NEVERMORE" is transferred, take your paper off and paint in the text. Repeat the process with a picture of a raven.

Lastly, because I like being "extra," I added a peekaboo side stamp to my drawer using a stamp and ink pad. If you have trouble finding the right stamp, check out page 211 where I'll show you how to make your very own.

Creepy Gift Tags

- Scissors
- Chipboard
- Book pages
- Hole punch
- Hole sticker
- Stamp and ink pad
- Fine-tip black marker
- Ribbon or string

We're making creepy gift tags! This is a quick and spooky project to give your gifts a touch of eerie charm! Say goodbye to those boring old presents because you're on your way to gift-giving with a creepy flair! Will people think you're peculiar? Absolutely! Will it scare Grandma? Most definitely! But normalcy is so overrated. Let's get creepy instead!

With scissors, cut a 2½ x 4–inch (6.3 x 10–cm) rectangle out of chipboard and a slightly larger rectangle out of a book page. Using a hole punch, punch a hole in the middle top of both. Place a hole sticker around the hole of both the chipboard and the book page.

(continued)

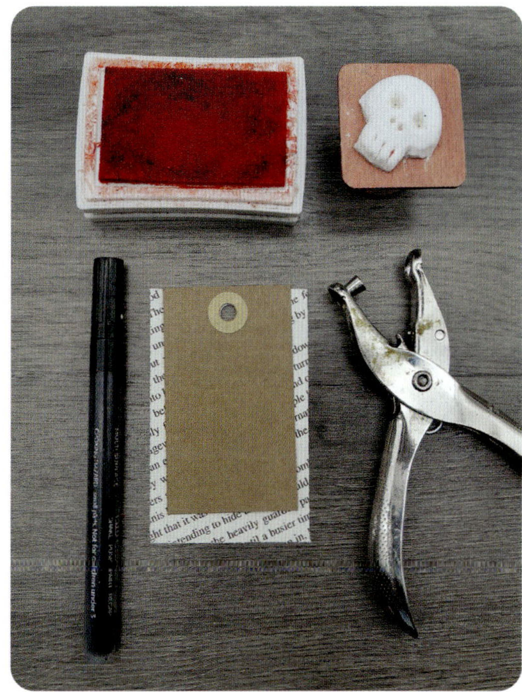

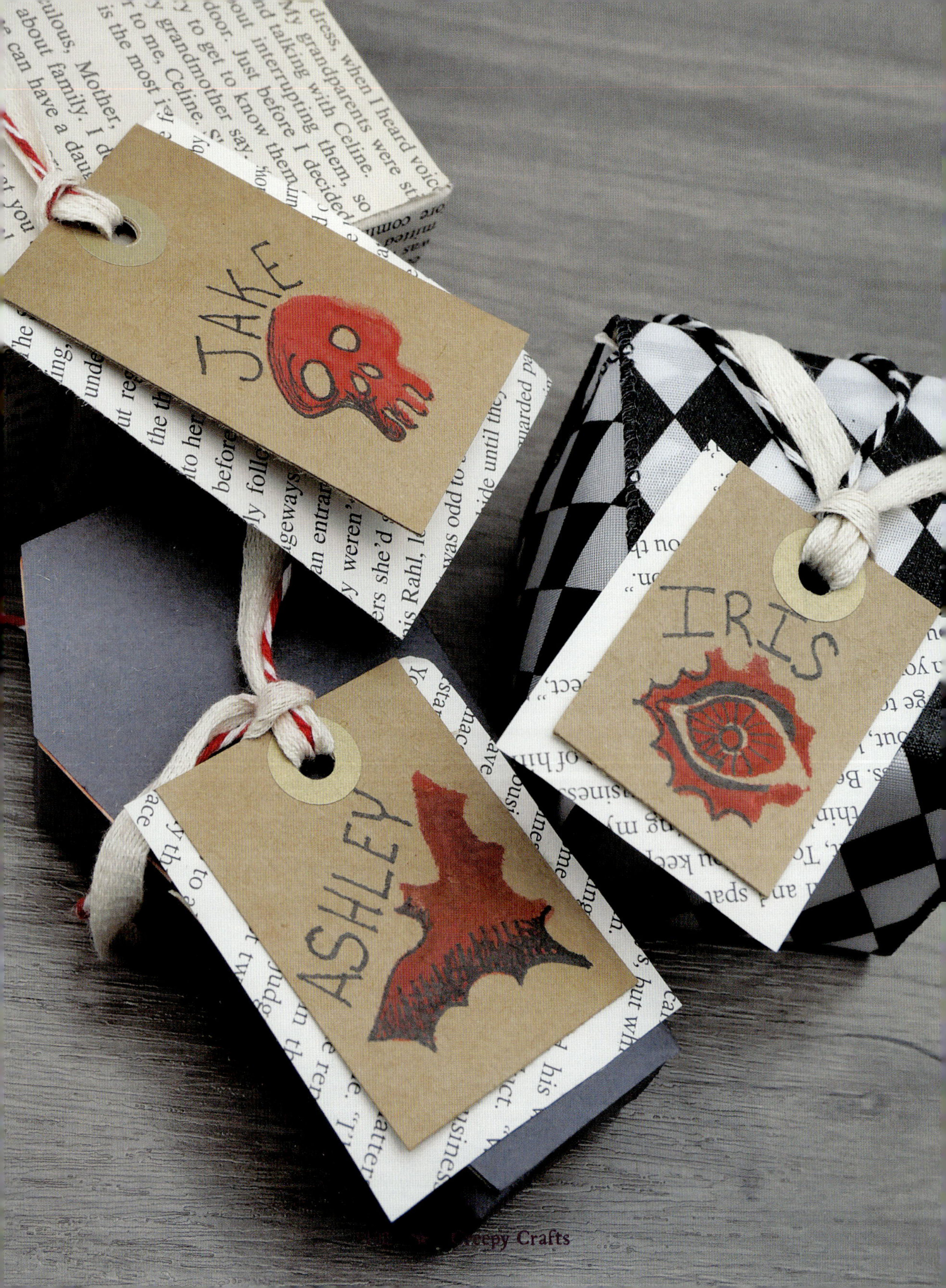

JAKE
ASHLEY
IRIS
Creepy Crafts

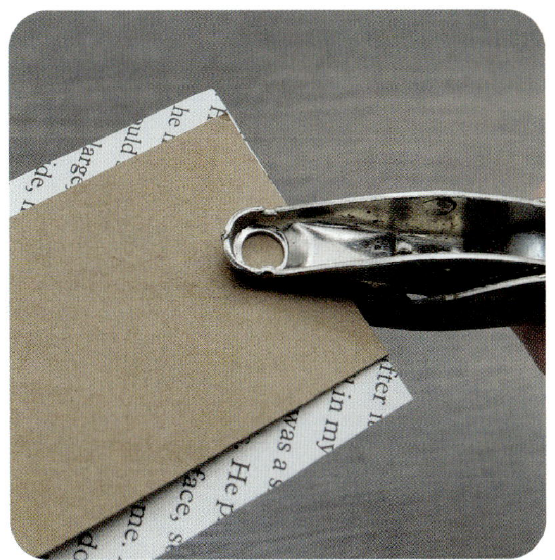

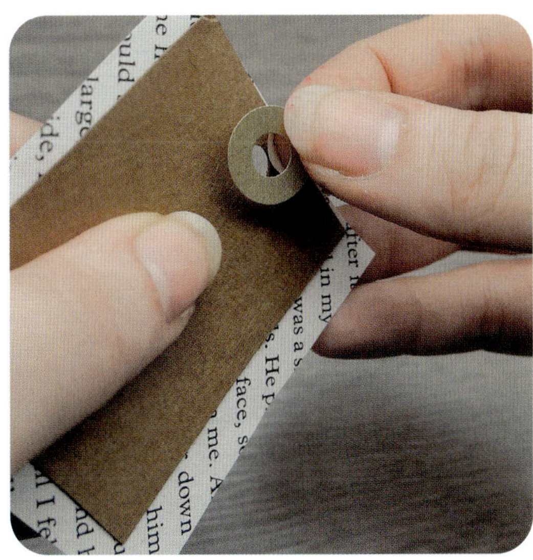

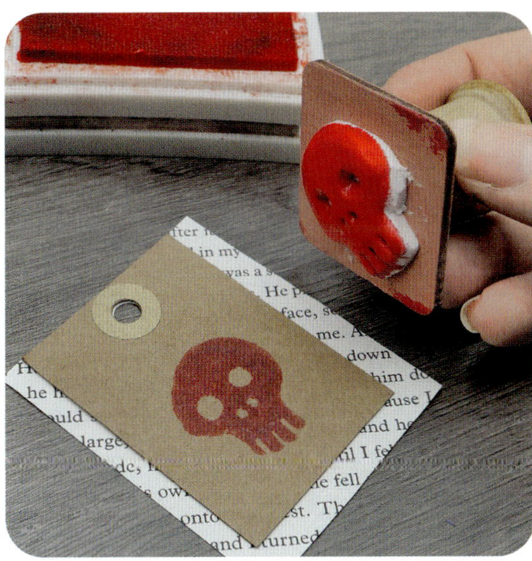

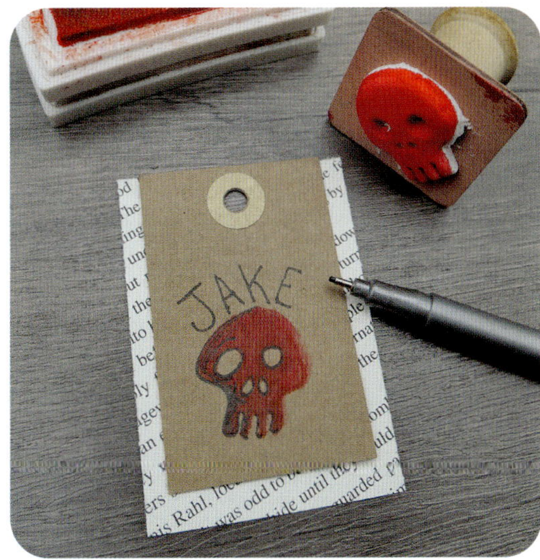

To make your own stamps, see the project for Spooky Skull Stamps (page 211). Stamp your chipboard with a stamp and ink pad. I went with red so that I could add black details, but you do you, boo.

Personalize your gift tag with a fine-tip black marker. I also added details to my stamp with the marker to add more depth and dimension to my tag.

Wrap ribbon around your gift and through the hole of your tag. Tie the whole thing off with a bow.

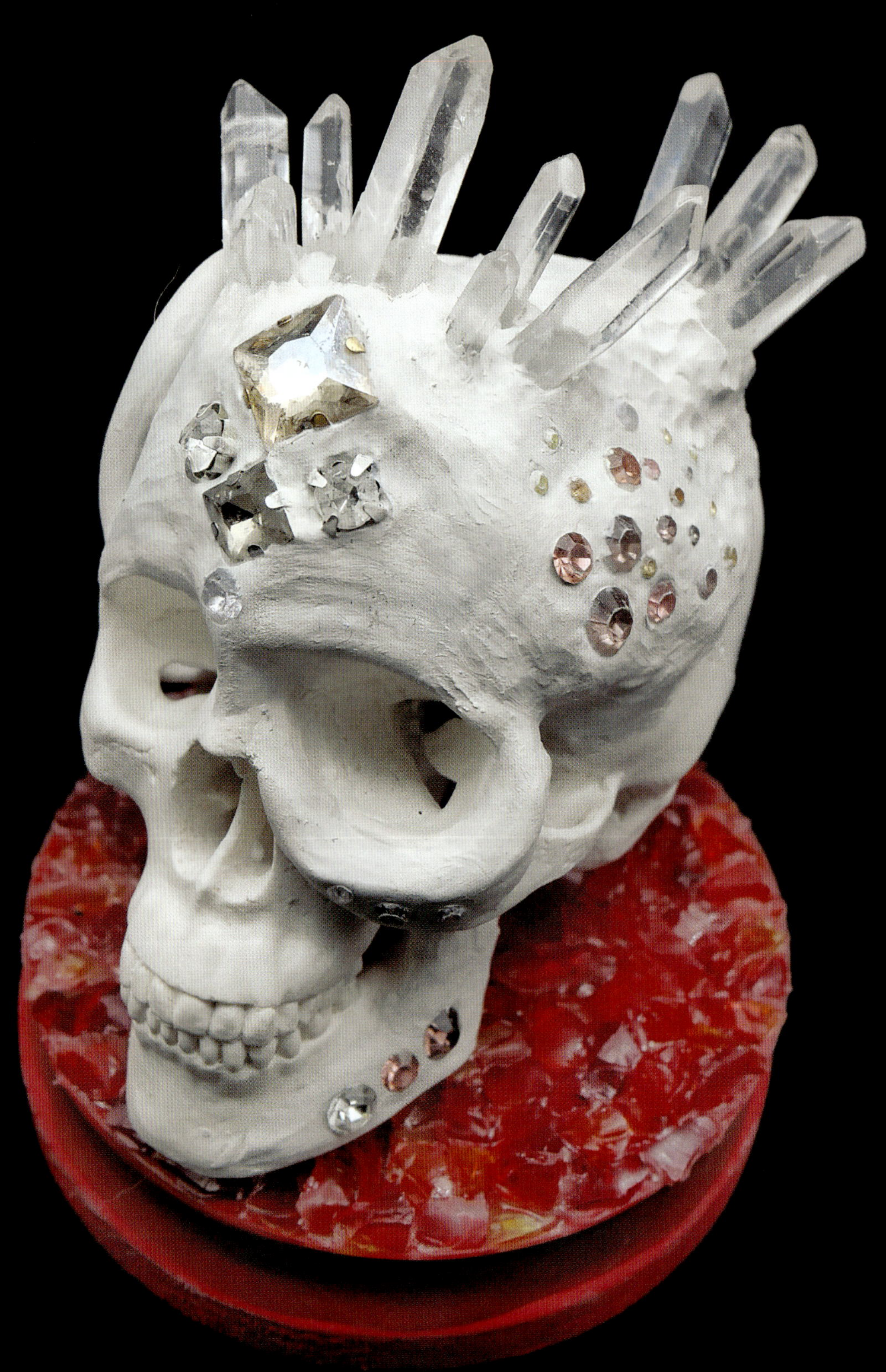

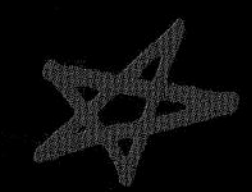

The Boneyard

Welcome to the Boneyard, where all the bone-chilling creepy crafts are made. I mean, let's face it: A creepy crafts book without bones is like eating boneless wings—they're just not as good compared to the bone-in versions.

In this section we'll be venturing into the world of bones, skulls and more, making crafts such as a mirror fit for the fairest bone queen and a stash of teeth that would make the tooth fairy jealous! Brace yourself as we dive into the Boneyard!

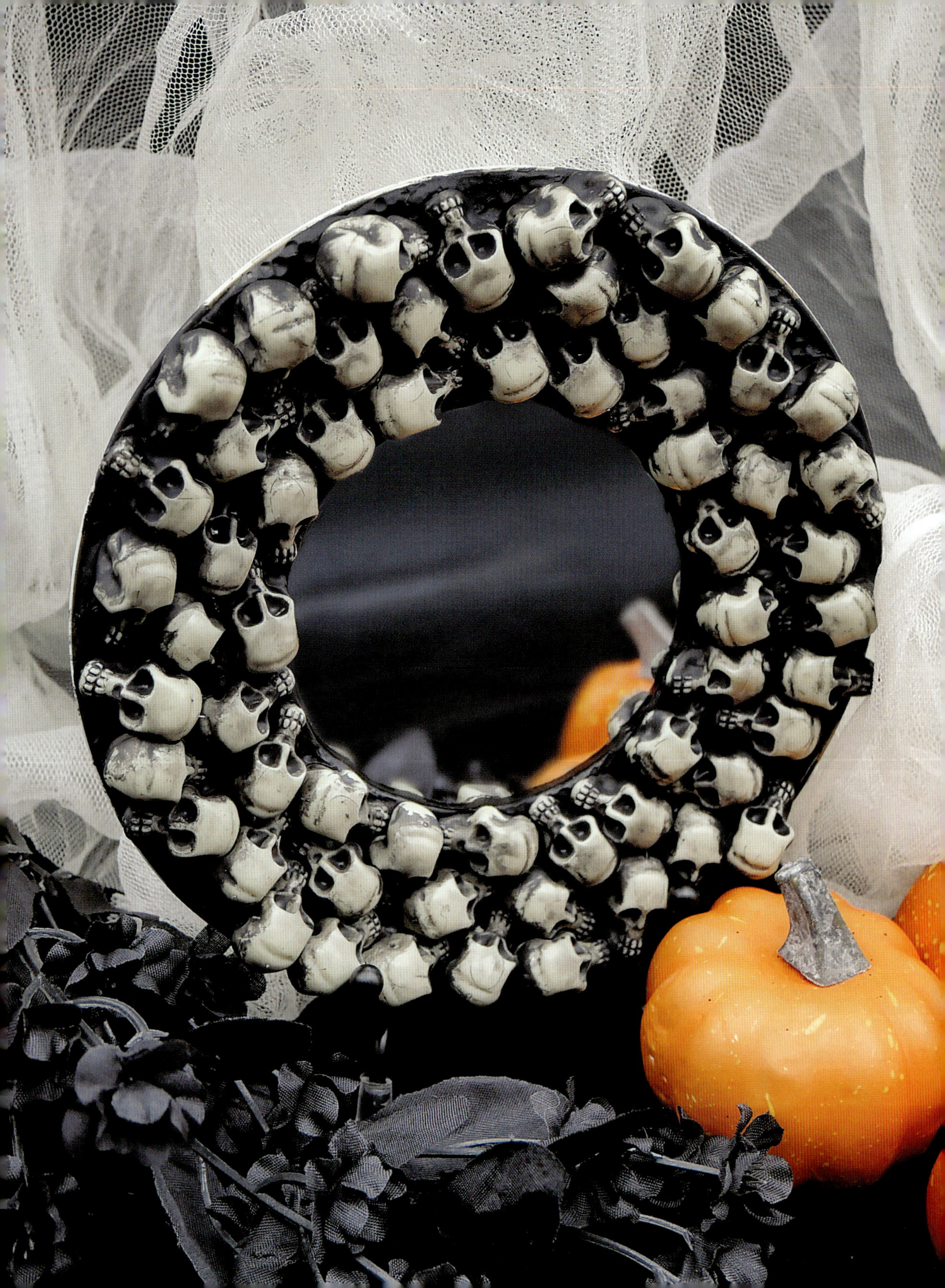

Skull Mirror

Is this what Grandma had in mind when she gave you all those old, dusty plates? Probably not, but I bet your grandma's one of those cool grannies who's proud of you for being so creative . . . or we just won't tell her. Either way, I'm proud of you for making something creative out of something you were (let's be honest) going to donate anyway.

Materials

- Silicone mat
- Disposable gloves
- Black epoxy clay (e.g., Apoxie Sculpt)
- Small saucer
- Small circle mirror (half as small as your saucer)
- Sculpting tools with round tip
- Tiny plastic skulls
- Acrylic paint and brush
- Paper towels
- Plate stand

Lay out your silicone mat and put on your gloves. Mix two golf ball–sized amounts of epoxy clay. Section out a small marble of clay and push it into the middle of the saucer. Press the small circle mirror onto the clay. Next, roll out a rope long enough to wrap around the outside of the mirror once. *You now have a mirror in the middle of a plate! Yay!*

(continued)

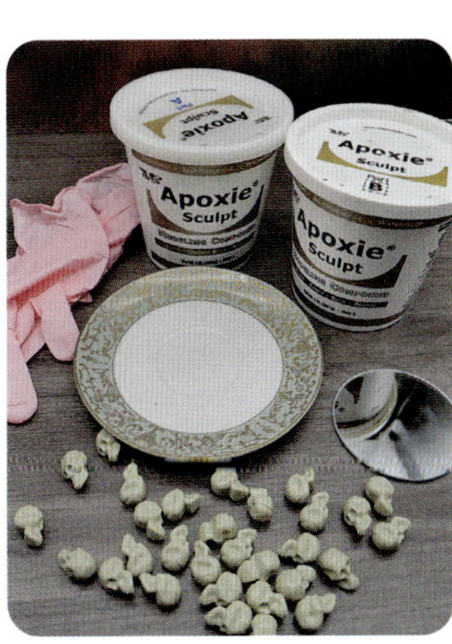 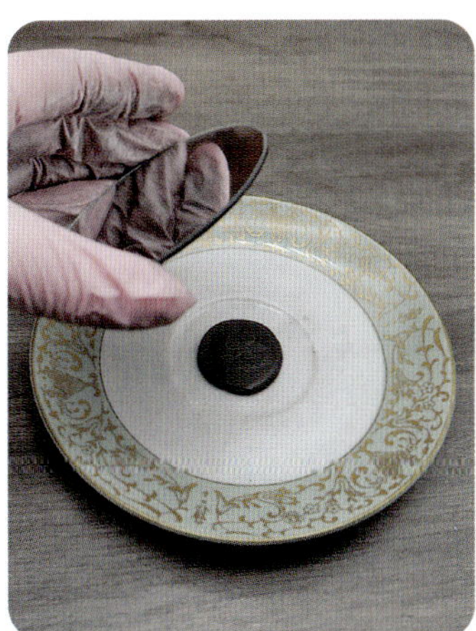 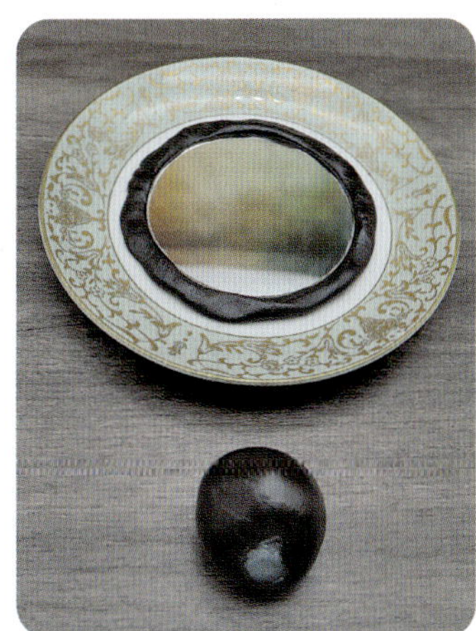

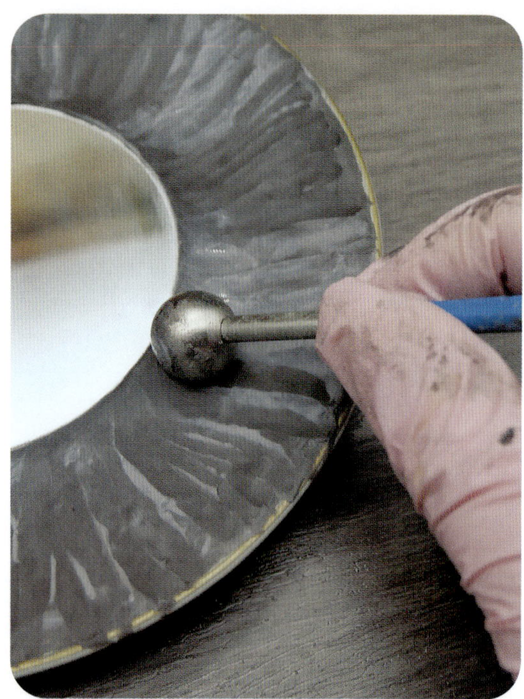

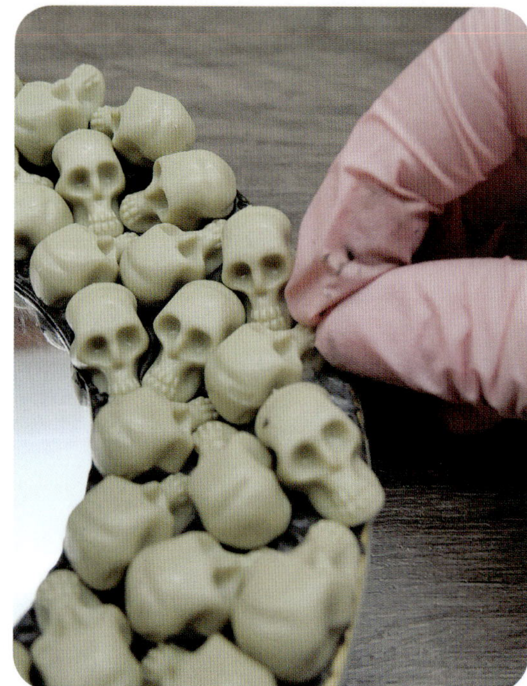

Cover the rest of the saucer with clay roughly ¼ inch (6 mm) thick. Smooth all the clay to the edge of the saucer with a larger round-tipped sculpting tool.

Press the skulls into the clay around the mirror. Face them every which way and keep them as tightly together as possible. Let this set for 2 or more hours.

Paint all the skulls and clay with black acrylic paint. While the paint is still wet, wipe away any excess with a paper towel. Place your mirror on a plate stand for displaying. *Now ask your mirror "Mirror, mirror on the wall, who's the creepiest of them all?"*

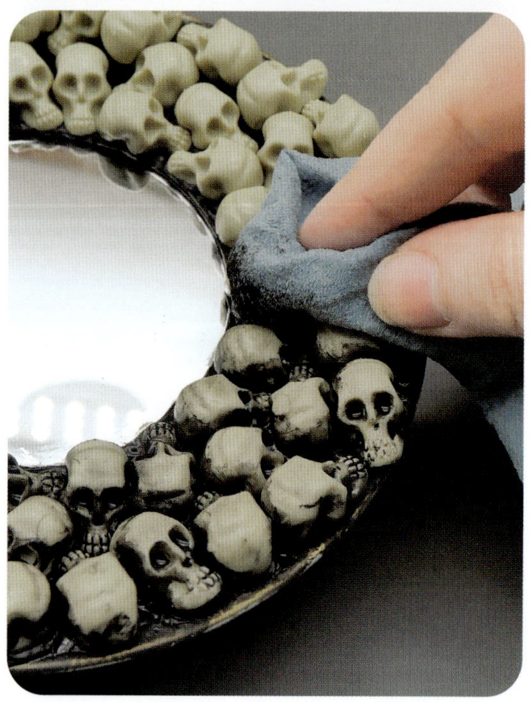

A Death Grip on Canvas

You can use either polymer or epoxy clay for this one. Epoxy clay will stick straight to your canvas without any glue, but it will be more difficult to plan out. On the other hand, you'll have to bake polymer clay before you attach it with glue to your canvas, but you can plan it out a lot easier. I will show you how to do this project with polymer clay.

Mix two parts Mod Podge with one part water in a small container. Dip your ripped-up pages into the mixture and place them on your round canvas. Cover the entire canvas, edges and all. Use a heat gun to dry it, being careful not to heat the pages too much and burn them.

(continued)

Materials

- Matte Mod Podge
- Water and small container
- Ripped-up book pages
- 6" (15-cm) round canvas
- Heat gun
- Acrylic paint and brush
- Barbed wire (see Barbed Wire Frame, page 67)
- Super glue
- 1 oz (28 g) white polymer clay
- X-ACTO knife
- Sculpting tools with round tip and silicone point
- E6000 glue
- Fun embellishments (optional)
- Twine or hemp

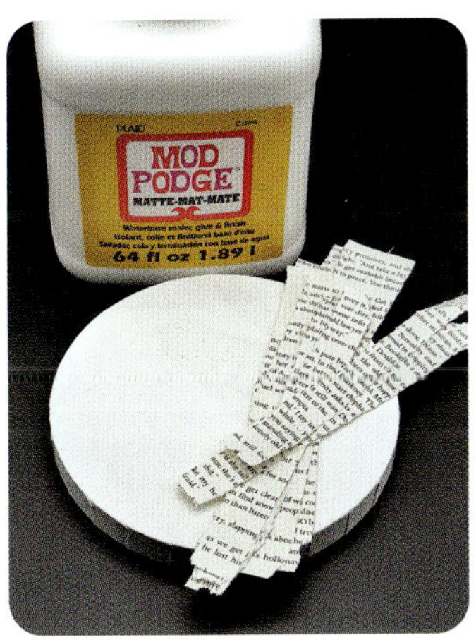

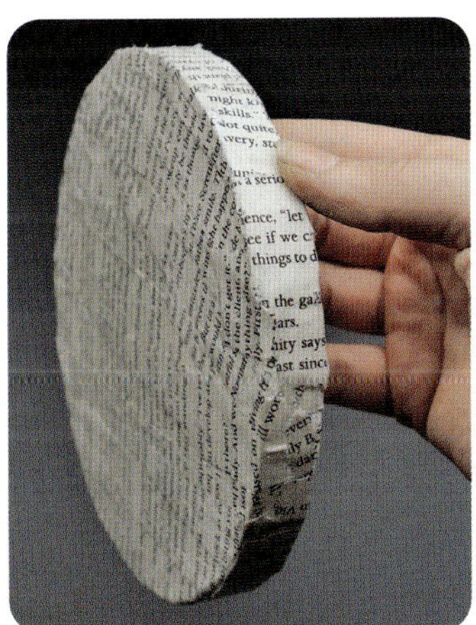

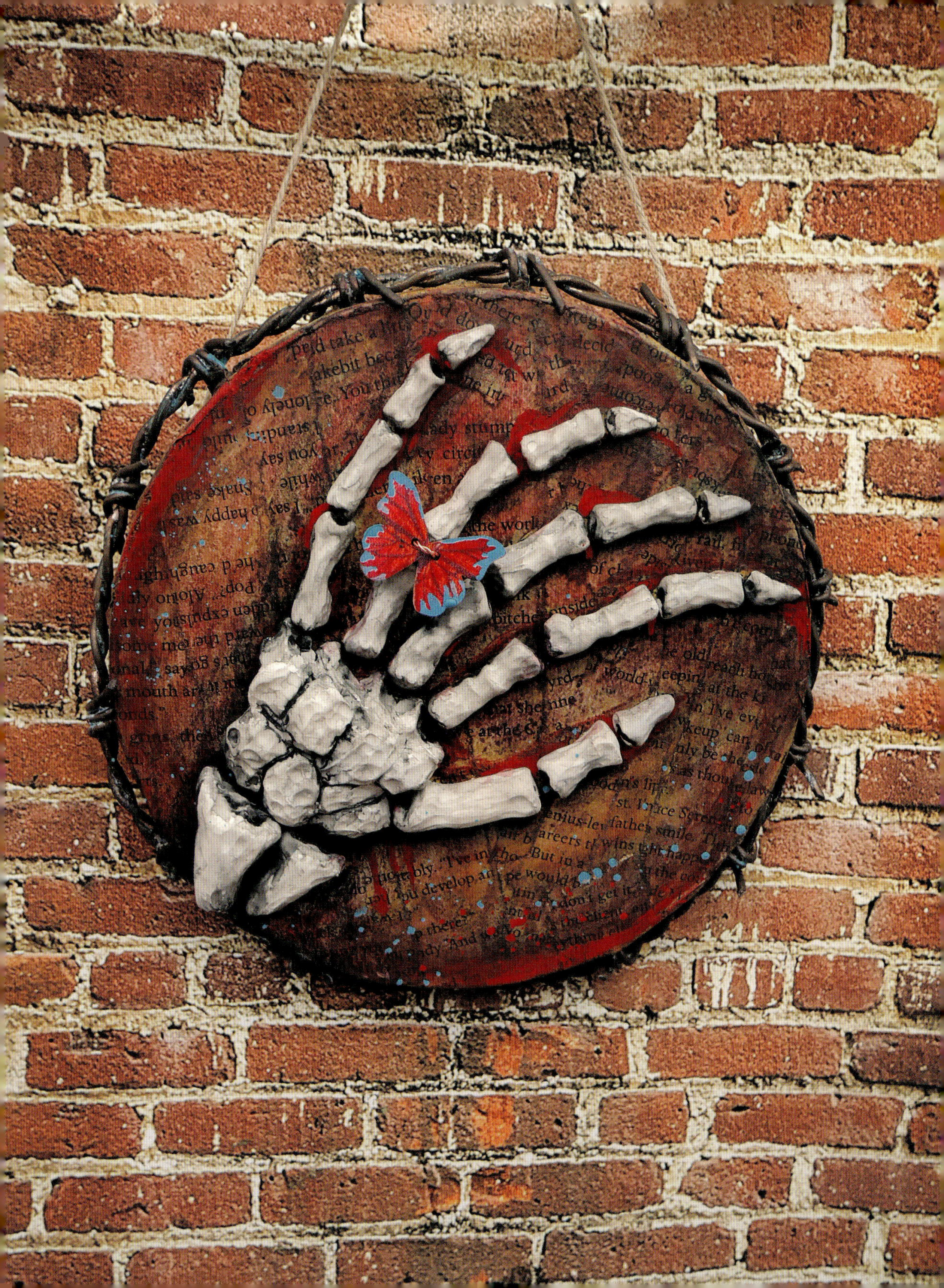

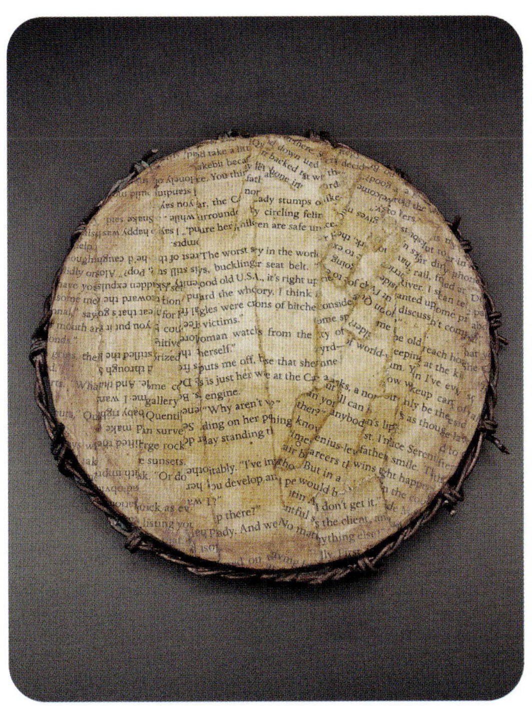

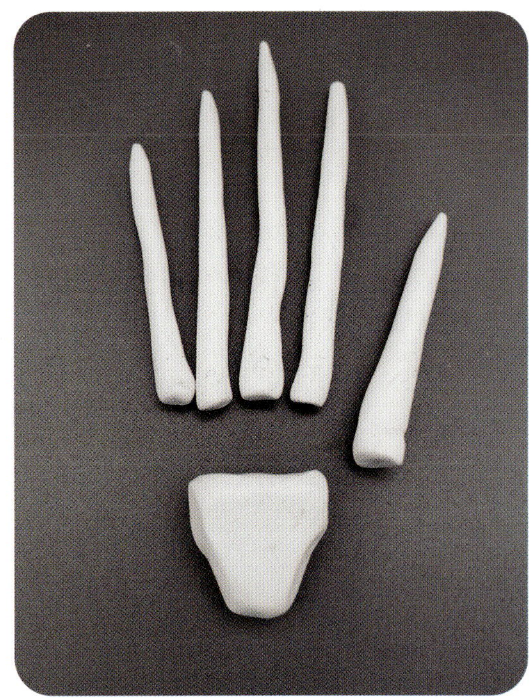

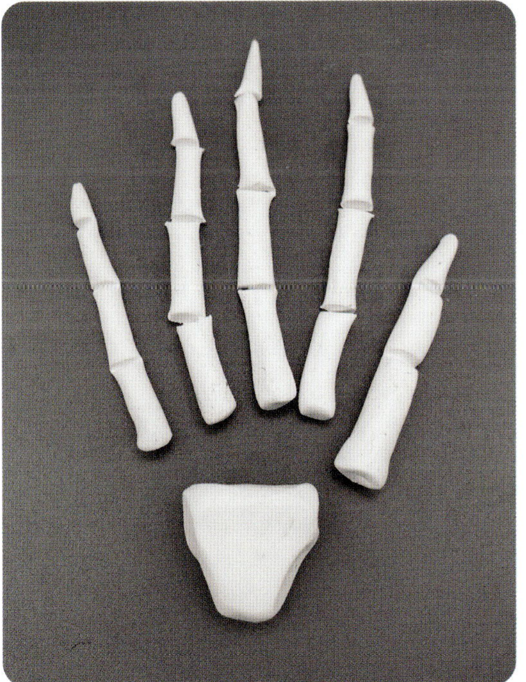

Tint your leftover Mod Podge mixture with a bit of brown acrylic paint and coat your canvas again. Dry with a heat gun.

Wrap barbed wire around your canvas and secure it with super glue. Let this set for 10 minutes.

Take your polymer clay and roll out five long, cone-shaped fingers and a block for the palm. With an X-ACTO knife, cut the fingers into four sections and the thumb into three.

(continued)

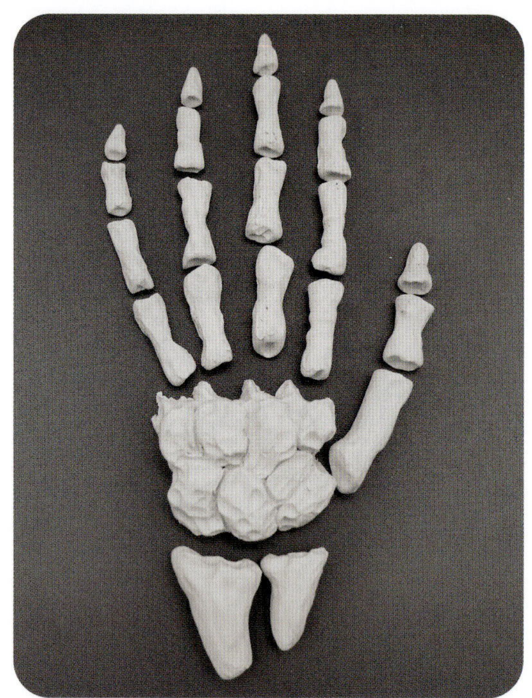

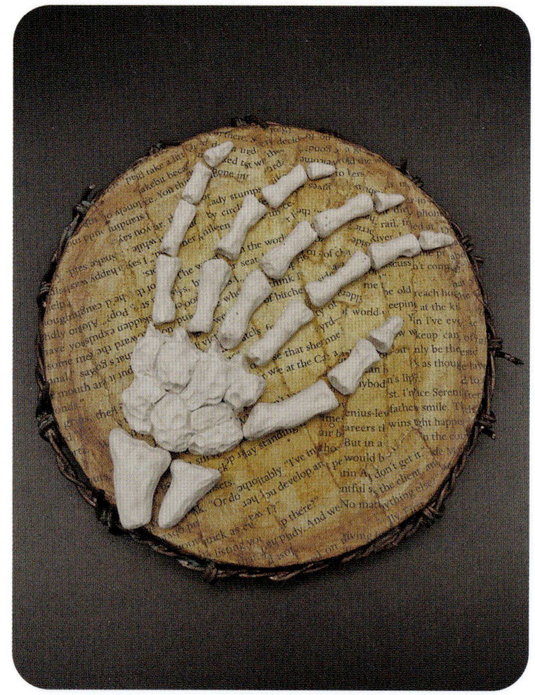

Using sculpting tools and your fingers, shape each section into a bone. Most finger bones flare out a little at the ends. To achieve this, roll them in the middle with a single finger, then use a round-tipped sculpting tool to push a dimple in each end. Sculpt the palm by adding a few bumps and dimples where the fingers would be. Bake according to the package instructions.

Be very careful when moving your bones, because you don't want them to roll around and get mixed up or else you'll have a hand puzzle to put back together!

Position each bone carefully on your canvas. Once you have the shape you like, glue each bone down with E6000. Wait 2 to 4 hours for your glue to dry.

Finish off your skeleton hand by adding colorful paint splatters to the background and fun embellishments like a butterfly ring. Use super glue to add twine to the back for hanging up.

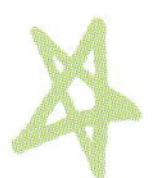

Rib-Vase

Are all your vases super boring? Yeah, mine too . . . Why not creep-ify them? I mean, at this point you should just be creep-ifying everything in your house! But if you're not quite ready for that commitment, let's just start with an easy vase.

Lay out your silicone mat and put on your gloves. Mix a small amount of epoxy clay. (Start with maybe a walnut-sized amount of clay; you can always mix more if needed.) Wrap the top of your vase with a thin ring of clay. Depending on your vase, it should be about the thickness of a shoelace.

With your fingers, sculpt a skinny diamond shape that is as long as the clay ring and press it on the middle of your vase.

Wrap three more rings of clay evenly spaced over the diamond and all the way around the vase. Push the edges of your rings down on two sides of the vase to make them droop a little. The last ring will actually be a C shape. Attach the ends of the C to the bottom of your diamond, touching the bottom ring, then droop the sides down and bring it back up in the back. This ring should look the droopiest. These should look like ribs.

(continued)

Materials

- Silicone mat
- Disposable gloves
- White epoxy clay (e.g., Apoxie Sculpt)
- Small glass jar or vase
- Sculpting tools with round tip, silicone point and wire brush
- Acrylic paint and brush
- Paper towels

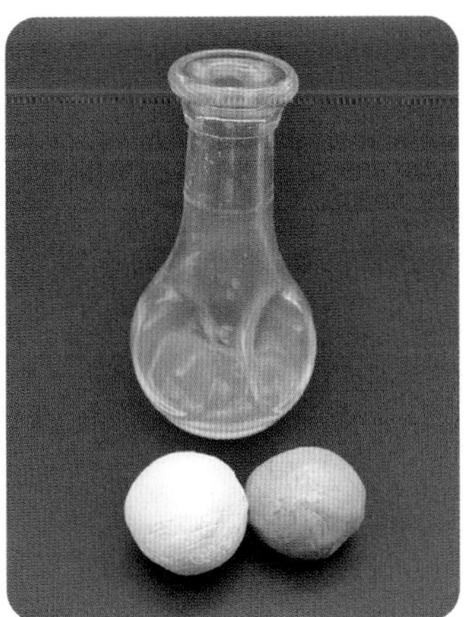
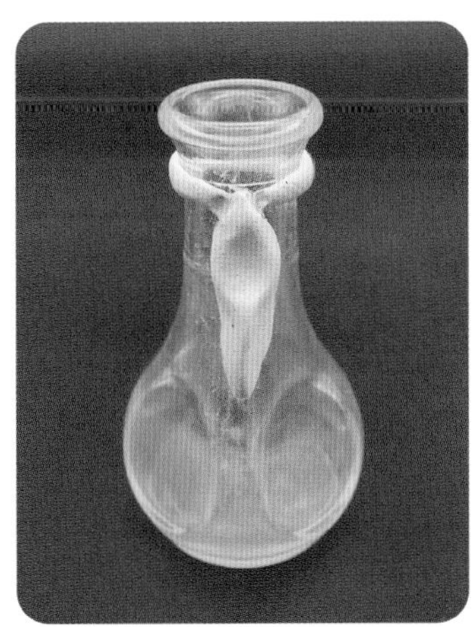
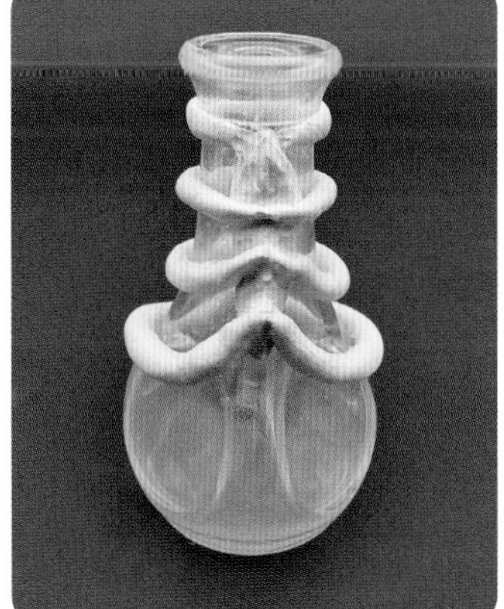

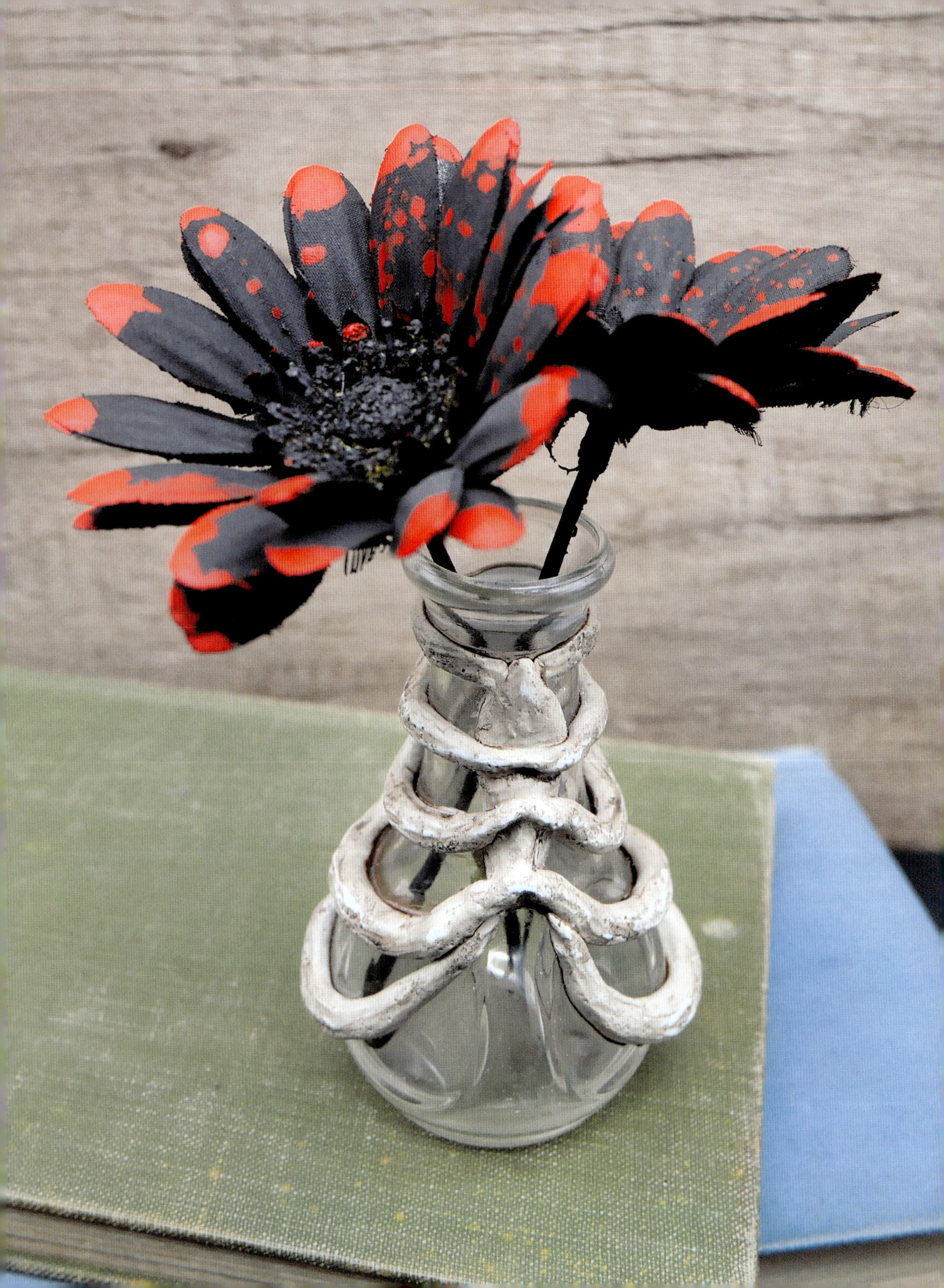

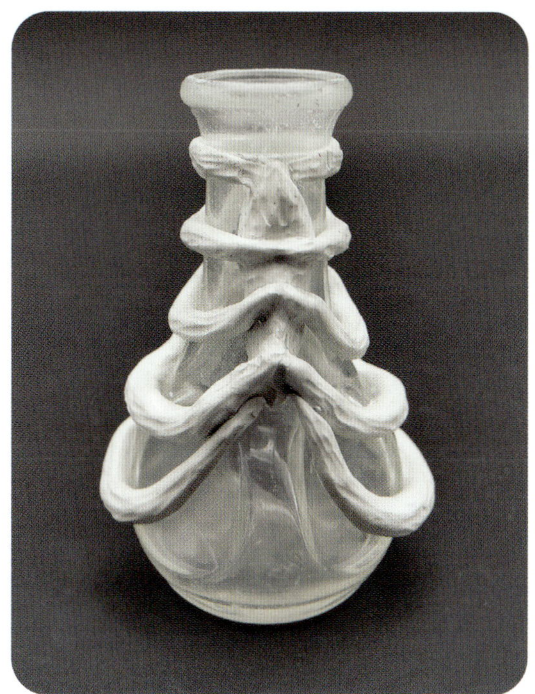 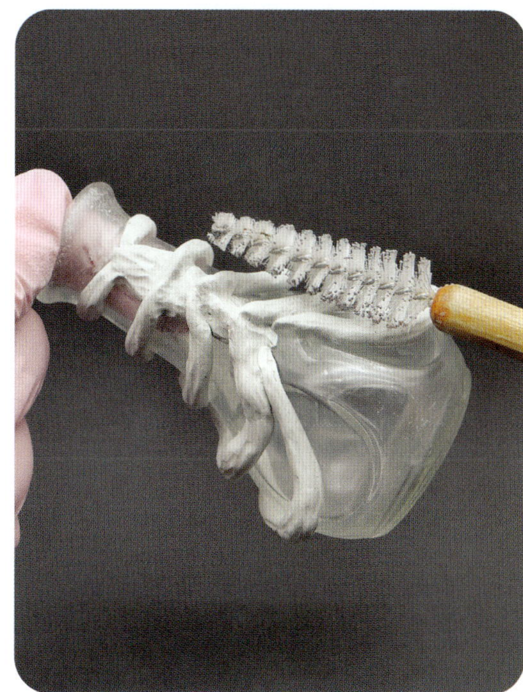

Texture all of your ribs using a round-tipped or silicone-point sculpting tool and drag it along the bones. Then add small texture holes to your ribs with a wire brush. Let this sit for 2 or more hours.

Water down a dark brown paint and paint over all your ribs. The paint should only stick to the crevasses and inside the holes, but if it is sticking more, then wipe it off with a paper towel and water down your paint more. Wipe any excess paint off of the glass.

Add the Bloody Pain-ted Flowers (page 167) for a complete look.

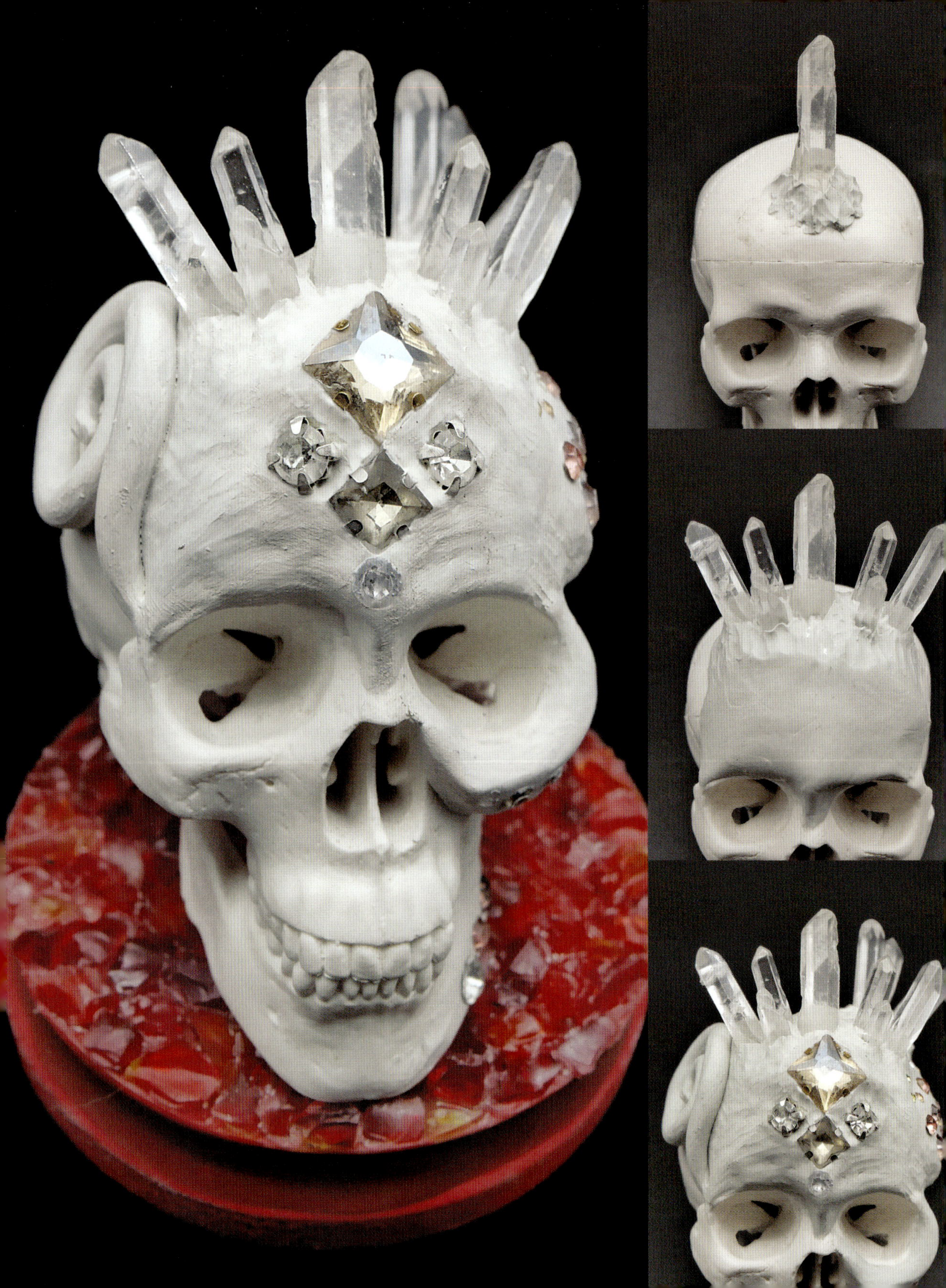

Crystal Skull

My dad used to say, "Sometimes I sit and think, other times I just sit." I feel like that explains this project perfectly because it is super easy and great for just playing around with clay and not thinking too hard. Sometimes my brain is tired, and I just want to sit and make pretty art! Also, everything is better with crystals! Especially skulls . . .

Materials

- Silicone mat
- Disposable gloves
- White epoxy clay (e.g., Apoxie Sculpt)
- Plastic skull
- Quartz crystals
- Sculpting tools with round tip and silicone point
- Assortment of embellishments, such as light-colored glass gems

Lay out your silicone mat and put on your gloves. Mix a golf ball–sized amount of epoxy clay and press a small dab of it onto the top of your skull's forehead. Press a large quartz crystal into the clay. Push the clay up around the bottom of the crystal with the sculpting tools.

Add more epoxy clay around the first crystal and extend it across the forehead, smoothing the edges with a wet gloved finger. Press a "crown" of smaller crystals on either side of the larger crystal, creating the appearance of a crystal crown.

Add more embellishments to the forehead. Depending on the embellishments you have you can create a pattern or make it look more haphazard. Remember, don't think too hard about it. Just have fun and stick pretty crystals in the clay. After all, skulls don't have brains, so why should you overthink it?

Smooth on a thin coat of clay around the eye socket and jawline, allowing you to press a few gems on there. I also added a spiral to the side of my skull, but you could make flowers or vines. Anything you like. Don't think about it, just do it.

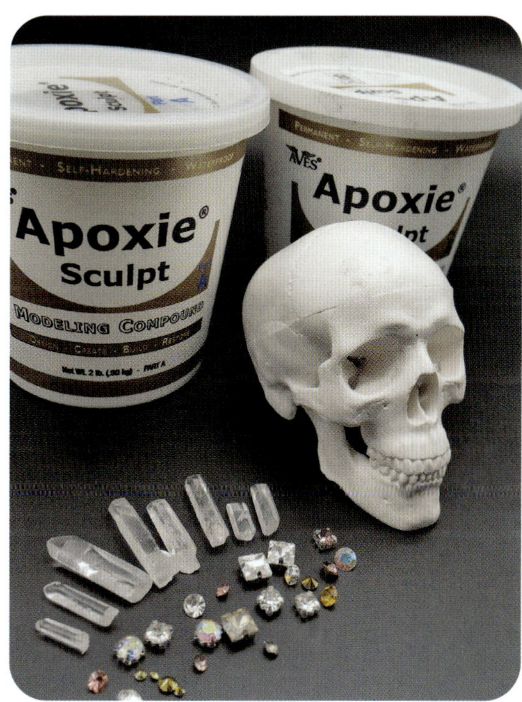

The Molten Lava Flow Display (page 213) makes for a great stand! I love how it makes the eyes glow red as if they were piercing through my soul.

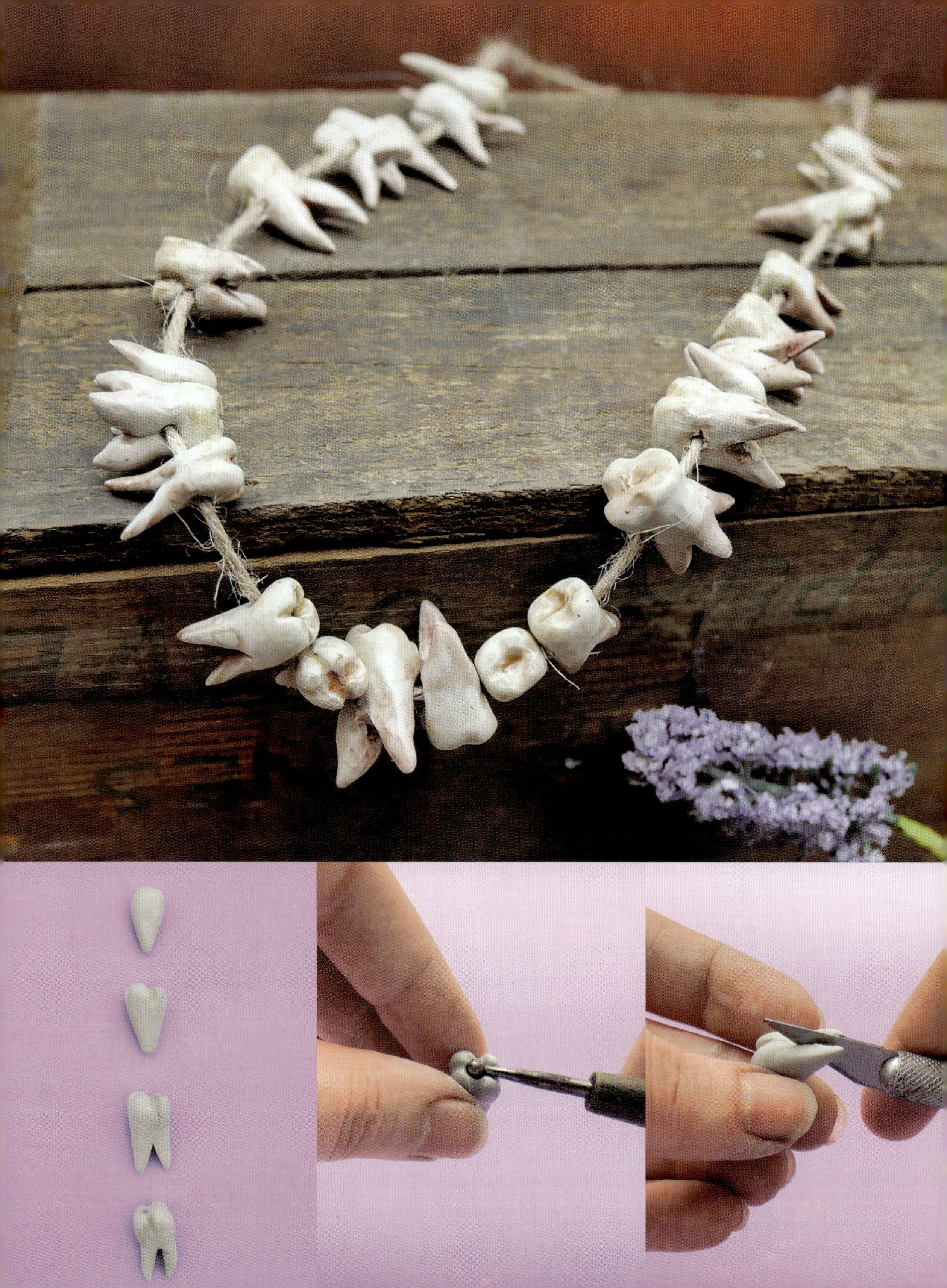

Tooth Fairy Stash

We all proudly want to display the teeth of our enemies. (No, just me?) Unfortunately, it may not be easy, ethical or legal to acquire real teeth . . . Instead, I offer a simpler solution in clay form! Sculpting a tooth is rather easy; the hardest part is preventing toothy flat spots.

You can alternatively use epoxy clay like Apoxie Sculpt for this; just don't forget your gloves and silicone mat.

Materials

- 1–2 oz (28–56 g) white polymer clay
- Sculpting tools with round tip
- X-ACTO knife
- Toothpick
- Acrylic paint and brush
- Paper towels
- Twine or hemp

Start off with a tiny bit of clay about the size of a large blueberry. Roll it on one end to make a teardrop shape. Then push a round-tipped sculpting tool into the larger end, making a dimple. Lean the ball tool on all four sides, making an ashtray-shaped ridge around the crown.

To make the roots, use an X-ACTO knife and cut the bottom. You can cut it into two or four roots, depending on your toothy preference. Pull the root legs apart a bit. Using a toothpick to put a hole through the side.

Make sure you set the teeth sitting on their crowns while they bake. This will prevent flat spots on the sides when they set. Bake according to package instructions.

Paint your teeth with a watered-down brownish-maroon color and wipe off any excess paint with paper towels.

After they're hardened, string twine through the holes and you've got teeth on a string! Now go hang them around your house!

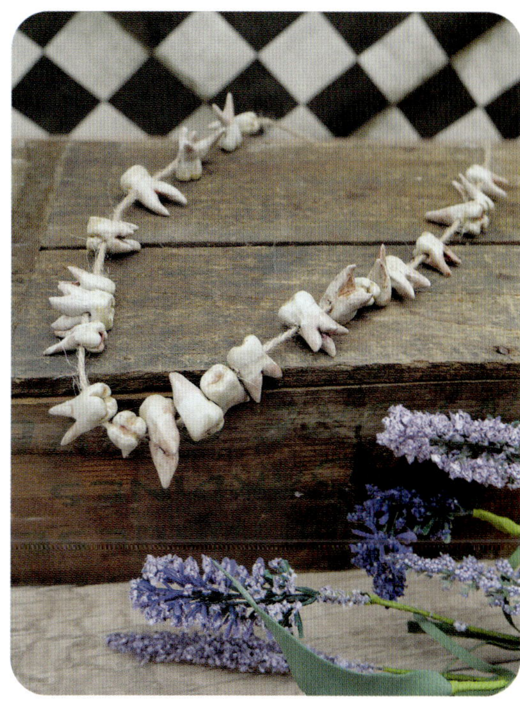

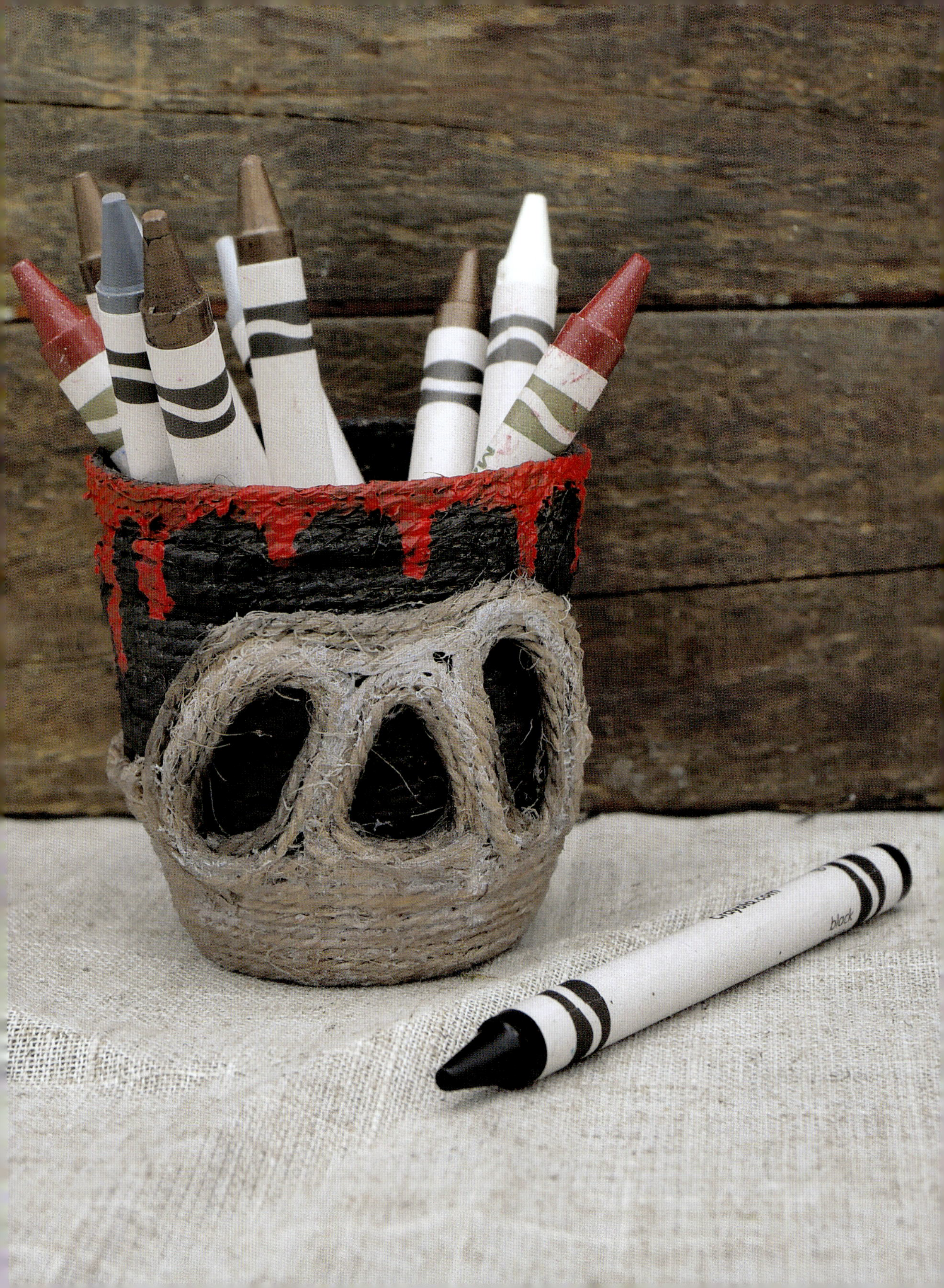

Crayola.com
black

Twine Skull Container

Forget buying hemp containers because, in no time, you will be able to make tons of budget-friendly ones by yourself! And these ones will have that creepy style I'm pretty sure you crave. I mean, if you don't crave creepy, then what are you doing here?

This project can be a bit tricky, and a lot messy, but it won't take long to get the hang of it and I promise it's totally worth it!

Materials

- Glass jar with straight-ish walls
- Permanent marker
- Tacky craft glue
- Hemp rope
- Mod Podge
- Old paintbrush
- Cotton swabs (if needed)
- Heat gun
- Acrylic paint and brush

Draw super simple skull eyes and a nose on the lower half of your glass jar using permanent marker.

Flip your jar over with its butt in the air. Using tacky craft glue, glue the end of your hemp rope to the bottom center of your jar. Smear glue onto the jar with one hand while rotating the jar with the other. Slowly work your way around the bottom and up the sides of your jar. Keep your rope tight but not overlapping.

(continued)

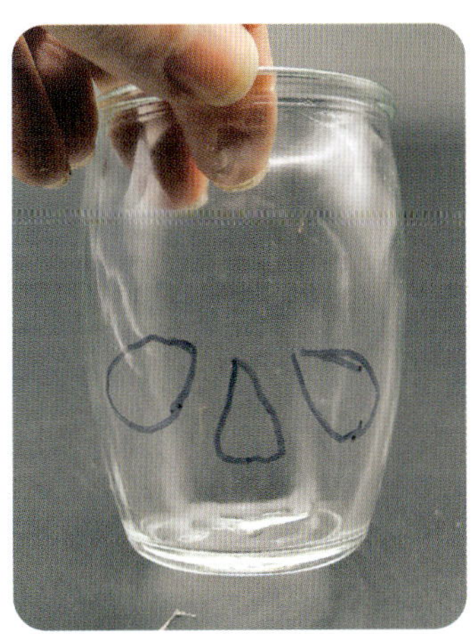

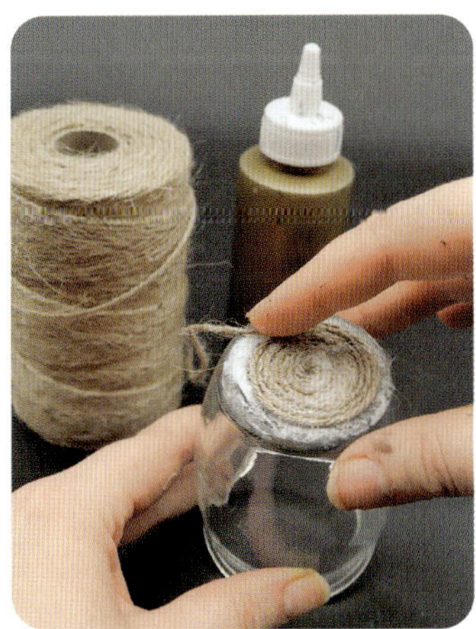

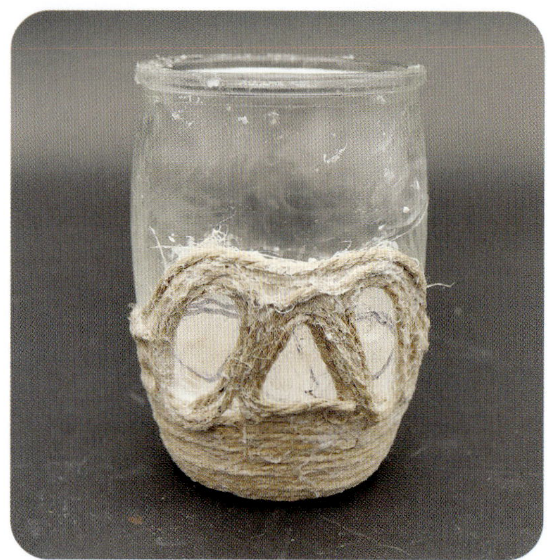 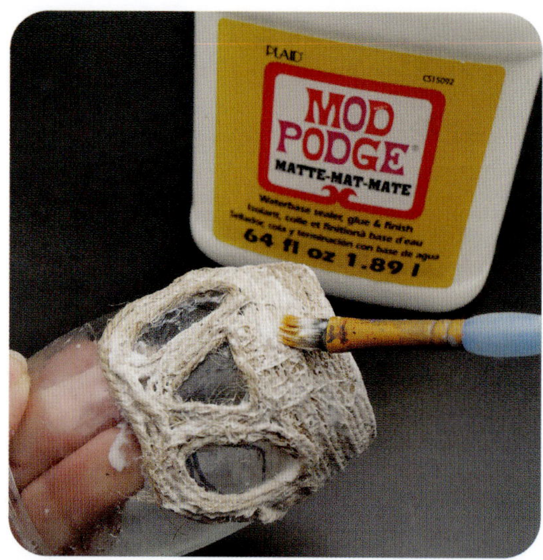

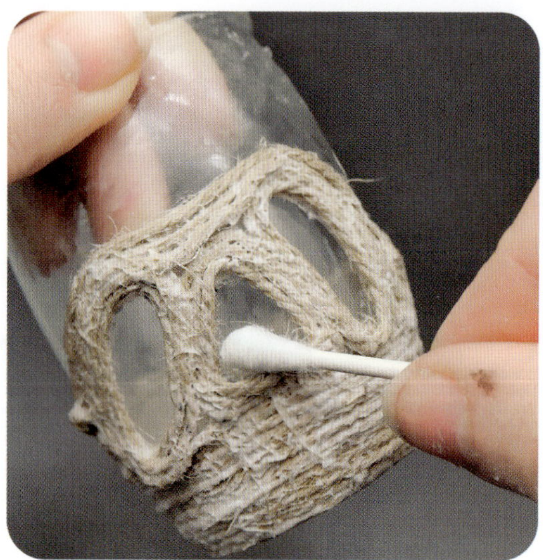 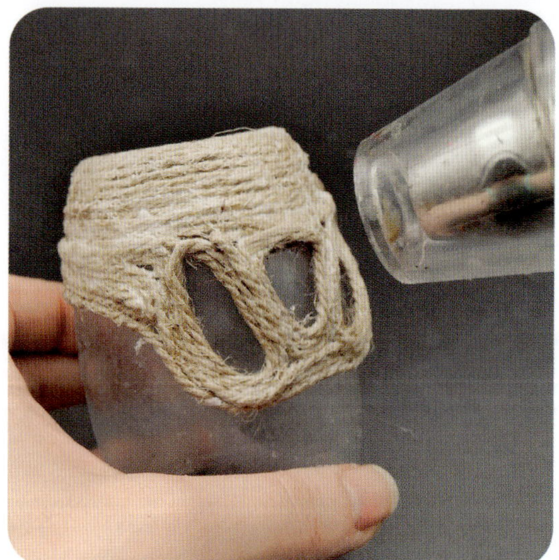

Once you reach the eyes and nose, glue the hemp rope around all three holes and around the back. You'll have to overlap it a bit, but keep it minimal. Use lots of glue and hold it in place with your finger. Once you have your shape, coat all of the hemp with Mod Podge using an old paintbrush.

Clean off any glue and Mod Podge on the jar around the hemp with a wet cotton swab. With your heat gun, dry just the surface of the hemp. You should still be able to see wet glue through the glass jar.

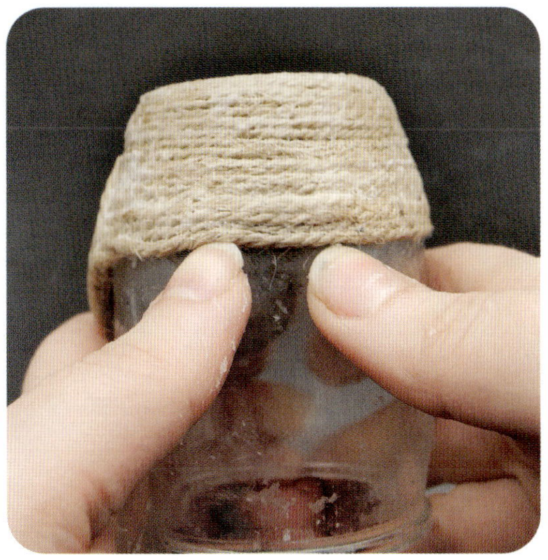

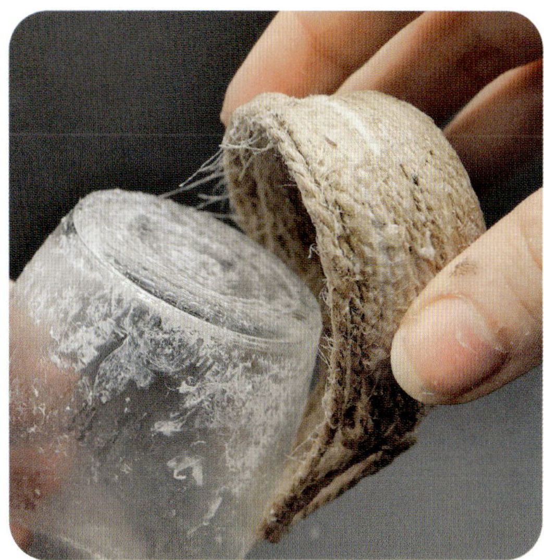

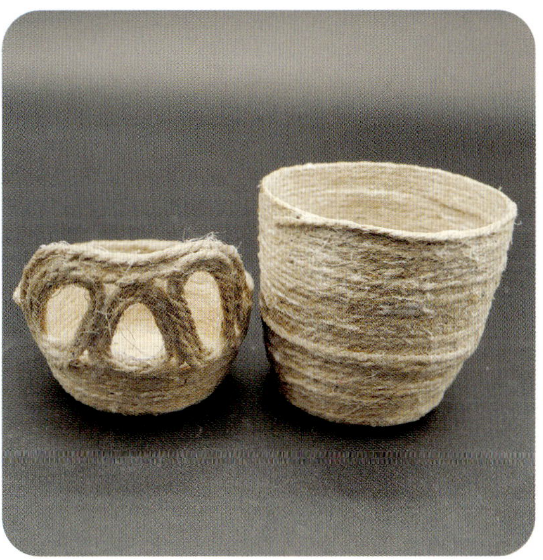

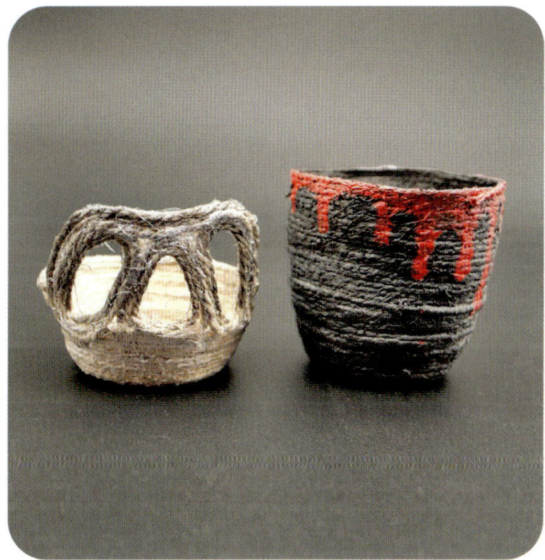

Take your fingernails and slowly pry the hemp off your jar. Start with the top edge and work your way down slowly. You can use a cotton swab and water to loosen the edges, but be careful not to saturate it with water or else your hemp will fall apart. Once you get your hemp loose enough, it should easily pull away from the jar.

Wash your jar off and repeat the steps for a second hemp jar without the eyes and nose. Ensure that this hemp jar is a little taller than the first one. Let everything dry. This could take a while, depending on how much glue you used. Mine took an hour or so.

Paint the taller hemp jar with black acrylic paint. Add colorful red drips down the sides. Place the taller hemp jar inside the shorter skull one.

You're finished; now go out there and make as many hemp containers as your little heart desires!

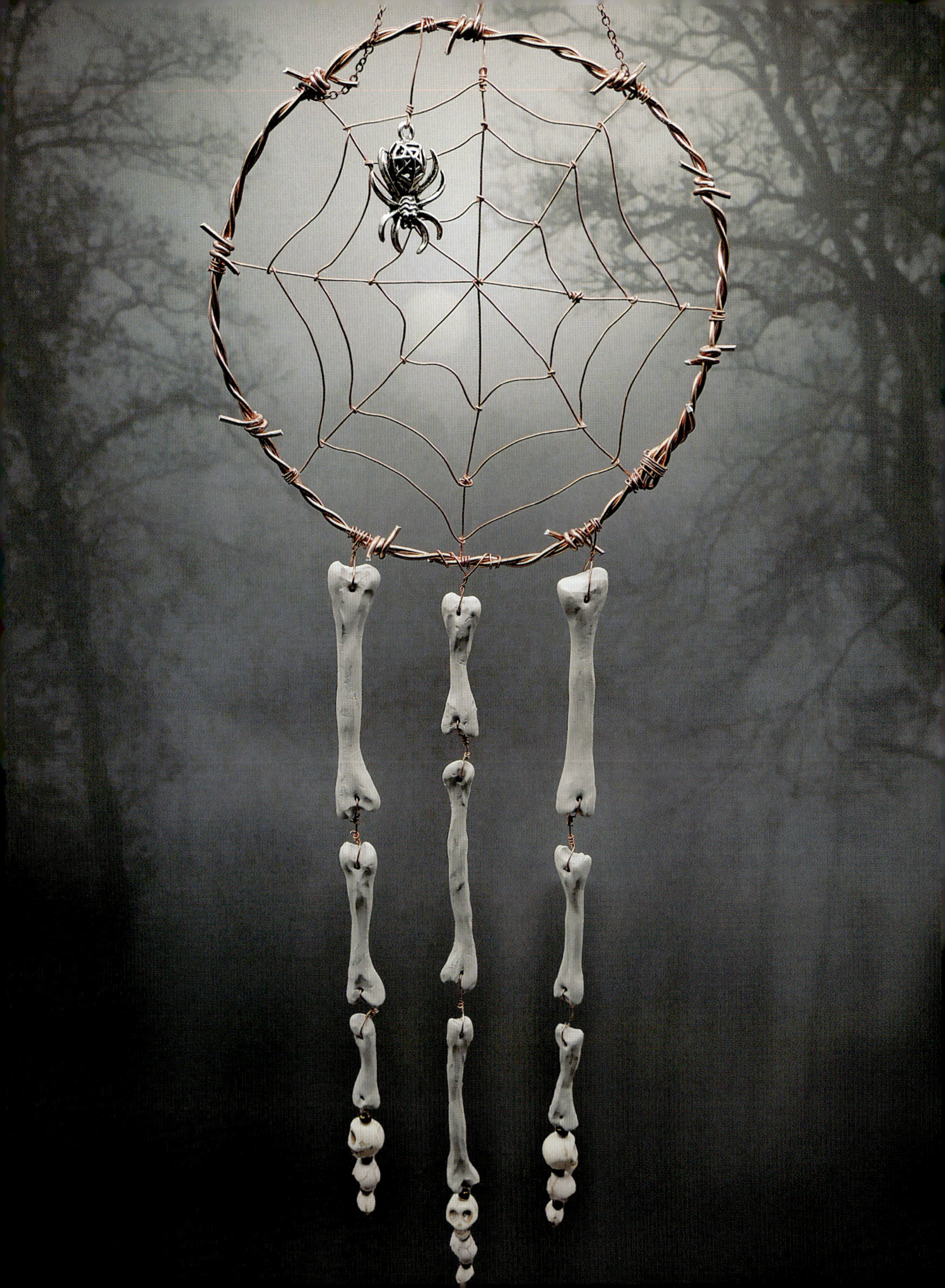

Webby Wires

In this project, we'll create a spiderweb from wire and hang bones from it. You may be asking yourself, "Wait a minute, did our spider hang those bones? Does it have a peculiar taste for macabre art, or was it simply eating lunch?" Either way, this eight-legged friend sounds both terrifying and fascinating! It will be a fantastic addition to any creepy crafter's home.

Take your barbed wire and make a 5- to 6-inch (12.7- to 15-cm) circle. (An easy way to make a circle is to wrap your wire around something cylindrical.) Secure the ends together with floral wire.

Now we'll make a web using floral wire, wire cutters and needle-nose pliers. Divide your circle in half and wrap the ends of the floral wire around the outside of your circle. Continue to divide your circle three more times. On the last one, make a loop in the center of your circle with your floral wire to secure all the wires in the middle.

(continued)

Materials

- Barbed wire (see Barbed Wire Frame, page 67)
- Matching floral wire
- Wire cutters
- Needle-nose pliers
- Super glue
- White polymer clay
- Sculpting tools with round tip
- Toothpick
- Fishing line
- 9 seed beads
- 9 skull beads
- Chain (for hanging)
- 2 jump rings (for hanging)
- Spider charm (optional)

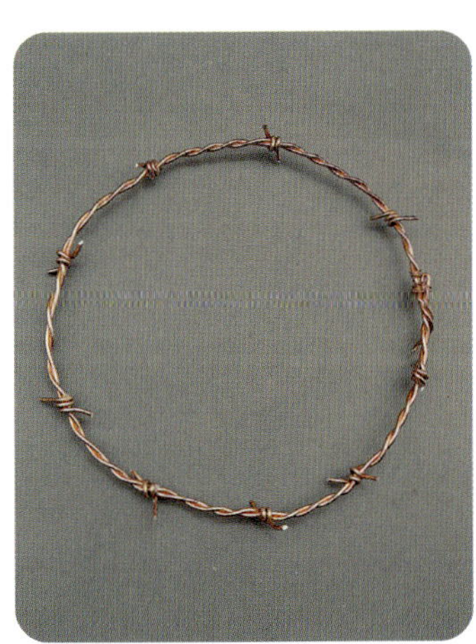
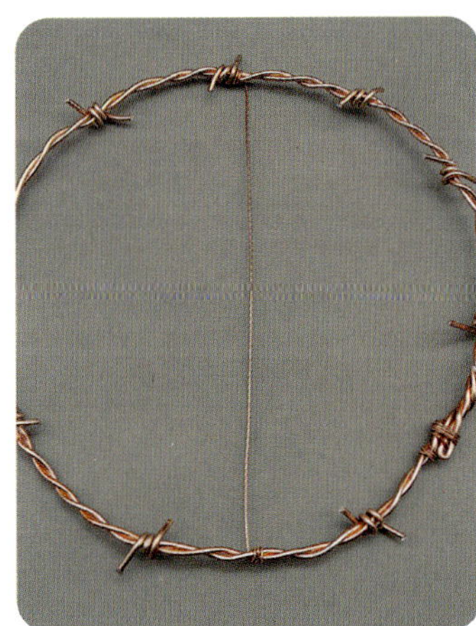
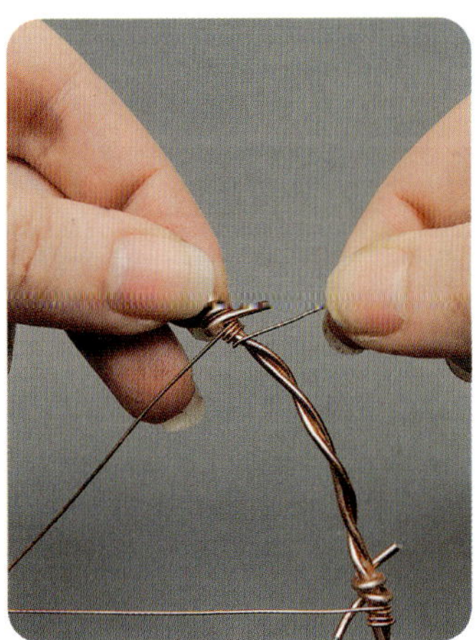

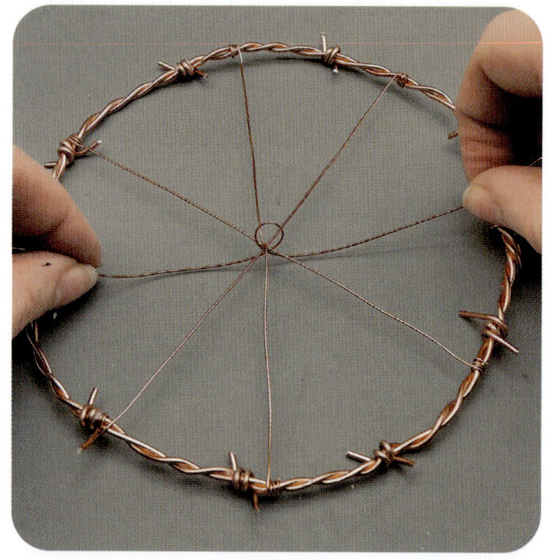 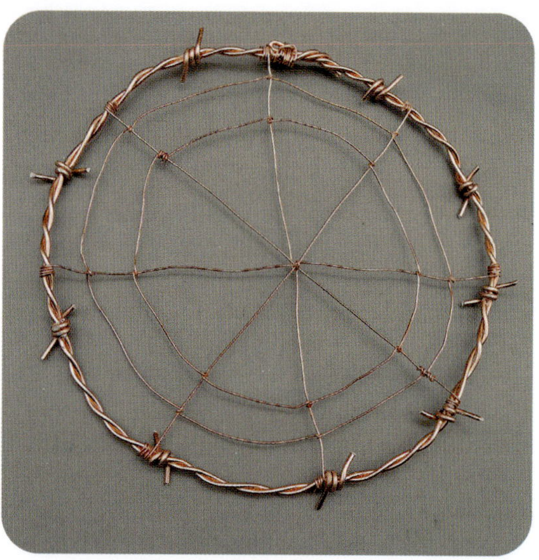

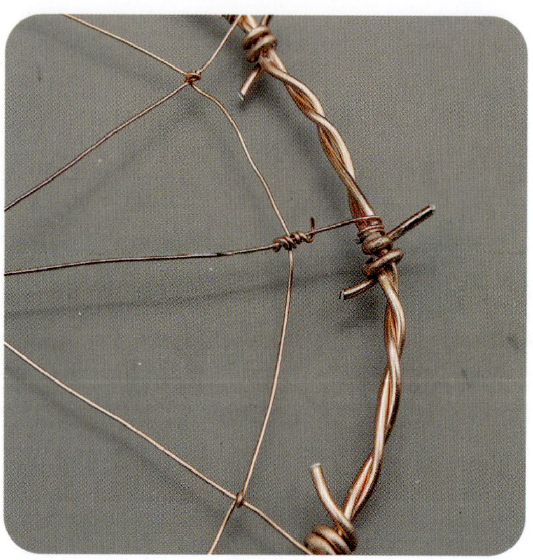 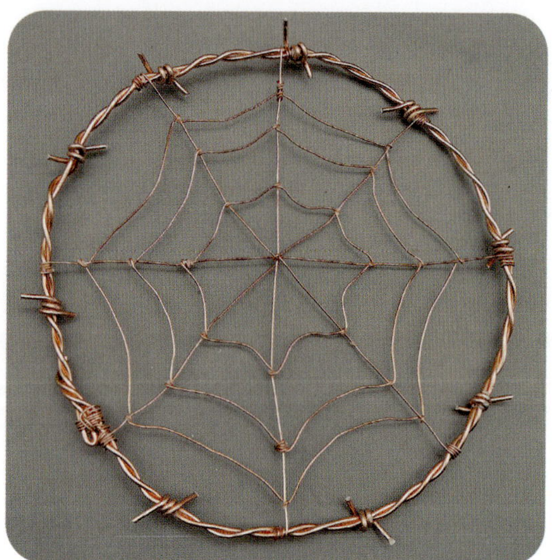

To finish off your web, make circles with the floral wire inside the barbed wire circle. Loop the floral wire around once at each divide. Make two or three circles of floral wire on the inside of the barbed circle. If the wires are loose and want to slip, use a small amount of super glue on each wire-wrapped intersection. Gently push the centers of the circle floral wires toward the middle to create a spiderweb look.

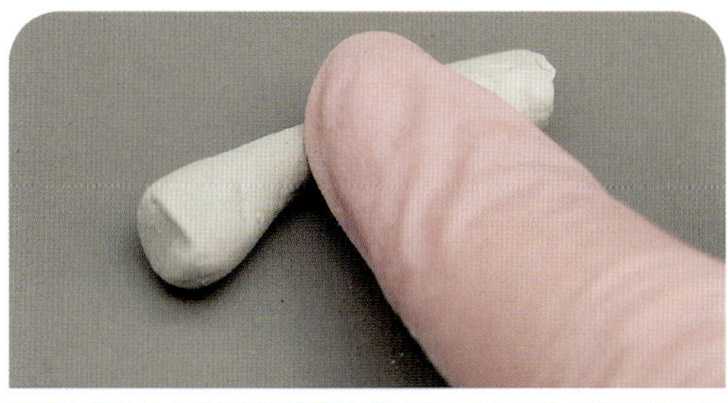

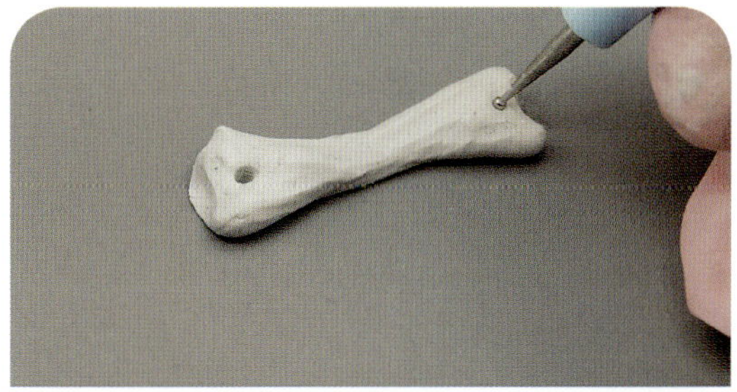

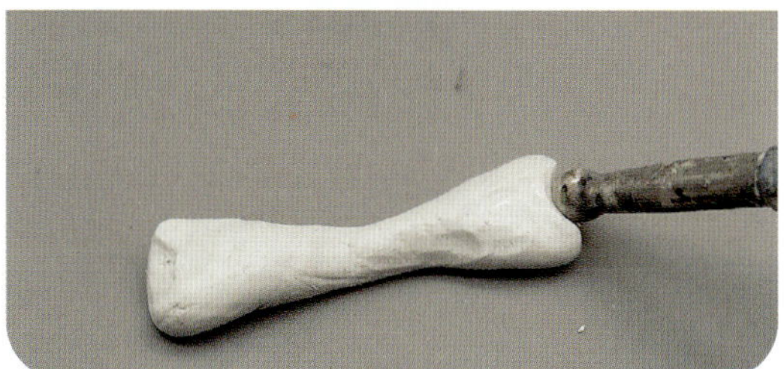

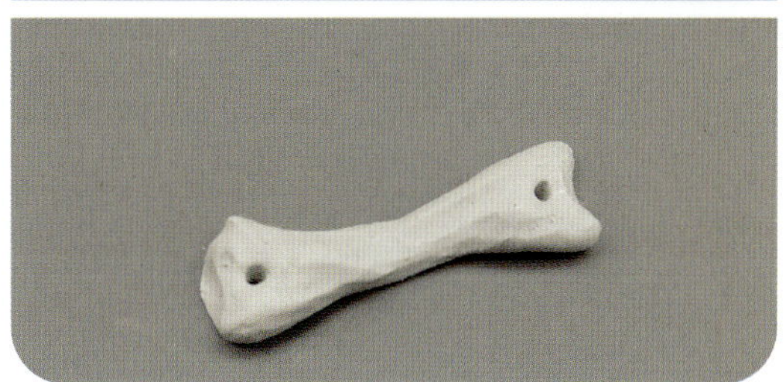

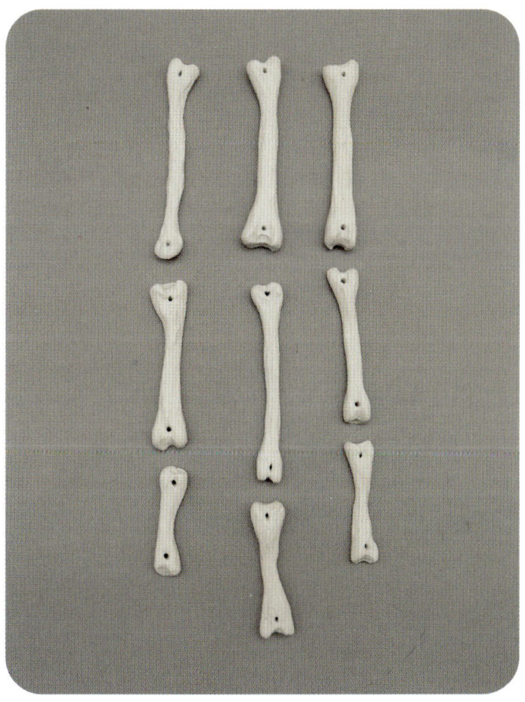

Let's add some bones using polymer clay. Take a blueberry-sized amount of clay and roll out a pencil-thick cylinder shape. Roll your fingertip in the middle of your bone to make the middle slightly skinnier. Add a dimple on each end with a round-tipped sculpting tool. Poke a hole in each end with a toothpick. Repeat until you have nine bones: three long, three medium and three small. Bake according to the package instructions.

(continued)

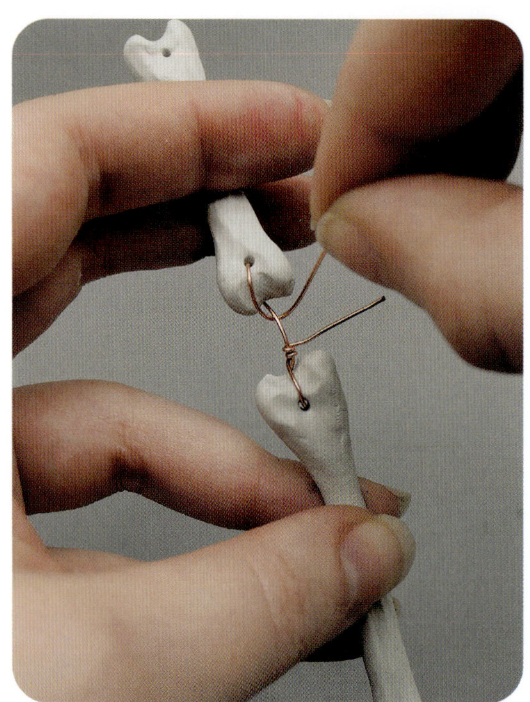

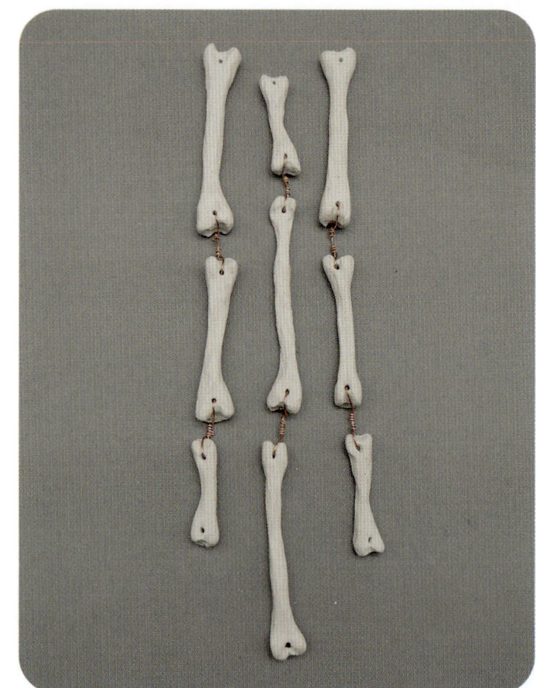

String together three bones—one small, one medium and one large—with a small piece of floral wire. Attach each bone by making a figure eight with your wire through the holes. Repeat until you have three bone strings. Attach all three bone strings to the bottom of the web with more wire.

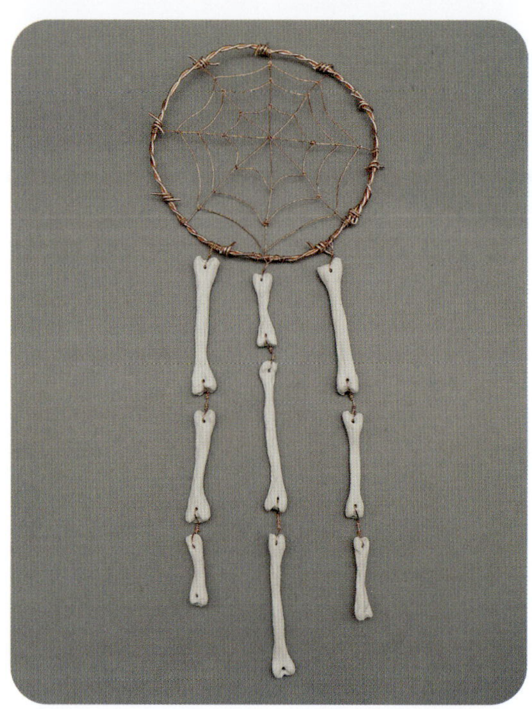

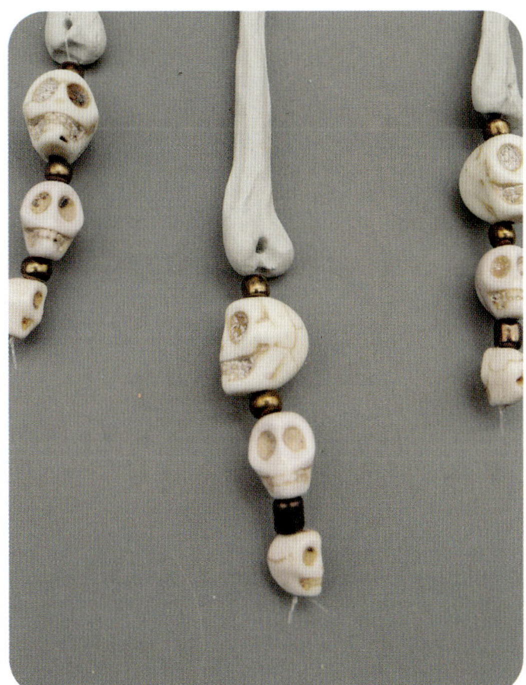 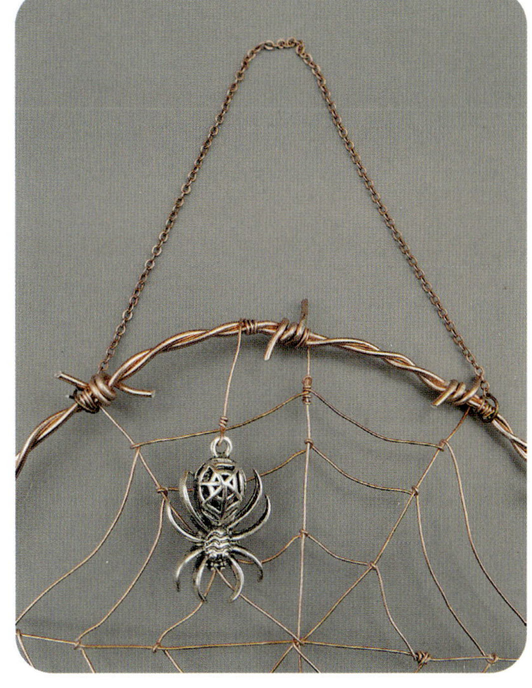

On the ends of the three bone strings, tie fishing line and make a pattern of seed beads and skull beads. Finish off the end by wrapping the fishing line around the last bead a few times and tying it off. Use a small amount of super glue on the knots to keep them from slipping.

Attach a chain to your web with jump rings. Optionally, you can attach a spider charm with wire to the top of your web.

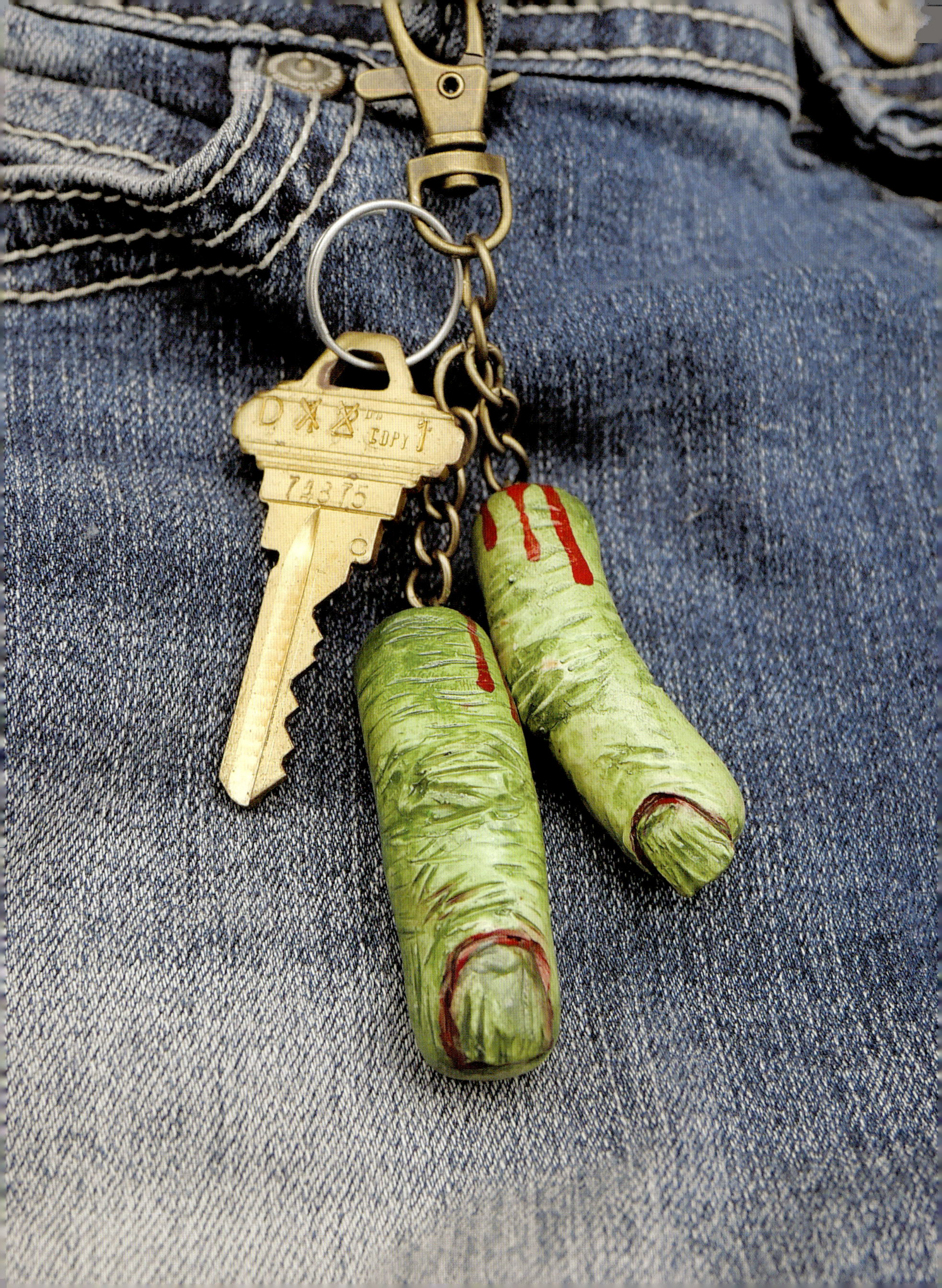

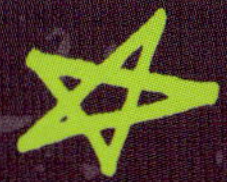

Gravedigger

When you think of a gravedigger, what comes to mind? A muddy hole and coffin, right? Well, in this section we're not digging graves (because that would be gross), but we are crafting things you might find in one. Yup, you heard that right! I'll guide you on how to sculpt the creepiest body parts, including ears, tongues, fingers and hearts. Because, let's be honest, who's ever heard of a spooky knee-cap or elbow? But don't worry, you'll dig how awesome they look hanging on your wall or pinned to your shirt! Without further ado, let's unearth your creepy corpse creativity!

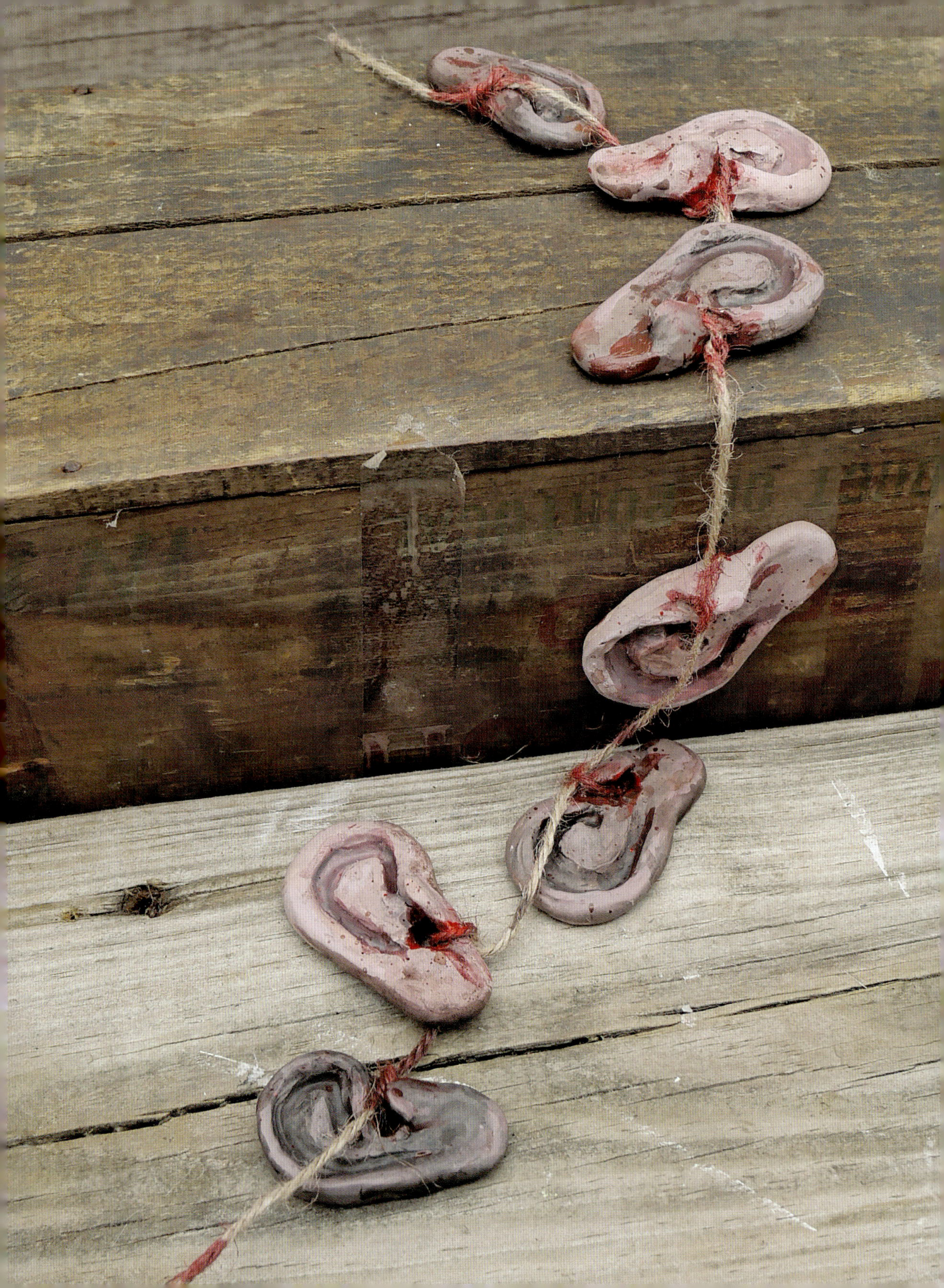

Severed Ear Chain

Materials

- ½ oz (14 g) polymer clay (for each ear)
- Sculpting tools with round tip
- Acrylic paint and brush
- Paper towels
- Hemp or twine

Yes, this is BY FAR the creepiest project in the book! And with it being so easy to do, I highly expect you to have at least one severed ear hanging in your closet. What? You say having a severed ear hanging in your closet is weird? You don't want the cops called on you again? Well, fine, hang it on your fridge like a "normal" person . . . What do you mean, that's not normal either? Well, maybe this project isn't for you! In fact, maybe you should have bought a book about rainbows and unicorns instead!

You could use epoxy clay like Apoxie Sculpt instead; just remember to wear gloves.

Using polymer clay, create a rough ear shape about ¼ inch (6 mm) thick. Run a medium-sized round-tipped sculpting tool along the top of the ear, following the curve. Using a larger round-tipped sculpting tool, push a divot into the right side of the ear.

(continued)

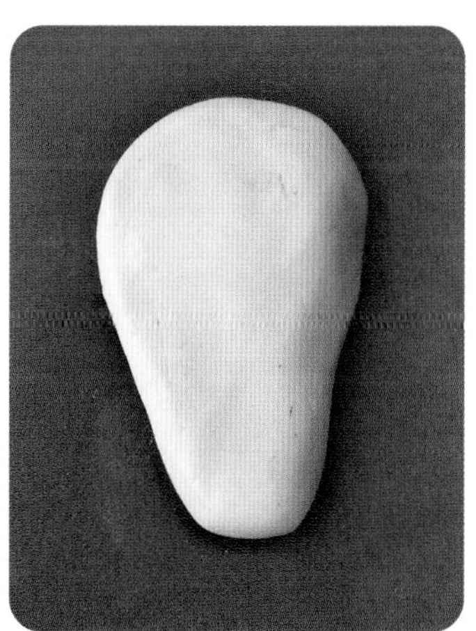
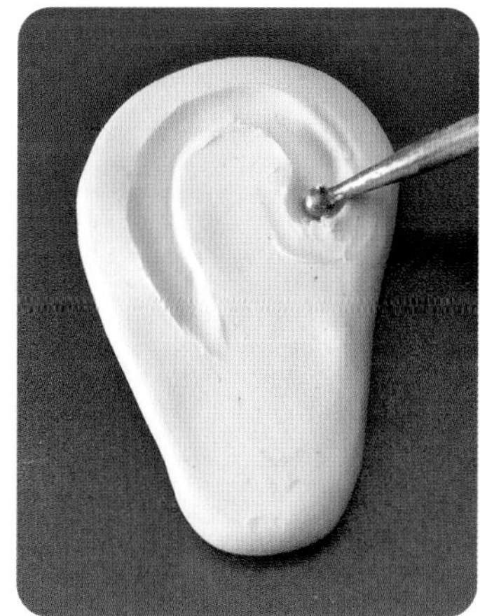
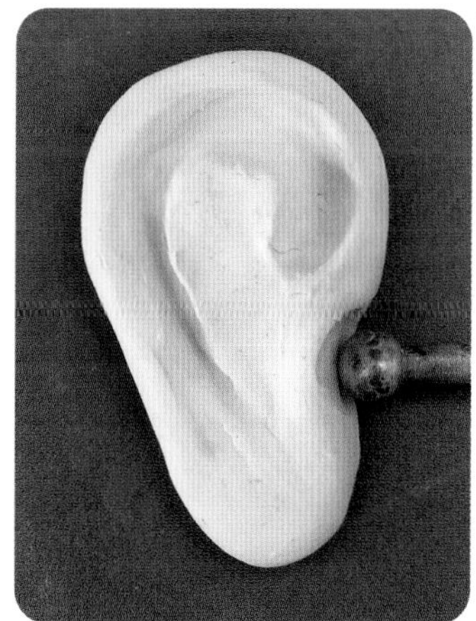

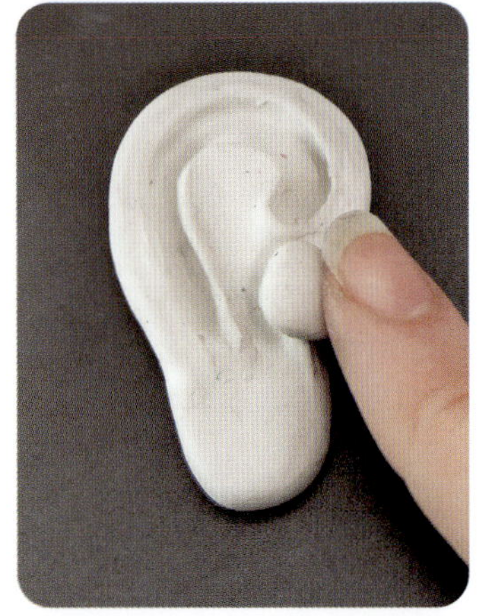 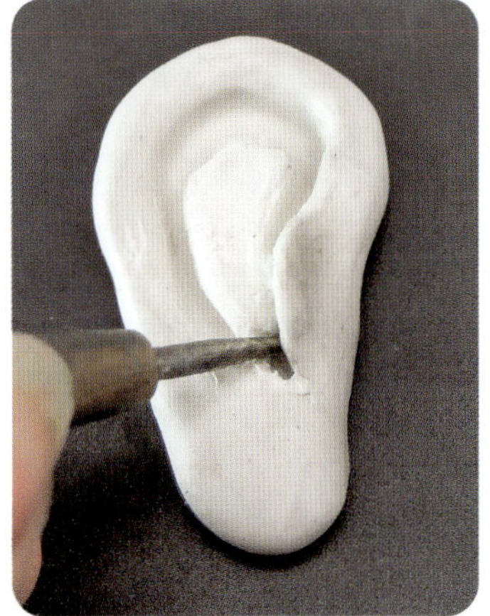 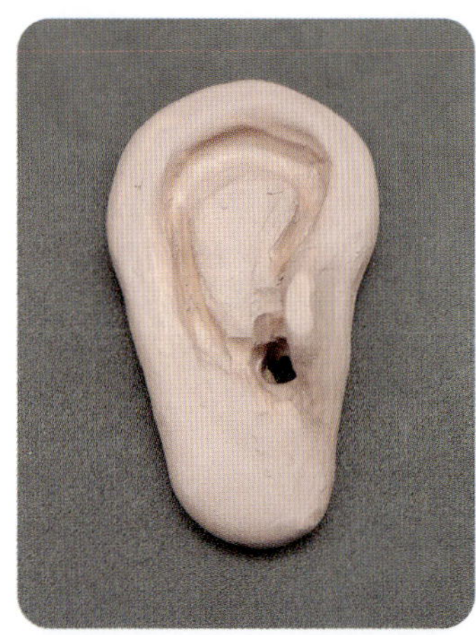

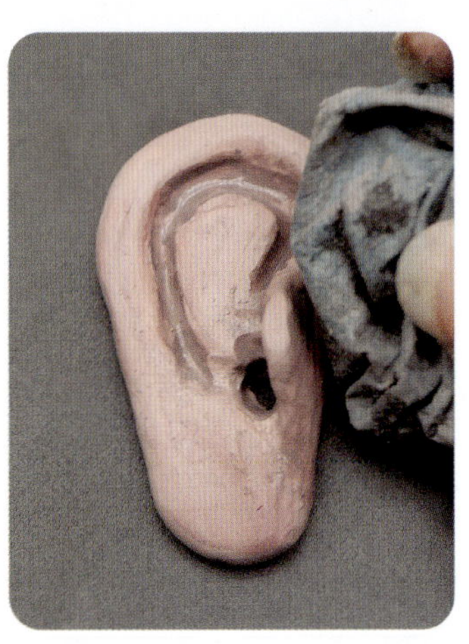 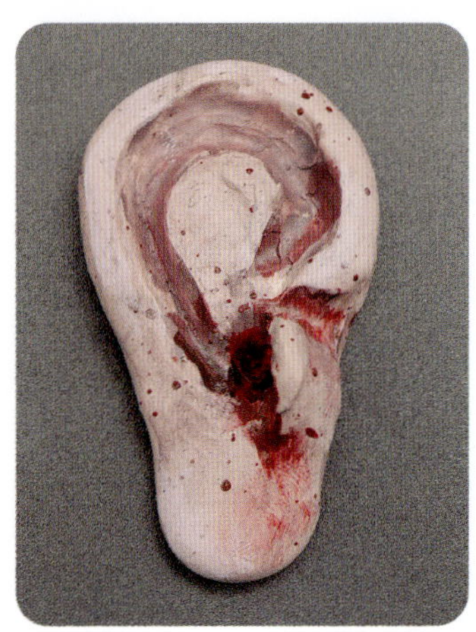 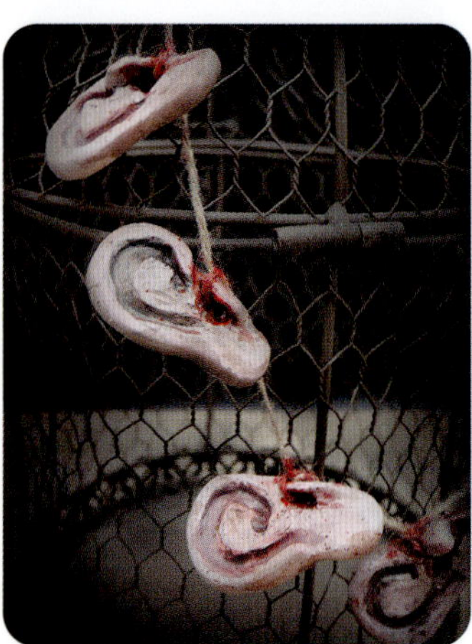

Roll a pea-sized ball of clay and push it on top of where you just pushed your ear in. Smooth the edges with your round-tipped sculpting tool.

Poke a hole where your ear hole would be using a round-tipped sculpting tool. Make sure your hole goes all the way through and is no bigger than the width of a pencil. Bake according to package instructions.

Paint your entire ear the skin tone of your choice. Water down a darker version of your skin tone and fill in all the crevasses. Wipe away any excess with a paper towel. Splatter red paint on your ear and fill in the ear hole with red.

Loop hemp though your ear hole and paint the hemp around the hole red. Loop on even more ears to make it look like you're a crazed cannibal!

Finger Key Chain

Give somebody the finger. Now, hold on a minute, before you assume anything rude. I'm talking about sculpting a finger key chain and merely presenting it as a gift to someone. And the best part is they'll never know which finger you gave them. I mean, unless they're your frenemy . . . then they probably know.

Using polymer clay, roll out a cylinder in the shape and size of a finger and press your key chain into the bottom. Using your round-tipped sculpting tool, create a divot where the nail bed should be. Add texture by sweeping your round-tipped tool across the finger.

(continued)

Materials

- ½ oz (14 g) white polymer clay
- Key chain
- Sculpting tools with round tip and silicone point
- Liquid polymer glue
- Acrylic paint and brush
- Paper towels
- Polymer glaze

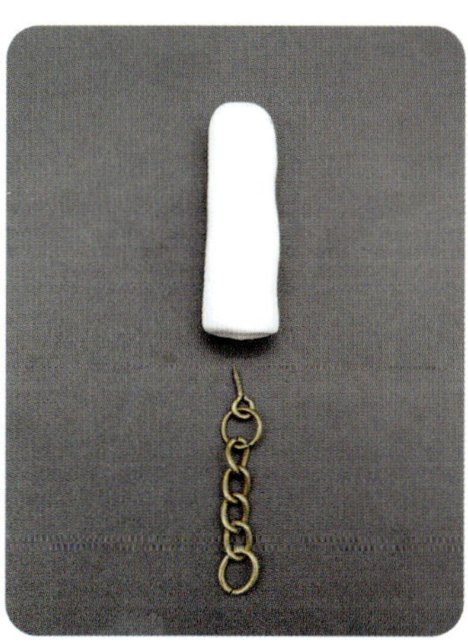
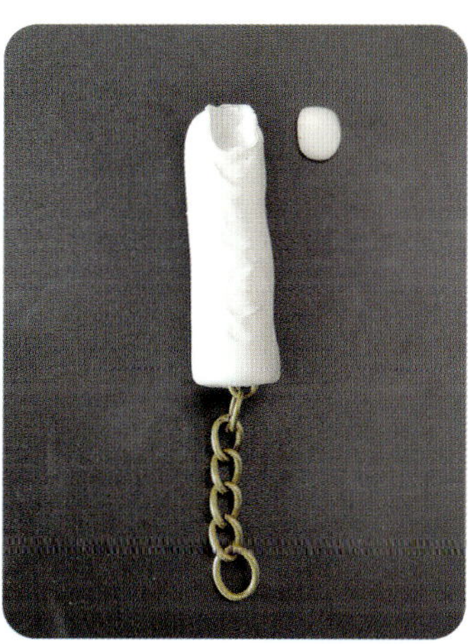
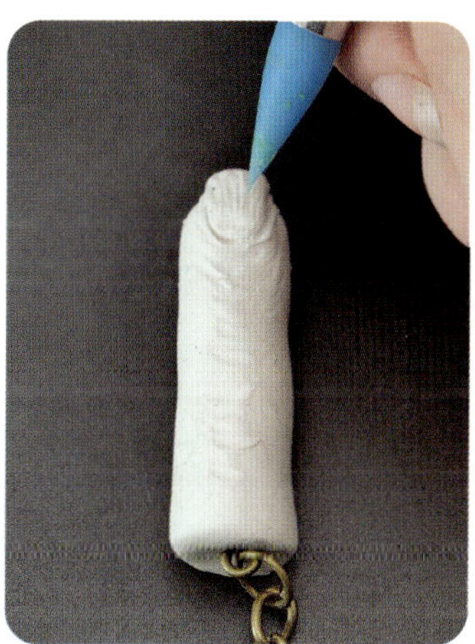

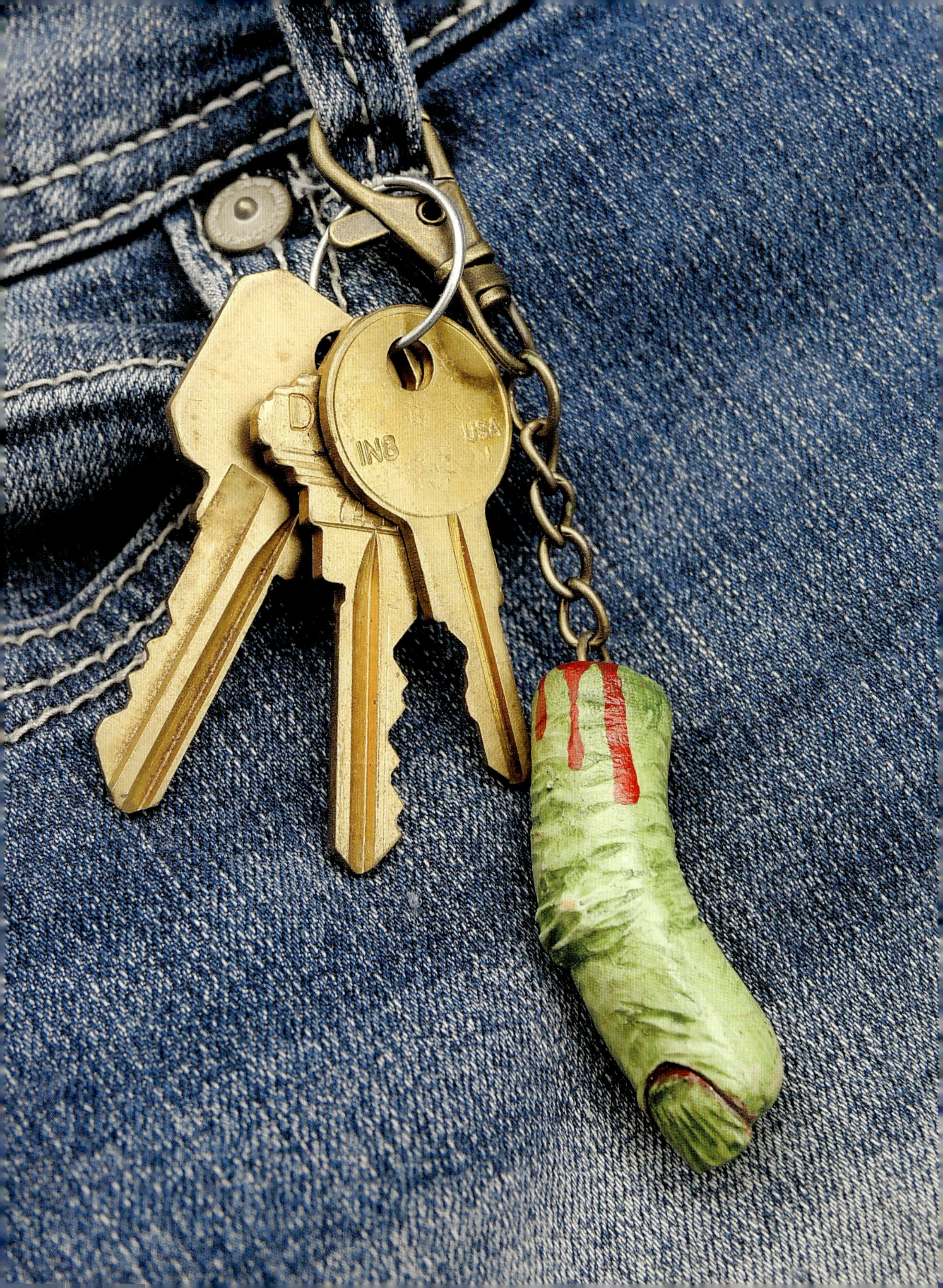

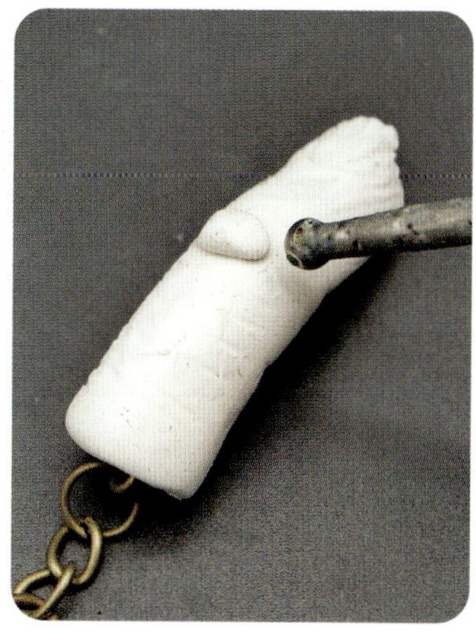
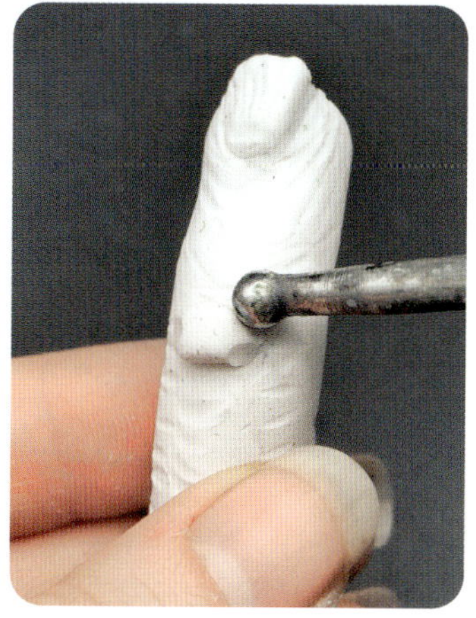
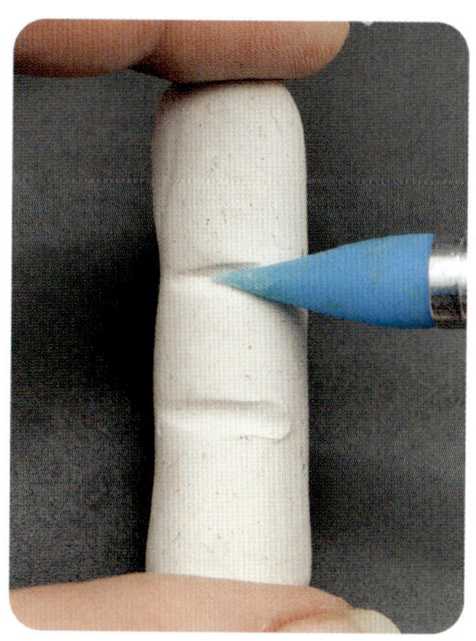
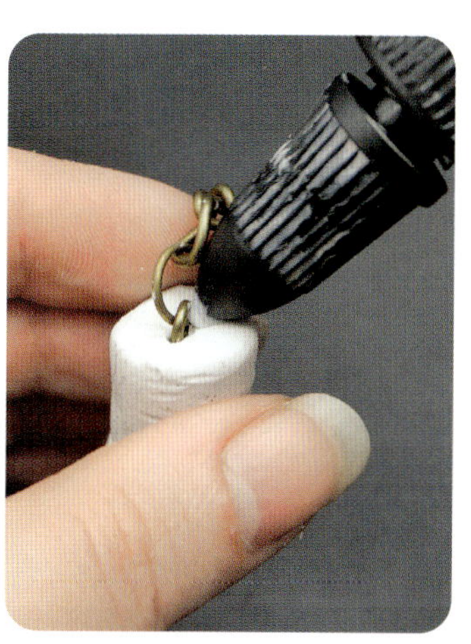
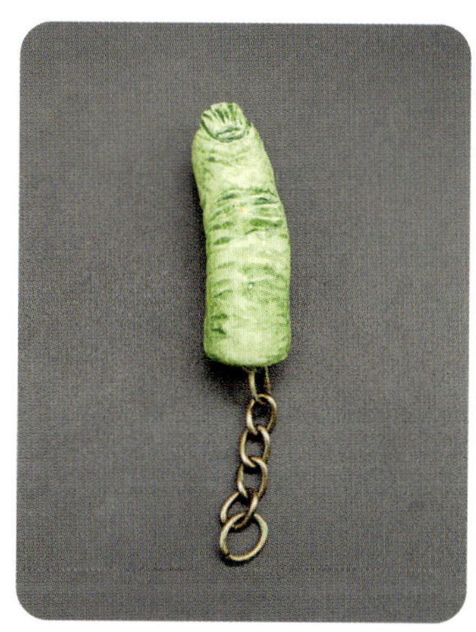
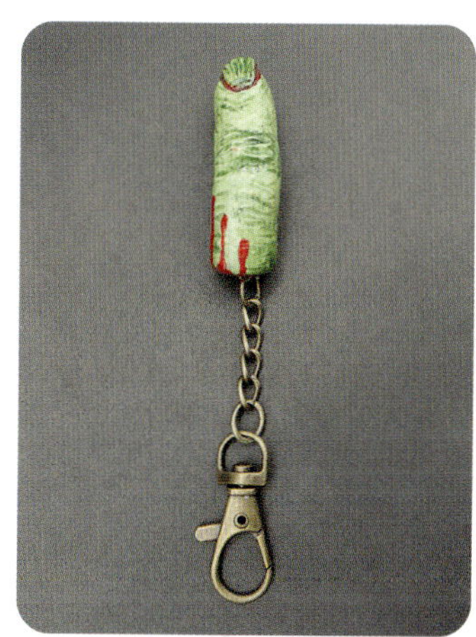

Roll a pea-sized amount of clay and smash it flat to make a nail. Then press the nail inside the nail bed. Using a silicone-point sculpting tool, create indents in the nail and around the nail bed.

Press a pea-sized amount of clay on top of the sculpted finger where the first knuckle should be. Smooth it out using a round-tipped tool.

Flip your finger over and create creases where the finger would bend using a silicone-point sculpting tool.

Once you're ready to bake, squeeze a small amount of liquid polymer glue around where the key chain is poking in. Bake according to the package instructions.

Paint the entire finger dark green and wipe off any excess paint with a paper towel. Then mix together red paint and polymer glaze and outline the nail bed. Using this mixture, paint the bottom where the key chain is and add red drips going down the side.

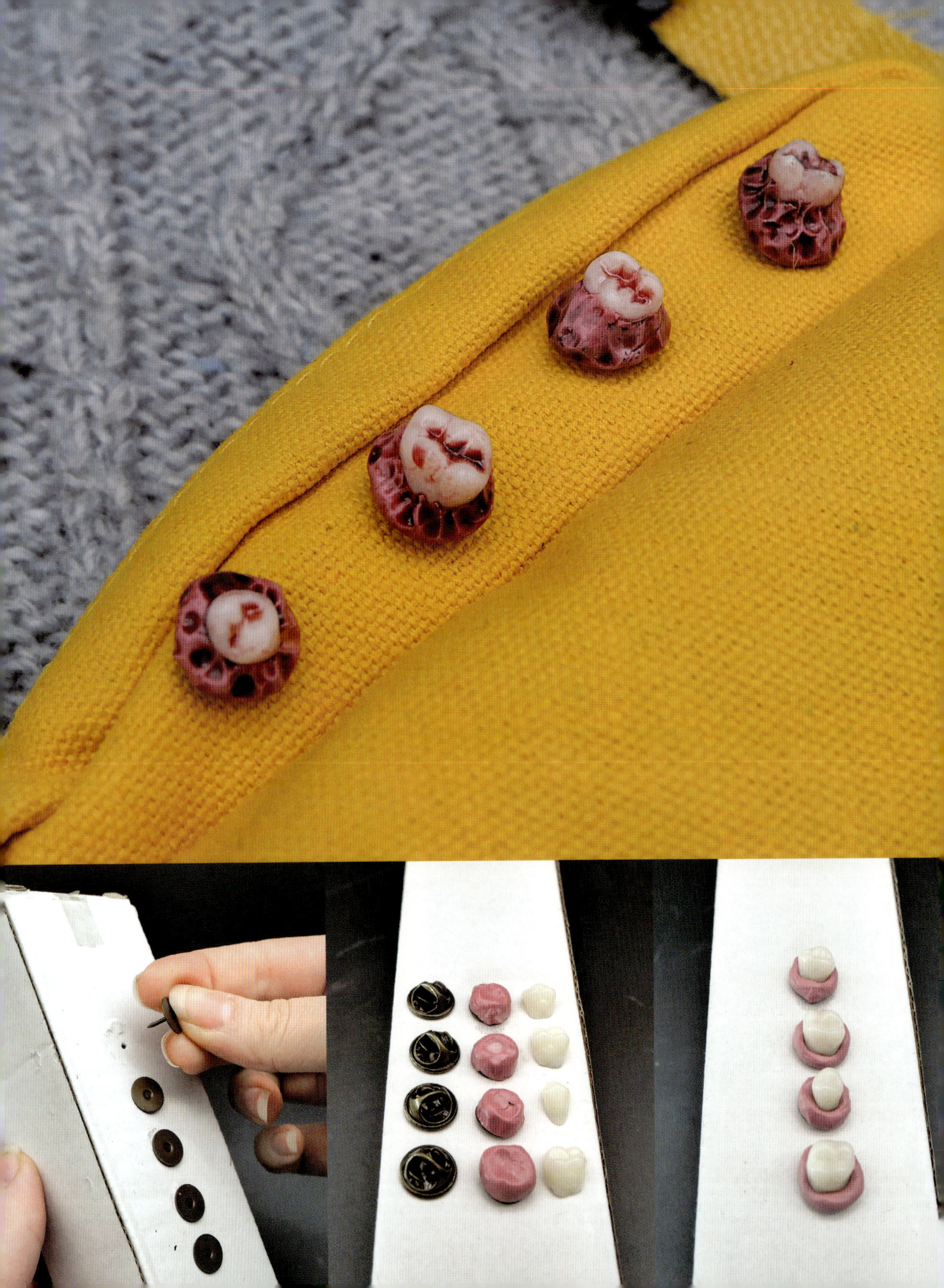

Teeth Pins

Freaking out people as I walk by is one of my favorite pastimes! One way you can achieve this is by making teeth pins to wear on your coat, backpack or purse. People will be much less likely to approach you if you're wearing a tooth pin, and it's so easy to do!

Push your butterfly pin into a cardboard box. This will hold your pin still while we work.

Lay down your silicone mat and put on your gloves. Mix a blueberry-sized amount of epoxy clay. *I didn't have pink epoxy clay, so I took white and red and mixed it together. Or you can also paint it afterward if you don't have red.*

Place a small cylinder glob of clay on top of your pin and push a fake tooth into it. Using your round-tipped sculpting tool, push the clay up and around your tooth. Add a dimple texture along the sides. Let this sit for 24 hours to harden.

Mix together blood red acrylic paint and gloss Mod Podge and paint the gums and teeth. Let this dry completely before moving your pin. Ta-da, you're finished!

Pair it with the Tongue Pin (page 141) for a more put-together look.

Materials

- Butterfly-back pins
- Cardboard box
- Silicone mat
- Disposable gloves
- White and red epoxy clay (e.g., Apoxie Sculpt)
- Fake resin teeth
- Sculpting tools with round tip
- Acrylic paint and brush
- Gloss Mod Podge (e.g., Magic Modge)

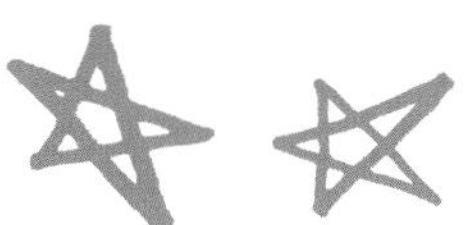

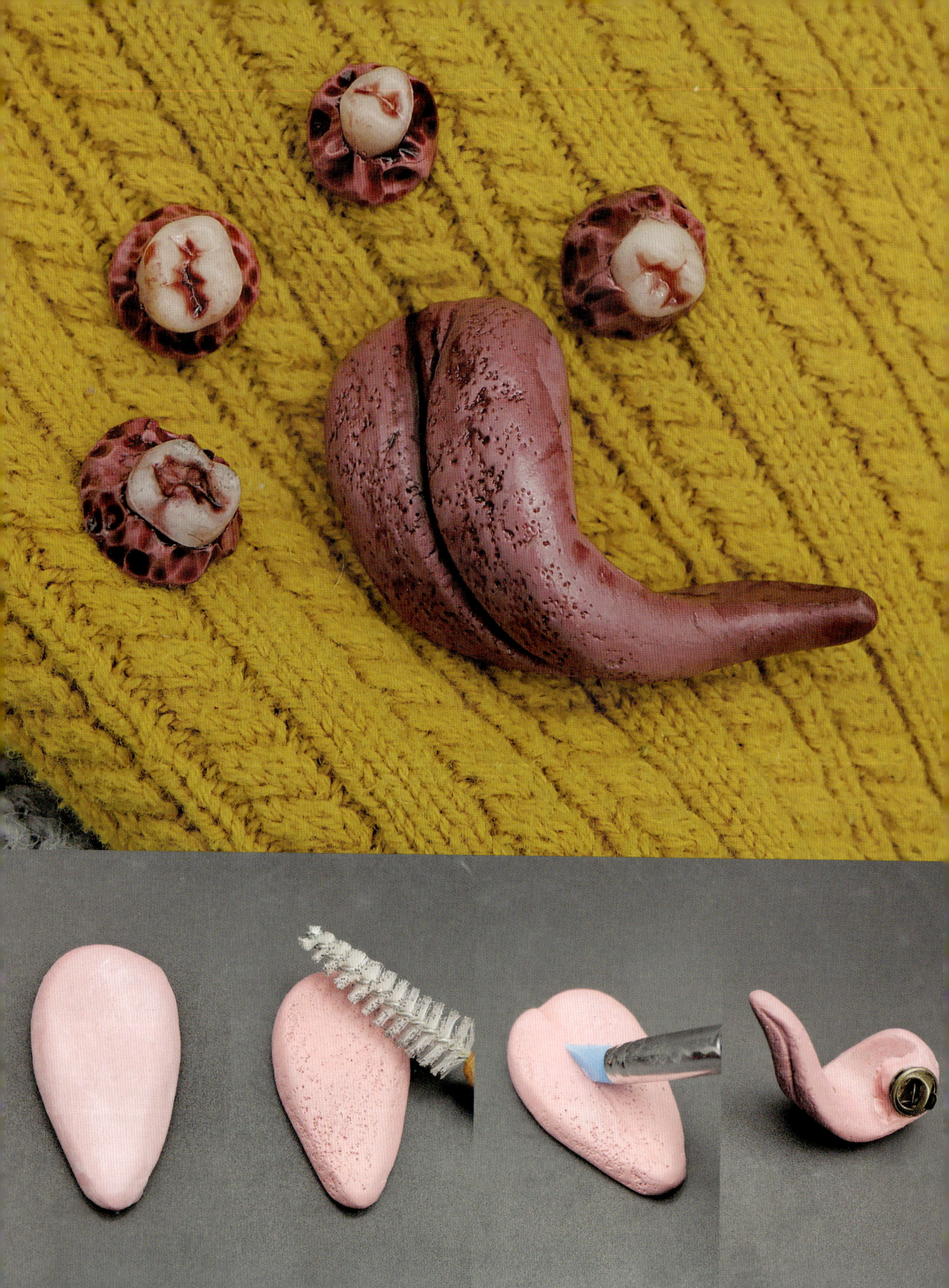

Tongue Pin

Are your teeth pins feeling lonely from the last project? Don't worry, let's make them a friend with a tongue pin! Now your pins can chat away or perhaps become the talk of the town! This is an easy project that can be done with polymer or epoxy clay. I'll show you how to do it with polymer clay, but if you decide to use epoxy, just wrap your rolling pin in cling wrap and remember to wear gloves.

Using pink polymer clay, mold a tongue-sized amount of clay into the shape of a large pumpkin seed. Using your wire brush sculpting tool, tap on your tongue to add texture. This makes it look more real. Take a silicone-angled sculpting tool and drag it down the center to make a line.

Drape the tongue onto your acrylic rolling pin and heat it up for a minute or two with your heat gun on low heat. Keep your heat gun moving; don't let it sit in one place for too long or you'll burn it. We're not trying to bake it completely; we just want it to keep its shape while it bakes in the oven. Slide it off your rolling pin and very carefully add your butterfly pin to the back using a small glob of clay and polymer glue. Bake it according to package instructions.

Create a mixture of one part maroon paint to one part polymer glaze and coat your entire tongue. Wipe off any excess with a paper towel. Finish off your entire tongue with polymer glaze to make it look wet.

Pair it with the Teeth Pins (page 139) for a more put-together look.

Materials

- ½–1 oz (14–28 g) pink polymer clay
- Sculpting tools with wire brush and silicone angle
- Acrylic rolling pin
- Heat gun
- Butterfly-back pin
- Polymer glue
- Acrylic paint and brush
- Polymer glaze
- Paper towel

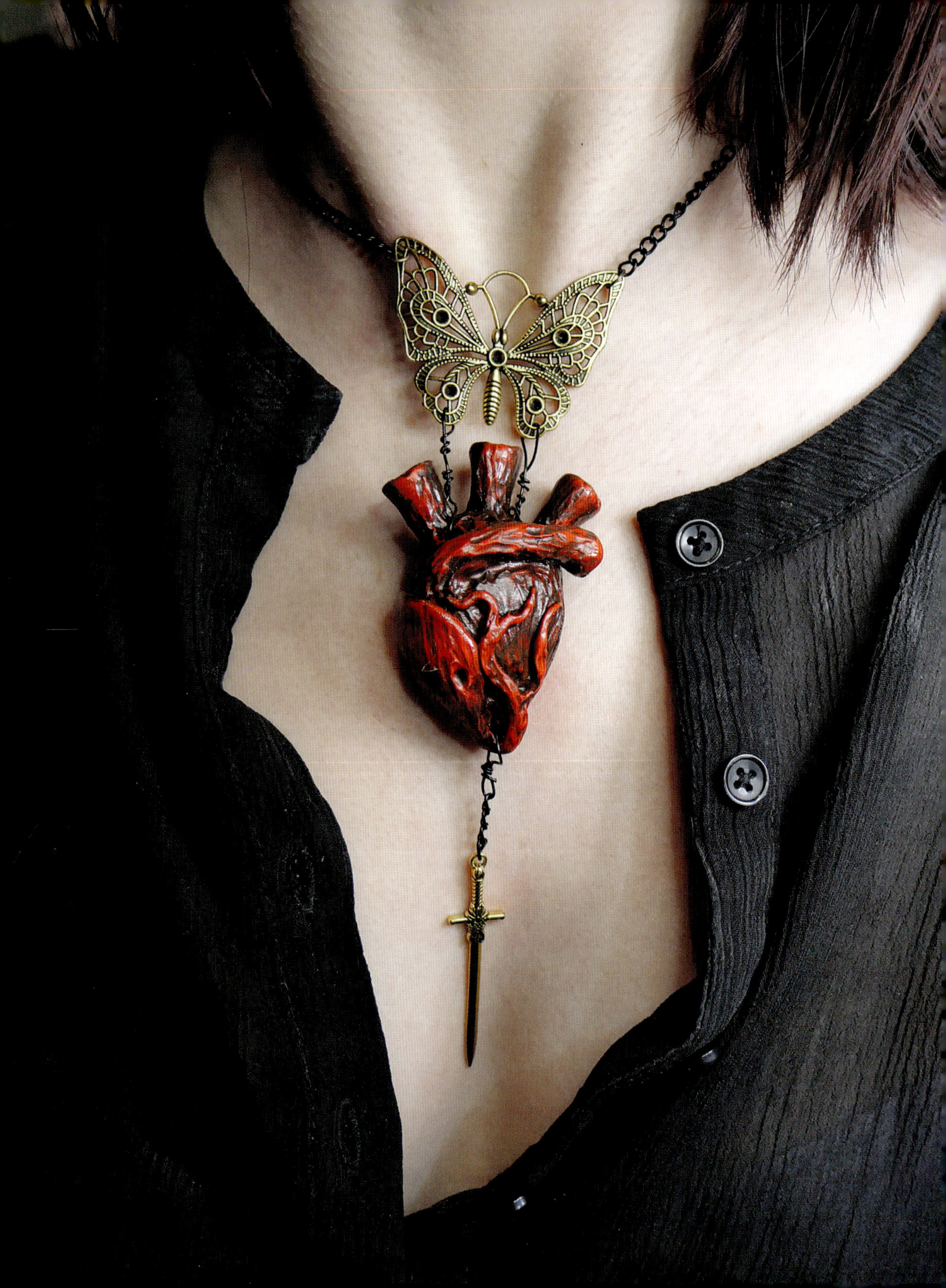

Clay Heart

Do you wear your heart on your sleeve? How about your neck? That is such a weird saying! Anyway, in this project I'll show you how to make a clay heart, and if you want to put it on a necklace, then let's do it!

Alternatively, if you want your necklace to hold up longer, you can use epoxy clay (like Apoxie Sculpt) instead of polymer. Just be sure to work on a silicone mat and wear gloves.

Materials

- 2 oz (56 g) polymer clay
- Sculpting tools with round tip
- Acrylic paint and brush
- Heat gun (optional)
- Paper towels
- Black floral wire
- Necklace chain
- Metal pendant
- Butterfly pendant (optional)

With your polymer clay, form a puffy seed shape roughly 2 x 1½ inches (5 x 3.8 cm). Roll three small cylinder-shaped nubs about ½ inch (1.3 cm) long for the top of the heart and attach them using a round-tipped sculpting tool. Blend the seams together.

(continued)

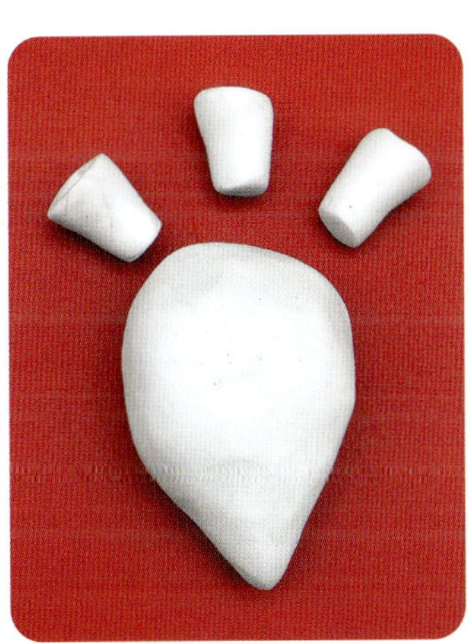
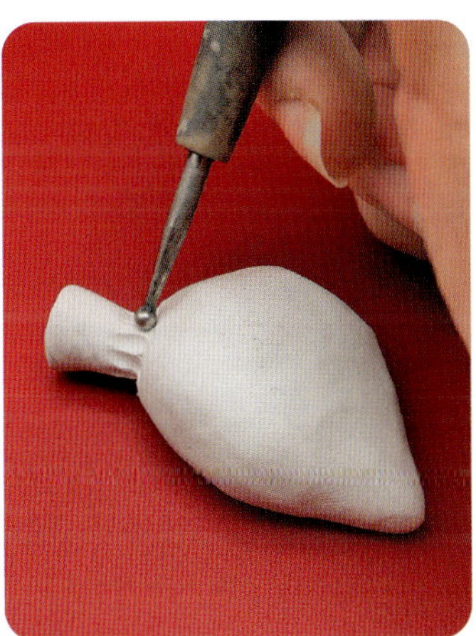
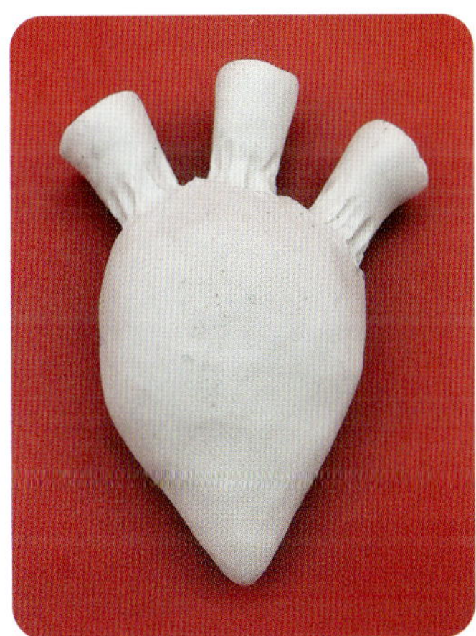

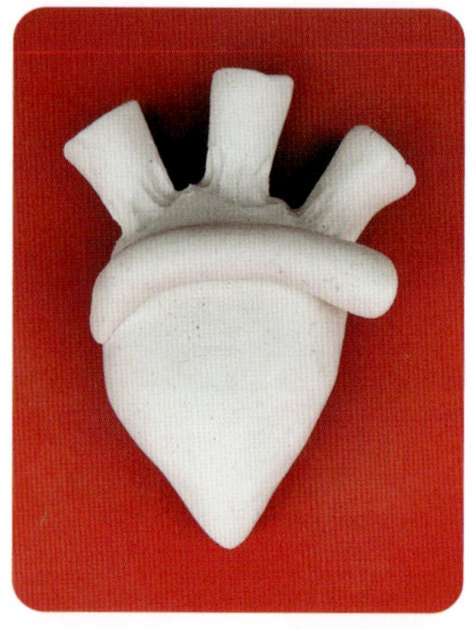
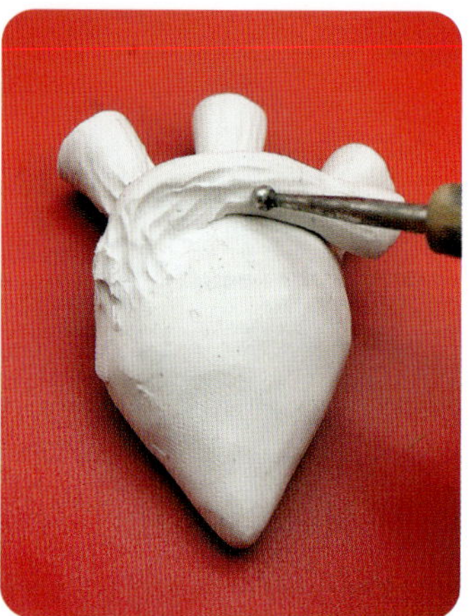
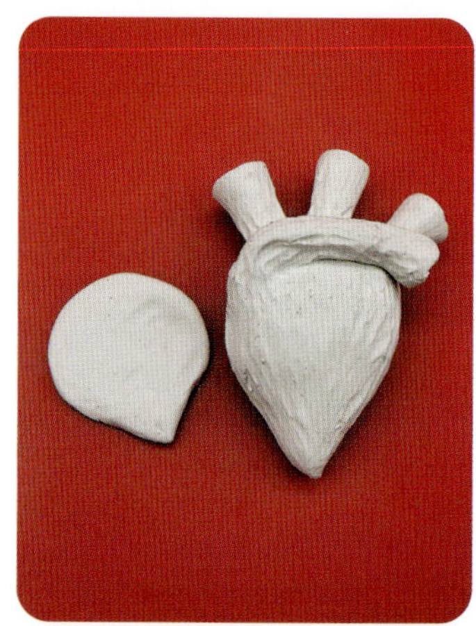

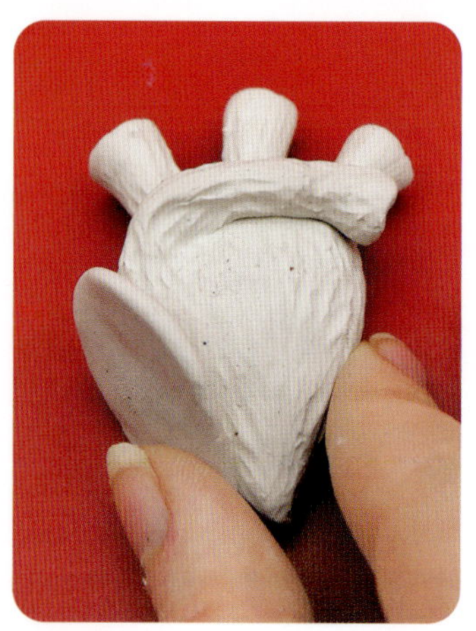
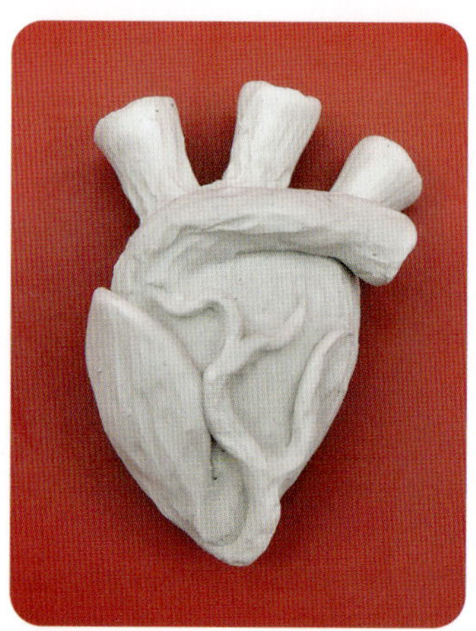
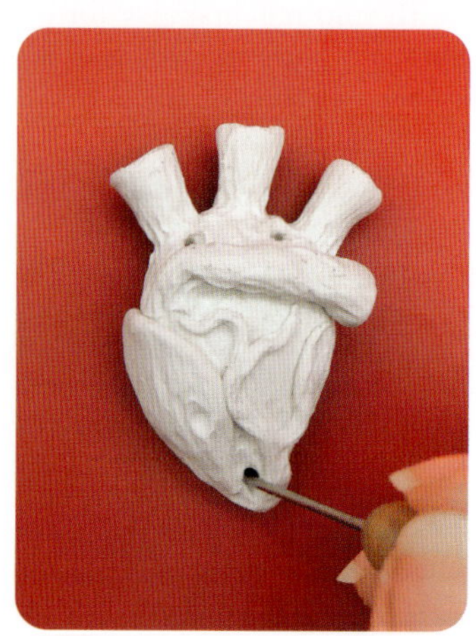

Roll another piece about 2 inches (5 cm) long and place it arching across the front of your heart, just below the nubs. Securely attach it using a round-tipped sculpting tool, blending the seams together like you did for the top nubs. Jab the round-tipped sculpting tool into the top of each nub to make a dent. *This makes them appear more artery-like.* Score the outside of your heart with your round-tipped sculpting tool to add a wood-carved texture.

Shape a flat disk roughly 1½ x 1½ inches (3.8 x 3.8 cm) with a point on one end. Press it onto the side of your heart point down and texture it to match your heart.

Roll out small ropes about the thickness of a pea and snake them up the front of your heart. These will be the veins. Don't go too crazy; just make a few that come up from the bottom like vines or upside-down roots.

Let's poke some holes in your heart! (*Don't worry, your heart won't feel it.*) Poke two holes at the top and a hole at the bottom. *Be careful not to poke the holes too close to the edge of your heart because polymer clay can crack with stress.* Bake your heart according to the package instructions.

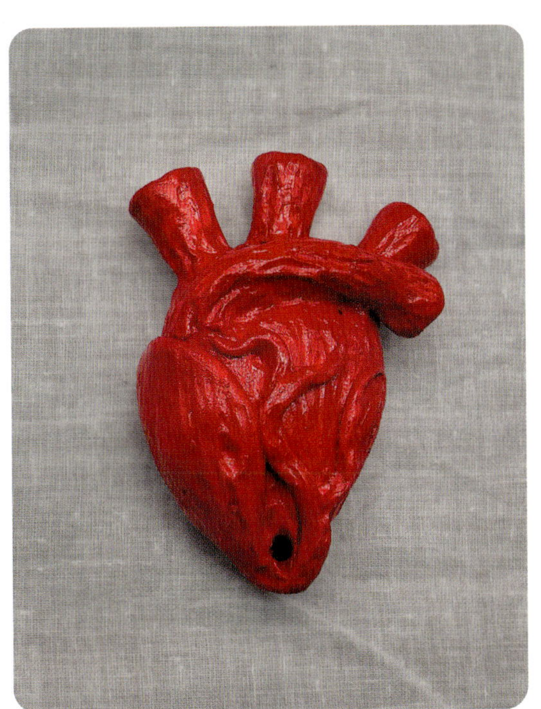

Paint your entire heart red and let it dry completely. Depending on your paint and how thick you laid it on, this can take 5 to 20 minutes. *You can speed up drying time with a heat gun if you have one, or just blow on it as hard as you can.* Once the red has dried, cover it with a watered-down black paint and wipe off any excess with a paper towel. The black should just fill in the details, making your heart appear less "flat."

Lastly, let's add it to a chain with embellishments. Using black floral wire, attach your chain through the top holes of your heart. In the bottom hole, hang your pendant with additional floral wire. Optionally, you can place a butterfly pendant between the heart and the chain, but if you don't have one it will look just as good without it.

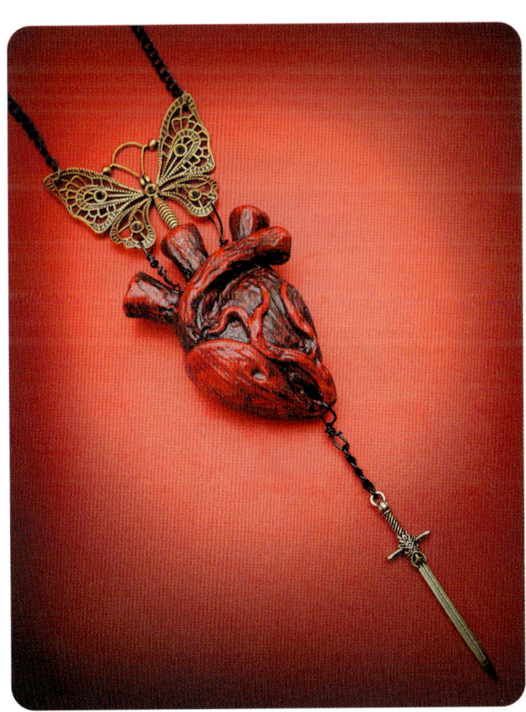

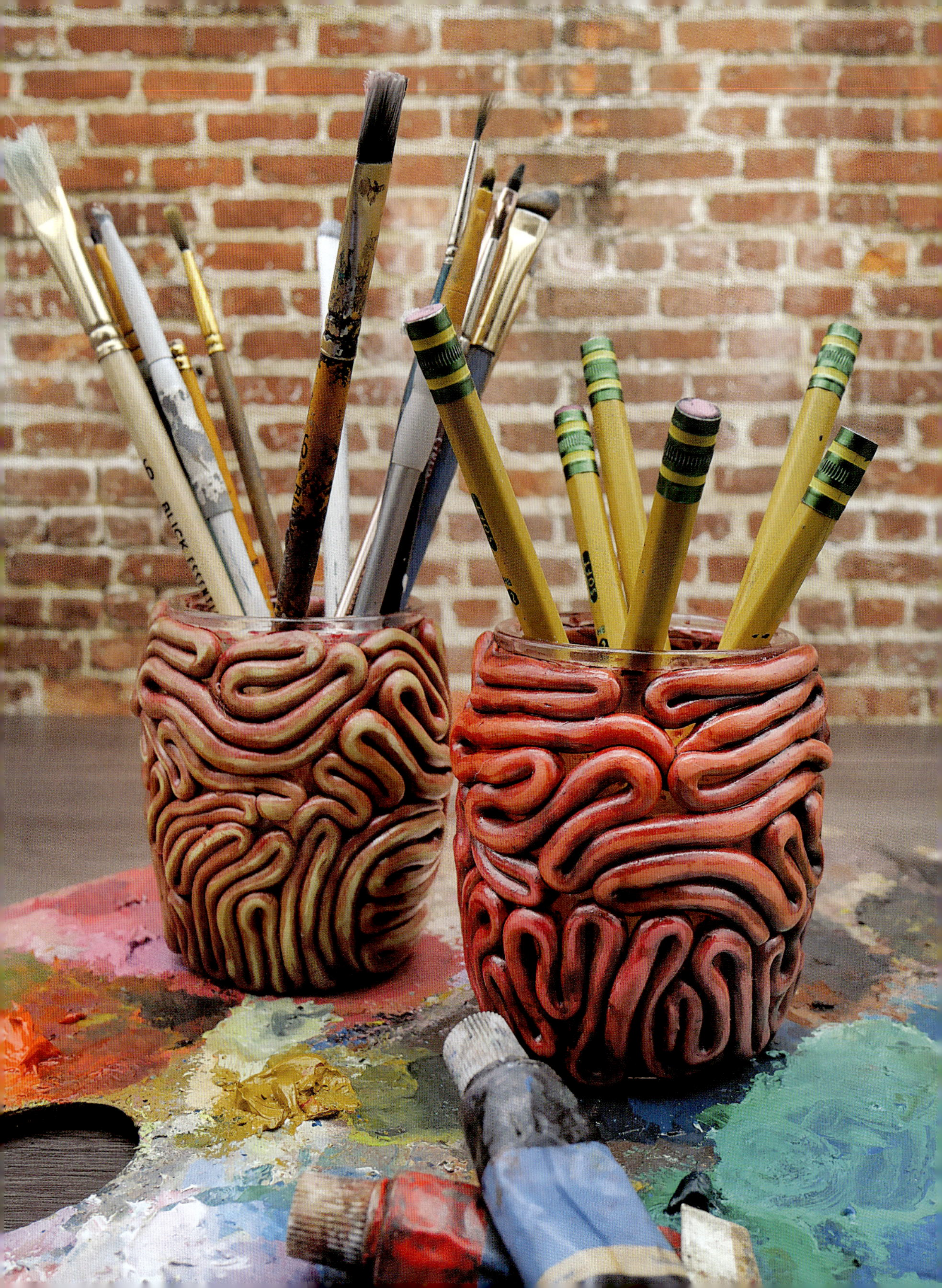

Why throw away your trash when you can make it into art? This idea delights the hoarder in me and makes my husband groan.

So, what is good trash?

Glass jars, boxes, tins, chopsticks, craft sticks, fruit bags, matches, pressboard, buttons, toothpicks, perfectly cracked walnuts, broken pots, corks, bottle caps, toilet paper rolls, scrap wood, broken jewelry and the list keeps going! The trick is to limit yourself to one box of trashy treasures and it's a "one in, one out" situation once that box is full. Of course, nobody said how big the box had to be . . .

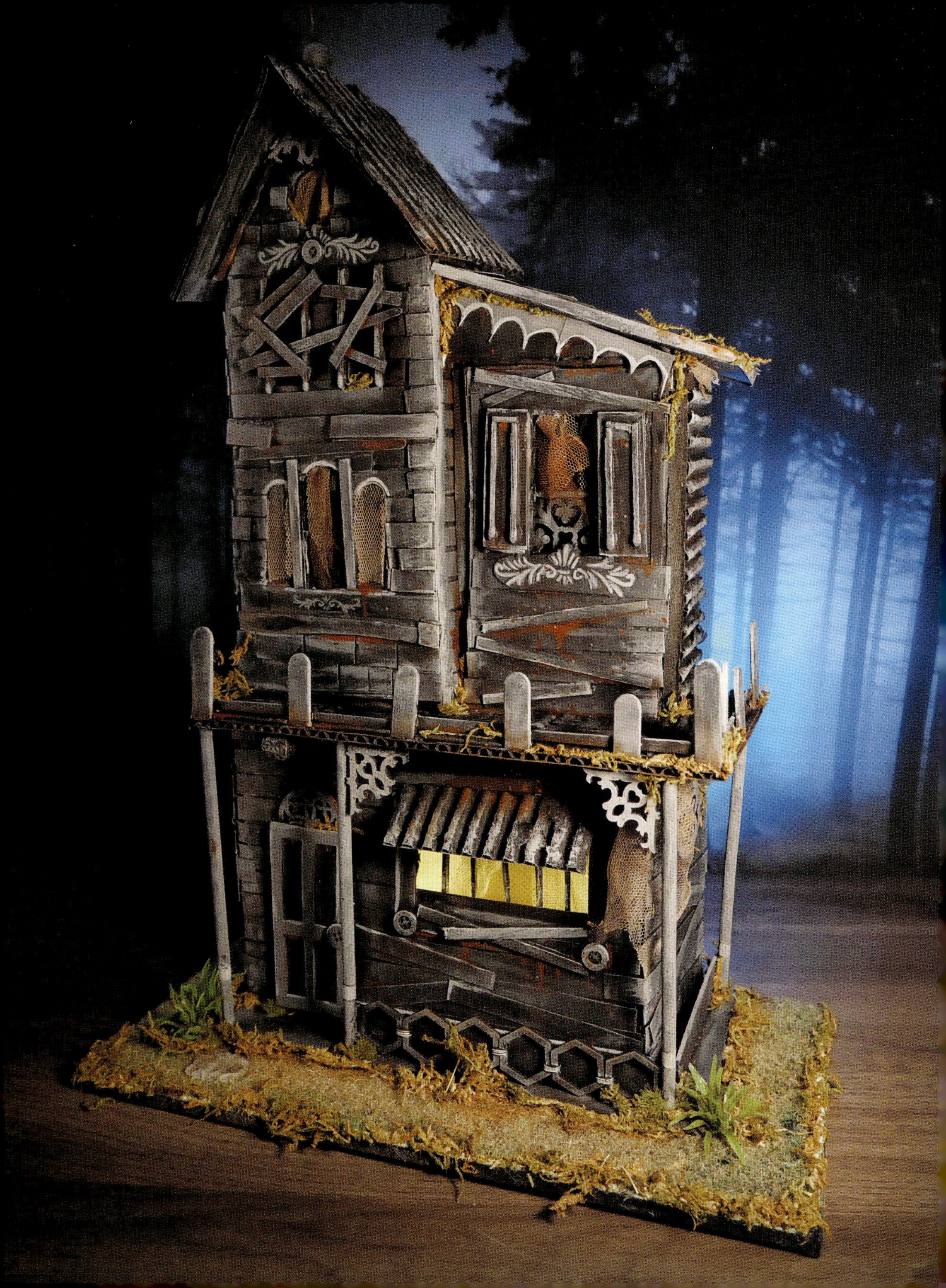

Haunted House

Do you ever say to yourself, "Wow that's a good box"? If you do, then welcome to adulthood! I was not prepared for how much of adulthood is saving boxes to store your junk in. Let's face it, your stash is overflowing and you're never going to do anything with that iPhone 5 box. With a trashy haunted house, you're going to finally put all those "good boxes" to good use! Well, maybe not ALL of them, because you've been stashing them like some sort of weird little box squirrel for a while now.

Start by grouping your boxes together and planning out your house. Draw inspiration by looking up old Victorian houses online. *Don't glue your boxes together just yet; it's easier to cut out windows and holes when your boxes are lying flat.*

(continued)

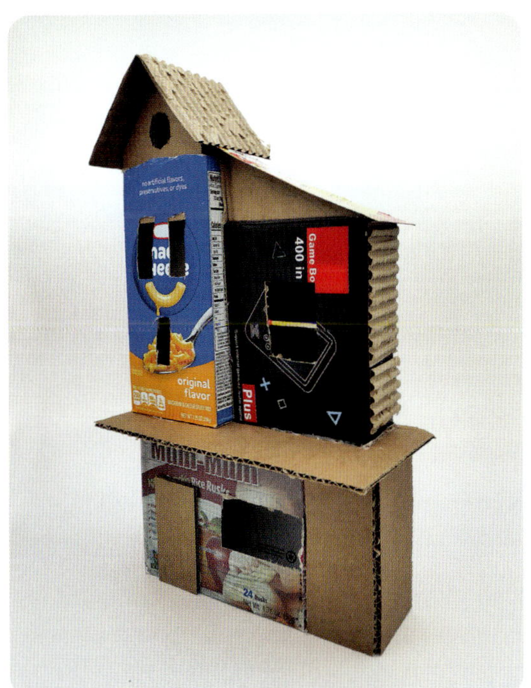

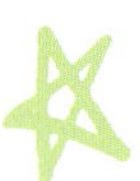

Materials

- Small empty boxes (various sizes)
- X-ACTO knife and/or scissors
- Hot glue and gun
- Interesting trash (e.g., cardboard, craft sticks, matches, buttons, chopsticks, etc.)
- Precision craft glue (e.g., Bearly Art)
- Corrugated cardboard (optional)
- 1 sheet of balsa wood
- Chopsticks (optional)
- Matte black spray paint
- Acrylic paint and brush
- 2 electric tea lights
- Moss and grass flocking

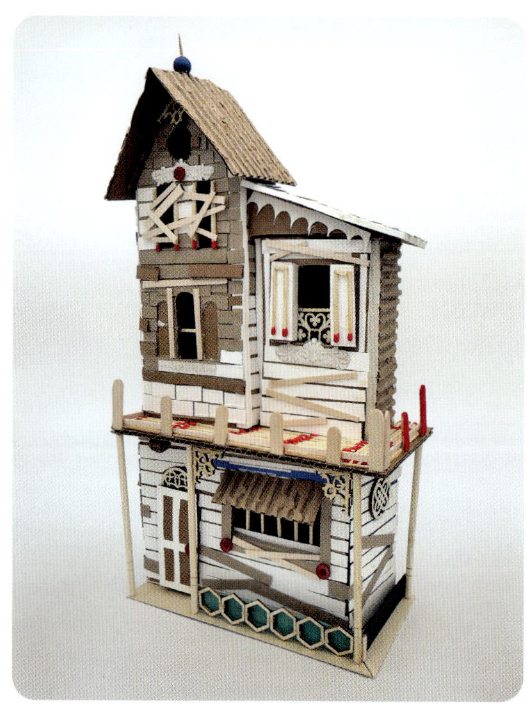

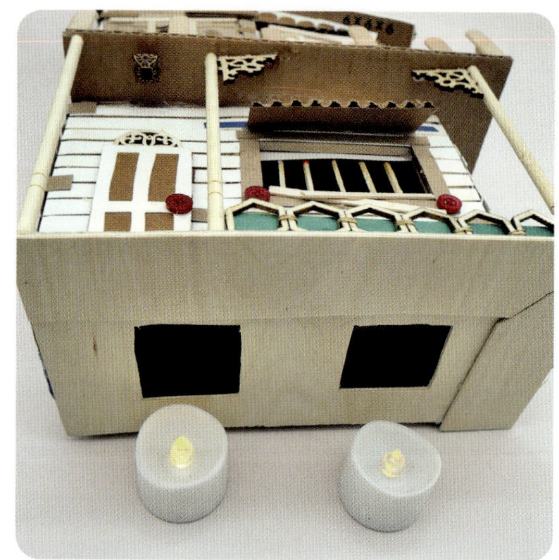

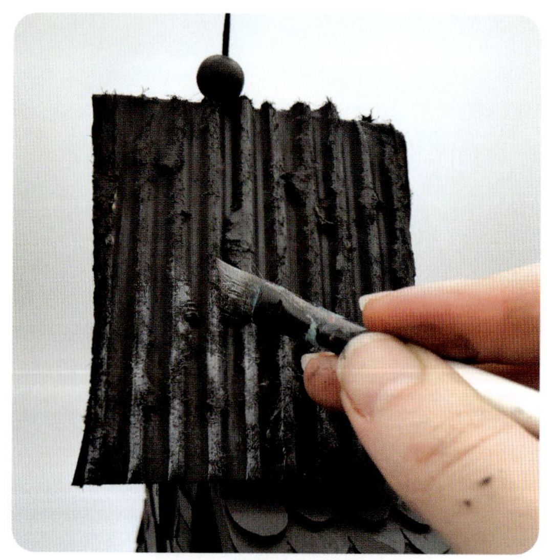

With your X-ACTO knife, cut out windows. I suggest adding a circle window or two. If you plan on lighting your house, cut a hole through all the floors from the first to the attic. This lets the light shine though.

Once you have all the holes for windows and lights cut out, hot glue all your boxes together.

Now let's add some curb appeal! Use your interesting trash items to add some detail to your house. Use hot glue for the bigger objects and precision craft glue for the smaller, lighter ones. Corrugated cardboard makes a great roof if you peel the first layer of paper off. *Luckily you don't have to be a perfectionist here because who's ever heard of a perfect haunted house? The trashier, the better!*

Using your X-ACTO knife, cut two square holes in your balsa wood big enough for your electric tea lights to fit. Cut matching holes in the bottom of your house, then hot glue your house to the wood. This will give your house a porch or deck. You can use chopsticks here to make

porch posts if you like or maybe this will be a yard. You can make your own story.

Once all your trash has been added to your house, spray-paint the entire thing matte black and allow it to dry completely, usually 30 to 60 minutes. Make the details pop by dry brushing them with light gray acrylic paint. Dry brushing is when you take a dry paintbrush, dip the tip into paint and lightly sweep it over the surface.

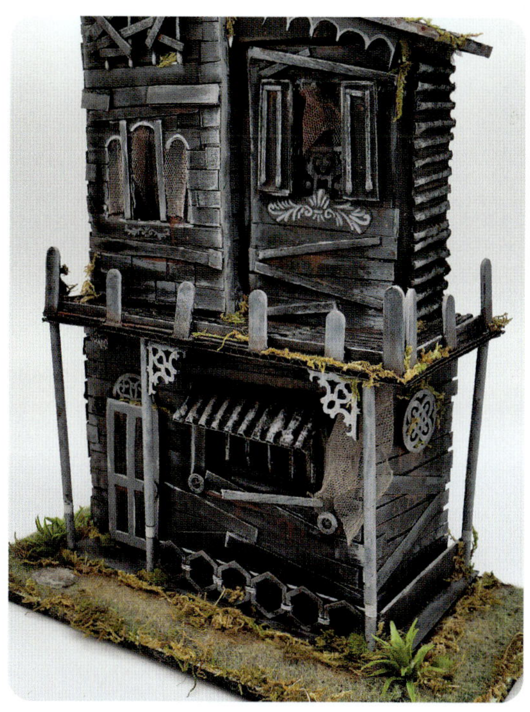

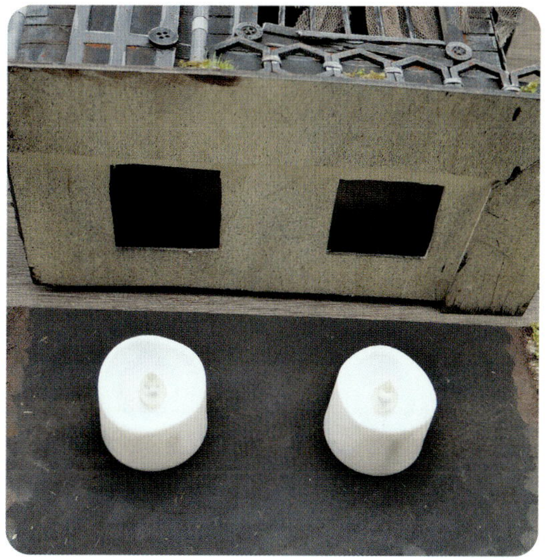

Add your last finishing touches by adhering grass flocking and moss around your house. Also let's make it look dirty by watering down brown paint and flicking it at your house to create a splatter effect, or paint drips of rust running down the sides. Really just have fun with all the little details.

And you're finished! This project is a great way to reduce waste and make a creepy Halloween or year-round decoration at the same time!

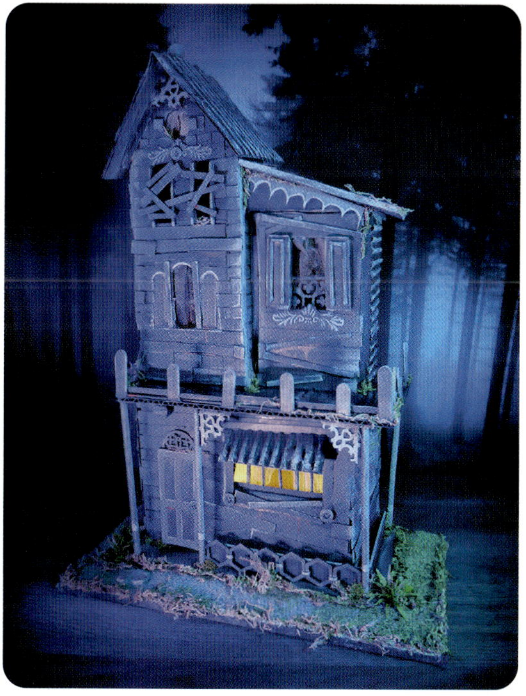

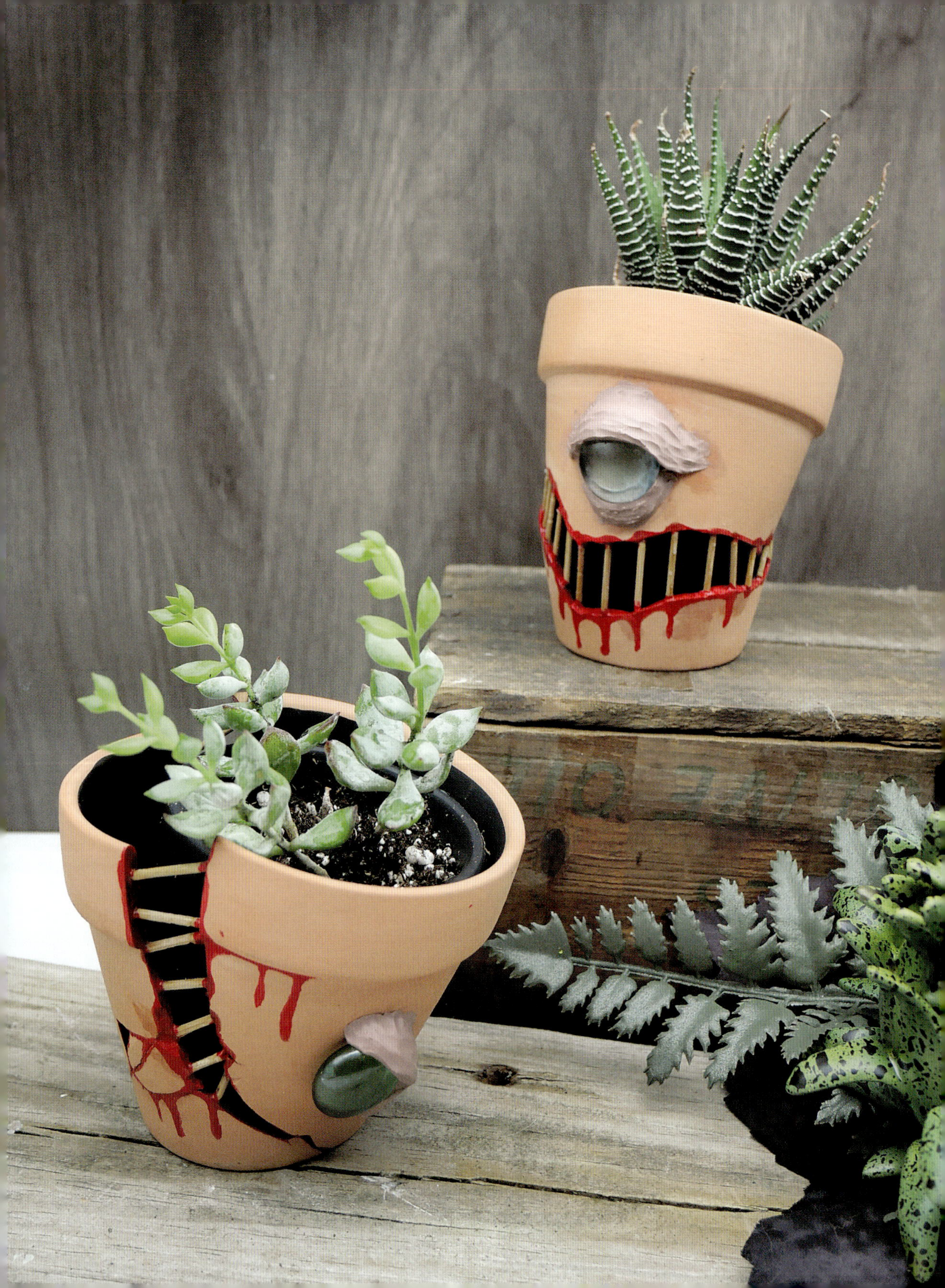

Terrifying Terra-cotta

Are your plants bored with their pots? I know my plants are constantly complaining about their homes! Actually, they complain more about the cats trying to eat them, but that's a completely different matter.

I came up with this project when my cat Emily pushed a plant over trying to be mouth friends with it (according to Emily). However, Jim the plant had a different story . . . After saving Jim from the floor, I decided to upgrade his living situation.

Hopefully you have a broken pot, but if not, you could ask a friendly cat for help. Wrapping the pot in a towel and hitting it once with a hammer will also do the trick.

Materials

- Broken terra-cotta pot
- Masking tape
- Wire cutters
- Toothpicks
- Super glue
- Precision craft glue (e.g., Bearly Art)
- Acrylic paint and brush
- Silicone mat
- Disposable gloves
- Epoxy clay (e.g., Apoxie Sculpt)
- Flat glass bead
- Sculpting tools

Hover your broken pot pieces together to envision how you'd like it to look. Take a little masking tape and hinge it on the back. The tape will be removed later; this is just for planning purposes. If your break is vertical instead of horizontal, tape the bottom. Hopefully your pot is broken in only two pieces, but it's okay if it's broken in more. You can glue the smaller pieces together to add a cracked texture.

(continued)

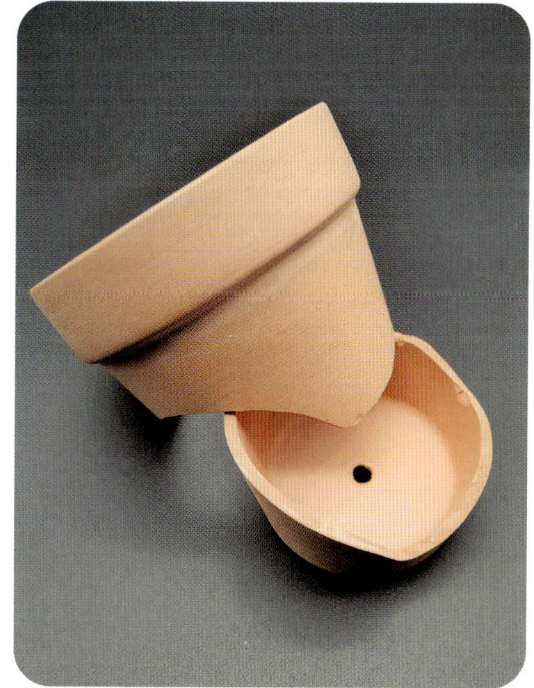

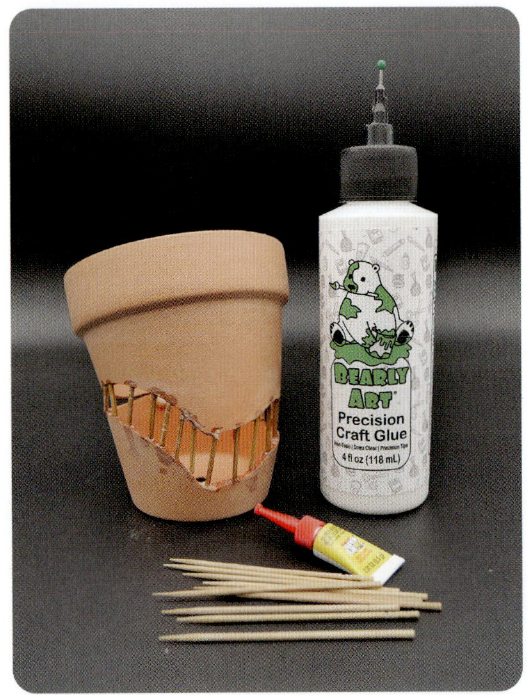 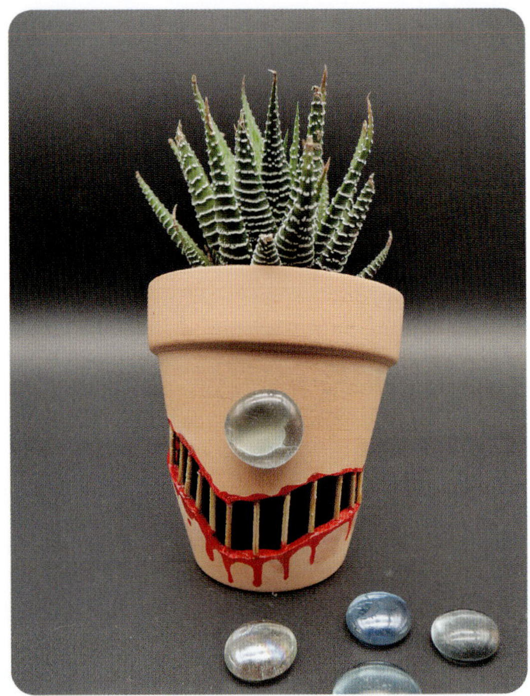

With wire cutters, cut a toothpick ¼ to ½ inch (6 to 13 mm) long. Starting on the middle front and working your way back, hold a toothpick up to the crack, mark the correct length and then cut it to fit before super gluing it in. Use a small amount of super glue at first just to hold it, and then go back over it with precision craft glue for a better hold. Do this all the way around until you reach the back on both sides.

Now that the hard part is done, the only thing left to do is dress it up! Paint red drips coming out of the gaping grin. Lay out your silicone mat and put on your gloves. Mix a marble-sized amount of epoxy clay. Using the clay, adhere a flat glass bead for an eye and sculpt an eyelid with your sculpting tools. Let the epoxy clay set for 2 to 4 hours and then paint the eyelid to match.

Tip: When adding your plant back in, place the plant in a slightly smaller black container before putting it in the new pot. That way dirt doesn't fall out of its mouth. If you don't care about a little dirt, you can just put your plant straight into your new pot.

Tinned Tentacles

Do you feel bad about throwing out food that's past the expiration date? Well, rather than risk it on a tin of sardines, just make it into art! Upcycling trash is a fun way to keep garbage out of the landfill.

Since we aren't made of clay money, fill the back half of your empty sardine tin with aluminum foil. Glue it in place with a tiny amount of hot glue. *Be careful not to use too much! This is just meant to keep things from slipping while we work. The polymer clay will be what actually holds it in place.*

Mix small amounts of purple and pink into your translucent polymer clay until it makes the color you desire. Press a flat chunk of the clay onto the exposed aluminum foil shoved inside your tin.

(continued)

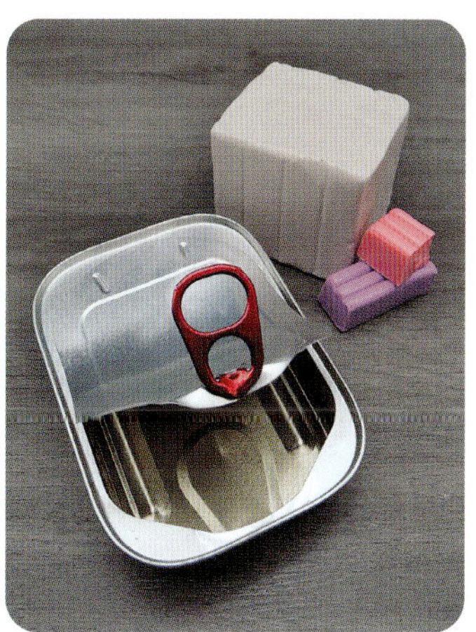

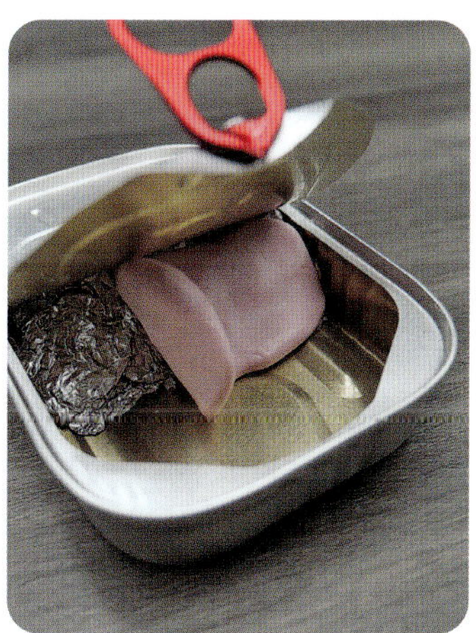

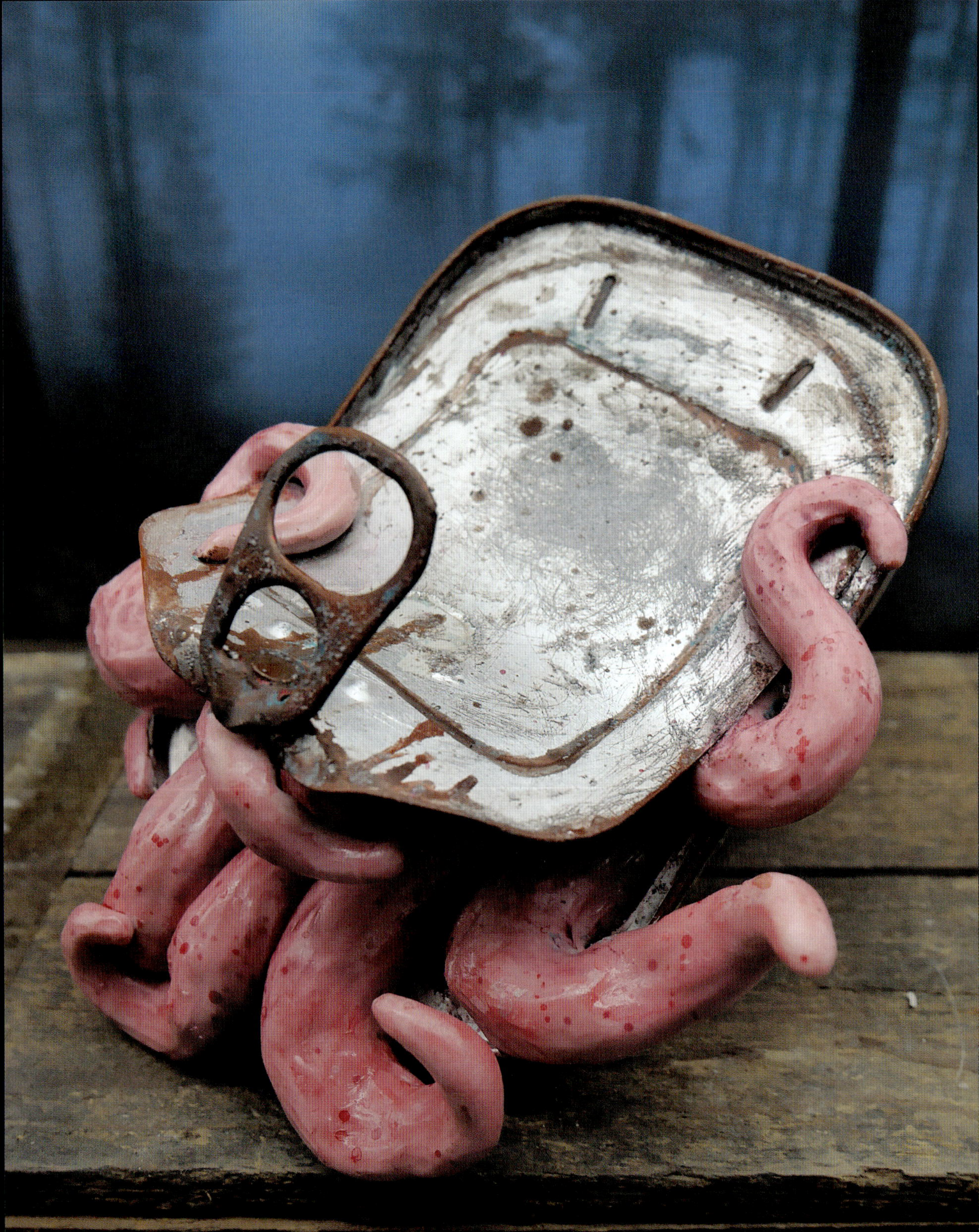

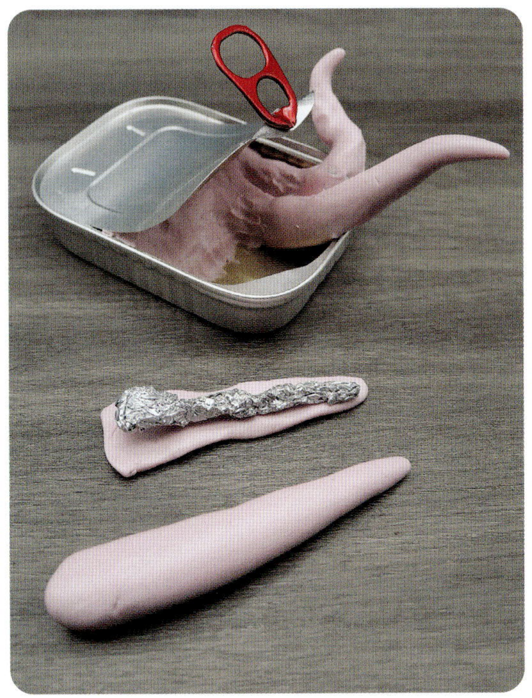

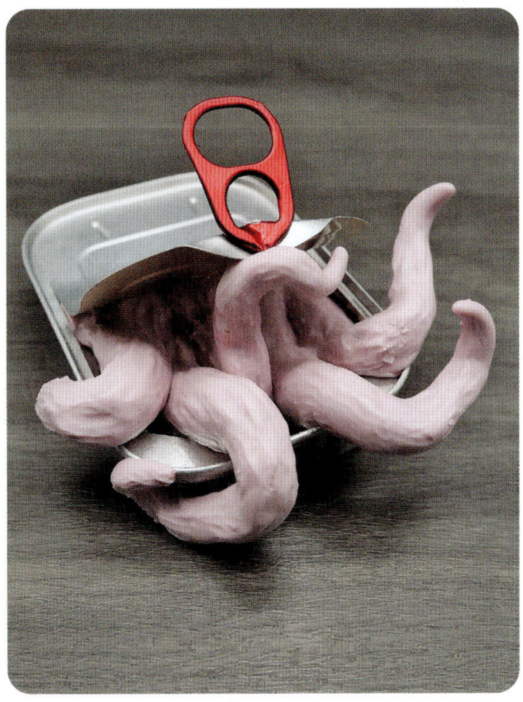

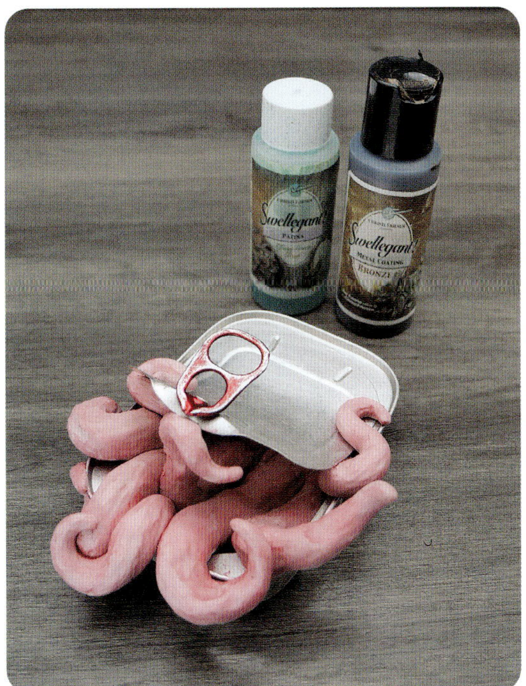

Tightly crumple up aluminum foil into a small, skinny tentacle, 3 to 4 inches (7.5 to 10 cm) long and no thicker than a pencil. Wrap it with your clay and attach it to the clay inside your tin. Use a round-tipped sculpting tool to smooth out any seams or fingerprints.

Repeat until your tin is full of tentacles. It usually takes four to six tentacles to fill a tin. Bend your tentacles into the desired shapes. Bend one tentacle up in the air, holding the lid open. Bake your horrifying clay creation following the package instructions.

Once your monster has cooled off, use sandpaper to sand all the metal on your tin. You don't have to go crazy, just enough to rough it up.

Splatter red acrylic paint on your tentacles and coat them in polymer glaze to make them wet. Paint the edges of your tin and the tab with bronze metal coating and let them dry. Then coat the entire tin with patina. After sitting overnight, the patina will age any metal it touches.

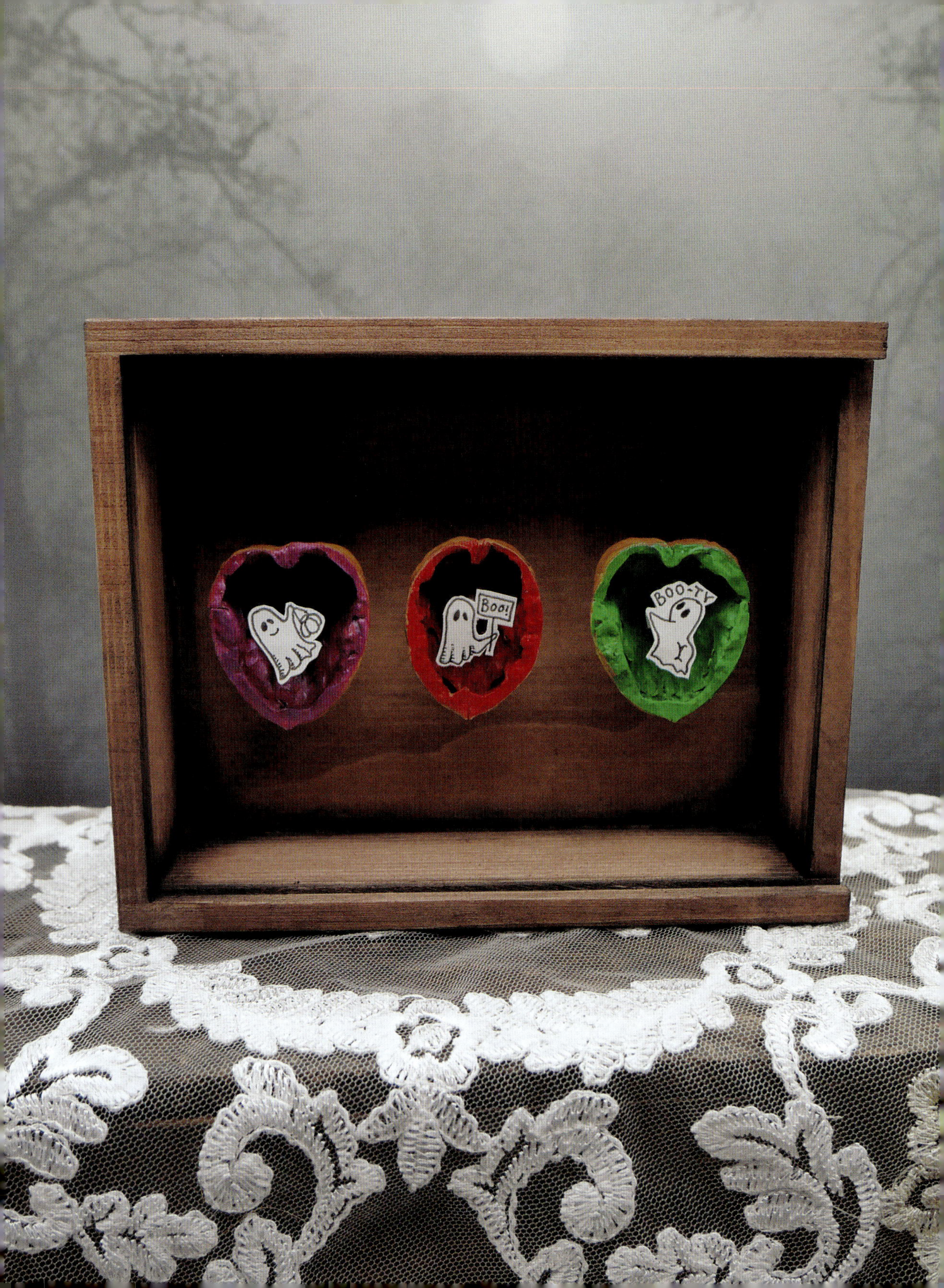
Boo!
BOO-TY

Tiny Walnut Ghosts

Warning, this project contains nuts! We're making something so nutty it will spook you right out of your shell! So, gather your walnuts and let's get cracking as we turn them into the most charming little haunts you've ever seen. *Did you like all my nutty puns?*

Tip for Cracking: Cracking walnuts down the middle can be quite tricky! If you're having issues, try using a wedge and hammer. Place your wedge along the seam and gently tap the wedge with a hammer. Go slow; it might take a few tries.

Let's set the stage for our ghosts. Paint the inside of the three walnut half shells. I went with purple, red and green, but feel free to make it your own.

(continued)

Materials

- 3 half walnut shells
- Wedge and hammer (if needed)
- Acrylic paint and brush
- Pencil
- Drawing paper
- Fine-tip pen
- X-ACTO knife
- Cutting mat
- Craft glue
- Hot glue and gun
- 6" x 4½" (15 x 11.3–cm) frame or shadow box
- Black mica powder (optional)

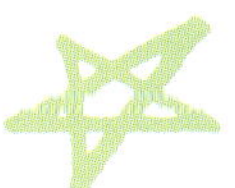

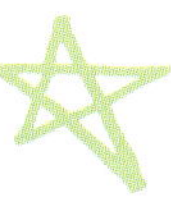

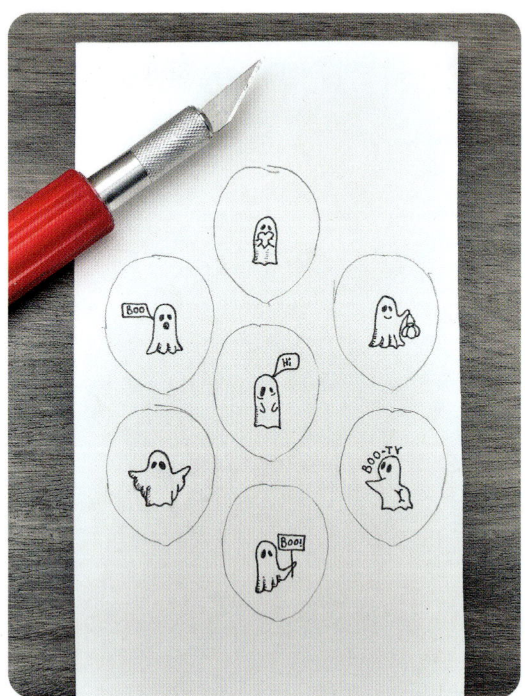

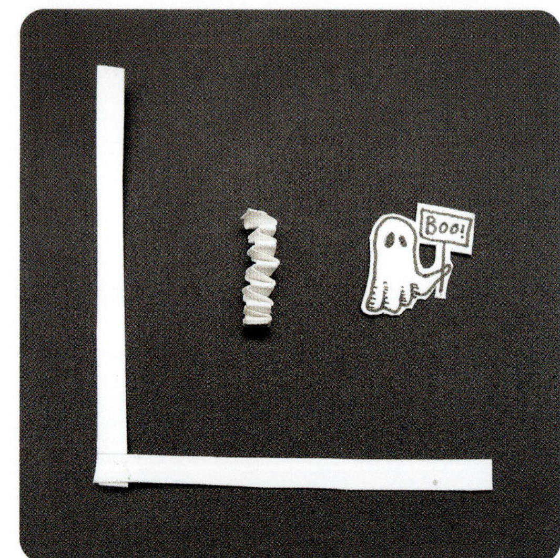

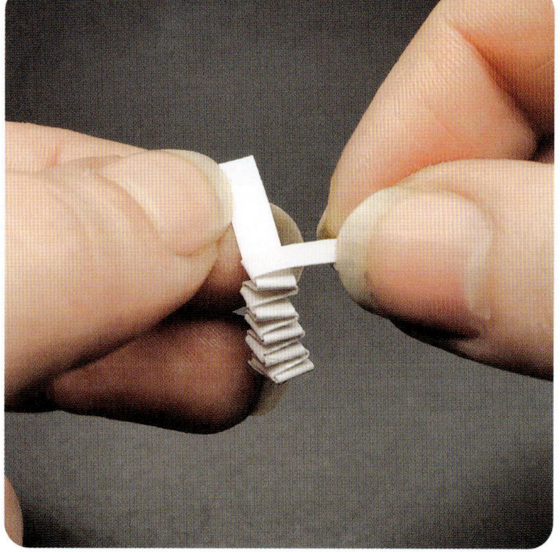

With a pencil, trace the flat side of each shell onto a piece of drawing paper. You only need to do this three times, but I got a little carried away. Draw a tiny ghost inside each of your traced shells, leaving about a ¼ inch (6 mm) of space around the edge. Trace your ghosts with a fine-tip pen. Cut out your ghosts using an X-ACTO knife and a cutting mat, leaving a small white border around each ghost.

Next, we need to make paper springs. Cut out two thin strips of drawing paper. Using craft glue, glue the ends together to make an L shape. Fold each piece accordion style. Glue the two ends together to complete your spring. Attach one of your ghosts to the end of your paper spring. Repeat this step for the remaining two ghosts. Then use craft glue to adhere your ghosts inside your painted walnuts.

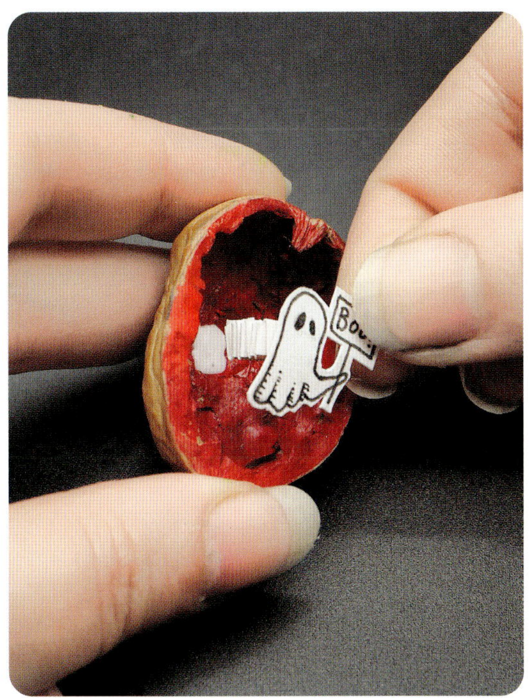

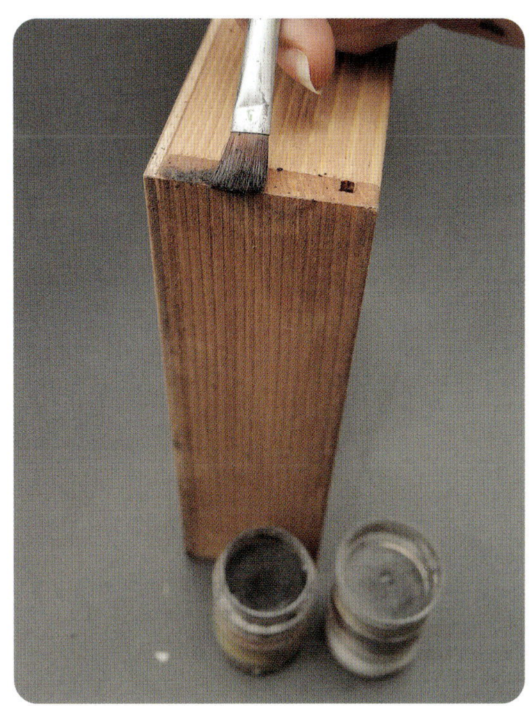

Hot glue your walnuts inside your frame, spacing them out evenly. You can use black mica powder to darken up the edges of your box to create a creepy dramatic effect.

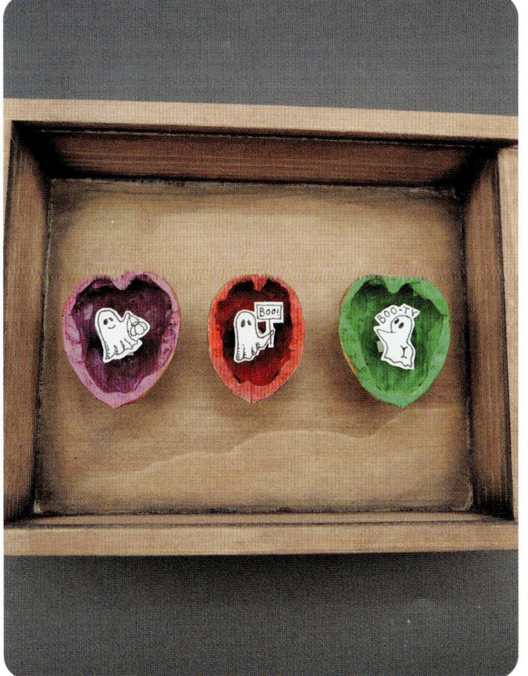

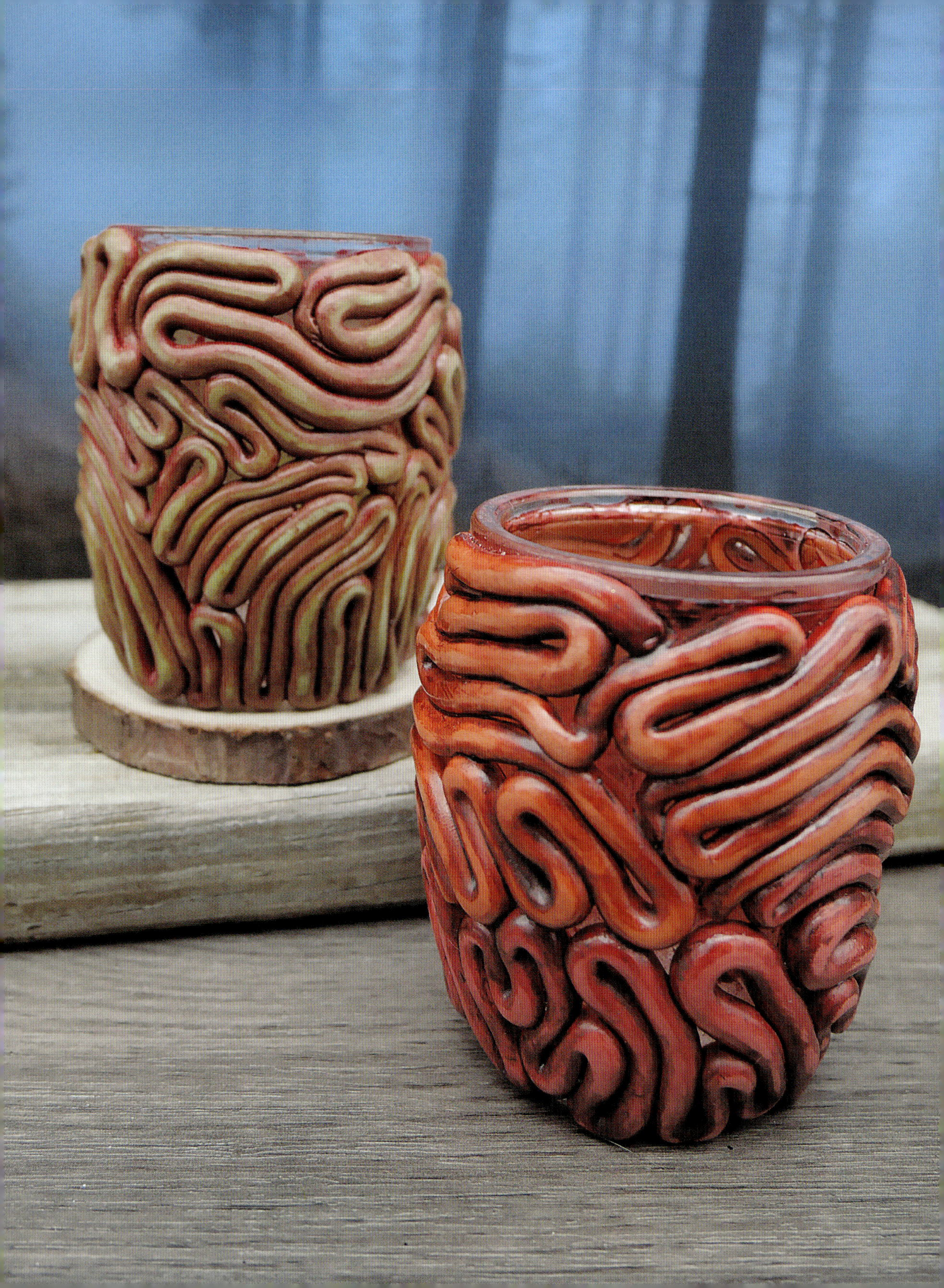

Smart Jars

This is a super easy project! It's smart not only because we're turning jars into brains but also because we're saving jars from the trash! I highly recommend using glass yogurt containers, small jelly jars or spice bottles. Reduce, reuse and recycle!

I used translucent and red polymer clay to make pink. But if you only have white, use that. You can always paint it at the end.

Roll out your polymer clay with the palms of your hands into a long rope a little thinner than a pencil. You can have multiple ropes or just one long rope. I find it easier to work with multiple small ones.

(continued)

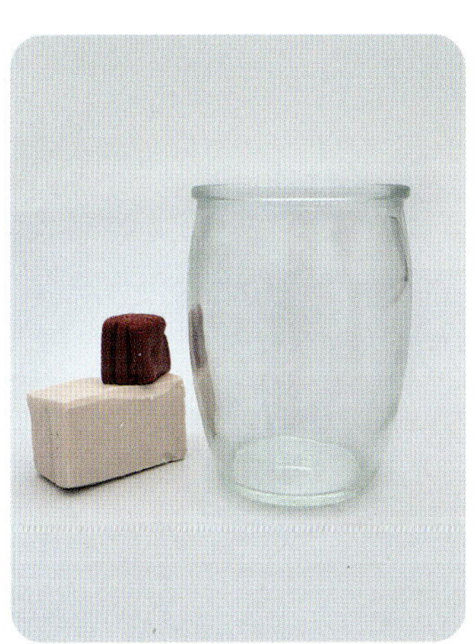

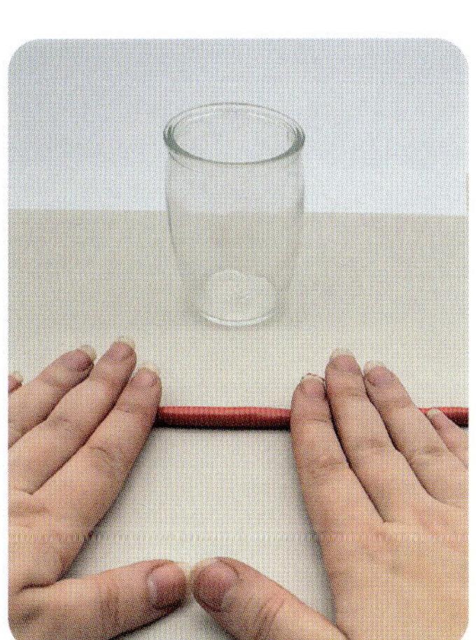

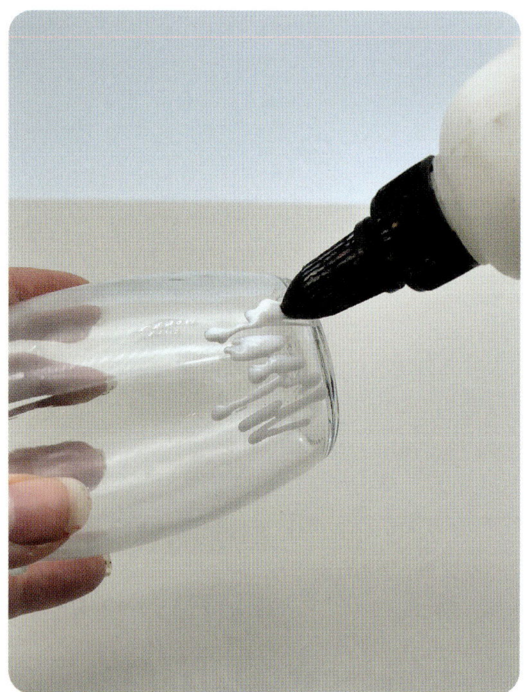

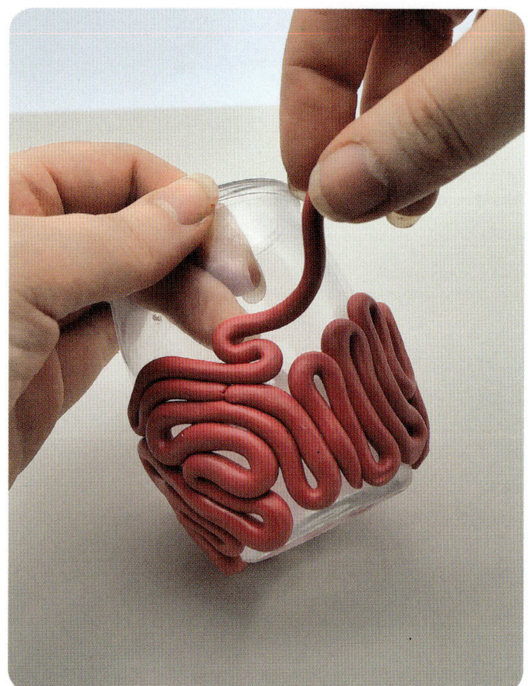

Take your clean glass jar and coat the bottom half with liquid polymer glue. Smear it around with your finger. Take your clay rope and start winding it all around the jar like a brain. Don't go all in one direction. You'll want it to twist and wind in different directions. Repeat for the top half of the jar. Bake according to the package instructions.

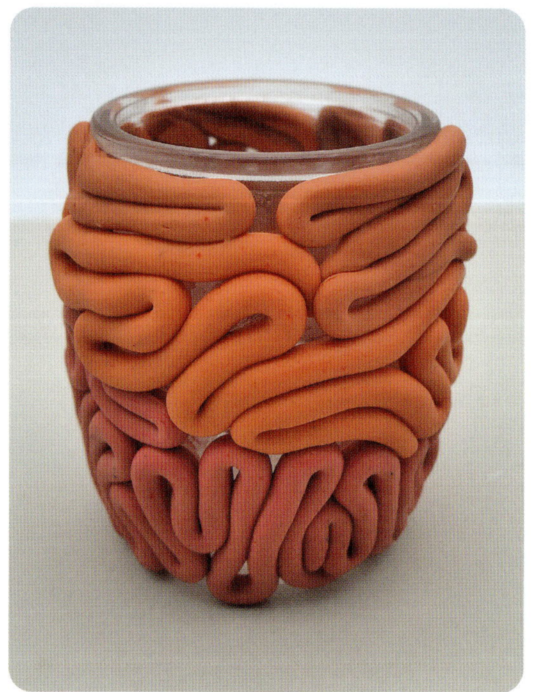

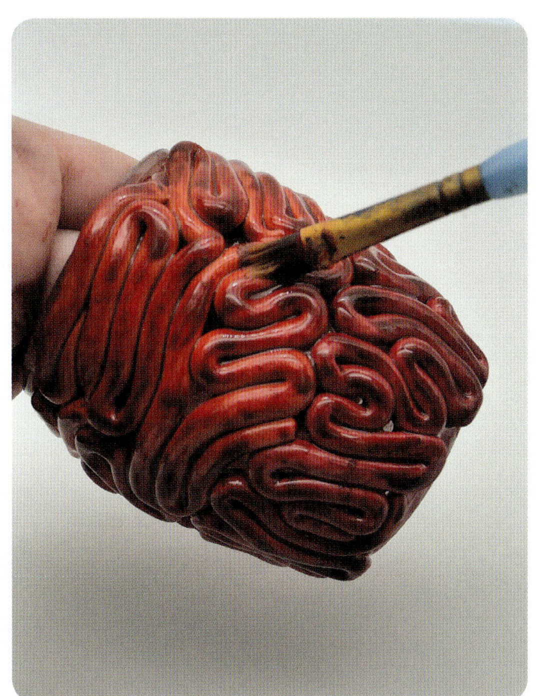

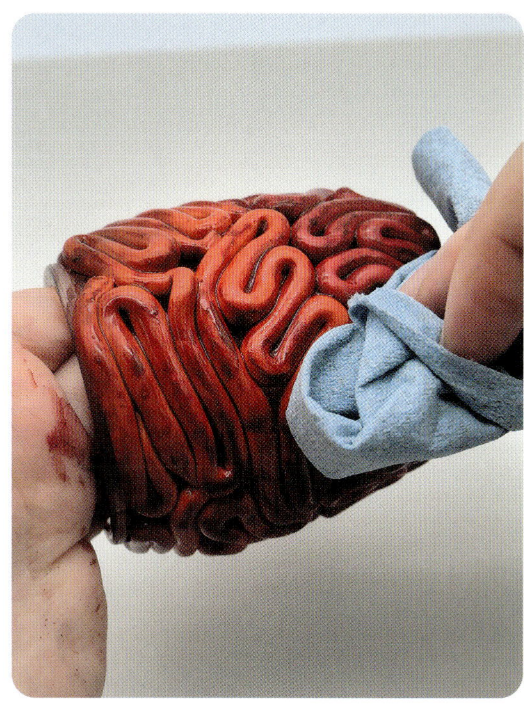

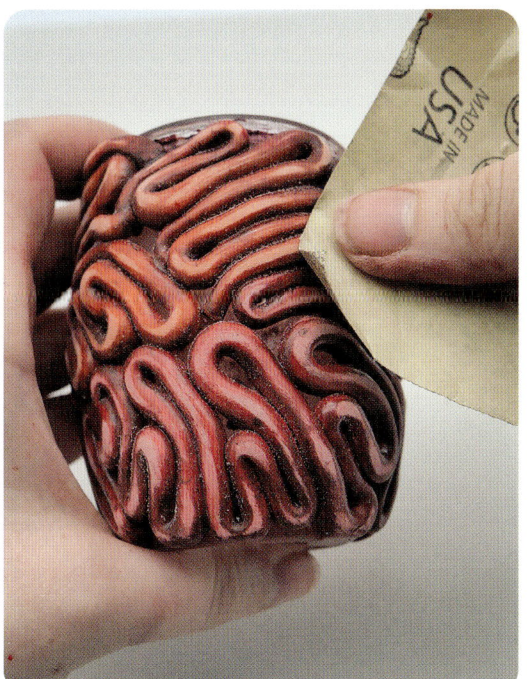

If you used white clay, paint your brain pink and let it dry before adding any more colors. Water down maroon paint and drip it into all the little holes and folds. Before the maroon dries, wipe off any excess paint that has oozed out or dripped onto the surface of the brain with a paper towel.

Let your paint dry for 10 to 30 minutes (depending on how watered down your paint was), then lightly sand the surface of the clay. We just want to reveal the color on the very tops of the folds. Wipe away any clay dust and coat your entire brain with clear polymer glaze for that fresh brain look.

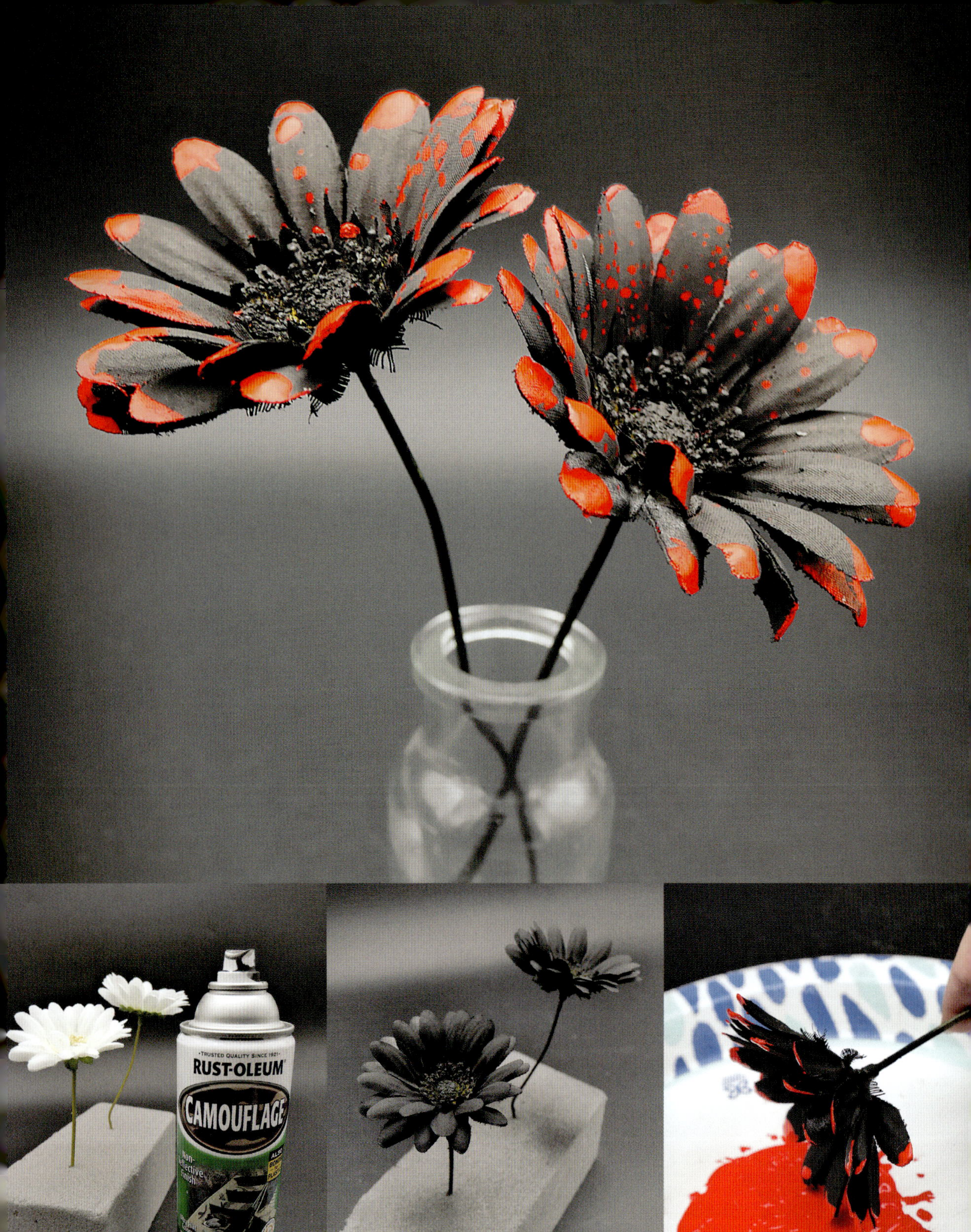

Bloody Pain-ted Flowers

Materials

- 1–4 fake flowers
- Styrofoam or floral foam
- Matte black spray paint
- Red acrylic paint
- Paper plate

Are your flowers looking too lively? Do you wish these fake flowers would just die already because they are clashing with your macabre lifestyle? That's only a little weird, but I get it.

Well, don't throw them away because we're about to paint your fake flowers! This is a rather simple way to update your décor. Say goodbye to boring and hello to creepy! I promise people will be talking about these bloody painted flowers!

Take your boring flowers and poke the stems through your Styrofoam so they are standing upright.

Spray-paint your flower petals with matte black paint. Let them dry for 10 to 30 minutes.

Add a glob of bright red paint to the center of a paper plate and dip the edges of your flower petals in. Stick your flower back in the foam to dry, 5 to 20 minutes.

Place your flowers in a glass jar or make the Rib-Vase (page 113) for that "not so fresh" look.

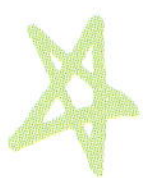

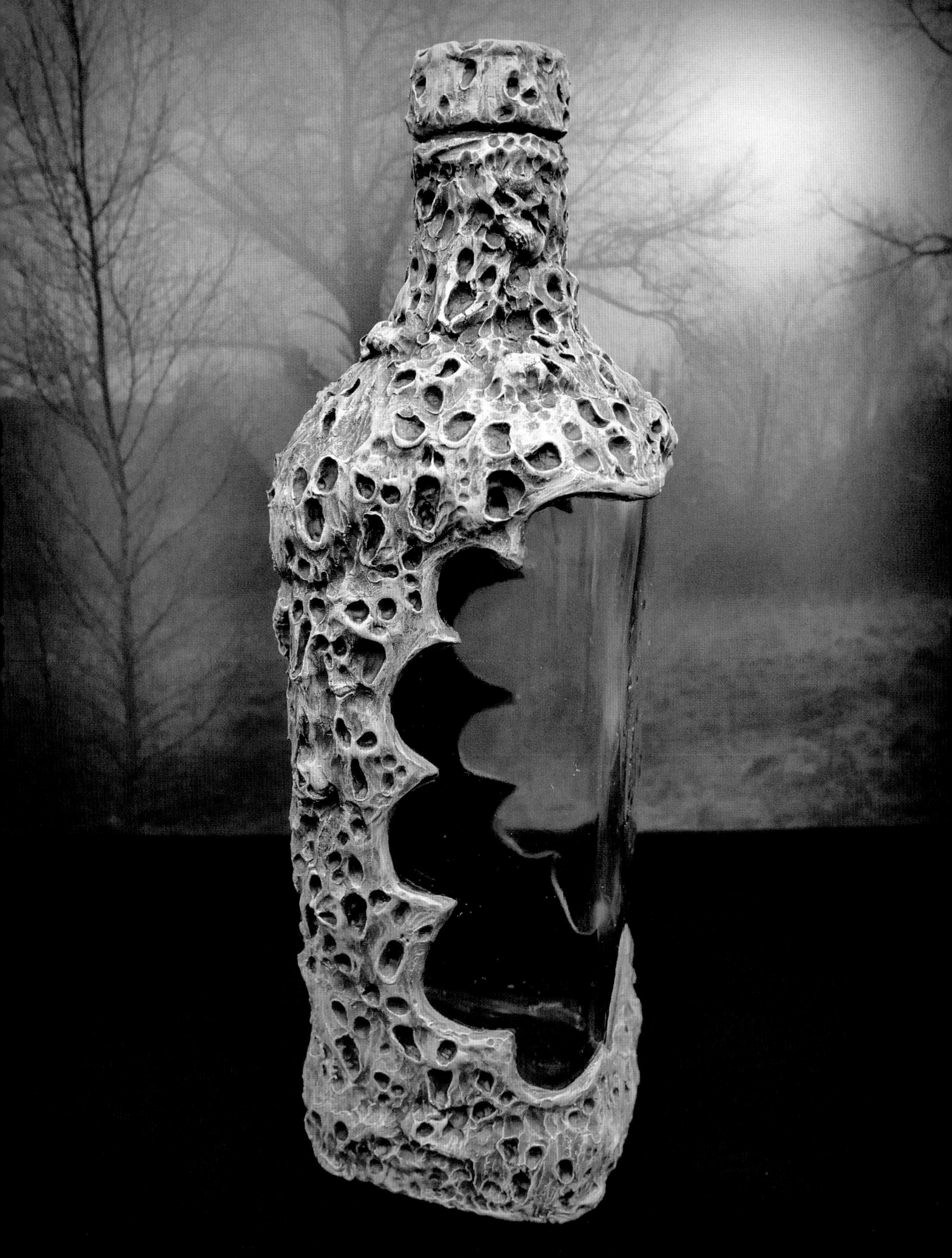

Bottle of Lost Souls

Are you looking for the perfect place to keep all your lost souls? Of course you are! After all, you're not a monster! Though, I can't help but wonder where you got so many souls. No matter! Grab a bottle, grab some clay and let's give them the home they deserve!

A little note about the materials: I used an empty liquor bottle, but as long as your bottle is clear you can use whatever bottle you like. If you don't have black epoxy clay, you can paint it black after it's hardened and then dry brush your details on. I just find the black clay makes it a whole lot easier.

Tape off three sides of your empty bottle with masking tape. Using a marker, draw a bite/flower shape on the two opposite taped sides and connect them with a straight line. Trace your drawn-on pattern with the X-ACTO knife and peel off the excess tape.

(continued)

Materials

- Clear empty bottle
- Masking tape
- Marker
- X-ACTO knife
- Black matte spray paint
- Old paintbrush
- Matte Mod Podge
- Silicone mat
- Disposable gloves
- Black epoxy clay (e.g., Apoxie Sculpt)
- Sculpting tools with round tip
- Acrylic paint and brush

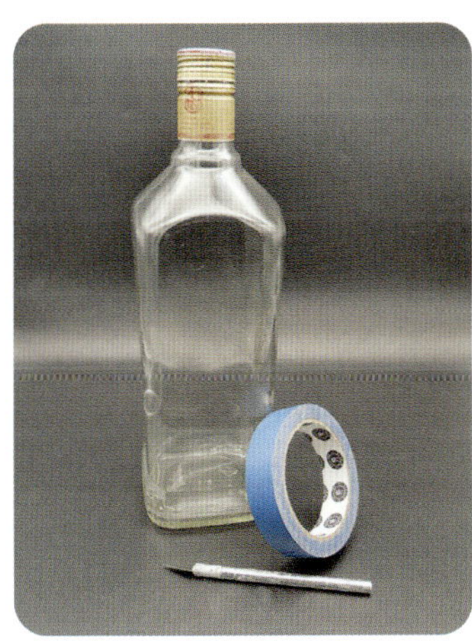
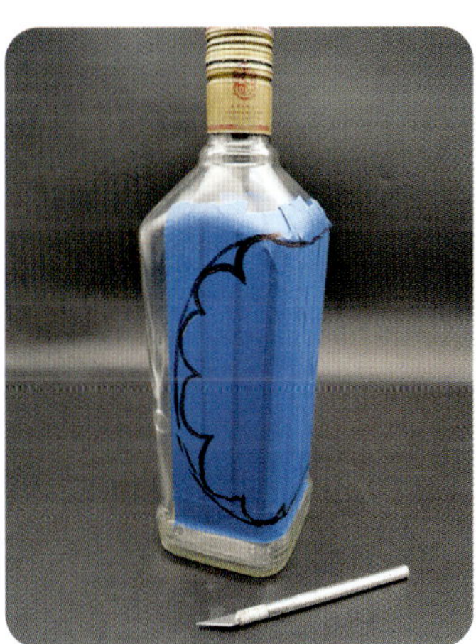
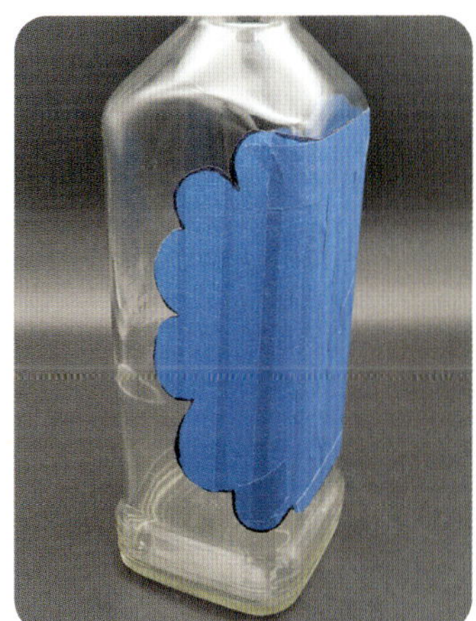

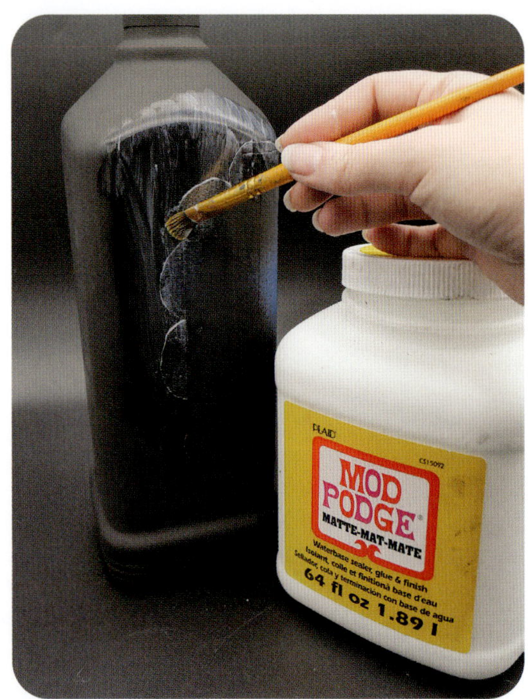

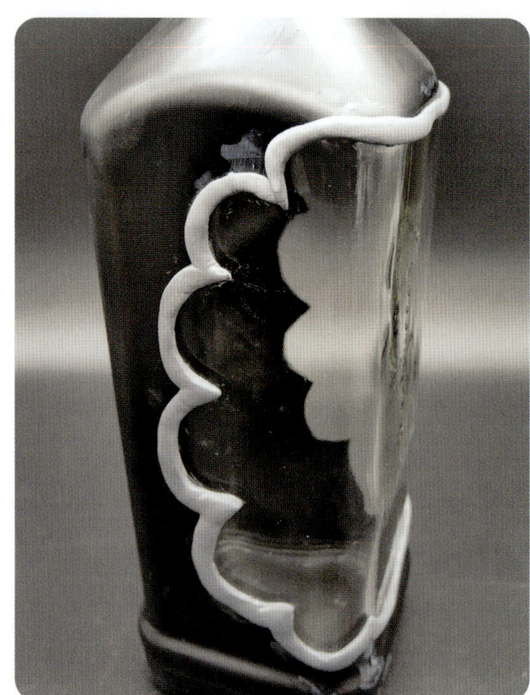

Spray-paint the entire bottle with black matte paint and wait for it to dry, usually around 10 minutes.

Using an old paintbrush, paint over all of the black spray paint with matte Mod Podge and peel off your tape. *You now have a super cool window in your bottle.*

Lay down your silicone mat and put on your gloves. Mix together a golf ball–sized amount of black epoxy clay and roll out a long, skinny rope not quite as thick as a pencil. Trace the outside of your bottle "window" with your clay rope.

Next, we're going to make small faces on your bottle. You'll want to mix clay as you go in golf ball–sized amounts because if you mix too much clay, it will harden before you're finished sculpting.

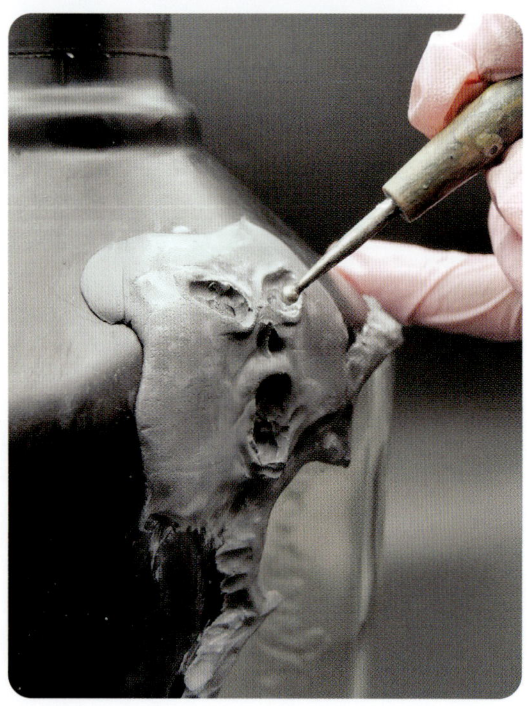

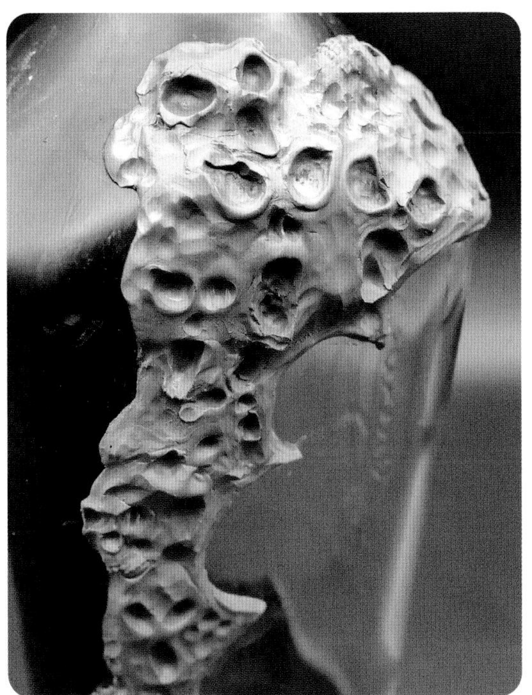

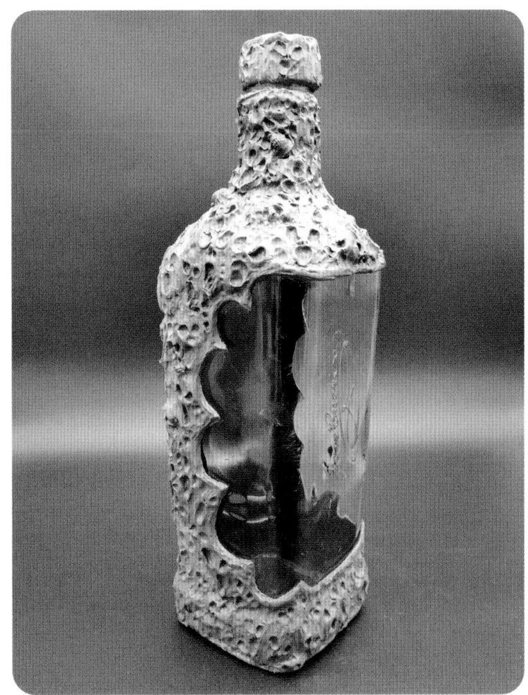

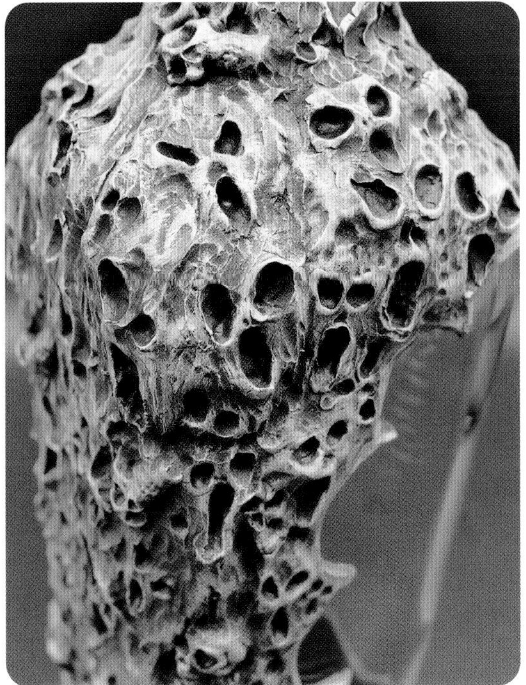

Flatten out a half dollar–sized disk of clay and press it onto the painted side of your bottle. Using your round-tipped sculpting tools, sculpt a crude screaming face. *Don't add too much detail, we're just looking for two eyes and a mouth. On some of them you can add two nostril holes, but don't go crazy. I promise no one will notice.*

Keep adding more and more faces until the entire black side of your bottle is covered. Let sit overnight to harden.

Dry brush light gray acrylic paint on all the little details. Dry brushing is when you take a dry paintbrush, dip the tip into paint and lightly sweep it over the surface.

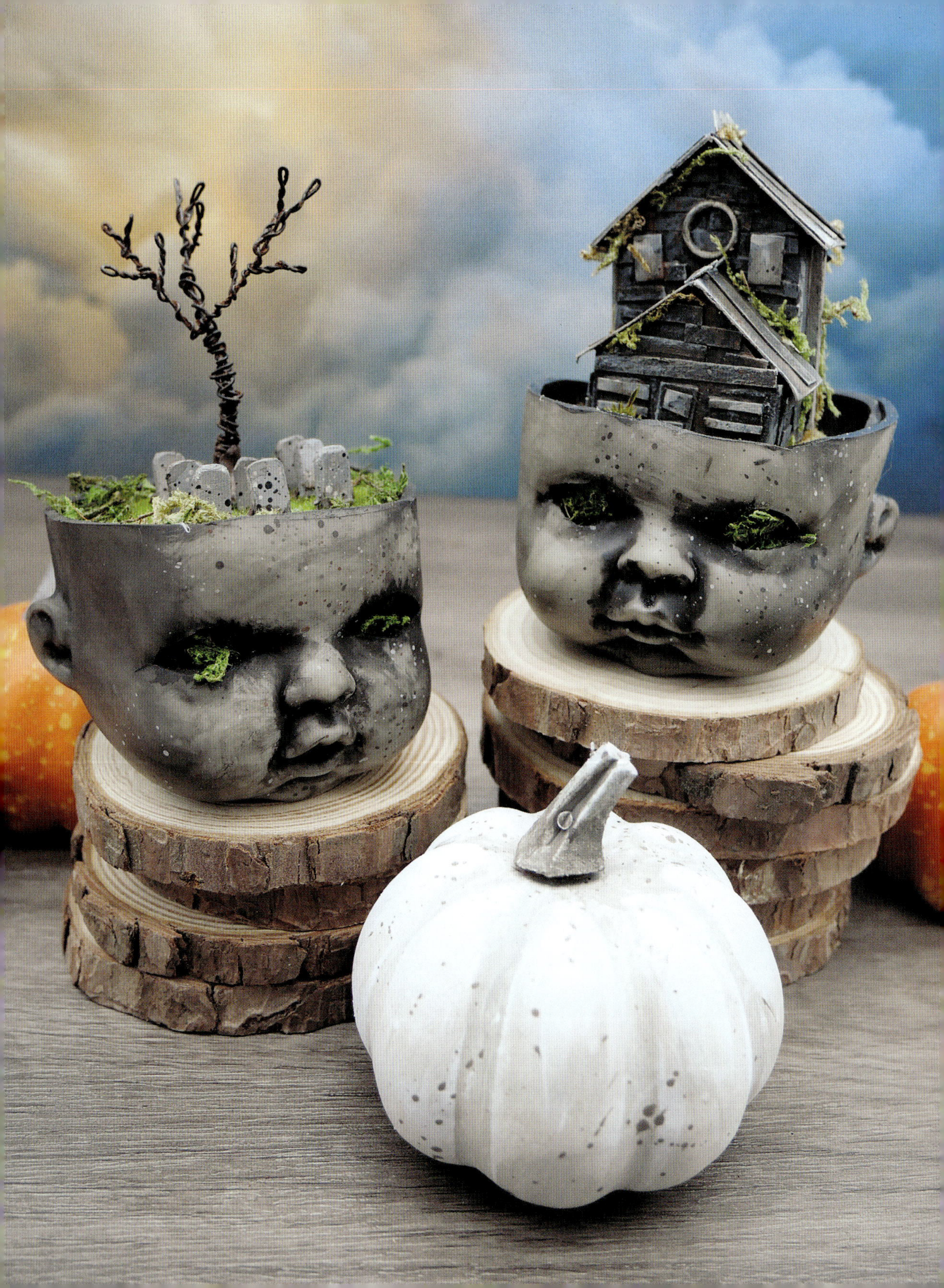

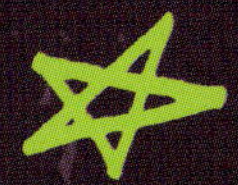

Macabre Miniatures

Get ready, we're diving into the world of macabre miniatures, where we'll craft itty-bitty cursed or magical (take your pick) creations! Try your hand at a tiny fairy mortuary encapsulated in glass bottles, a minuscule witch's station complete with all the clutter essential for spell casting or the tiniest (probably not haunted) dollhouse inside a doll's head! What more could you ask for? It's tiny, it's cursed and it's awesome!

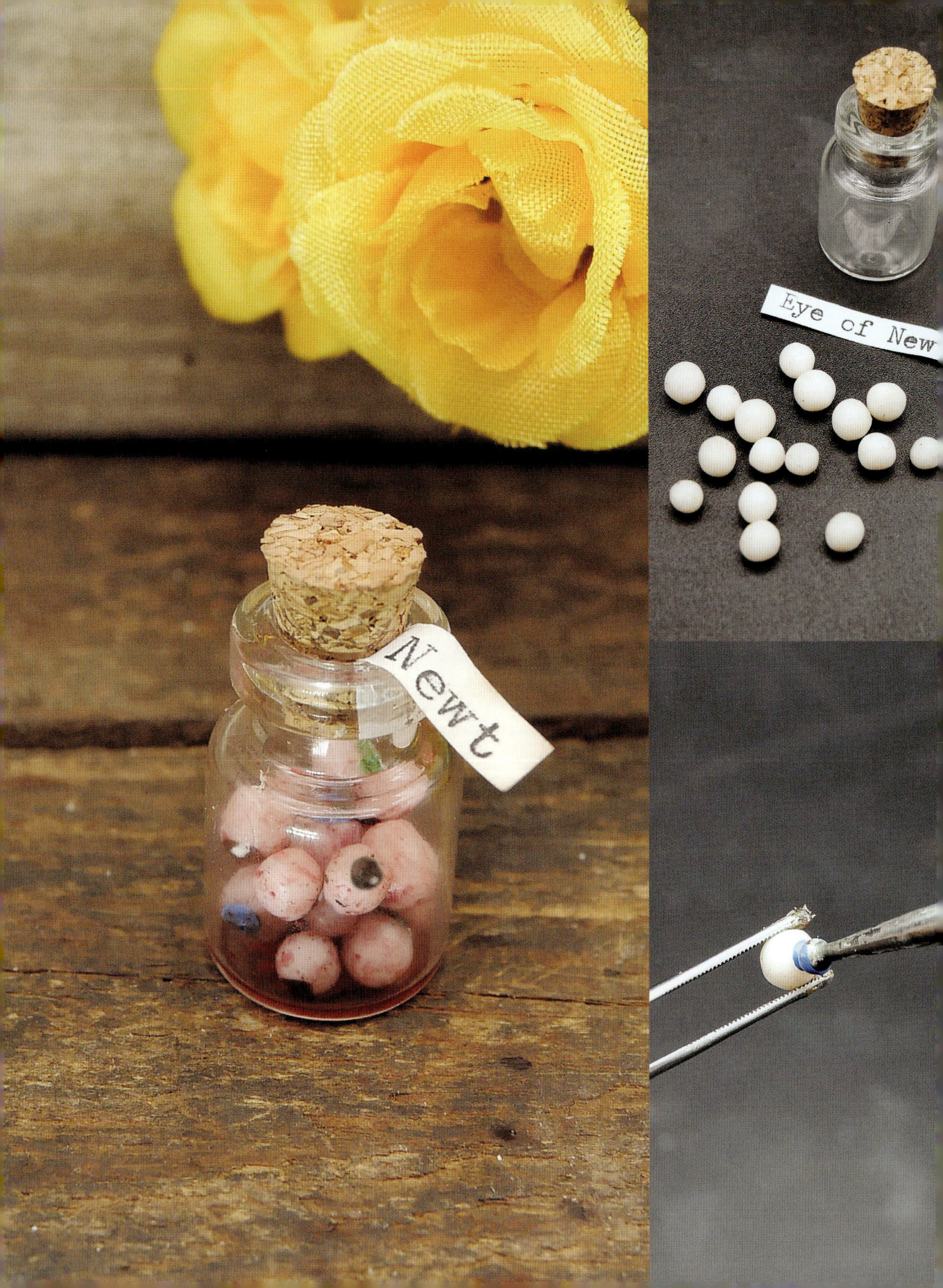
Eye of New
Newt

Eye of Newt

Ever wonder what the heck "eye of newt" is? I know, it sounds like some fancy ingredient witches use in the movies, maybe made of lizard's eyes? Well, you're not wrong, but hey, we don't have to stick to boring lizard eyes here. Let's make up our own story. Maybe it's the eyes of that tiny fairy who overcharged for fairy dust that one time when we were in a pinch (never forget!). Whatever story you come up with will make your eyes more personal to you, and you'll have a great story to tell people who ask WAY too many questions.

Take your polymer clay (preferably translucent but white works too) and roll tiny peppercorn-sized balls. The size of your glass bottle will determine how many you'll want to make. Err on the side of more because you *will* lose a few while trying to paint them. Bake according to the package instructions.

Grasp one of your balls with tweezers (ouch). Dip a medium-sized round-tipped sculpting tool in blue paint and dab it in the middle of your ball. Blow on it to dry the paint so you don't smear it when you set it down. Alternate between blue, green and brown paint. Once you have a pile of eyeballs, add black to the center. If you find adding black too tedious, you can skip this part. They still read as eyeballs in your jar even without irises.

Mix together red acrylic paint and polymer glaze and coat your eyeballs with the mixture. Add this mixture to the bottom of your bottle as well. Add your eyes to your glass bottle.

If you have a typewriter, that's great; if not, just use a pen. Type out the word "Newt" on a piece of paper and cut it out. Tuck one end of your paper strip inside your glass bottle next to the cork.

Materials

- ¼ oz (7 g) translucent or white polymer clay
- Tweezers
- Sculpting tools with round tip
- Acrylic paint and brush
- Polymer glaze
- Mini corked glass bottle about 1" (2.5 cm) tall
- Typewriter or pen
- Paper
- Scissors

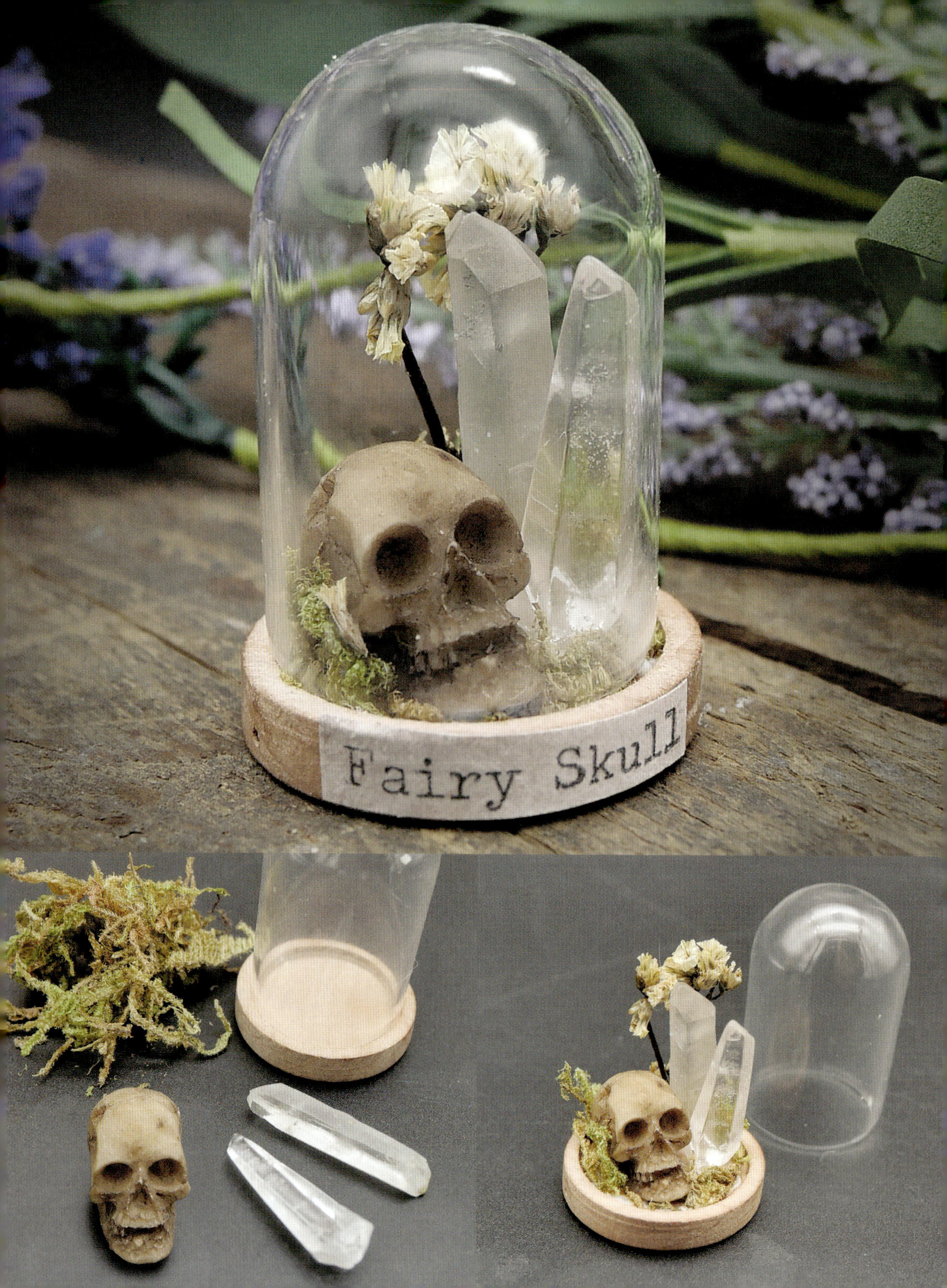

Fairy Skull

Fairy Skull

Aha! Remember when we made those tiny eyeballs in the last project (page 175)? Of course you do, it was just on the last page … Well, in this project, we're proudly displaying the skull of that pesky fairy who thought it was fine charging two crystals when we only had one! The joke's on her because she now has her crystals for all to see under a tiny cloche along with her head. Am I going too far with this weird story? Yup! But that's the fun of it! Also, how amazing will this fairy skull look next to the eyeballs? It'll be pretty sweet.

Hot glue your skull and two crystals under your tiny cloche. Make sure you can still easily close it.

Using precision craft glue, glue moss and/or dried flowers around the skull and crystals. *You don't want to use hot glue on moss because it can destroy moss and make it brittle.* Go ahead and close your cloche once you have it looking good. You may need to stuff some of the moss under the glass as you close it. If you like, you can glue it shut using a little craft glue, but I just left mine unglued in case I ever want to change it out.

Type or write the words "Fairy Skull" on a piece of paper and cut them out. Using craft glue, adhere your paper to the bottom of your cloche.

Materials

- Hot glue and gun
- ½" (1.3 cm) skull
- Two 1" (2.5 cm) quartz crystals
- 2" (5 cm) glass cloche
- Precision craft glue (e.g., Bearly Art)
- Moss and/or dried flowers
- Typewriter or pen
- Paper
- Scissors

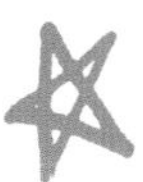

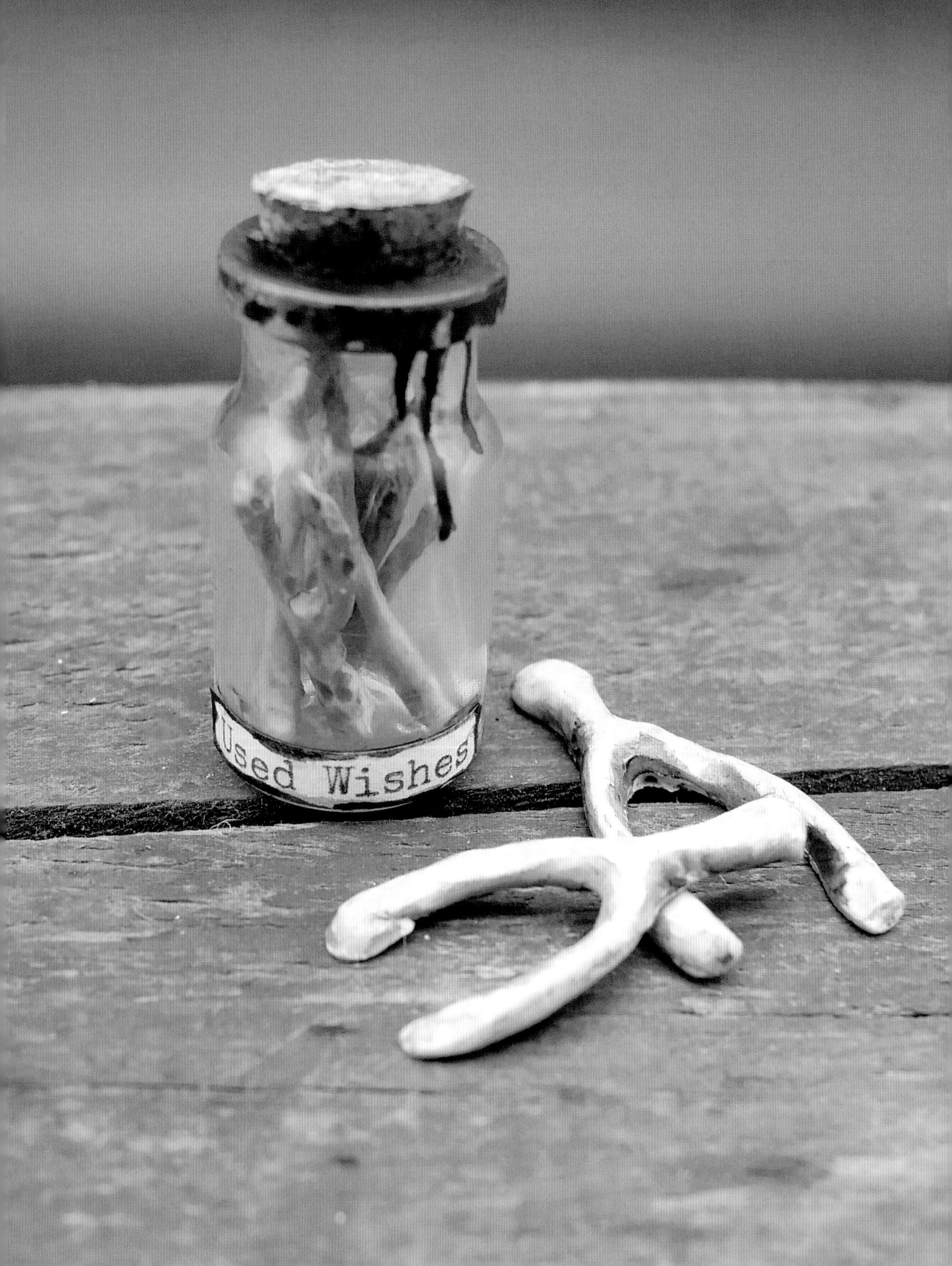
Used Wishes

Used Wishes

Is taking a fairy's wishbone going too far? Depends on what they did. I mean, if they are jacking up the prices on fairy dust when they know I need it, then maybe they have it coming. Just saying . . . In this project, we'll be crafting itty-bitty wishbones you can stash in a bottle, right next to that Fairy Skull (page 177) and Eye of Newt (page 175) you made in the previous projects. It'll be like a mini fairy museum right on your shelf. Or did I mean to say mausoleum?

Materials

- ¼ oz (7 g) white polymer clay
- Sculpting tools with round tip or silicone point
- Acrylic paint and brush
- Paper towels
- Typewriter or pen
- Paper
- Scissors
- Precision craft glue (e.g., Bearly Art)
- Mini corked glass bottle 2" (5 cm) tall

Roll out a long cylinder of polymer clay shorter than the height of your mini corked glass bottle. Use a round-tipped or silicone-point sculpting tool to texture your bones by running it up and down the length. Squish the ends to make them slightly thicker and bake according to the package instructions.

Water down brown acrylic paint and paint your bones, wiping off any excess paint with a paper towel. We're just looking to stain them a bit because clean bones would be boring.

Type or write the words "Used Wishes" on a piece of paper and cut them out. Using craft glue, adhere your paper to the bottom of your bottle.

Place the bones into your mini corked glass bottle and close it with the cork. On the outside of the bottle paint dark brown drip marks coming out of the opening down the sides of your bottle. Outline the label with the same color to make your label appear dirty.

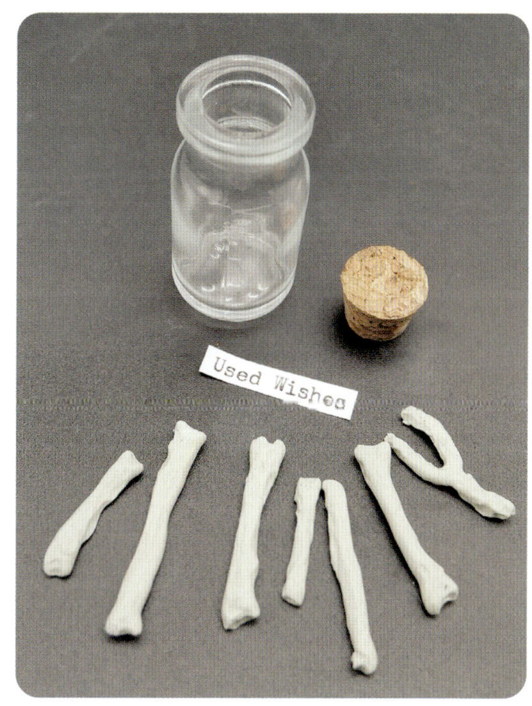

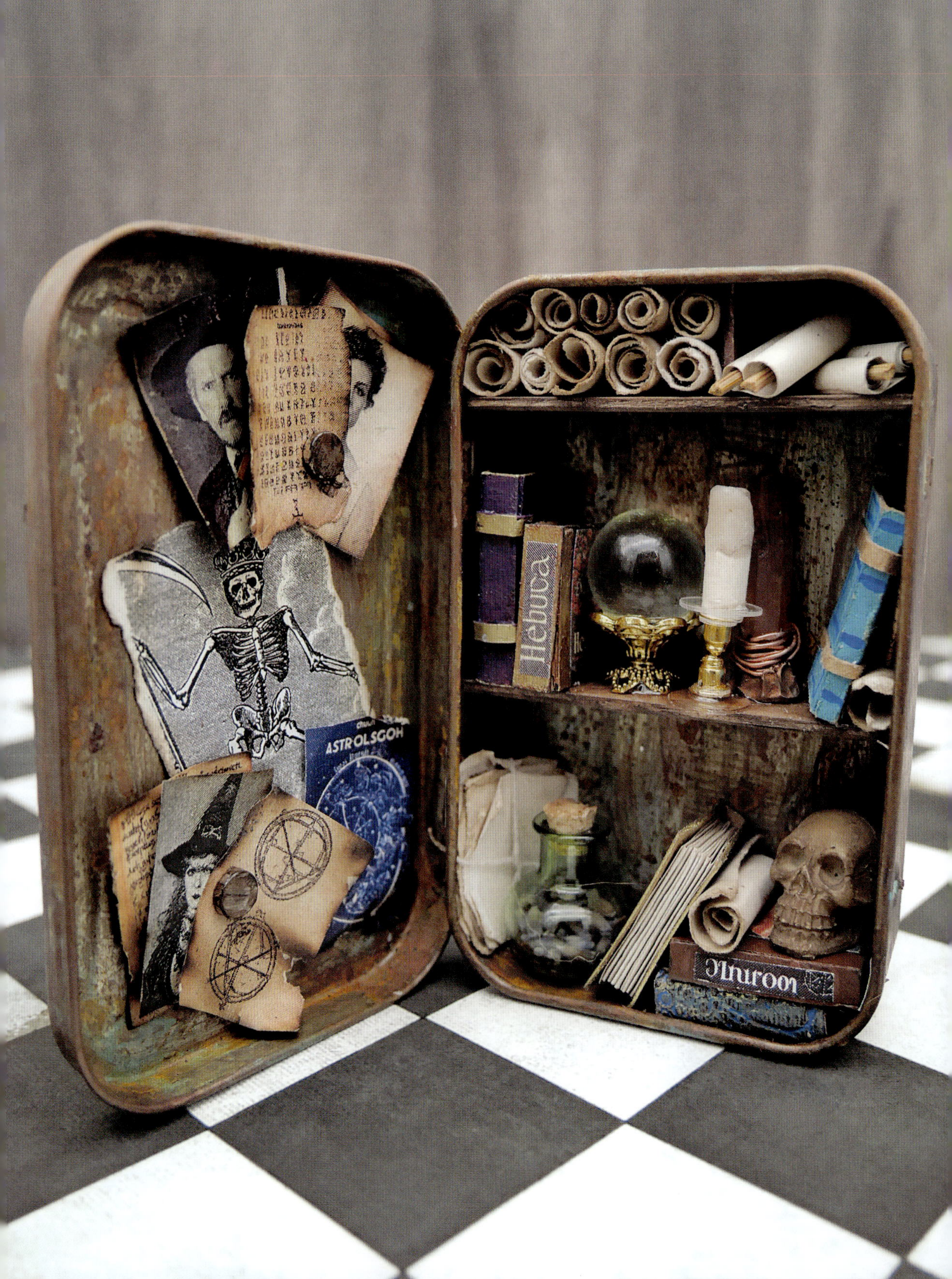

The Witch's Station

This project is designed to make the teeny tiny witch within you cackle with delight! Because even the tiniest witches deserve a cozy little station to conjure their potions. This station comes equipped with a cabinet, spell books, crystal ball and witchy documents. I guess even the tiniest witches can't escape tiny magical paperwork!

The Cabinet

Where your witch will keep all her goodies.

Sand the Altoids tin inside and out. We want to remove some of the paint and rough it up a bit.

Paint the entire tin with Swellegant copper metal coating and let it dry, 5 to 30 minutes. Paint over the copper with Swellegant patina. After a few hours this will start to age the copper color and make it look rusty. Once you're happy with the amount of patina, clear coat it with matte Mod Podge.

Let's install some shelving! Using an X-ACTO knife, cut two small shelves out of balsa wood to fit inside your tin. You may need to sand the edges a little to make it fit. Paint your shelves chocolate brown and secure them with super glue.

Materials

- Sandpaper
- Altoids tin
- Paintbrush
- Swellegant copper metal coating
- Swellegant patina
- Matte Mod Podge
- X-ACTO knife
- Balsa wood
- Acrylic paint
- Super glue

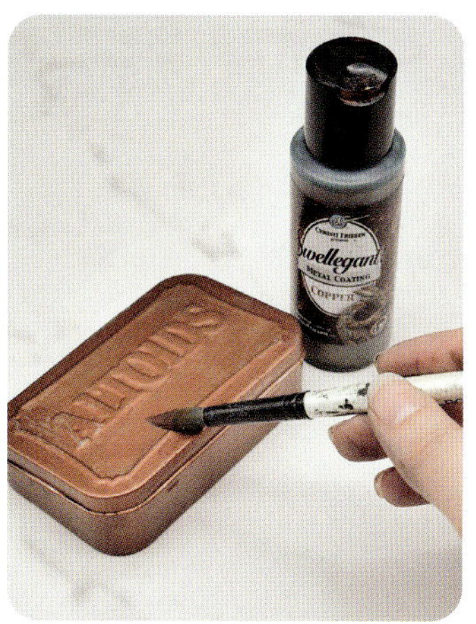

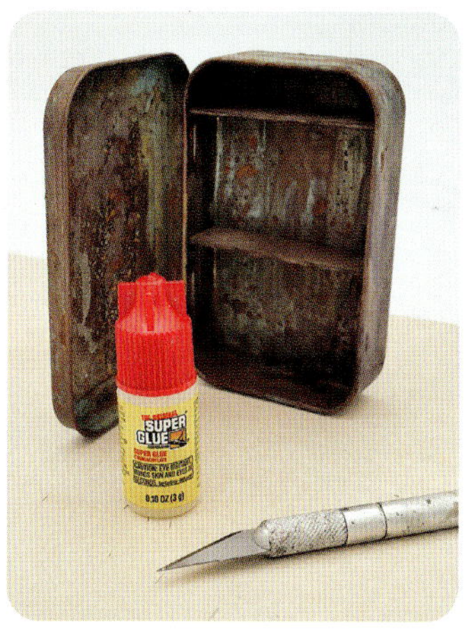

Tiny Library

Every witch has a spell book! Let's give her a library of spell books!

Put a sheet of white paper in a baking pan and pour in your strong brewed coffee. Let this sit for 5 to 10 minutes and pull it out. Lay it flat on a hard, nonporous surface and let it dry for 24 hours.

> **Tip:** Only put one sheet in the pan at a time. If you do multiple, they will stick together.

Cut a ¾-inch (2-cm)-wide strip off the long side of your coffee-stained paper, and accordion fold the strip in ½-inch (1.3-cm) intervals.

Materials

- White paper
- Baking pan
- 1 cup (240 ml) strong brewed coffee
- Scissors
- X-ACTO knife
- Chipboard
- Craft glue
- Chip clip
- Acrylic paint and brush

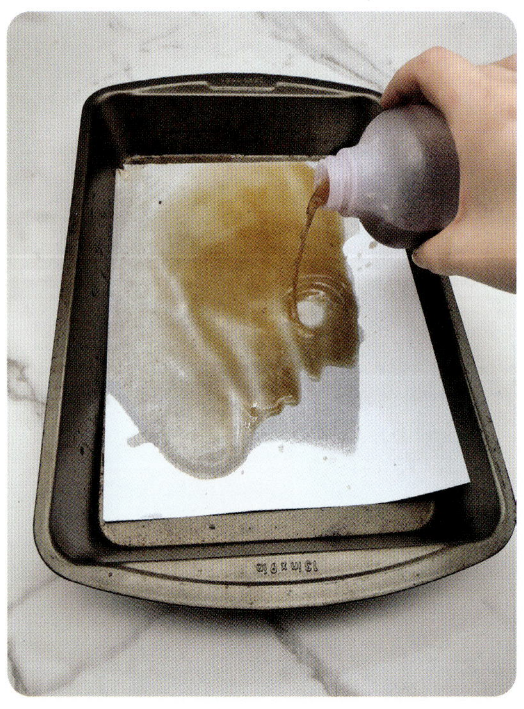

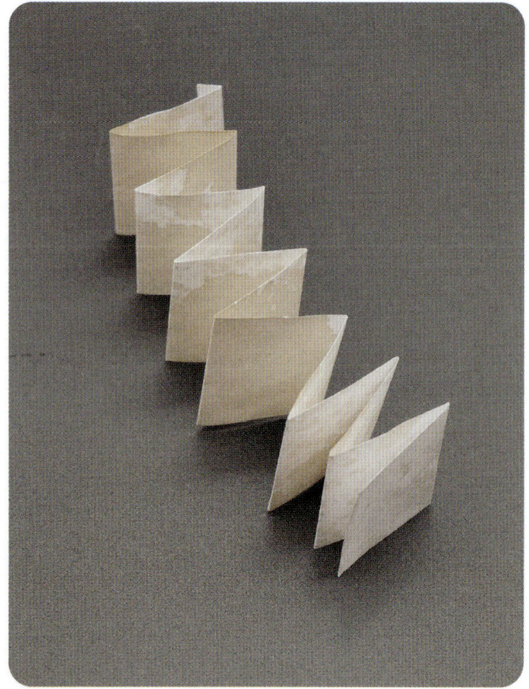

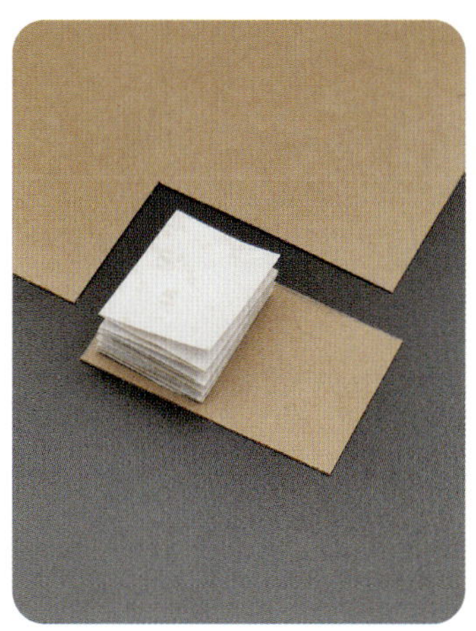 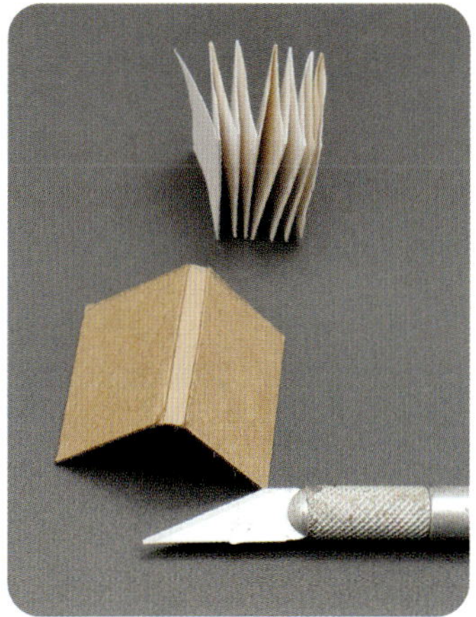 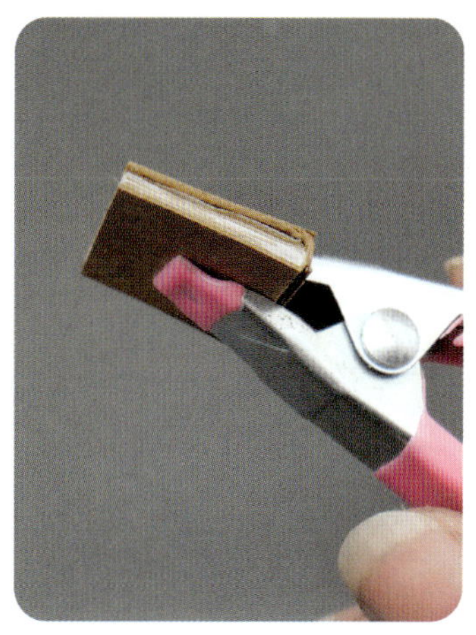

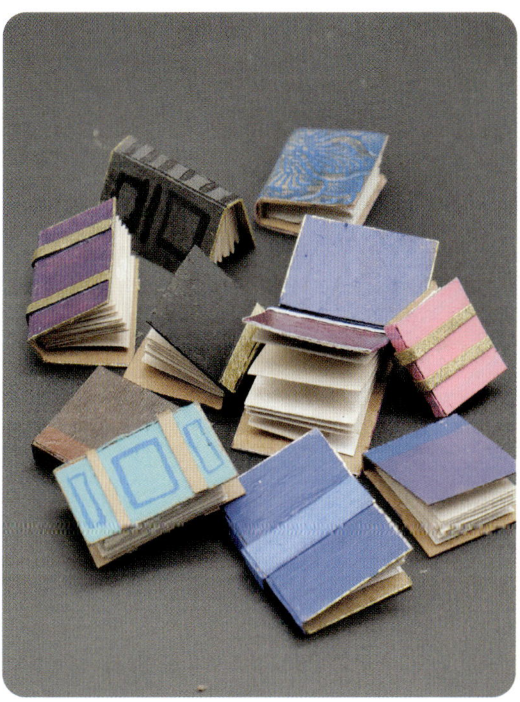

With an X-ACTO knife, cut a 1½ x 1–inch (3.8 x 2.5–cm) rectangle out of chipboard. Score two lines in the center back of the chipboard about ⅛ inch (3 mm) apart. This is for the book spine. Fold the flaps to make the book cover.

Use craft glue to adhere the accordion-folded pages onto the spine of the chipboard and clamp it all together with a chip clip. Wait 10 to 15 minutes to dry.

Paint the covers on your books to give them style. Or print some covers out and glue them on.

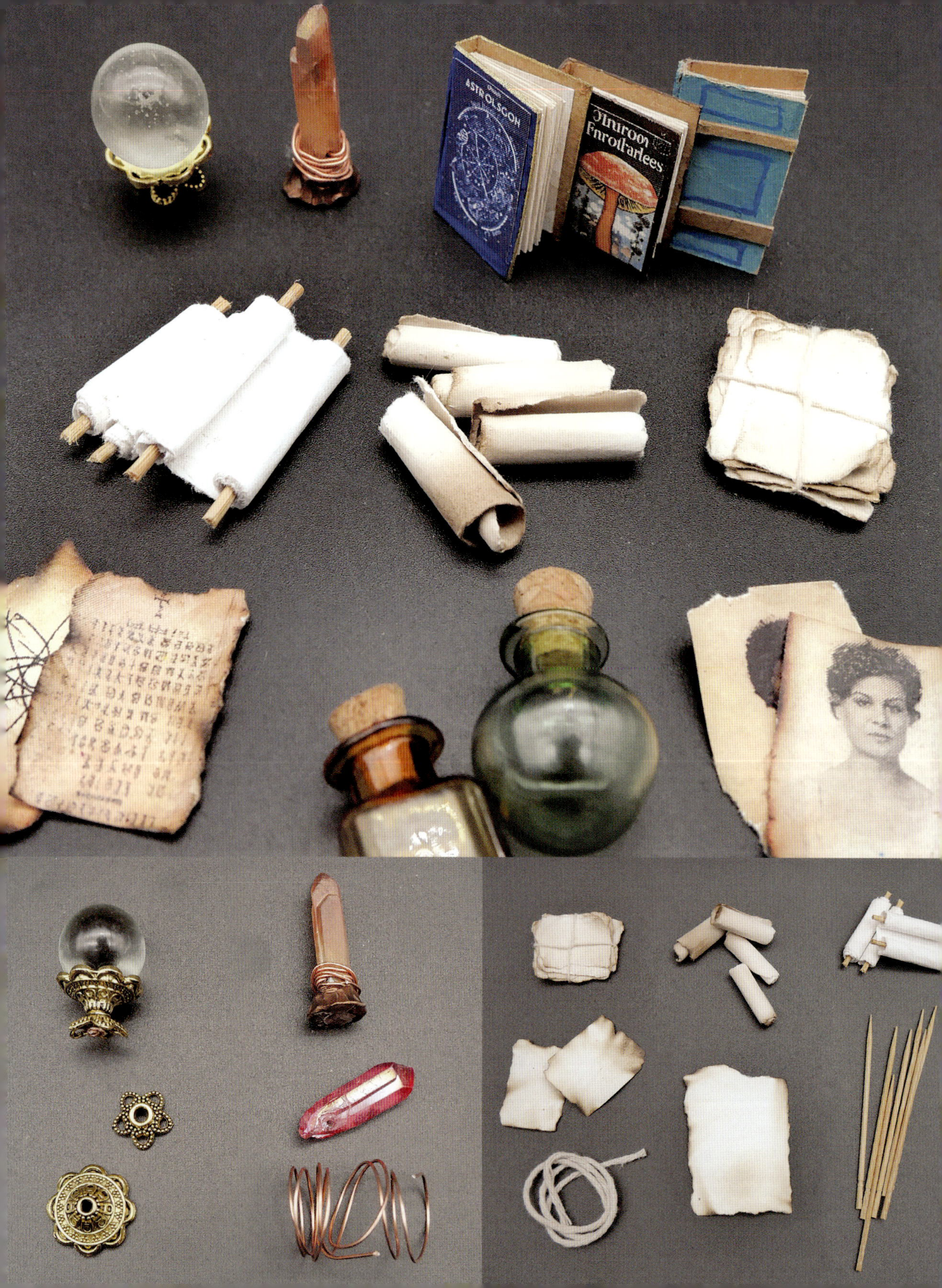

Witchy Clutter

Everyone has clutter, and the most magical clutter is witchy clutter!

Crystal Ball

To make a crystal ball, super glue the holes of two bead caps together. Allow to dry for 30 minutes. Then super glue a clear marble inside one of the bead caps. BAM! Super easy crystal ball!

Crystal Statue

Wrap a small amount of floral wire around the bottom of the quartz bead, feeding it through the hole. Sculpt a small amount of clay to the bottom and shape it so the bead sits up straight. Bake according to the package directions. Paint the clay brown or bronze.

Scrolls

Rip ½-inch (1.3-cm)-wide strips of paper. Wrap the short ends of the paper strip around two toothpicks and glue in place. Roll it up like a scroll. Trim the toothpicks with wire cutters. Alternatively, you can roll without the toothpicks to create single rolled scrolls.

Stacks of Paper

Rip small sheets of paper roughly ¾ x 1 inch (2 x 2.5 cm) and carefully burn the edges with a candle. Tie together with string to make a stack of important witchy documents.

Materials

- Super glue
- 2 bead caps
- Clear marble

- 5" (12.7 cm) of floral wire
- 1" (2.5-cm) quartz crystal with hole
- ¼ oz (7 g) polymer clay
- Acrylic paint and brush

- Paper
- 2 toothpicks
- Precision craft glue (e.g., Bearly Art)
- Wire cutters

- Paper
- Candle
- String

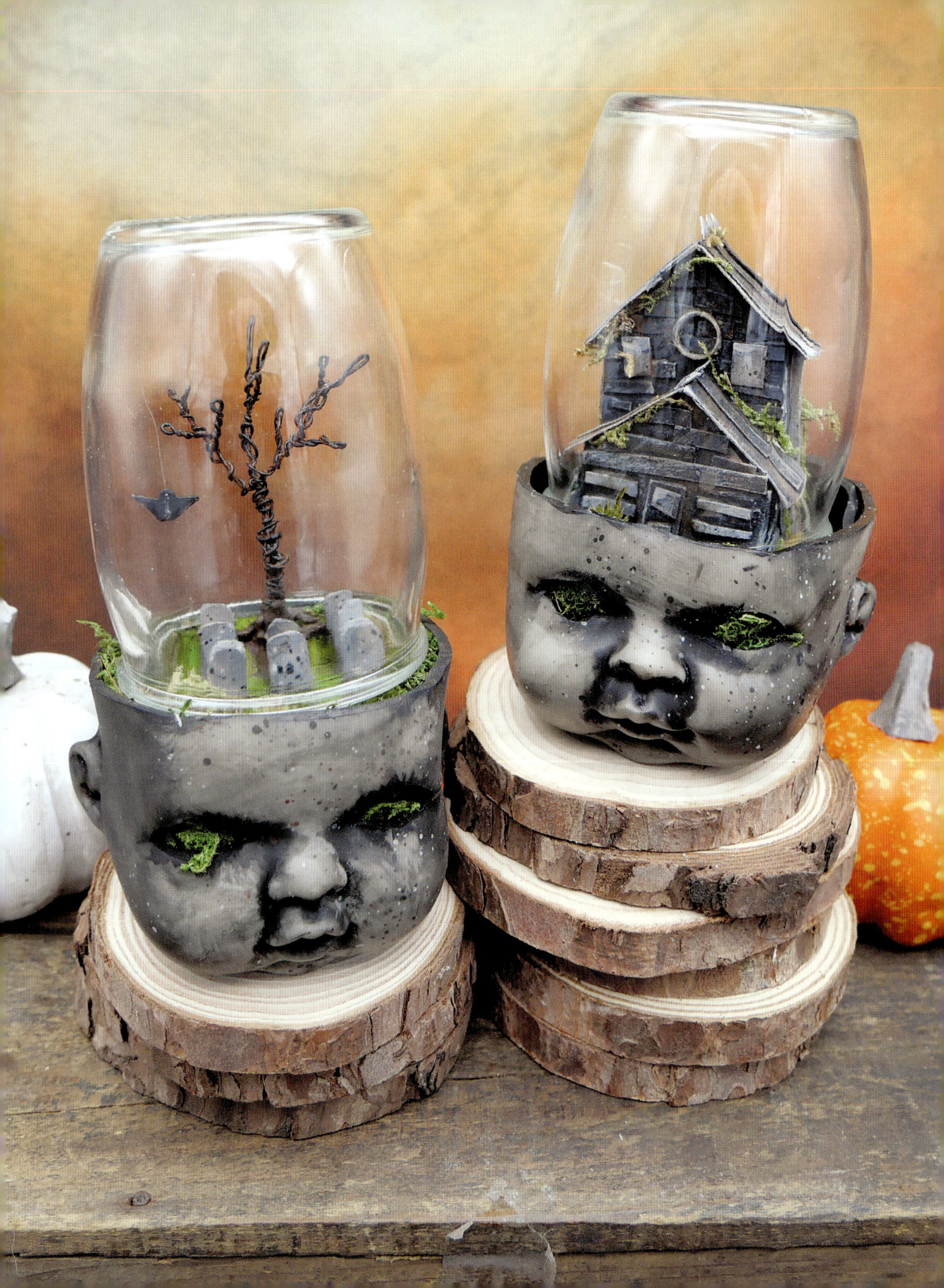

Disturbing Dollhouse

Have you ever found a random doll head? If so, it's probably not haunted or anything, so don't even worry about it! This project is a lot like the previous Haunted House project (page 149), only on a much smaller scale, inside a toootally *NOT HAUNTED* doll's head.

Using masking tape, tape a circle around the very top of your doll head near the hairline. This will serve as your cutting guide. Hold your doll head tightly, because you don't want it escaping! Using an X-ACTO knife, carefully cut along the edge of the masking tape. If your doll doesn't have eyeholes, use the X-ACTO knife to cut those out too.

Paint the bottom portion of your doll head with black acrylic paint. Use a paper towel to wipe away any excess paint, creating an aged look. Paint the top head piece green. Paint both insides solid black. Set aside to dry.

(continued)

Materials

- Masking tape
- Doll head about 3" (7.5 cm)
- X-ACTO knife
- Acrylic paint and brush
- Paper towels
- 1 small sheet of balsa wood
- Tacky craft glue
- Paper
- Grass flocking
- 2 small matchboxes
- Hot glue and gun
- Embellishments (optional)
- Moss
- Aluminum foil
- Small glass jar (optional)

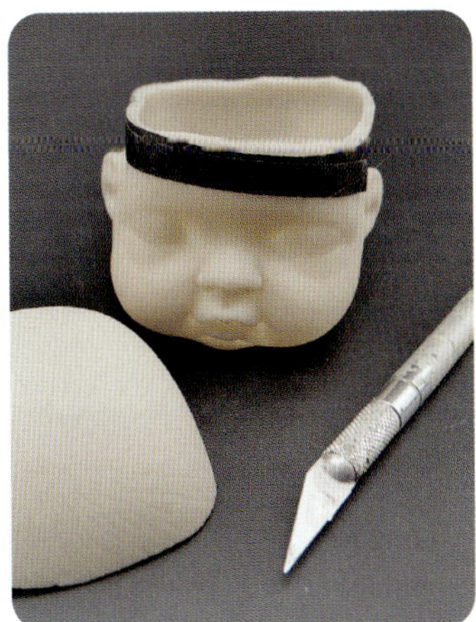

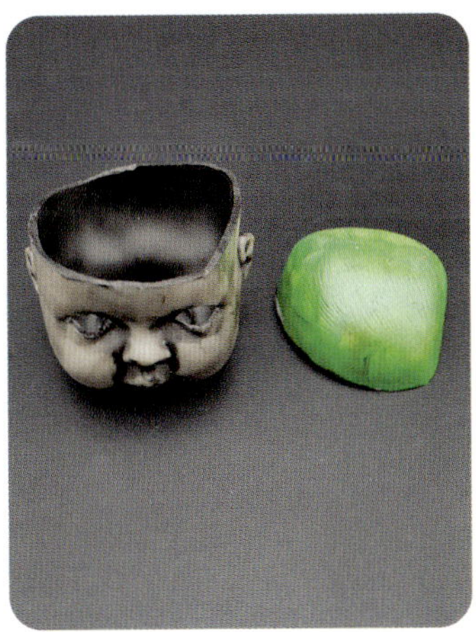

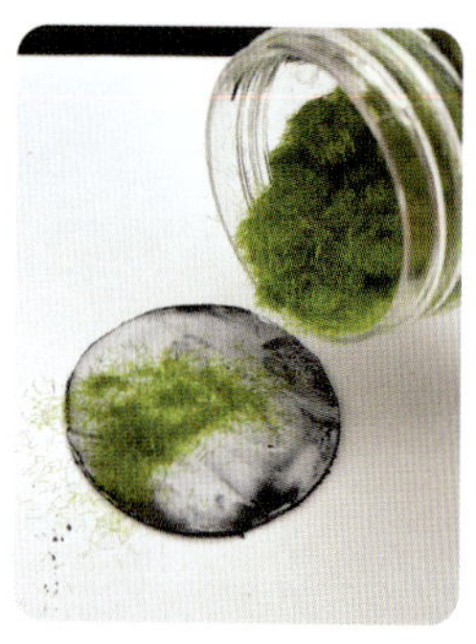 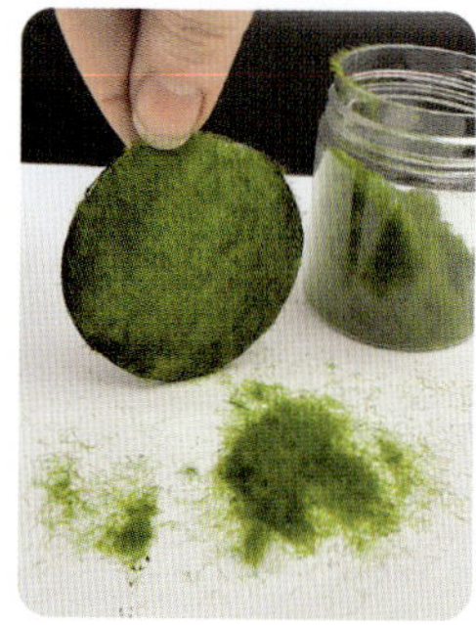 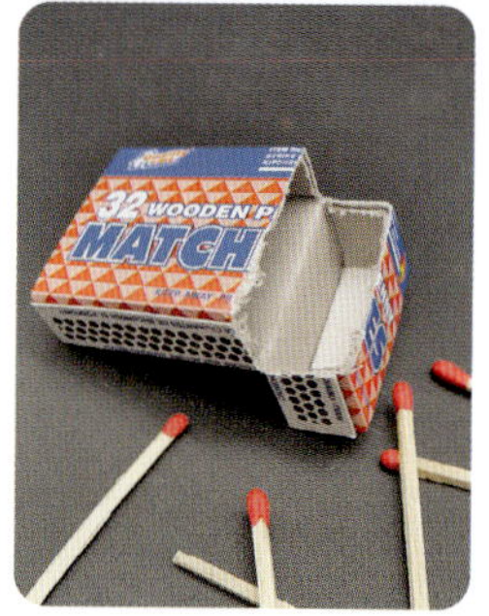 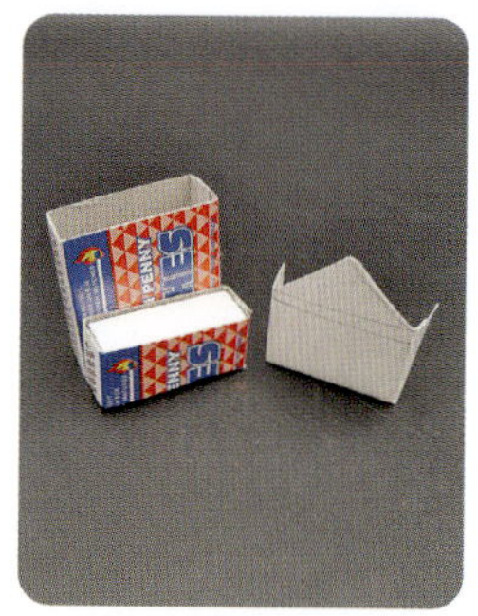

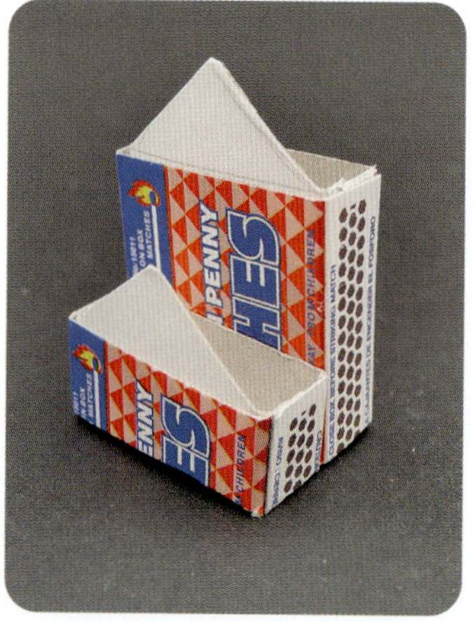 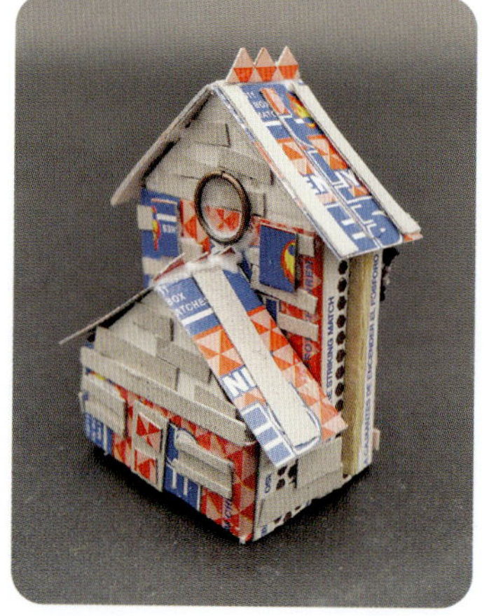 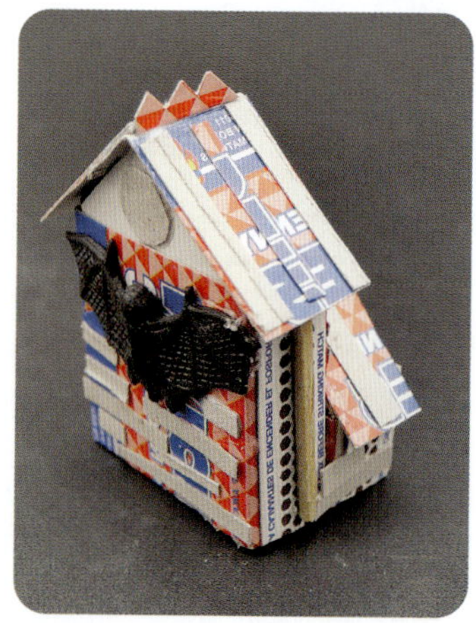

Cut a circle out of balsa wood with your X-ACTO knife the same size as the hole cut in the doll's head and paint it black. This will serve as a platform for your house. Coat the entire top of your wooden circle with a thin layer of tacky glue. Spread it evenly with your finger. While the glue is still wet, place your circle on top of a sheet of paper and sprinkle grass flocking onto the glue. Shake off the excess and funnel it back into the jar using the paper. Set your wooden circle off to the side to dry.

Using your X-ACTO knife, cut one of the matchboxes a fourth of the way up. Leave the back of your matchbox uncut so that you can fold it. Fold and hot glue together. Use the inside trays of the matchbox to make roof peaks and hot glue them in place.

Let's add some details! Using a second matchbox, cut out all the little details: roof, doors, windows, siding. Glue this all on using tacky glue. You can use the matches for some of the details. I glued a hoop ring to the front (*because I love a circle window*) but make it your own. *Remember, it doesn't have to be perfect. This is going to be an old, haunted house and haunted houses aren't perfect!*

Now it's time to add the paint. Paint the entire house black and let it dry for a few minutes. Dry brush a medium gray on all the details. (Dry brushing is when you take a dry paintbrush, dip the tip into paint and lightly sweep it over the surface.) Splatter brown and orange paint on your house to make it look dirty and aged.

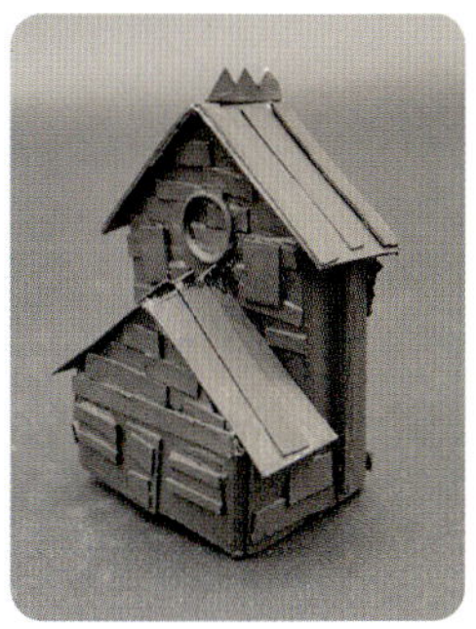
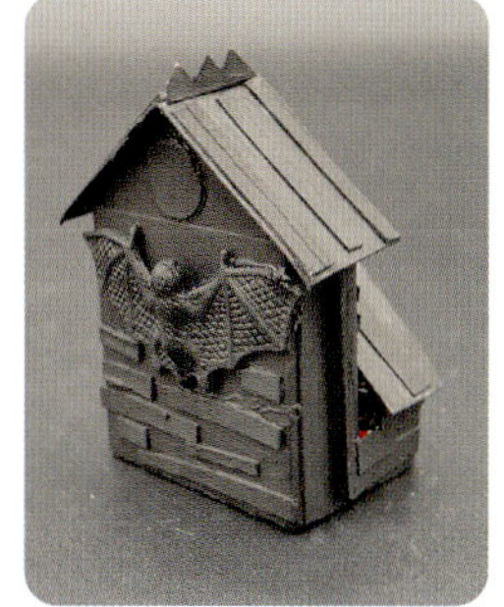
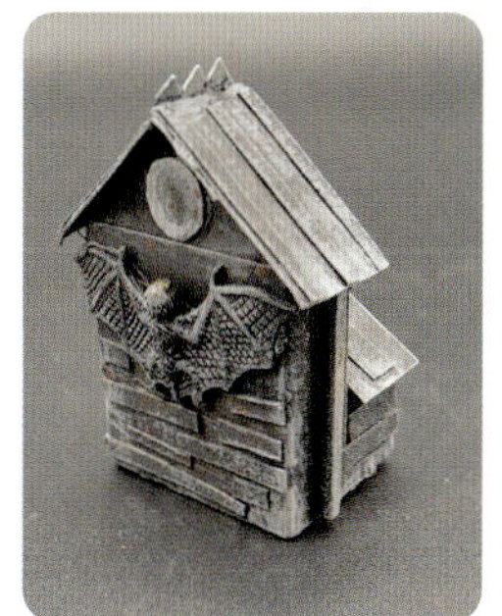
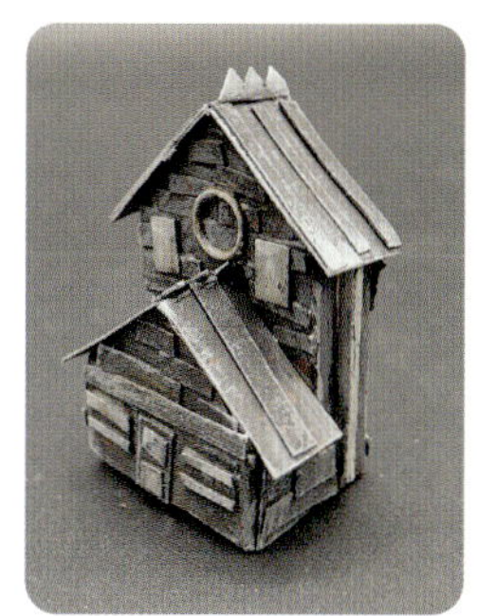

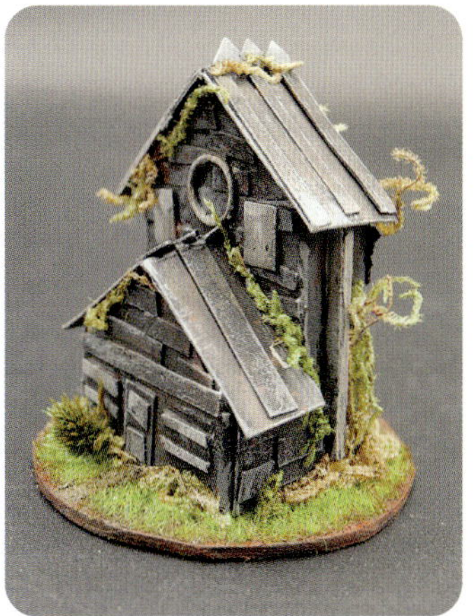
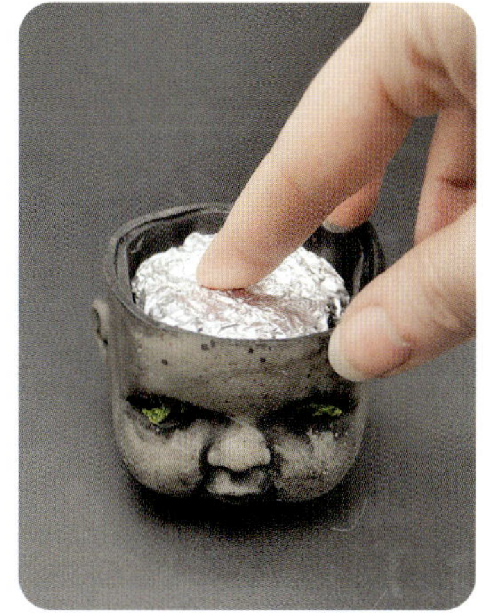
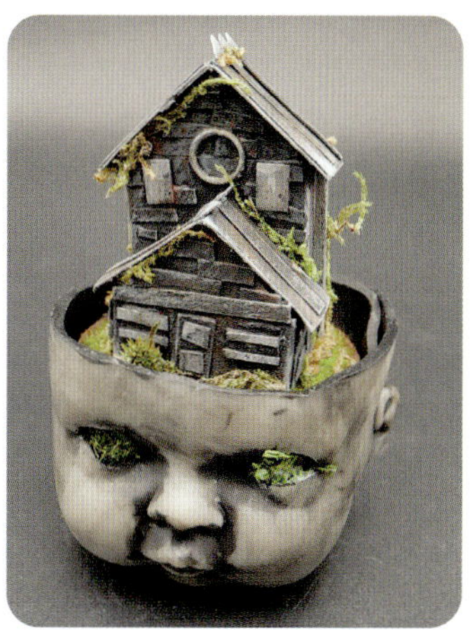

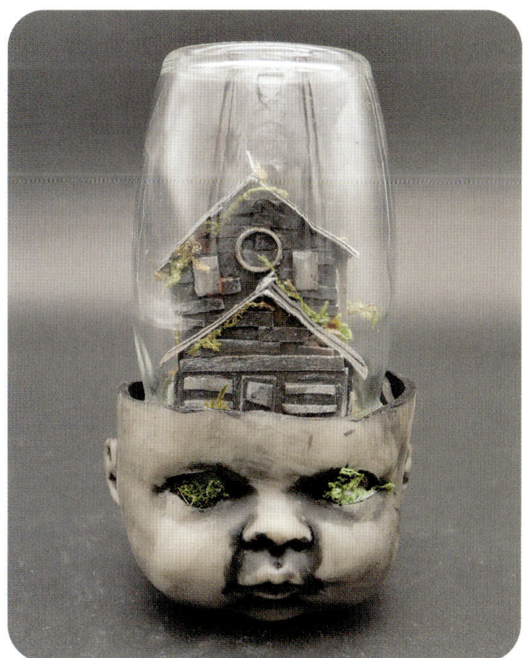

Hot glue your haunted house onto your grass disk and use tacky glue to adhere moss and any other small plants around the bottom of your house. Set this aside.

The doll head halves should be dry now. Take the green top and flip it upside down into the hole of the bottom half. Green should peek out behind those hollow eyes. Hot glue this in place.

Fill the eyeholes with moss. This gives it the illusion that your house goes a lot deeper.

Press aluminum foil into the cranium of your doll and hot glue it in place. Then hot glue your grass disk and house onto the foil.

If you want to protect your house, cover it with a small glass jar. I left this part optional because it's hard finding the right size jar that fits perfectly. I bought mine with pudding in it and saved it.

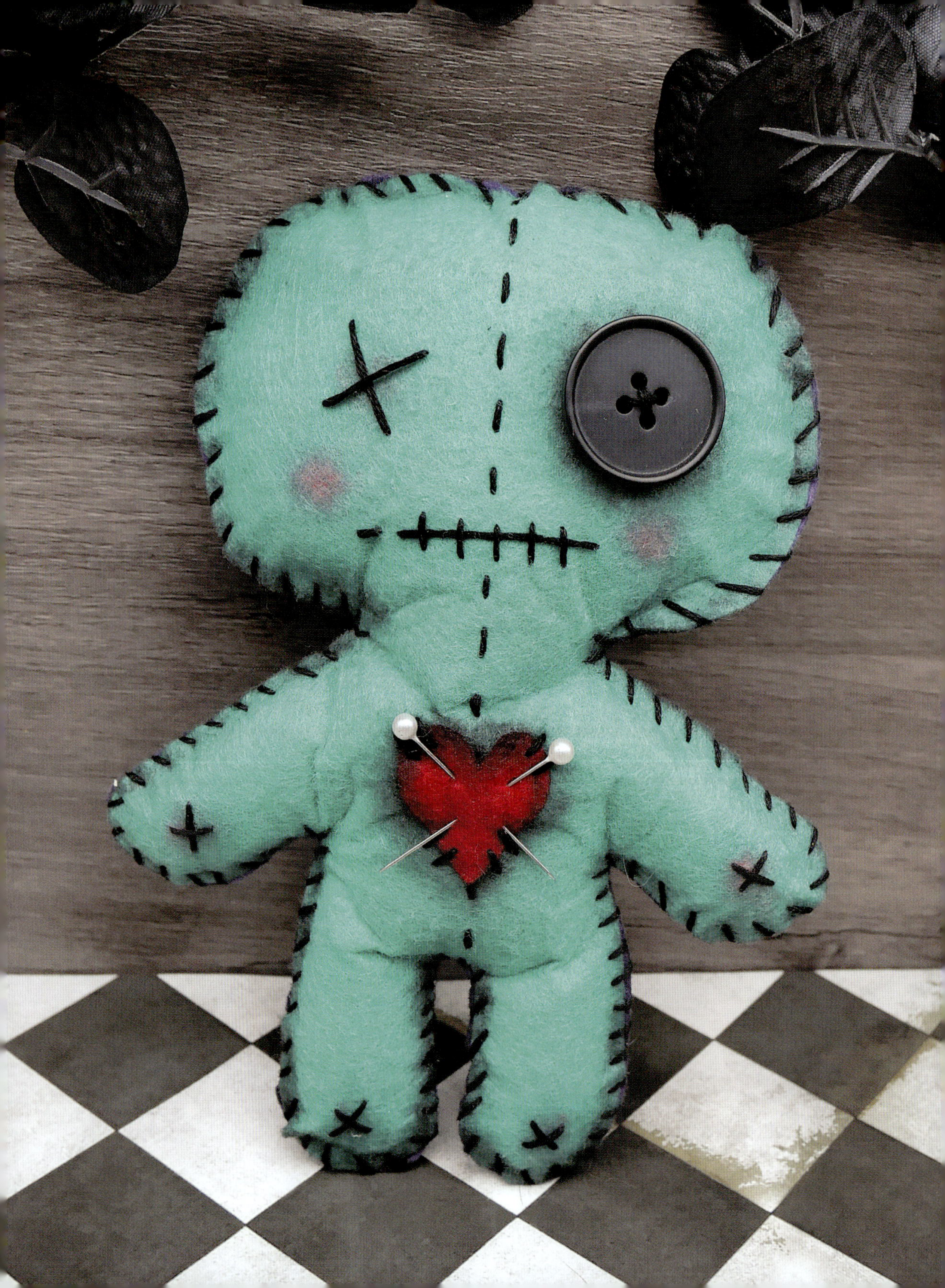

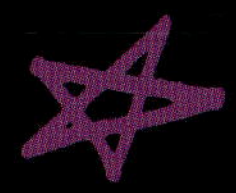

Odds and Ends

Welcome to the Odds and Ends section of this book, a collection of projects that are a bit more odd than ends. Actually, I'm not even sure what an "ends" is. Much like my own childhood, these misfit crafts are hard to categorize. But hey, here I am, still a misfit, BUT a misfit with a book! Aha! Take that, haters!

So, before you judge these misfits too quickly, consider that they may be the hidden gems of this book, or perhaps they'll go off and write their own DIY books! Okay, probably not, that was a peculiar thing to say. Regardless, we love all misfits here, so no bad-mouthing them! Especially the Octopus Canvas (page 193). He's a little delicate, but who can blame him? He's all washed up. Shhh, don't tell him I said that! And as for the Voodoo Doll (page 199), he seems friendly enough, but his silence will keep you on pins and needles all day! Yup, this is the Island of Misfits' portion of the book. So relax and enjoy.

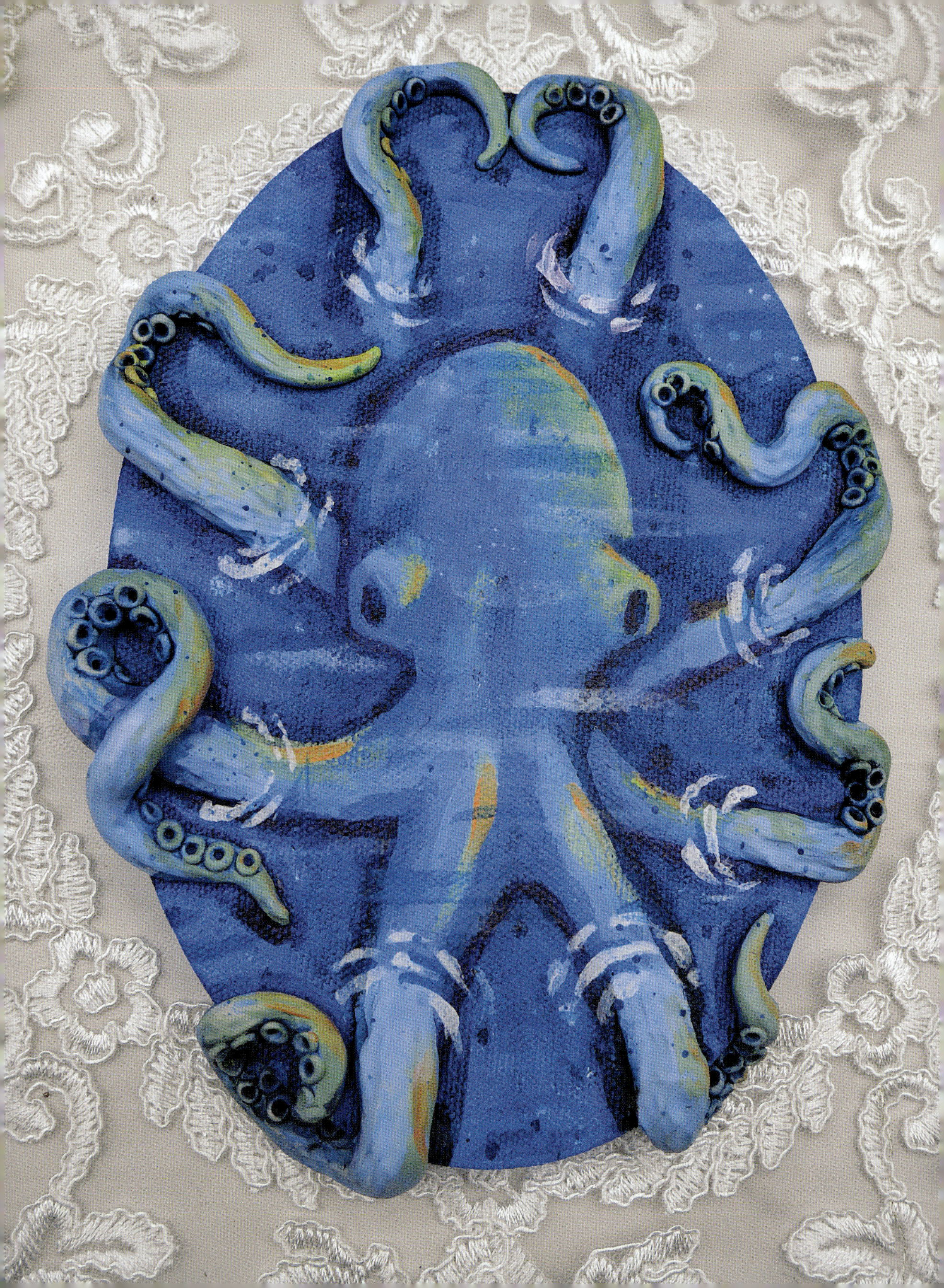

Octopus Canvas

You may be wondering, "Hey, what's this octopus doing in a creepy craft book? Octopodes aren't creepy." Heck yes, they are! They're freakishly smart, can change color, have three hearts, have blue blood and squirt black ink. Seems pretty terrifying to me! In this project I'll show you how to create one of these terrifying creatures right on a canvas.

Paint your oval canvas a solid blue color. Splatter dark blue and white speckles onto your canvas using your paintbrush. Let it dry.

Sketch a rough octopus in dark blue paint in the center of your canvas. Extend the arms to the edges.

(continued)

Materials

- 5" x 7" (12.5 x 18–cm) oval canvas
- Acrylic paint and brush
- Silicone mat
- Disposable gloves
- Epoxy clay (e.g., Apoxie Sculpt)
- Sculpting tools with round tip
- Paper towels

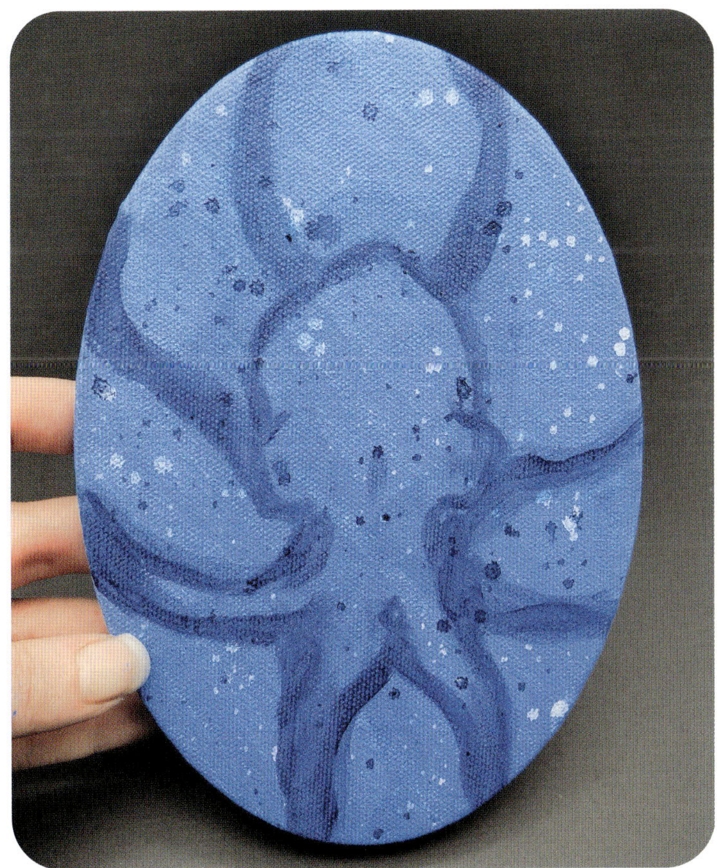

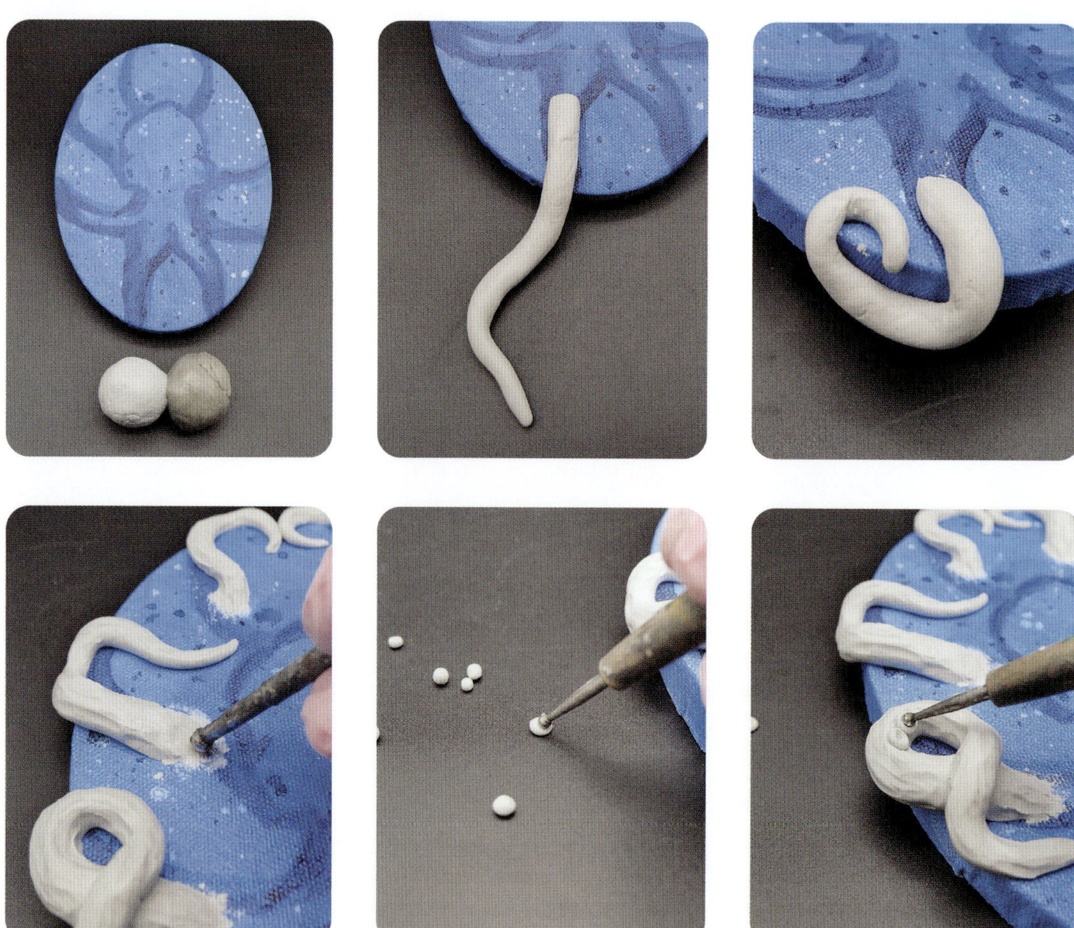

Lay out your silicone mat and put on gloves. Mix a golf ball–sized amount of clay and divide it into eight parts. Roll each part into 3- to 5-inch (7.5- to 12.5-cm)-long ropes. Taper the ends. These will be your tentacles. On your sketched octopus, place the tentacles a little way down the legs. You'll want your legs to appear as if they are emerging from the canvas about midway. Use a round-tipped sculpting tool to smooth the base of each tentacle into the canvas. Curl and loop some tentacles around and over the edge of your canvas.

Now for the suction cups! Mix a marble-sized amount of epoxy clay and create peppercorn-sized balls. Attach each ball to the tentacles by poking them with a small round-tipped sculpting tool. Cluster the suction cups inside the curves of each tentacle. Allow to set for 2 or more hours.

With light blue paint, paint your octopus and tentacles. Don't worry about getting paint inside the suction cups. We'll paint those next.

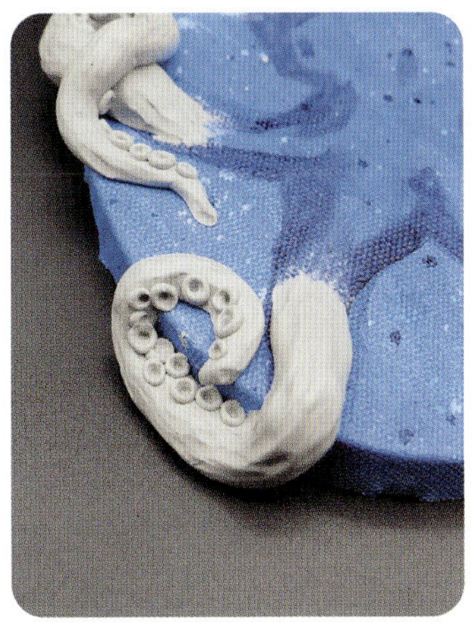
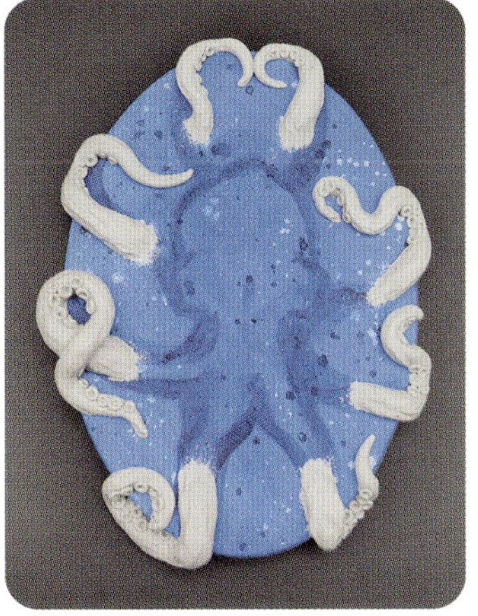
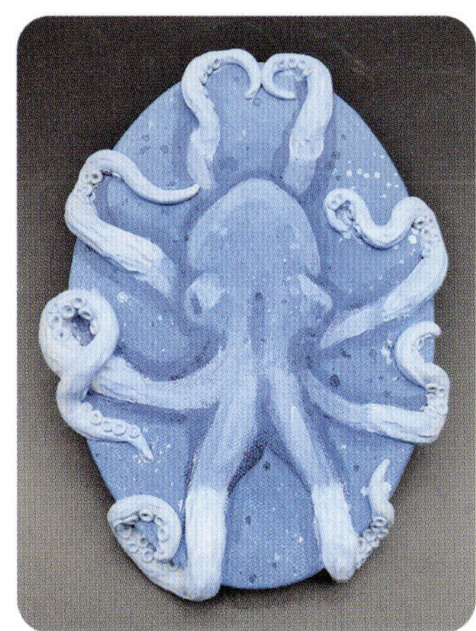

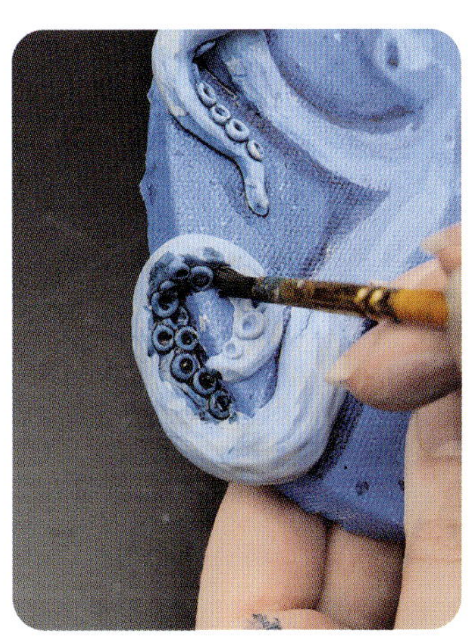
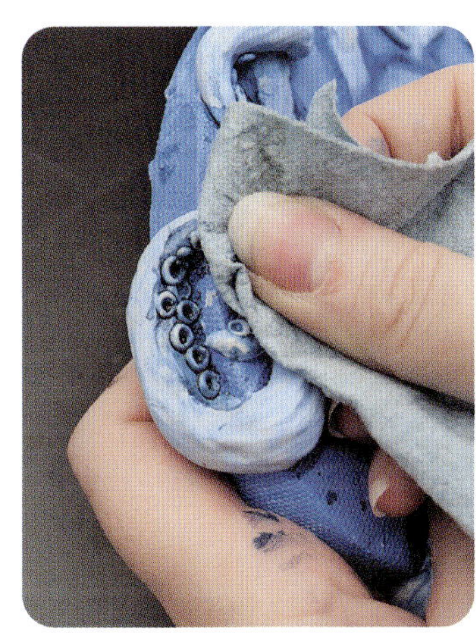
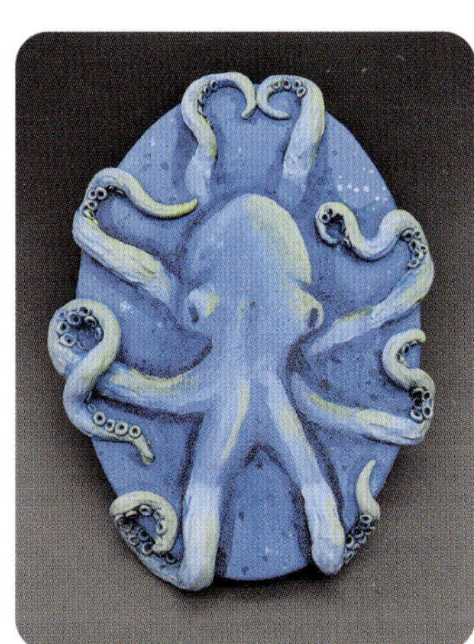

Using watered-down dark blue paint, fill the crevasses and suction cup holes with paint. Wipe off any excess paint with a paper towel.

Using yellow and/or light orange paint, add highlights on one side of the octopus both on the canvas and on the clay. *The best way to do this is to think about a light hitting your octopus and only paint the yellow where the light would be.*

Paint white water ripples near the base of your clay. This should look like rings of white around each tentacle where it's coming out of the water.

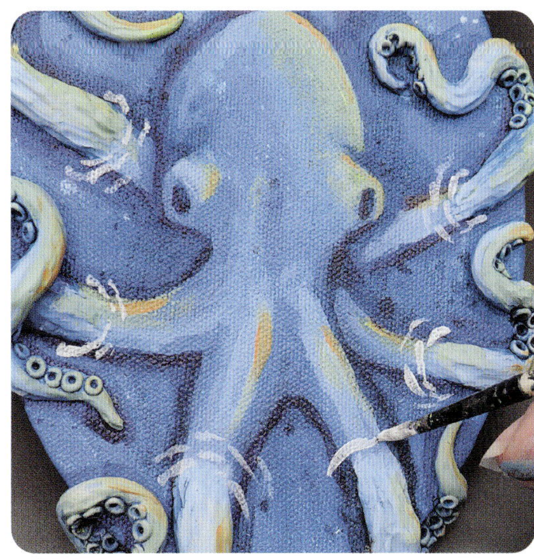

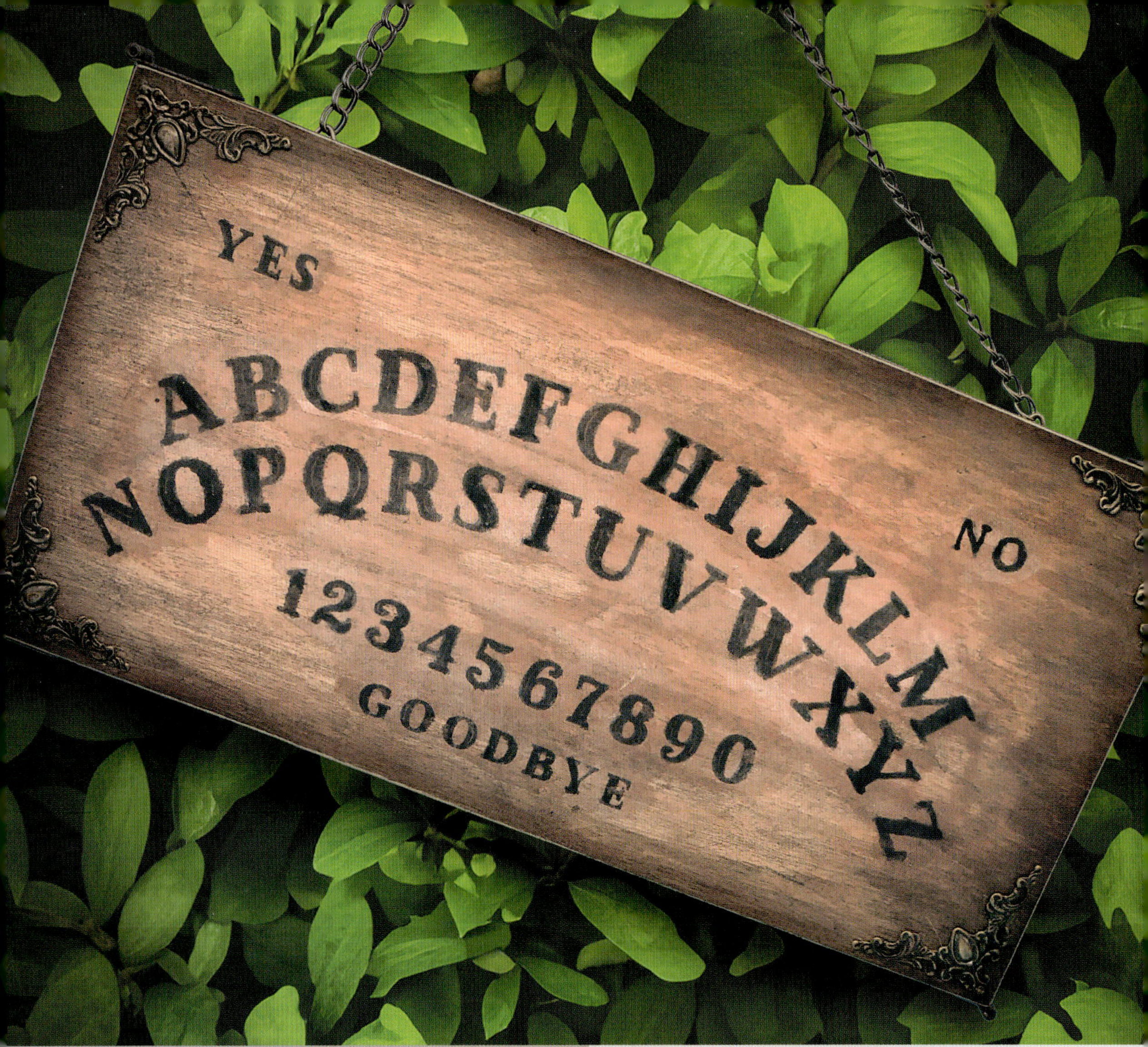

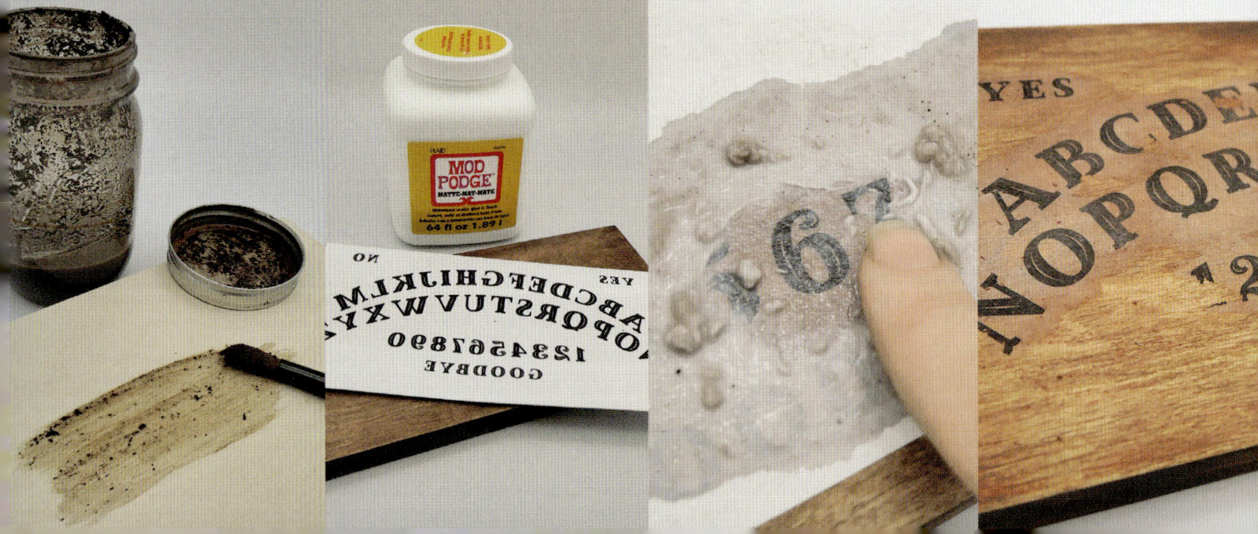

Spirit Board

Spirit boards aren't just a portal to the spirit world; they can also be a decorative conversation piece! Just be careful not to accidently summon a spirit when you are hanging it up. After all, we want your guests to be enchanted, not haunted!

Stain your wooden canvas by smearing on leftover coffee grounds and water. You could alternatively just use strong brewed coffee, but I like to drink my coffee. Keep adding the grounds until you get it the darkness you like. Wipe off and let it dry for an hour, or use a heat gun to speed up the process.

Using a laser printer and white paper, print out a backward black-and-white spirit board the size of your canvas. I typed mine out, but there are lots of options online if you want to download one.

Paint the canvas and only the front side of the paper with regular matte Mod Podge. Be extra careful not to get any Mod Podge on the back of the paper! It should be pretty wet when you lay the lettering face down onto the wood. Squeeze out any pockets of Mod Podge or air, being very careful not to squeeze it out onto the back of the paper. Let this dry for 4 or more hours.

Making sure the Mod Podge has dried completely, wet a little section of paper and slowly circle your finger, taking off just the top layer of the paper. Go slow; this will take some time. If the print starts to come off, stop and move on to a new section. Wipe away any excess paper and let it dry. *Don't worry if some of your print is missing; that just gives it a rustic feel.*

Sand just the edges of your board to smooth the corners. Glue on your metal corner embellishments with precision craft glue. Screw on your D-ring hangers to the back and add a chain.

Materials

- 6" x 12" (15 x 30–cm) rectangular wooden canvas
- Coffee grounds
- Heat gun (optional)
- Laser printer
- 20lb (75gsm) white printer paper
- Matte Mod Podge
- Sandpaper
- Metal corner embellishments
- Precision craft glue (e.g., Bearly Art)
- 2 D-ring hangers with screws
- Screwdriver
- 16" (40.5-cm) bronze chain

Note: *Using a laser printer instead of an inkjet printer will give you better results while transferring an image. Some people say you can use an inkjet printer, but I've never had good results. The image tends to bleed and smear.*

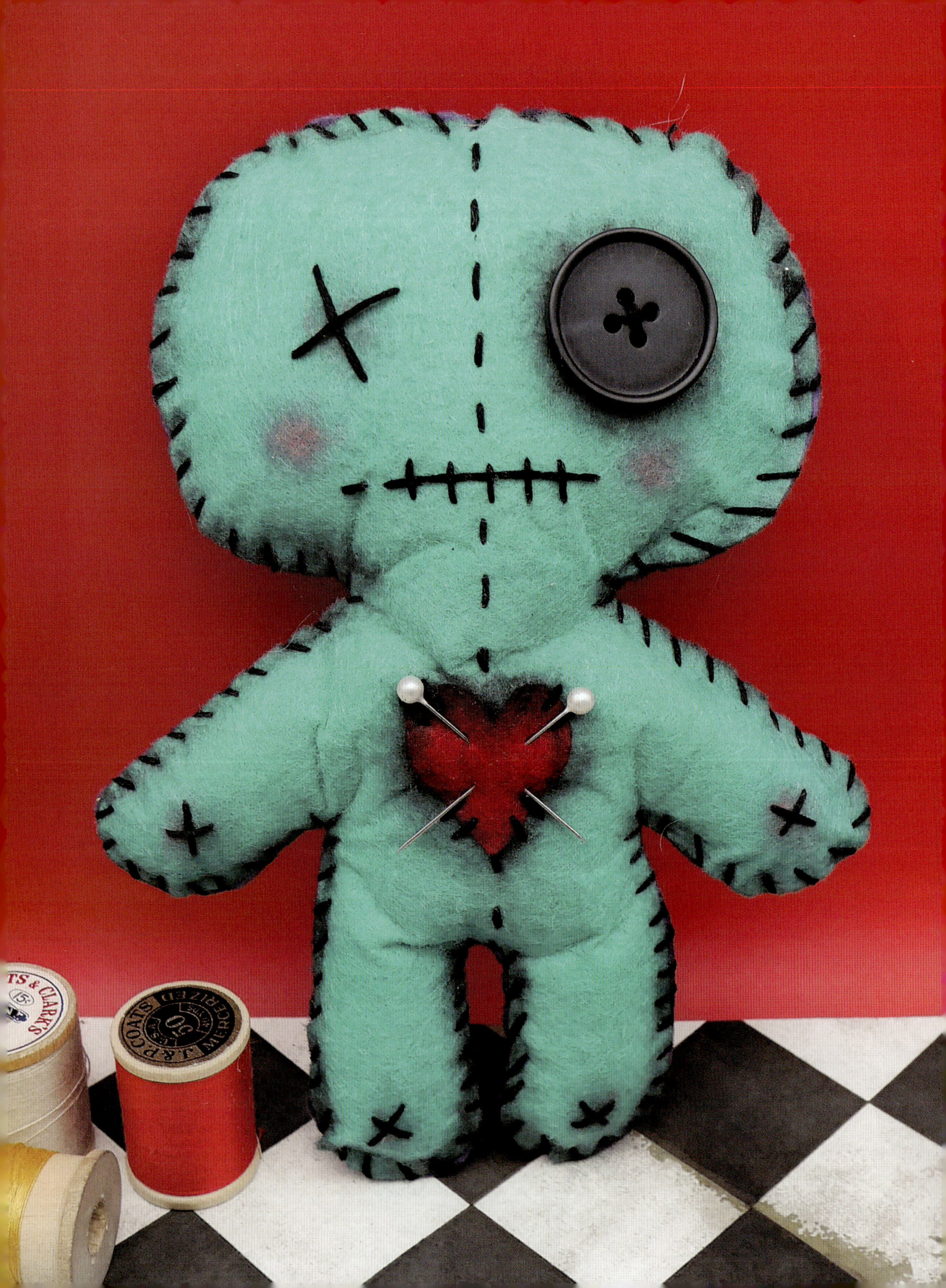
TS & CLARKS
15
J&P COATS MERCERIZED
50

Voodoo Doll

Who wants a "voodoo? Who do? You do . . ."?

In this project I'll guide you through the peculiar process of creating your very own voodoo friend out of felt. This little guy is not only adorable and friendly but also can't talk. What more could you want in a friend? Let's just say he's the strong silent type.

Start by folding a piece of printer paper in half. Draw half a person's shape along the crease. Make the arms and legs chunky and the head large. Cut out your person and unfold the paper. You may need to trim the head to make it more circular.

Pin your person template onto the turquoise and purple felt squares and cut out one of each color. (It's okay, he hardly *felt* it.) You should have two identical felt people.

(continued)

Materials

- Paper and pencil
- Scissors
- 8" (20-cm) turquoise, purple and red felt squares
- Sewing needle
- Black embroidery thread
- Black button
- Sewing pins
- Stuffing fluff
- Chopstick or pointy stick
- Black and red mica powder and brush
- Hot glue and gun (optional)
- Magnets (optional)

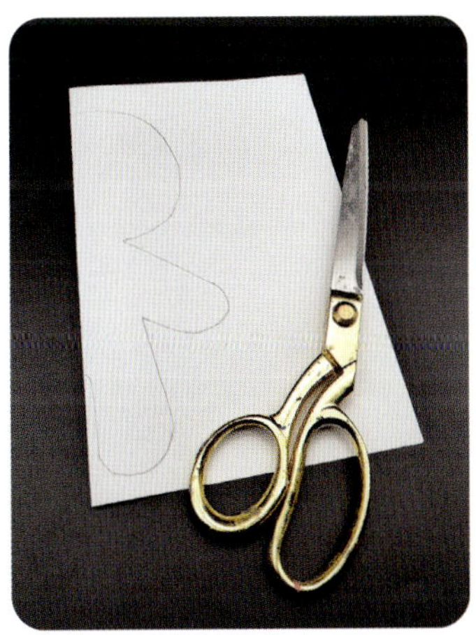

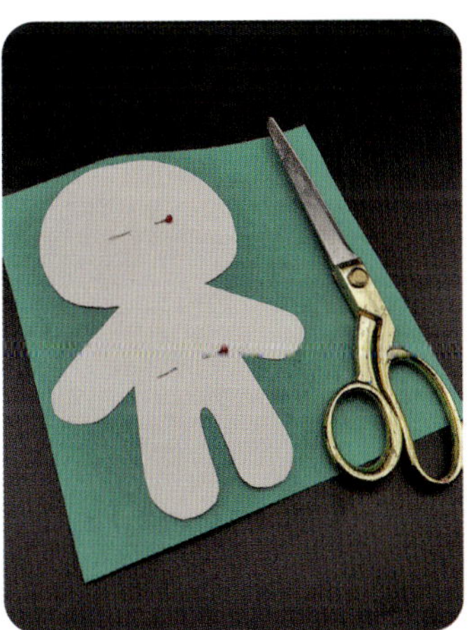

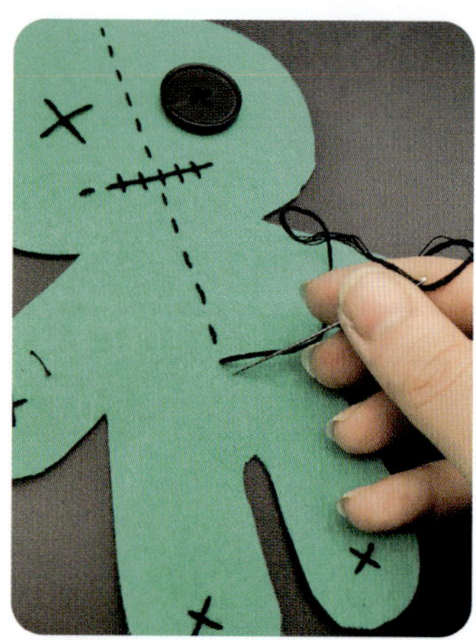

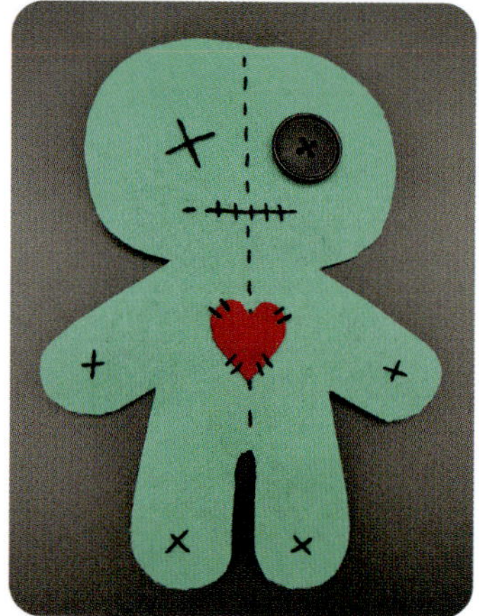

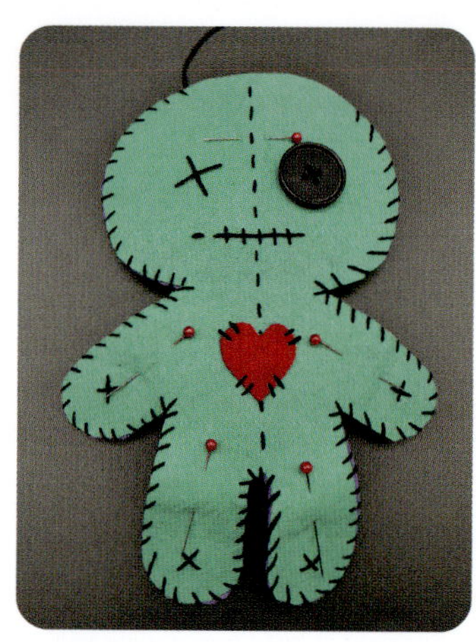

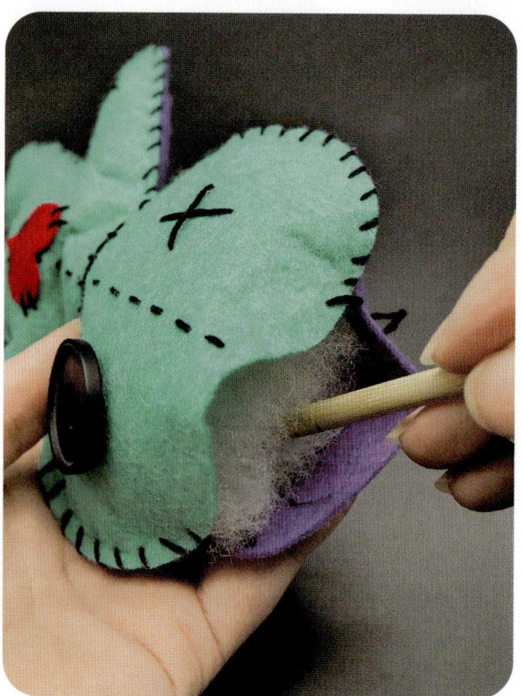

Thread your sewing needle with black embroidery thread and, on the turquoise doll, sew on all your details. I did one button eye, an X for the other eye, a stitched mouth, Xs for the hands and feet and a dashed line down the middle, but feel free to make it your own. Cut a heart shape out of your red felt and sew it onto the chest using big chunky stitches.

Pin the purple doll cutout to the back of your turquoise doll cutout. Starting on the right side of the head, loop stitches all the way around your doll with your needle, sewing the two halves together. Leave a 2-inch (5-cm) space at the top of your doll. Don't unthread your needle yet.

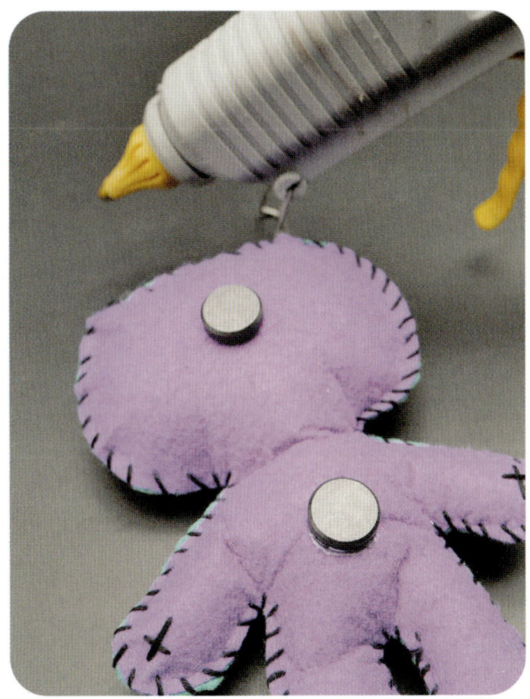

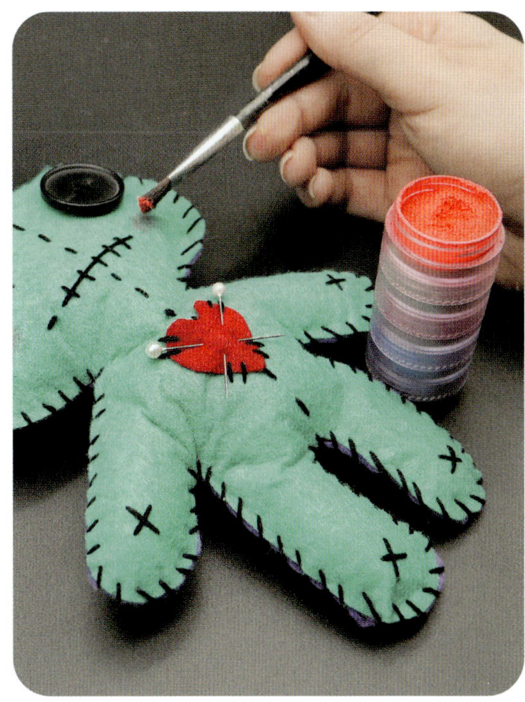

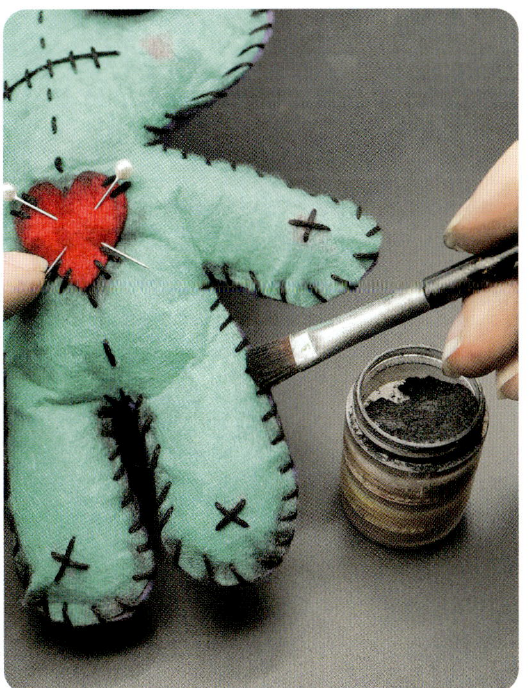

Unpin your doll and stuff it full of fluff. Use a chopstick to get the stuffing into the feet and hands. Be careful to not overfill your doll, or it might look crinkly. After stuffing, use your needle to sew up the opening.

To finish the look, brush black mica powder onto the edges of your voodoo doll, under the button eye and around the heart. Finish it off with red powder for the cheeks and the center of the hands and feet.

Optional: If you want to turn your voodoo doll into a magnet, hot glue magnets to the back.

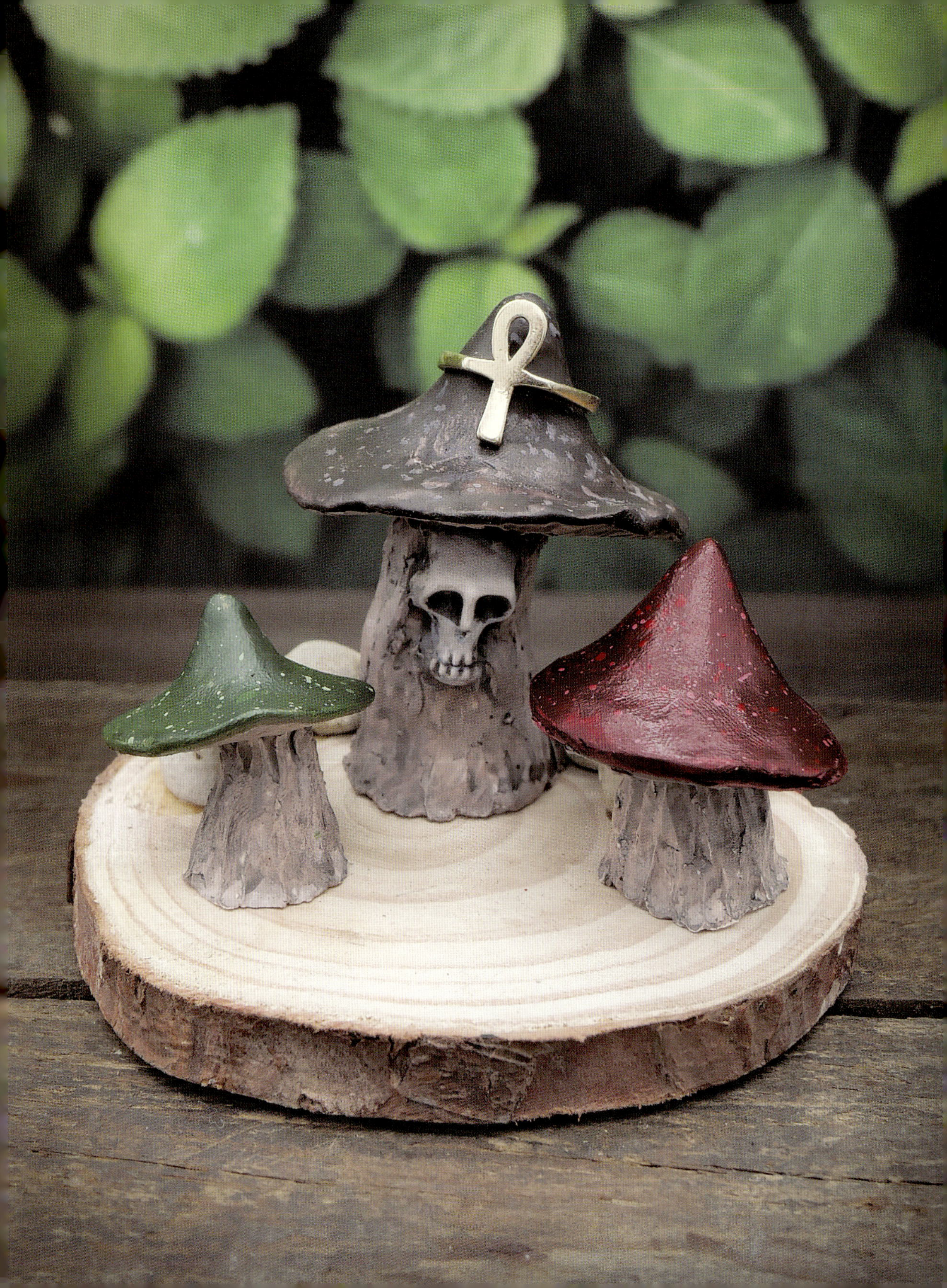

Death Mushrooms Ring Holder

Are you looking for a creepy solution to storing your rings while you're not wearing them? Death mushrooms make the perfect guardians for your precious jewels! With limited knickknack space, I love creating art with a purpose. I mean, you could add another shelf to the wall, but at some point, you WILL run out of wall space. So why not make art that you can actually use? That's why I came up with death mushrooms.

Materials

- 1–2 oz (28–56 g) white polymer clay
- Sculpting tools with round tip
- ½" (1.3-cm) skull
- Acrylic paint and brush
- Paper towels
- 3" (7.5-cm) circular wood slice
- E6000 glue

Flatten a ball of polymer clay into a disk about 2 x 2 inches (5 x 5 cm) and ¼ inch (6 mm) thick. Put this disk in your palm and press a large round-tipped sculpting tool in the center to mold the disk around. This will be the mushroom cap of our ring holder. Set this aside.

(continued)

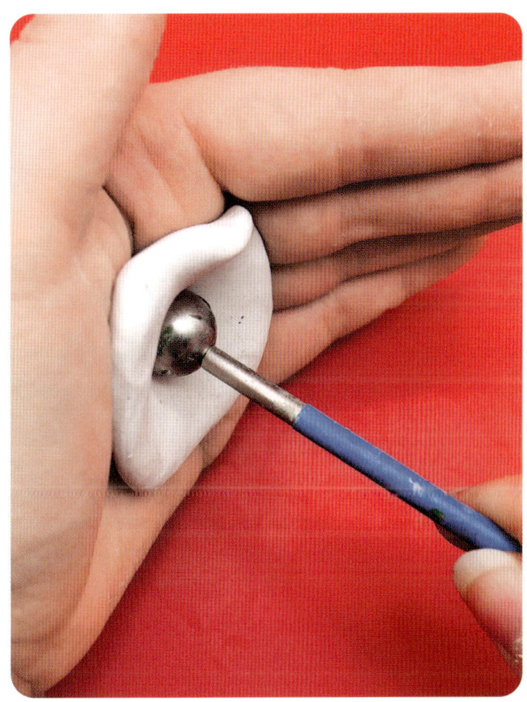

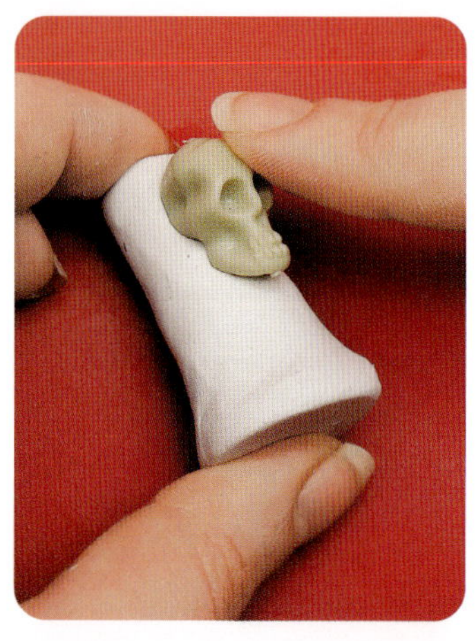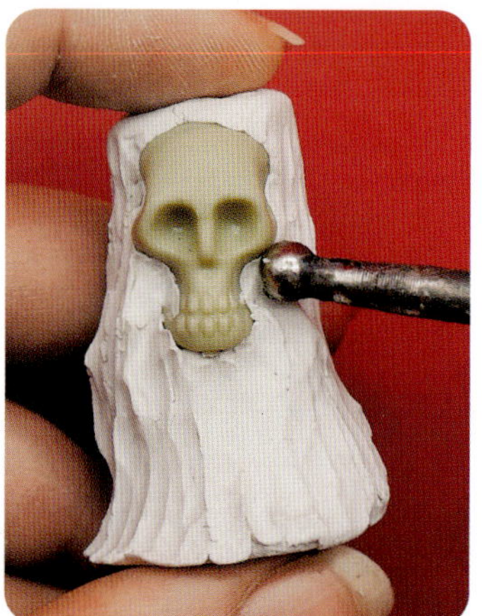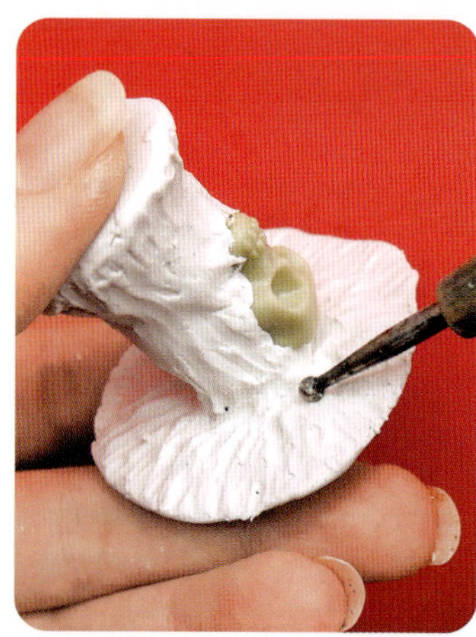

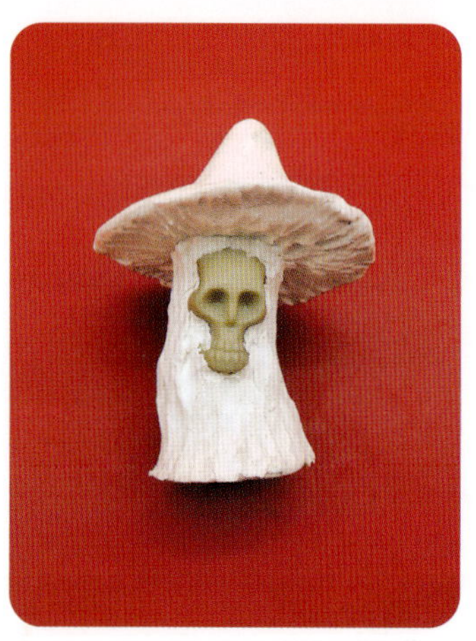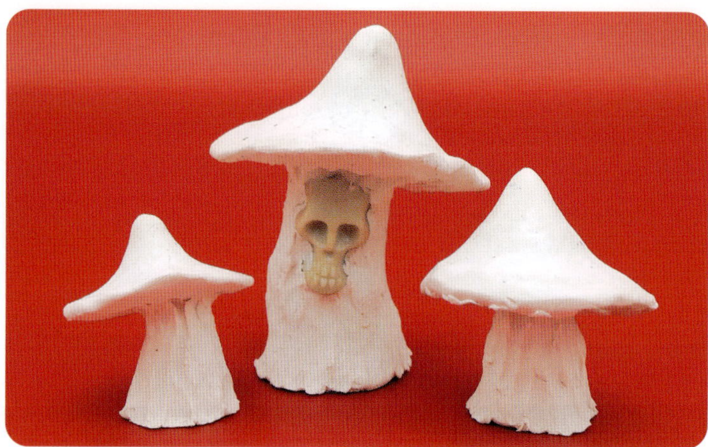

Roll a thick cylinder shape out of polymer clay about ½ x 2 inches (1.3 x 5 cm). Flare the bottom out by rolling the top half between your palm and a flat surface. This will be the stem of the mushroom. Press a small skull into the side of the stem. Drag a small round-tipped sculpting tool vertically along your stem to make it look like tree bark.

Press the cap and the stem together, holding it between your two fingers and thumb. Blend the two pieces together with a round-tipped sculpting tool. Drag your tool on the underside of the mushroom cap to create gills.

Now let's make two babies! Repeat the steps above, only about half the size and without the skull. Bake all the mushrooms according to the package instructions.

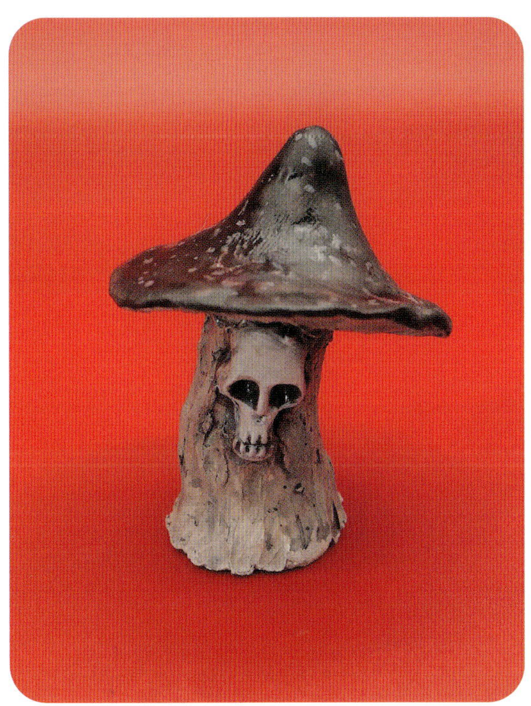

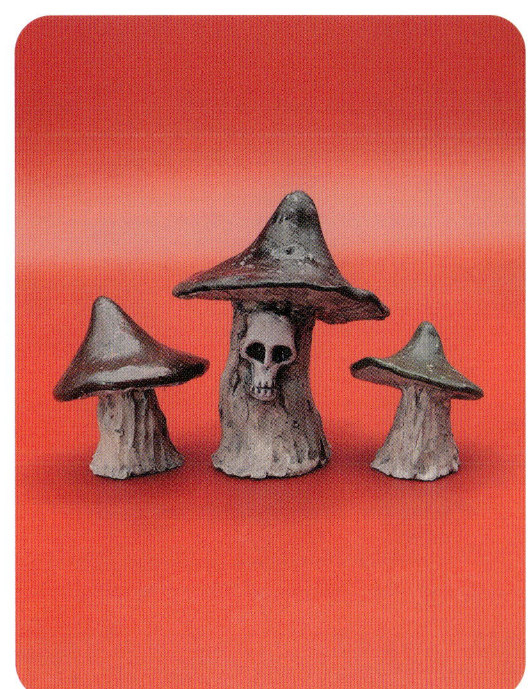

Paint your mushrooms a dark brown color and wipe away any excess with a paper towel. The color should just stick in the nooks and crannies of your mushrooms. Paint each mushroom cap green, brown and red. Splatter specks of light and dark paint on the mushroom caps to create texture.

Adhere all three mushrooms to the wood slice using E6000.

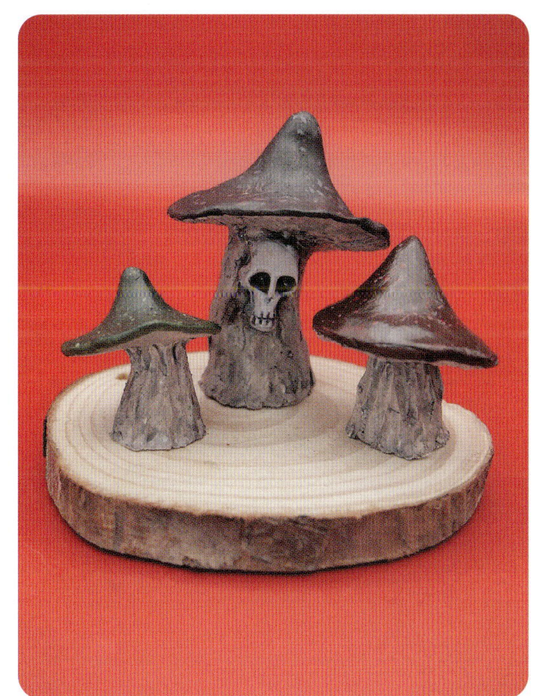

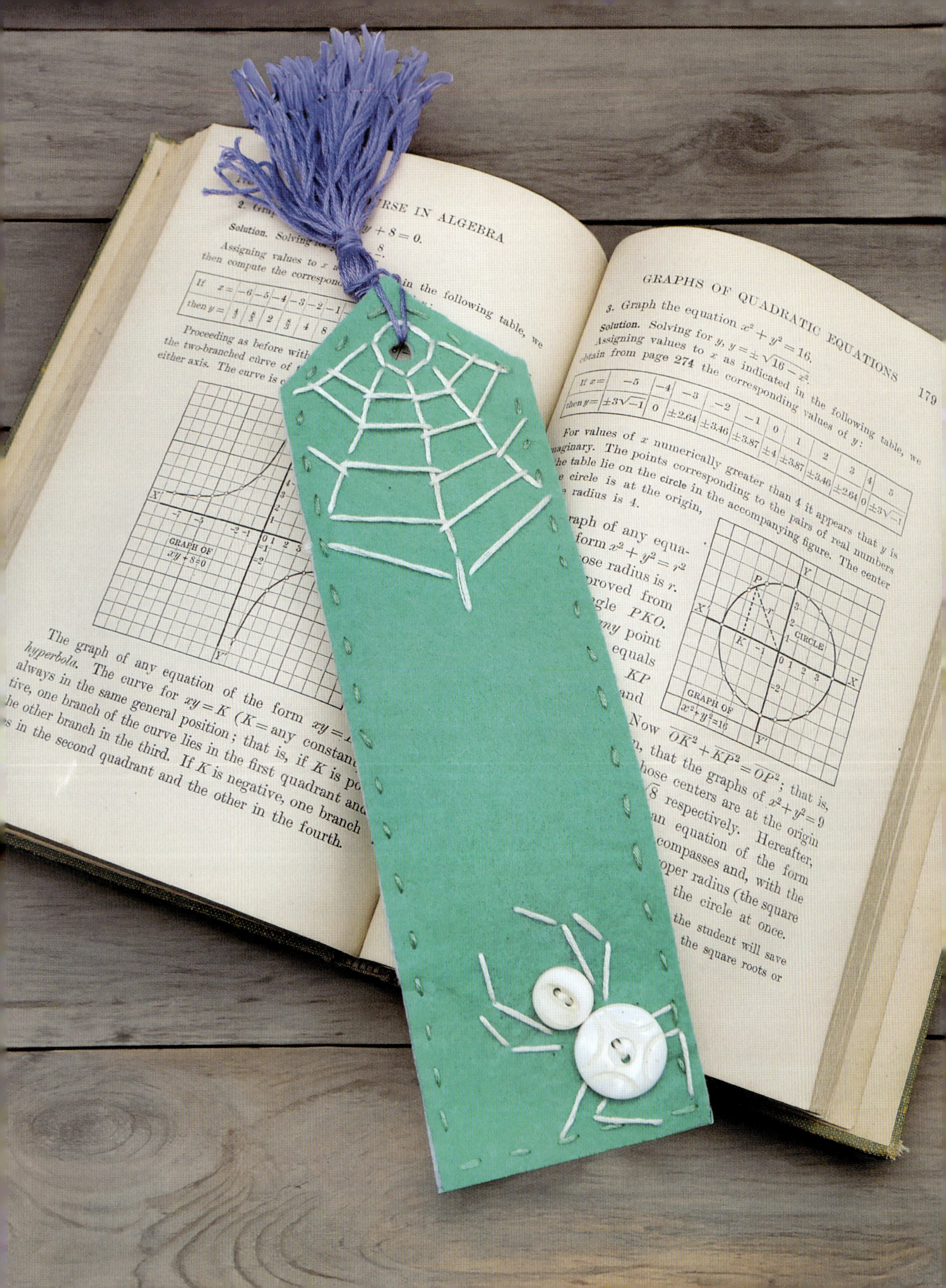
URSE IN ALGEBRA
2. Graph
Solution. Solving
Assigning values to x
then compute the corresponding
If x = | -6 | -5 | -4 | -3 | -2 | -1
then y =
Proceeding as before with
the two-branched curve of
either axis. The curve is
GRAPH OF
xy + 8 = 0
The graph of any equation of the form xy = K
hyperbola. The curve for xy = K (K = any constant
always in the same general position; that is, if K is po
tive, one branch of the curve lies in the first quadrant and
the other branch in the third. If K is negative, one branch
s in the second quadrant and the other in the fourth.

GRAPHS OF QUADRATIC EQUATIONS
179
3. Graph the equation x² + y² = 16.
Solution. Solving for y, y = ± √16 - x².
Assigning values to x as indicated in the following table, we
obtain from page 274 the corresponding values of y:
x = | -5 | -4 | -3 | -2 | -1 | 0 | 1 | 2 | 3 | 4 | 5
y = | ±3√-1 | 0 | ±2.64 | ±3.46 | ±3.87 | ±4 | ±3.87 | ±3.46 | ±2.64 | 0 | ±3√-1
For values of x numerically greater than 4 it appears that y is
imaginary. The points corresponding to the pairs of real numbers
in the table lie on the circle in the accompanying figure. The center
of the circle is at the origin,
the radius is 4.
graph of any equa-
form x² + y² = r²
whose radius is r.
proved from
angle PKO.
any point
equals
KP
and
Now OK² + KP² = OP²; that is,
that the graphs of x² + y² = 9
whose centers are at the origin
respectively.
GRAPH OF
x² + y² = 16

Webby Bookmark

Bookmarks are essential for keeping your place in a book. In fact, you could use a bookmark right here in this book. Oh wait, no you can't because you haven't made it yet. Well, let's get to crafting these webby bookmarks so you'll never lose your spot again.

With scissors, trim the corners off one side of your two felt strips to make a wide V. Using a hole punch, make a hole in the center of your V.

Using white embroidery floss and a sewing needle, sew a circle around the hole you just punched out and then lines radiating from the circle. Connect the lines going the opposite way and continue down until you get a spiderweb pattern. *Don't worry about what the back looks like; we'll cover it up.*

(continued)

Materials

- Scissors
- Two 6" x 2" (15 x 5–cm) felt strips
- Hole punch
- White embroidery floss
- Sewing needle
- 2 buttons, one smaller than the other
- Pins
- 2" (5-cm) piece of cardboard

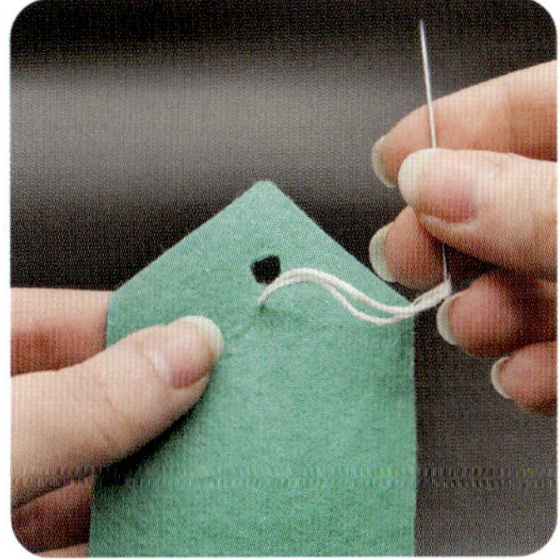

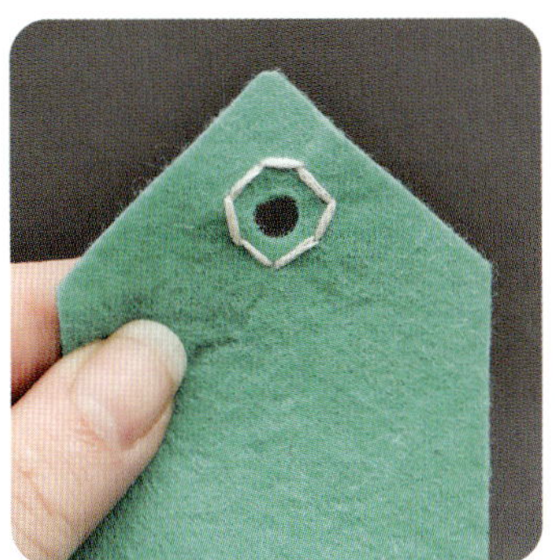

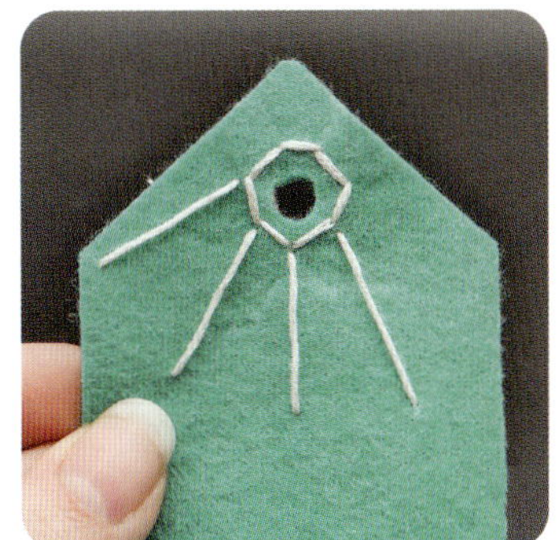

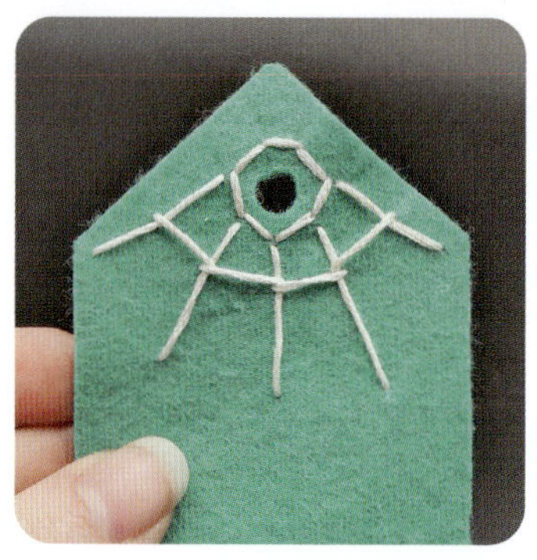
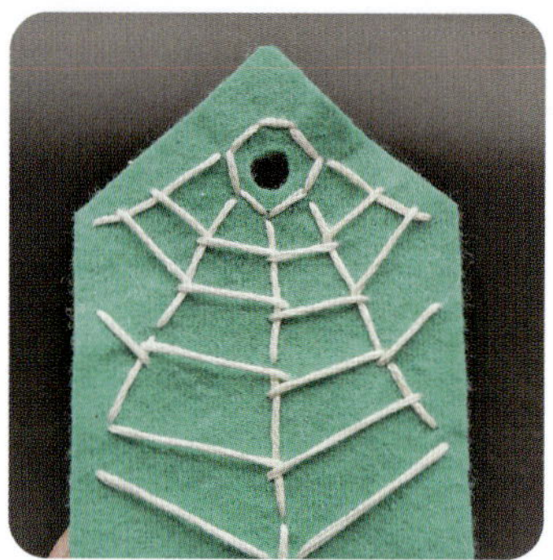
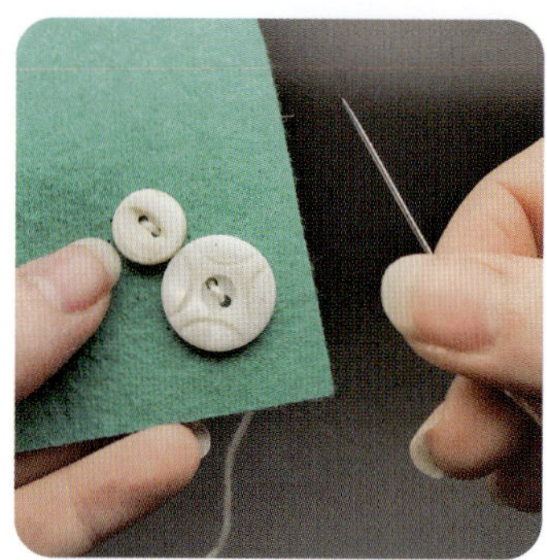

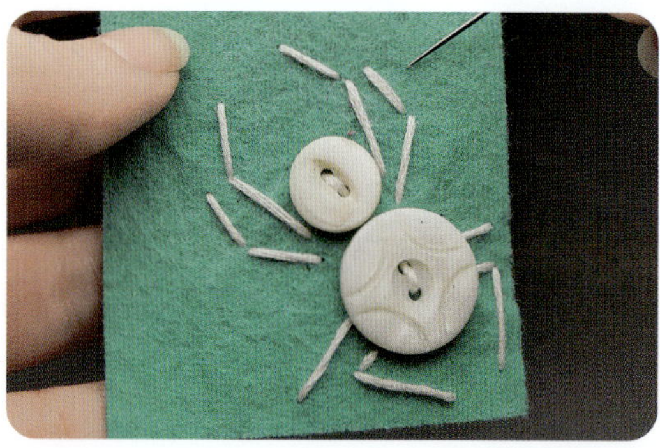

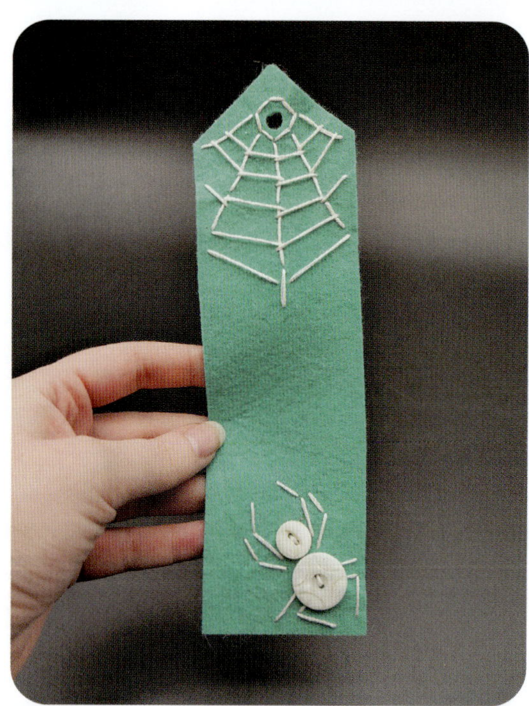

At the very bottom of your bookmark, sew on two buttons. This will be the spider's head and body. Leave enough room for legs. Stitch eight legs coming out of your spider: four front legs coming out of the middle and four legs coming out of the butt.

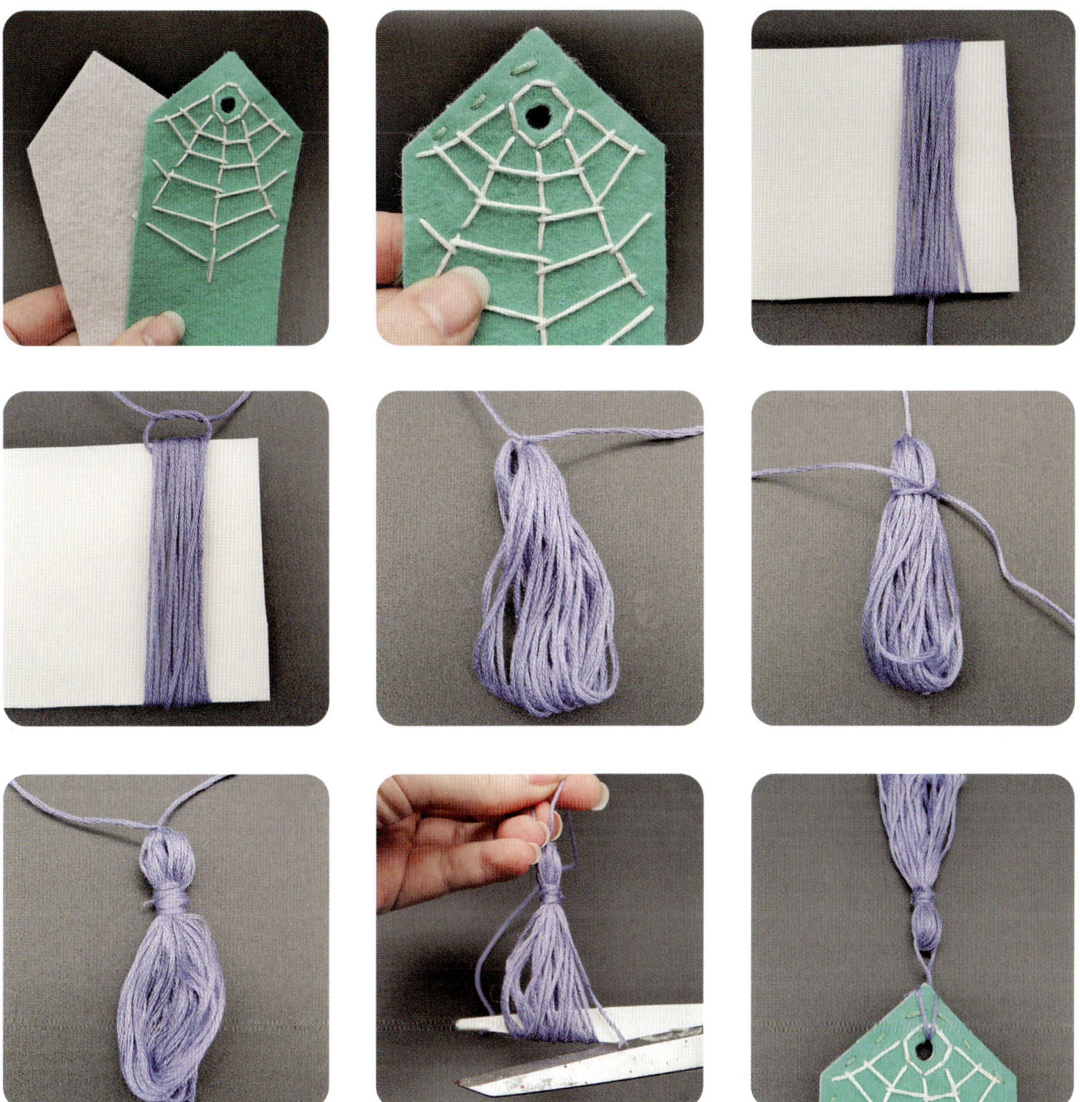

Once you have everything exactly the way you like it, let's cover up that mess on the back! Pin the second felt strip to the back and sew along the edges.

Let's make a tassel! Wrap embroidery floss around your piece of cardboard 15-ish times. Slip a new piece of floss through all the loops at the top and slip it all off the cardboard. Wrap an additional piece of floss a few times around the top portion about ½ inch (1.3 cm) down, knotting it off. Cut the bottom of all the loops free to make a tassel. Attach this through the holes in your felt.

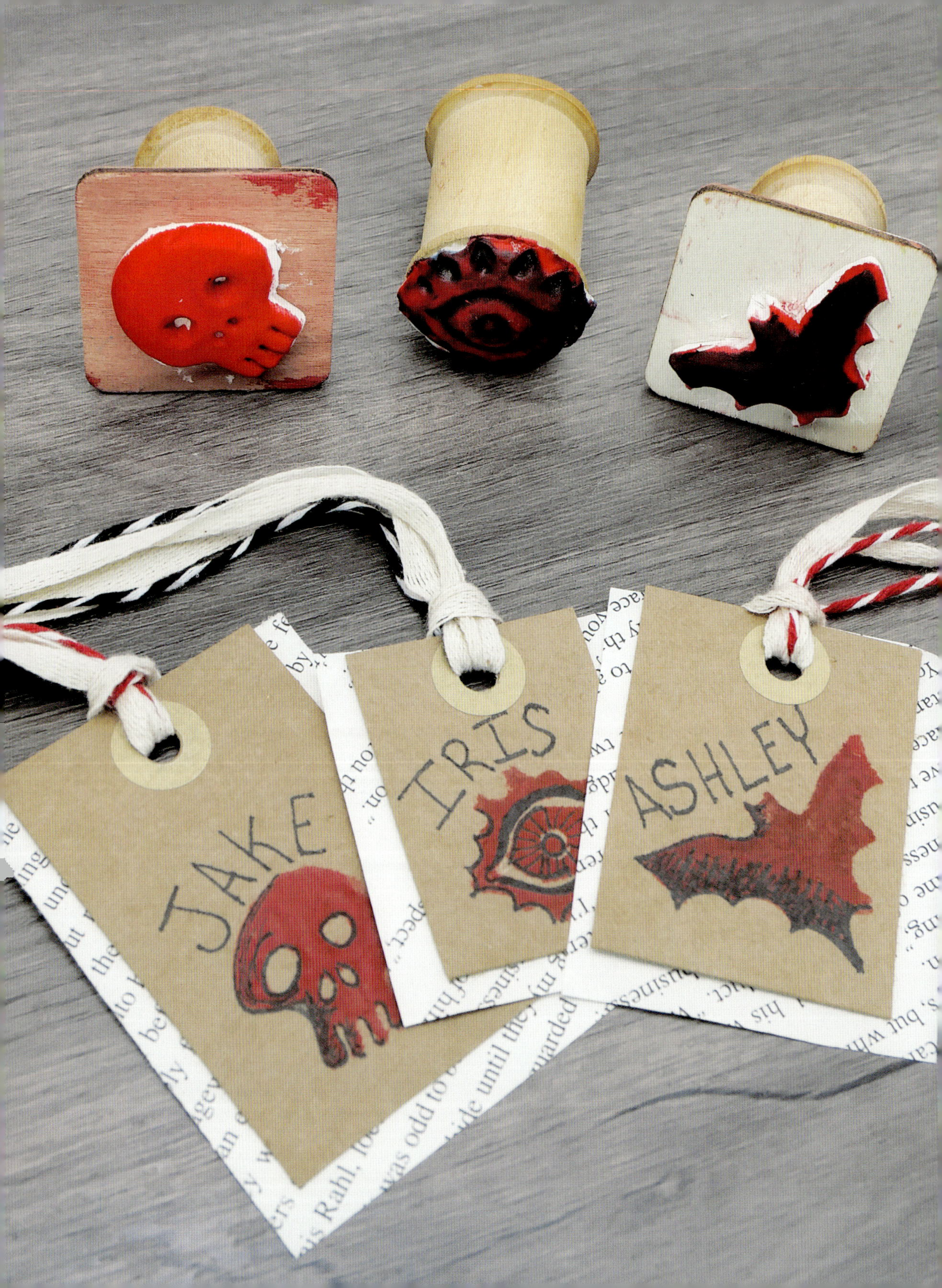

JAKE
IRIS
ASHLEY

Spooky Skull Stamps

If you've seen the cost of rubber stamps, I'm sure you've thinking, "What a rip-off!" I mean, what is it—a bit of rubber and wood? Well dang, let's just make our own! I'll show you how to make a skull stamp, but if you're feeling adventurous try other shapes. Just keep it simple because the foam clay doesn't take details well.

Materials

- 1½" x 1½" (3.8 x 3.8–cm) flat square of wood
- ¼ oz (7 g) foam clay
- Sculpting tools with round tip
- Hot glue and gun
- Empty spool of thread
- X-ACTO knife (if needed)
- Ink pad and paper

Take your wood square and press a marble-sized ball of foam clay into the center. Use a round-tipped sculpting tool to make two eyeholes and define the jaw. Use a smaller round-tipped sculpting tool and make the nostrils. Then press it into the bottom to make lines for teeth. Let the clay cure completely (read package instructions for times, but usually 24 to 48 hours).

(continued)

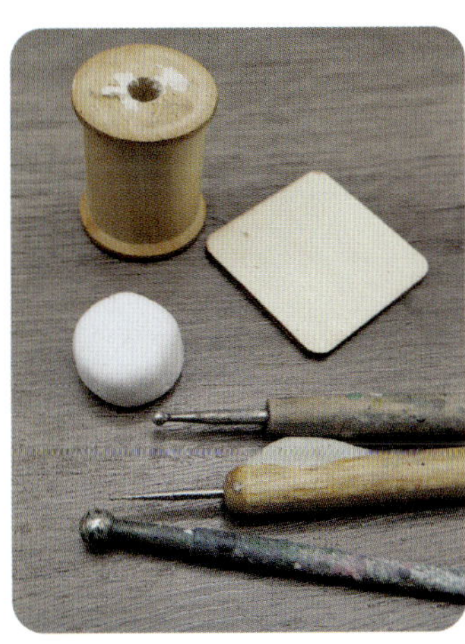
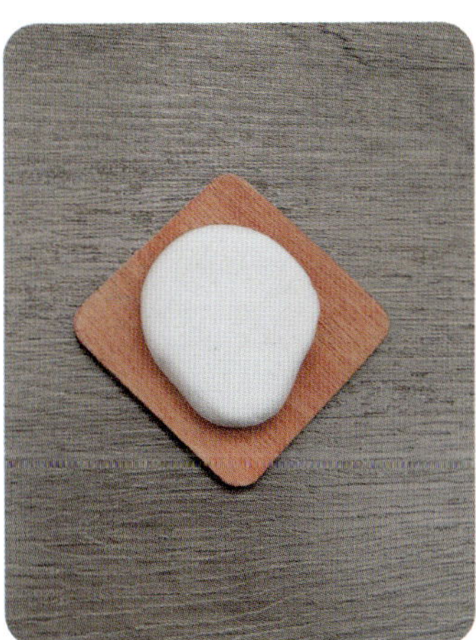
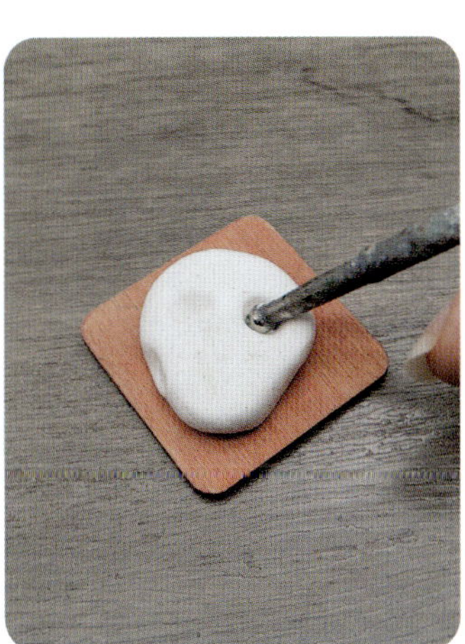

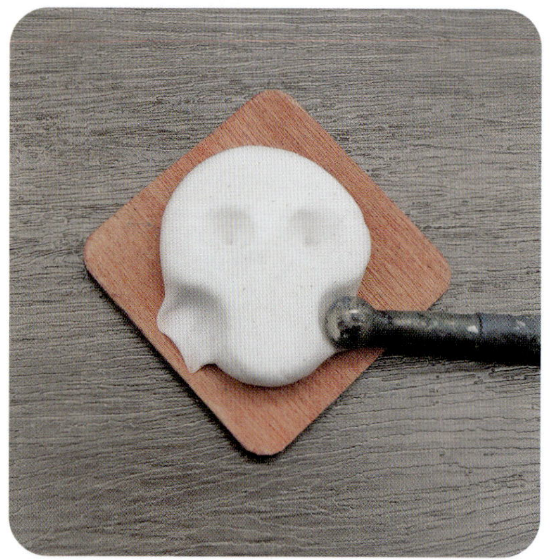
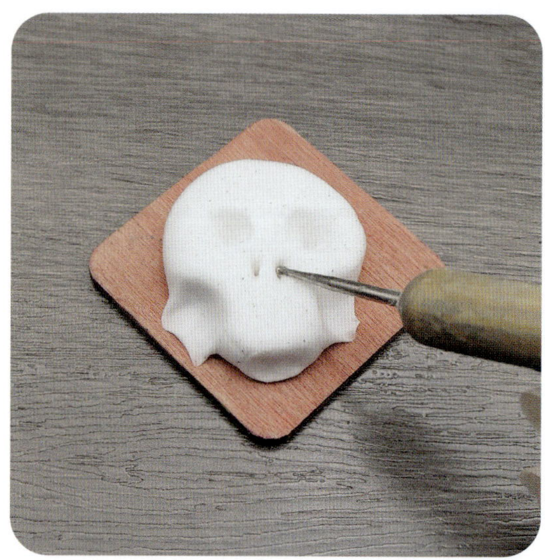
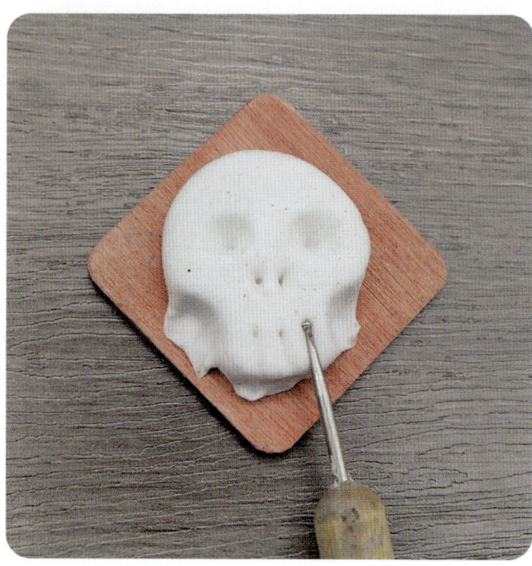
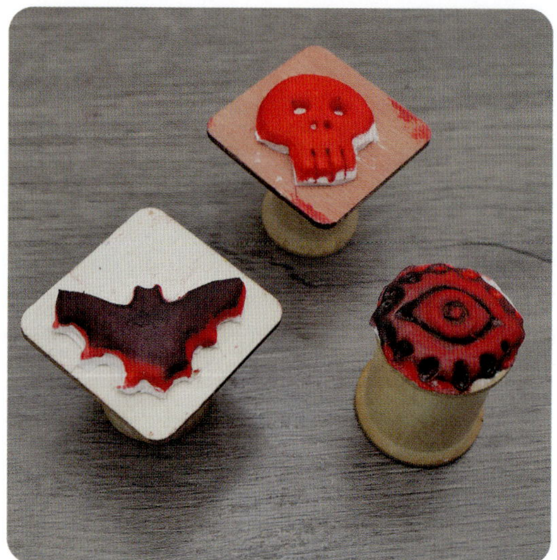

Hot glue the wood onto your empty spool of thread to make a handle. Try out the stamp with the ink pad and paper. If your stamp has any problem spots, use an X-ACTO knife or sculpting tool to deepen the lines.

Wrapping spooky gifts? Try using your stamps on the Creepy Gift Tags (page 101).

Molten Lava Flow Display

Have you ever wanted a unique way to highlight your knick-knacks or paddywhacks? You could buy a boring lighted platform, or you could create a molten lava one. After all, lava is guaranteed to be 93 percent more awesome!

Hot glue red and orange glass shards onto one side of your 4-inch (10-cm) clear acrylic disk. Cover the entire side and don't leave any large gaps. Set side.

Drill a hole ½ to 1 inch (1.3 to 2.5 cm) away from the edge of the 4-inch (10-cm) wood slice. Feed one end of the fairy lights all the way through. Use hot glue to attach the battery pack to the center bottom of the wood. Pile your lights in a circle on top of your wood ½ to 1 inch (1.3 to 2.5 cm) away from the edge and secure with hot glue. Glue the wood beads to the bottom of the round wood to serve as feet.

(continued)

Materials

- Hot glue and gun
- Red and orange glass shards
- 4" (10-cm) clear acrylic disk
- Drill and drill bit
- 4" (10-cm) red circular wood slice
- Red or white fairy lights
- 4 wooden beads
- Silicone mat
- Disposable gloves
- Red epoxy clay (e.g., Apoxie Sculpt)

Note: While some people put blood, sweat and tears into their art, let's keep the blood to a minimum! You can easily buy your glass shards at most craft stores or online, and they come in a variety of colors.

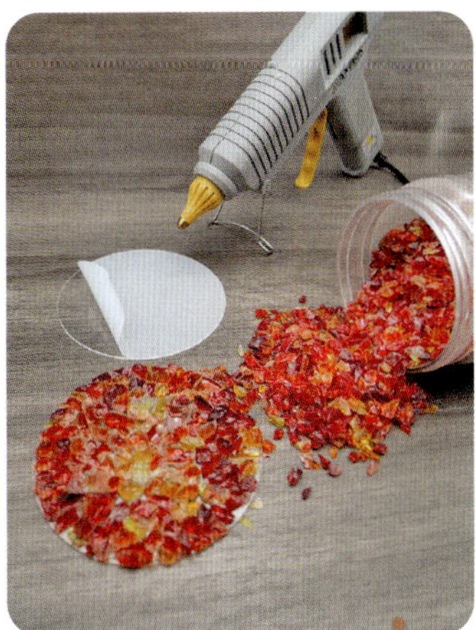

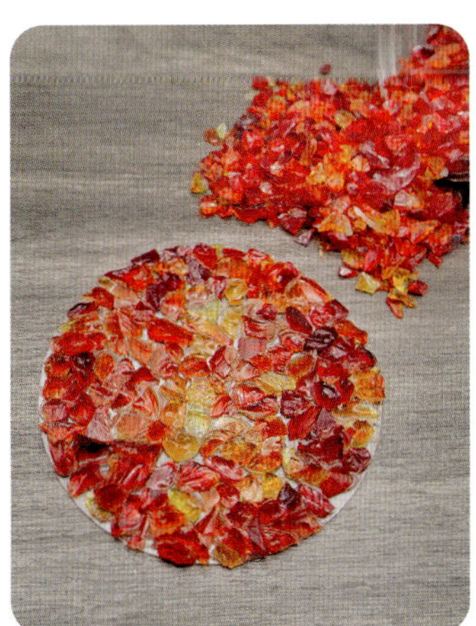

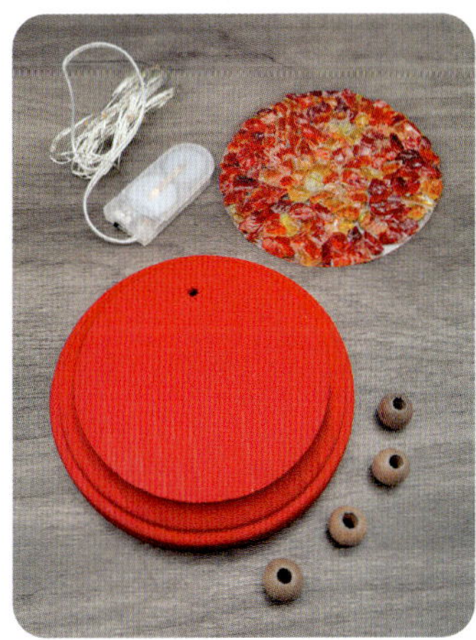

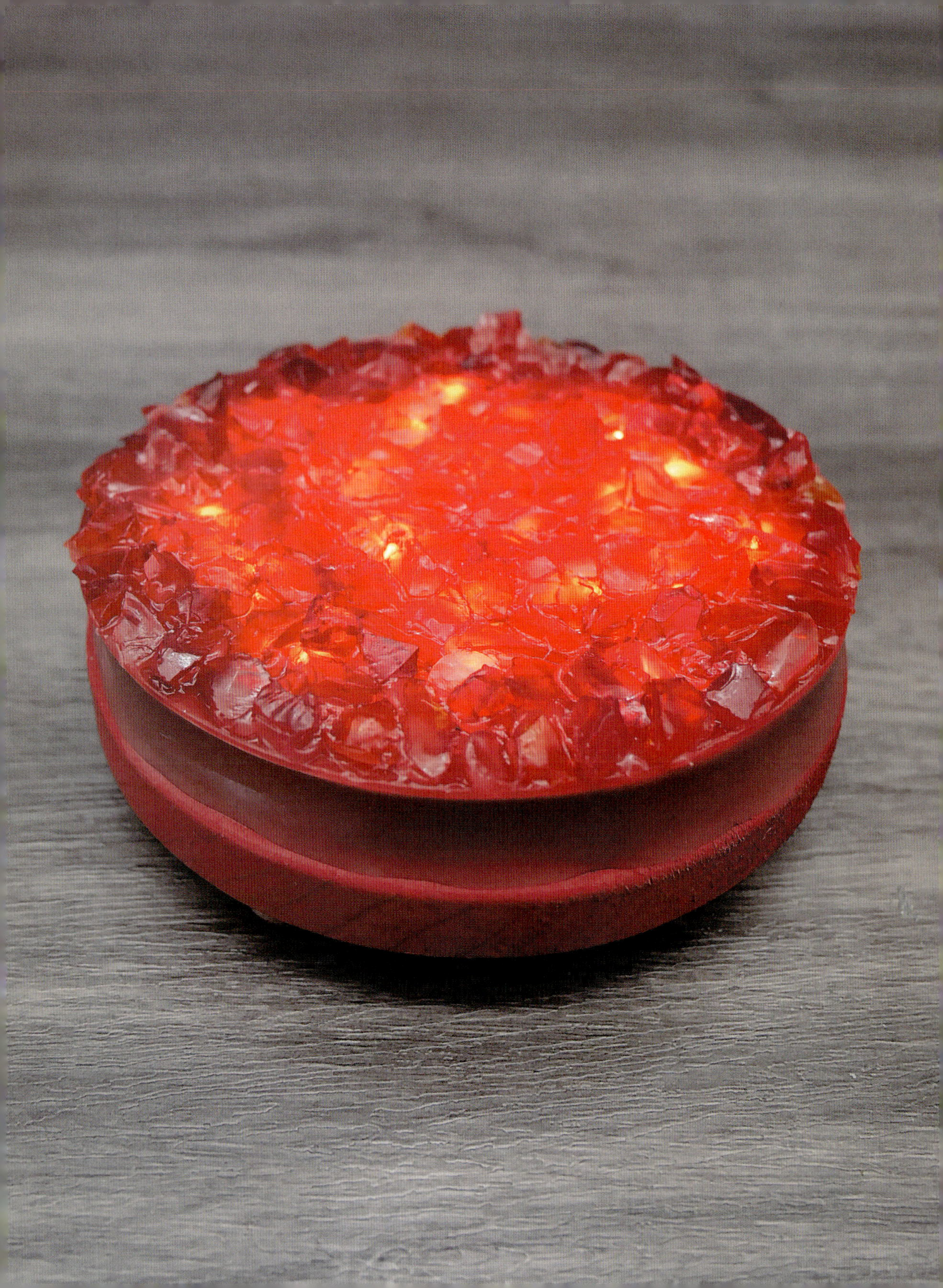

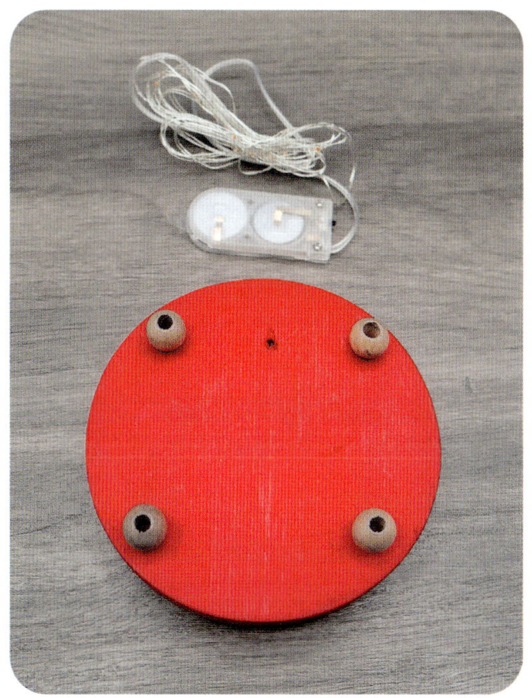 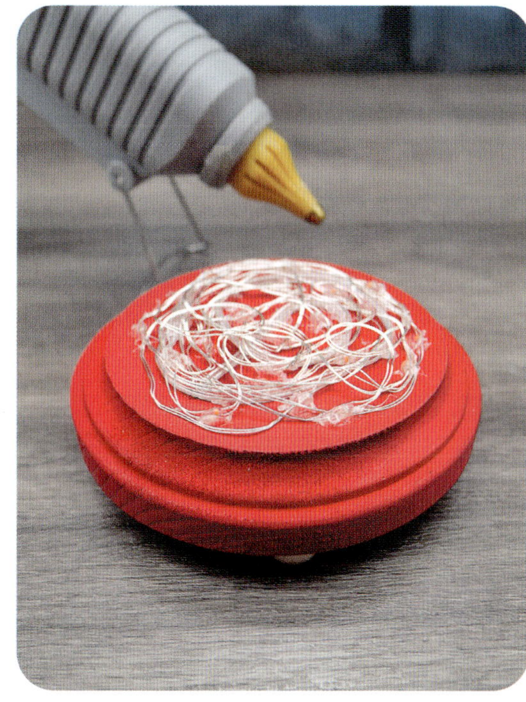

Attach the disk with glass shards to the top of the fairy lights with hot glue.

Lay out your silicone mat and put on your gloves. Mix a golf ball–sized amount of red epoxy clay. Roll out a long log that's as thick as the gap between the wood and the acrylic. Wrap the clay around, filling the gap between the acrylic and the wood. Be careful not to push the clay too deep into the gap. You can smooth your clay out with a wet gloved finger. Set aside overnight to cure.

Turn on your lights and watch the magma-ificent glow of your new lava display!

Acknowledgments

I would like to express my sincerest thanks to Marissa Giambelluca, Meg Baskis and Laura Benton at Page Street Publishing! You are all saints who I probably annoyed the crap out of with all my newbie questions. But especially Marissa, who first convinced me that writing a book was something even in my wheelhouse.

A HUGE thanks to my husband, who basically ran the house, cooked the meals, did the laundry and took care of our daughter and cats while I was shut up in my room writing and crafting.

Finally, I'd like to thank all the readers who may or may not have bought my book after seeing me create weird art on the Internet. Without you, I would be nowhere, and I owe all my success to you!

About the Author

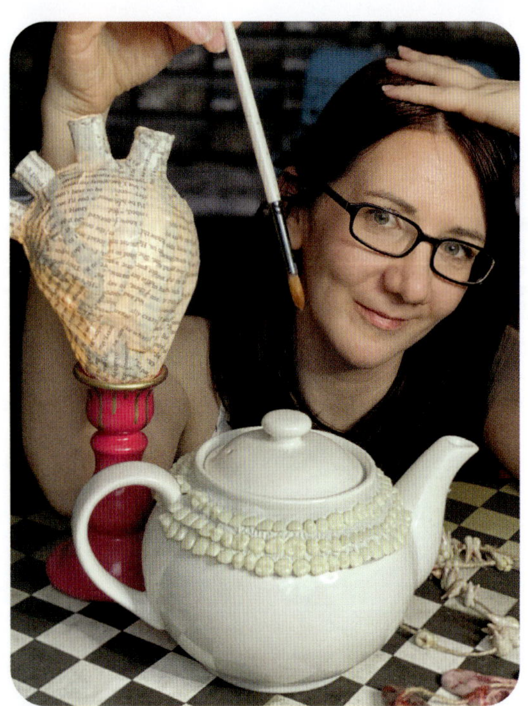

Hi, I'm Ashley Voortman, aka Peculiarly Ashley, and I've been making art for over 15 years. I've tried many forms of art over the years, including painting, drawing, sculpting, graphic design, screen printing, felting, sewing, jewelry making, animation and even that one time I tried knitting (never again . . .). Lately I've landed somewhere between content creation and sculpting. You might know me as the teapot/circle window/octopus lady.

To support my crafting habits, I sell my art on Etsy and share the process on TikTok and YouTube. Shockingly, over two million people have decided to follow me on TikTok to watch my sassy, artsy adventures. I know, I was surprised too! But I'm just so grateful to have them along, laughing and creating art with me!

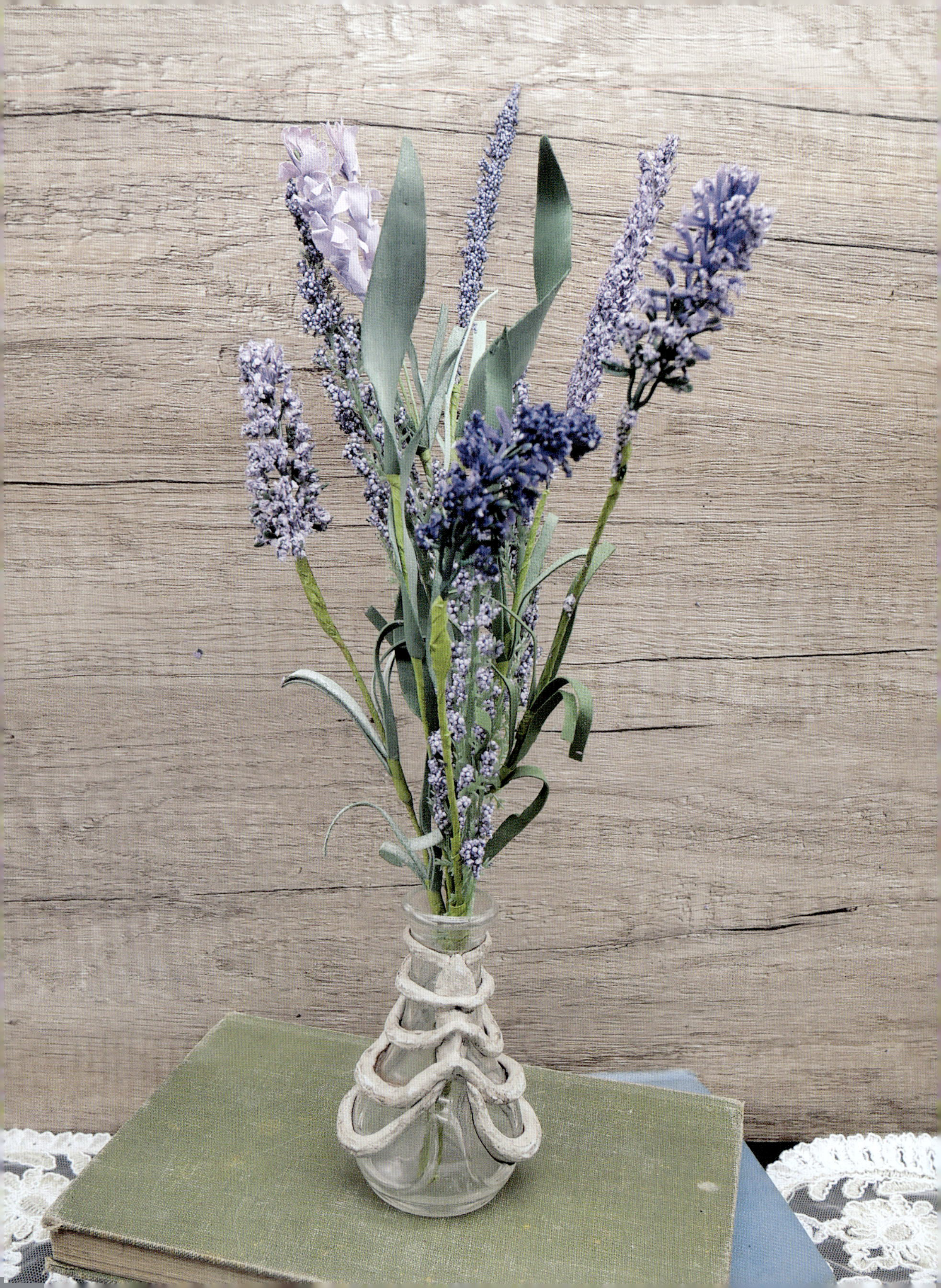

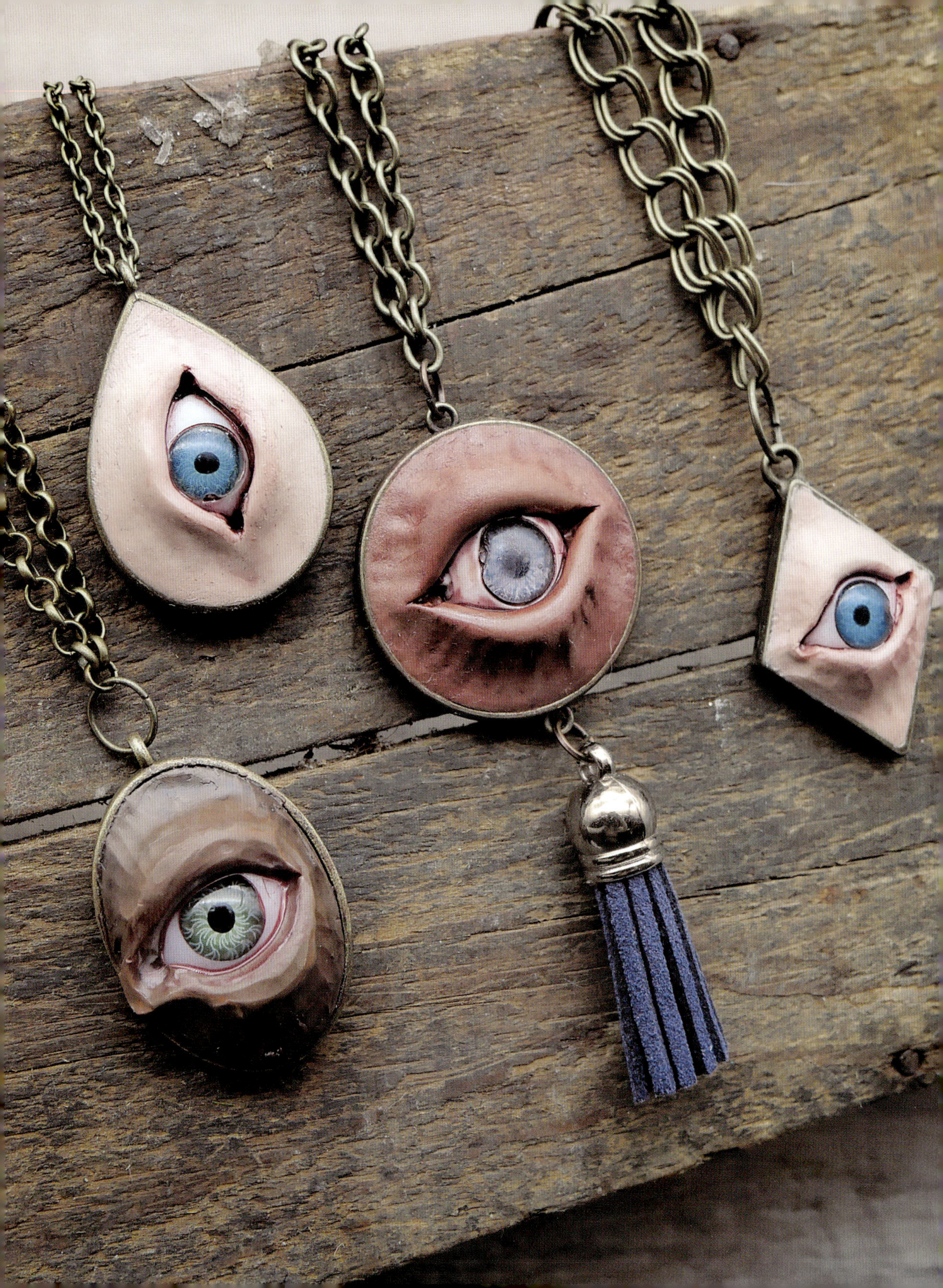